SAVIOR

TODD McFARLANE BRIAN HOLGUIN CLAYTON CRAIN

image

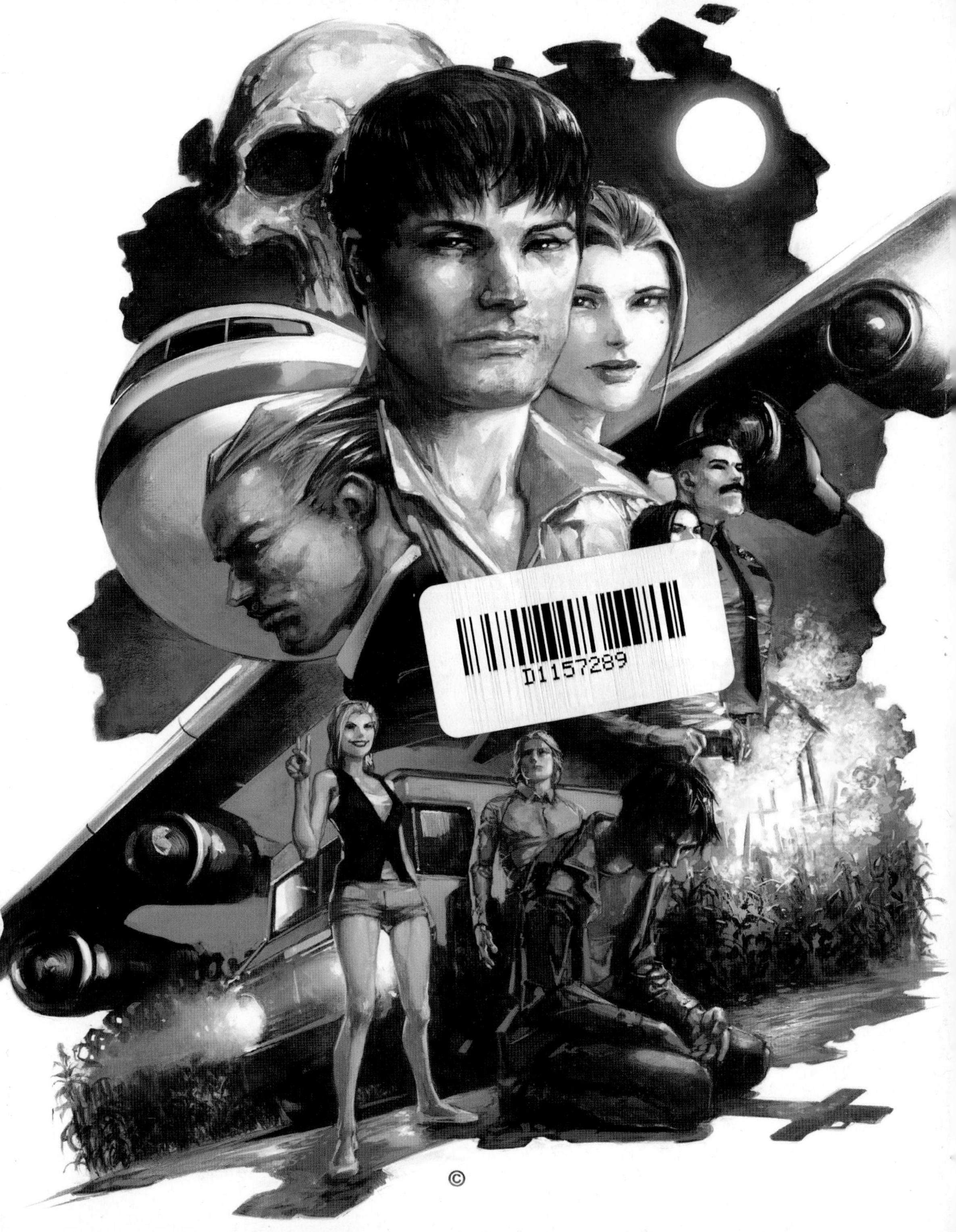

©

IMAGE COMICS AND TODD McFARLANE PRESENT

SAW

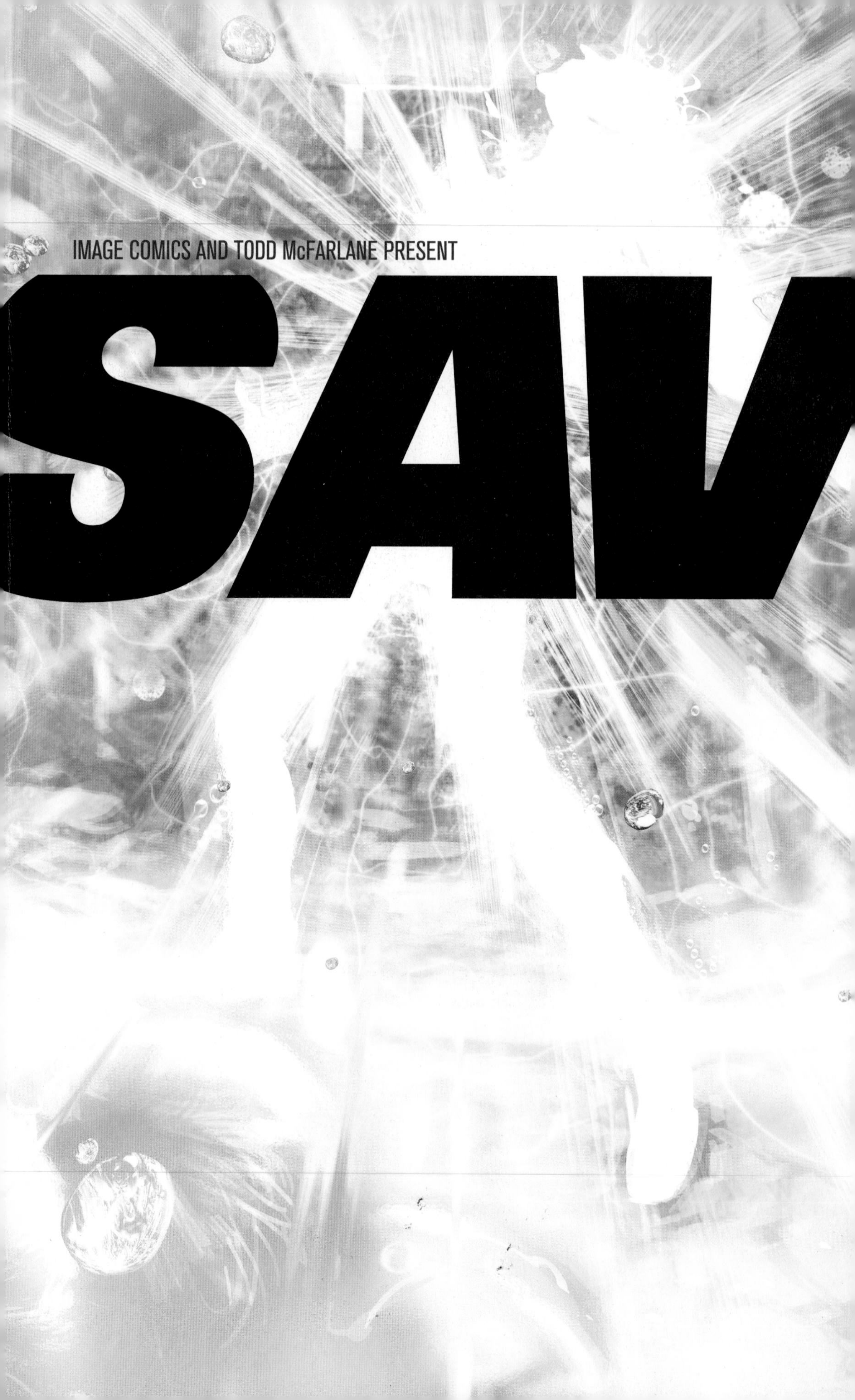

IOR

STORY

TODD McFARLANE
BRIAN HOLGUIN

COVER/STORY ART

CLAYTON CRAIN

LETTERING

TOM ORZECHOWSKI

EDITOR

TODD McFARLANE

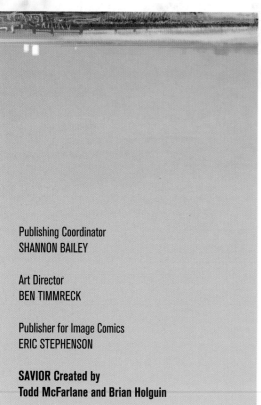

Publishing Coordinator
SHANNON BAILEY

Art Director
BEN TIMMRECK

Publisher for Image Comics
ERIC STEPHENSON

SAVIOR Created by
Todd McFarlane and Brian Holguin

TODD McFARLANE PRODUCTIONS

McFARLANE.COM

Savior. First Printing. Published by IMAGE COMICS, 2001 Center Street, Sixth Floor, Berkley, CA 94704 USA. **For information regarding the CPSIA on this printed material call: 203-595-3636 and provide reference #EAST – 671136.**

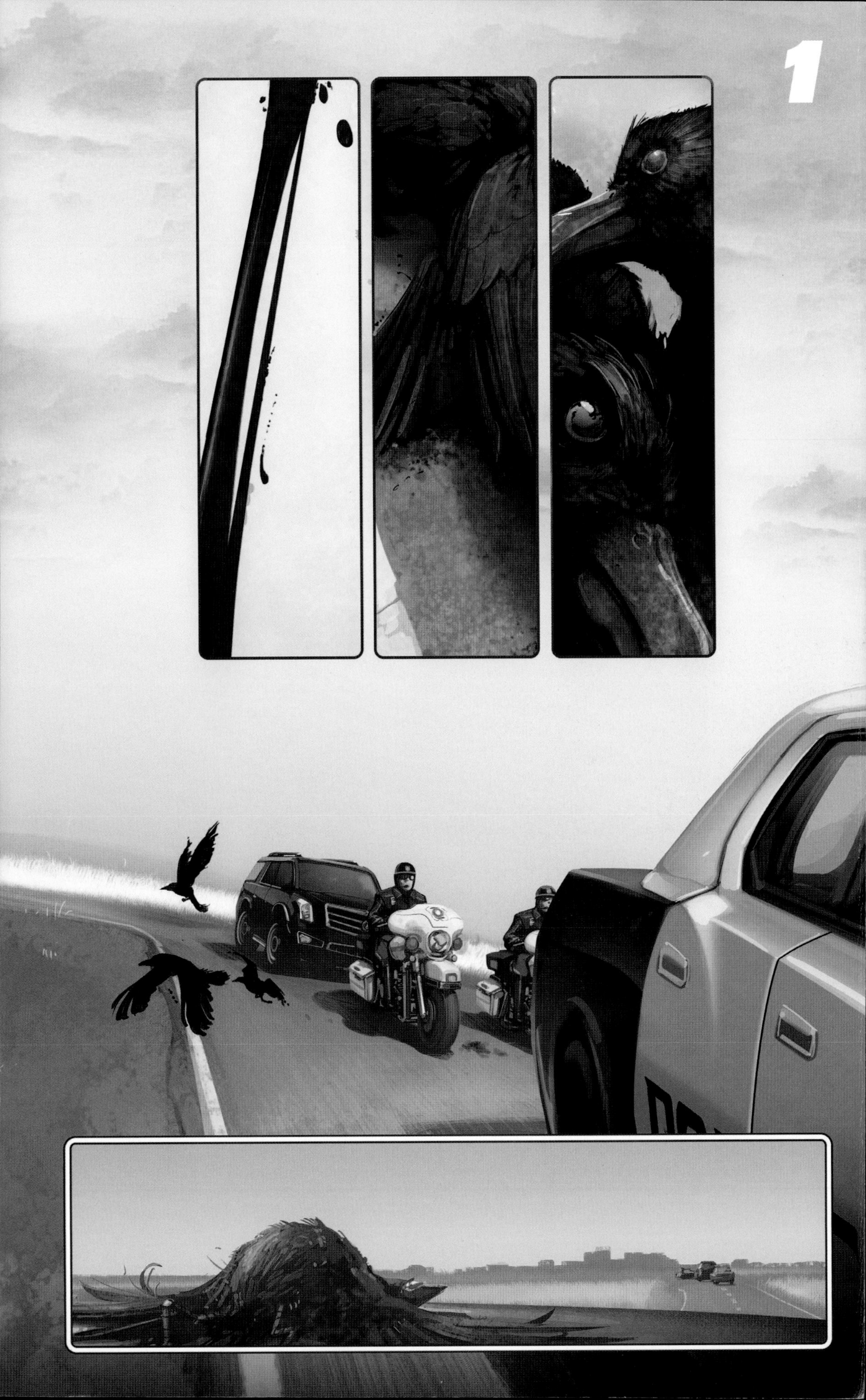
1

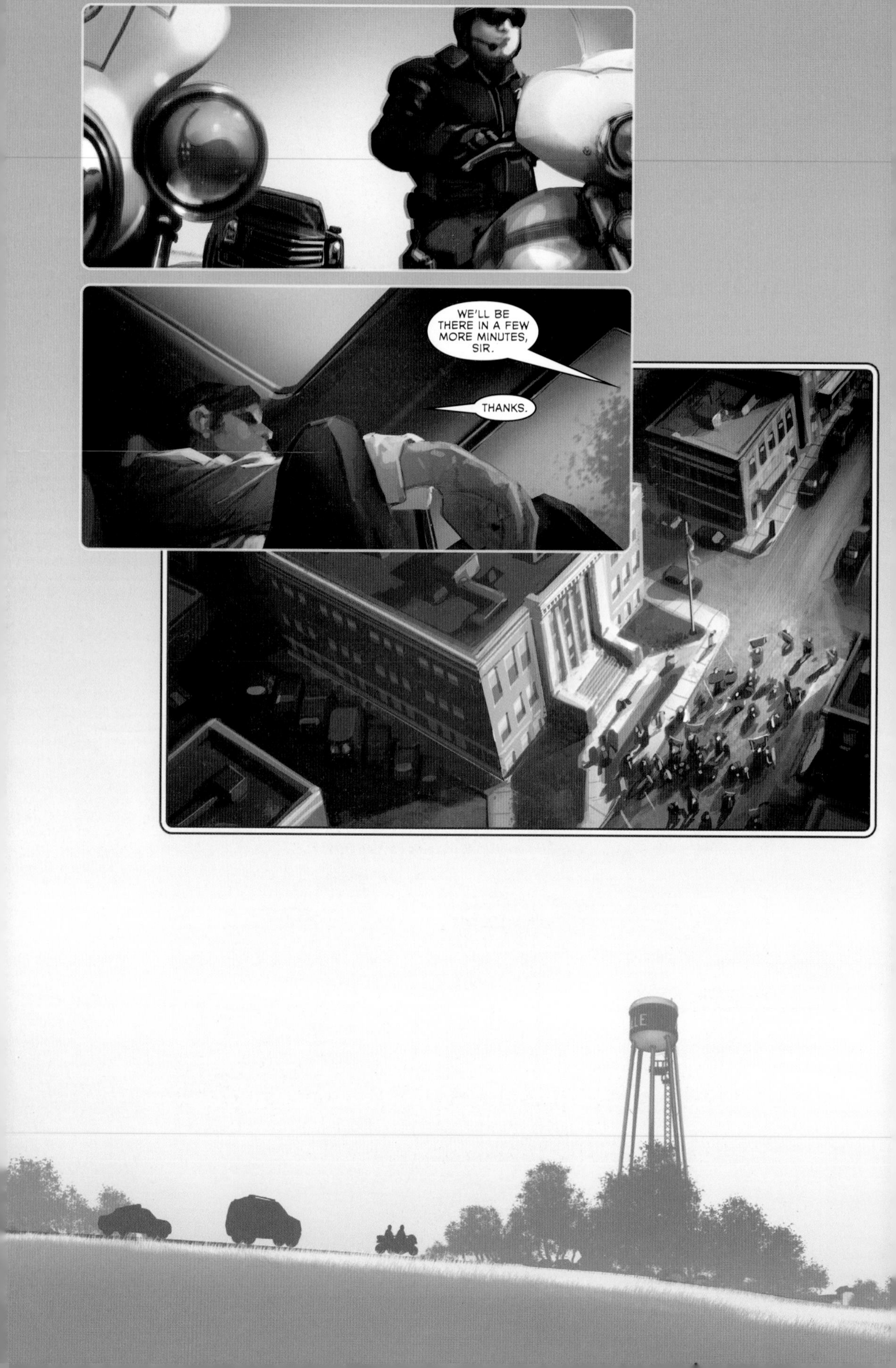
WE'LL BE THERE IN A FEW MORE MINUTES, SIR.
THANKS.

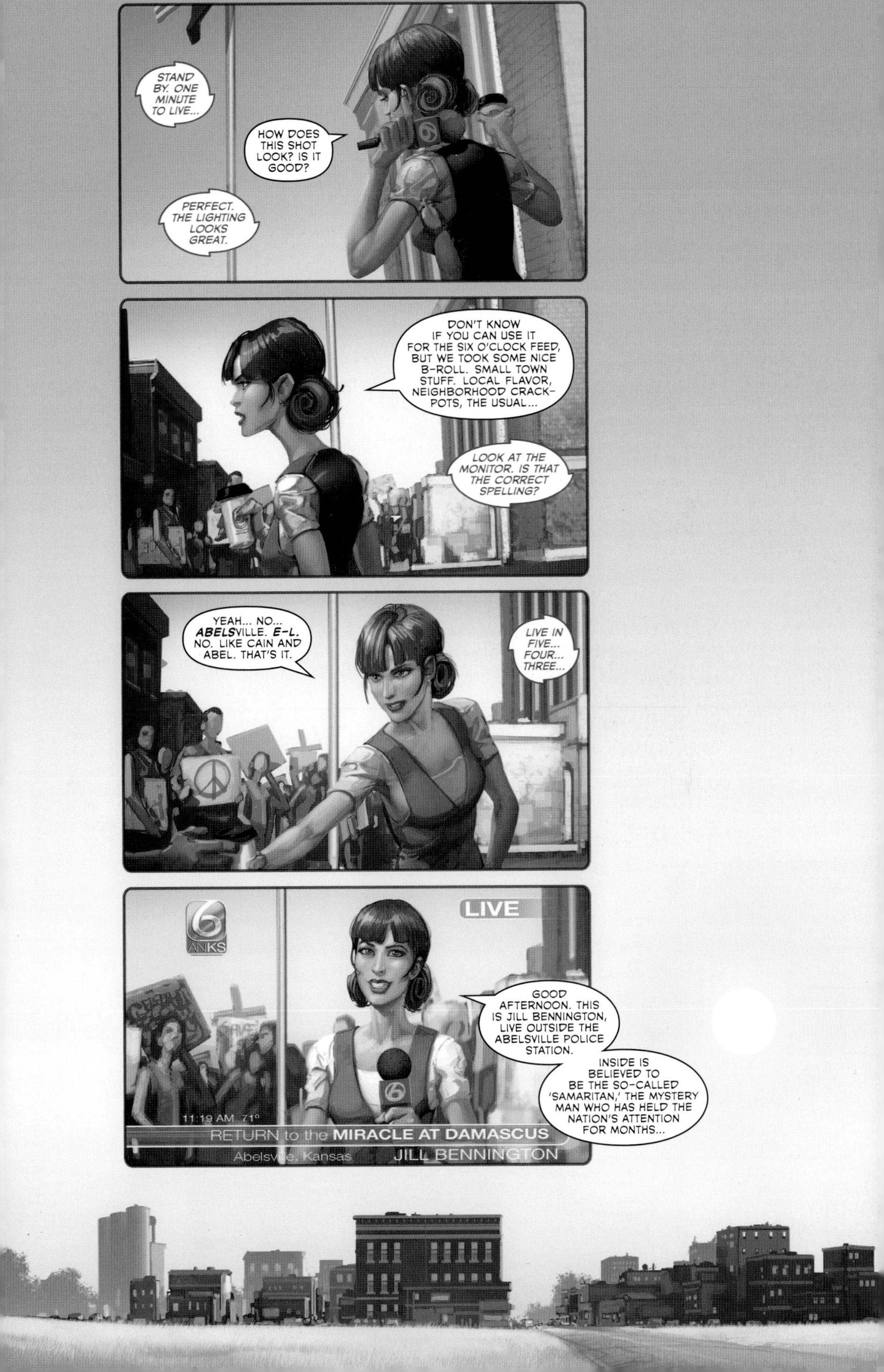
STAND BY. ONE MINUTE TO LIVE...
HOW DOES THIS SHOT LOOK? IS IT GOOD?
PERFECT. THE LIGHTING LOOKS GREAT.
DON'T KNOW IF YOU CAN USE IT FOR THE SIX O'CLOCK FEED, BUT WE TOOK SOME NICE B-ROLL. SMALL TOWN STUFF. LOCAL FLAVOR, NEIGHBORHOOD CRACK-POTS, THE USUAL...
LOOK AT THE MONITOR. IS THAT THE CORRECT SPELLING?
YEAH... NO... ABELSVILLE. E-L. NO. LIKE CAIN AND ABEL. THAT'S IT.
LIVE IN FIVE... FOUR... THREE...
LIVE
11:19 AM 71°
RETURN to the MIRACLE AT DAMASCUS
JILL BENNINGTON
GOOD AFTERNOON. THIS IS JILL BENNINGTON, LIVE OUTSIDE THE ABELSVILLE POLICE STATION.
INSIDE IS BELIEVED TO BE THE SO-CALLED 'SAMARITAN,' THE MYSTERY MAN WHO HAS HELD THE NATION'S ATTENTION FOR MONTHS...

VIEWERS MAY REMEMBER THE SO-CALLED MIRACLE AT DAMASCUS, WHEN AN AMATEUR VIDEO WENT VIRAL, FOLLOWING THE TRAGIC--
HOLD ON--SOMETHING'S HAPPENING. WE'RE GOING TO TRY GETTING A SHOT...
LIVE
11:22 AM 68°
RETURN to the MIRACLE AT DAMASCUS
Abelsville, Kansas
JILL BENNINGTON
6 ANKS
LIVE
IT APPEARS LIKE... YES! IT'S HIM. THE SO-CALLED MIRACLE WORKER? HE'S GETTING OUT OF A LIMO AND FEDERAL AGENTS, ALONG WITH LOCAL POLICE, ARE ESCORTING HIM TOWARDS THE TOWN'S COURTHOUSE.
11:24 AM 71°
RETURN to the MIRACLE AT DAMASCUS
Abelsville, Kansas
JILL BENNINGTON
6 ANKS
LIVE
BACK UP! GIVE US ROOM!
11:24 AM 71°
RETURN to the MIRACLE AT DAMASCUS
Abelsville, Kansas
JILL BENNINGTON
6 ANKS
LIVE
HE WON'T BE ANSWERING ANY QUESTIONS TODAY.
11:24 AM 71°
RETURN to the MIRACLE AT DAMASCUS
Abelsville, Kansas
JILL BENNINGTON

6 ANKS
LIVE
YOU FRAUD! YOU'RE JUST A FAKE. GOD'LL PUNISH YOU!
MY CHILD! HE'S SICK! PLEASE... WE NEED YOUR HELP!
TOUCH ME! TOUCH MY HAND!
11:24 AM 71°
RETURN to the MIRACLE AT DAMASCUS
Abelsville, Kansas JILL BENNINGTON
6 ANKS
LIVE
WE'RE PRAYING FOR YOU. STAY STRONG.
11:25 AM 71°
RETURN to the MIRACLE AT DAMASCUS
Abelsville, Kansas JILL BENNINGTON
EXCUSE ME! OVER HERE.
JILL BENNINGTON, CHANNEL SIX. I JUST HAVE ONE QUESTION.
6 ANKS
LIVE
DO YOU THINK YOU'RE *GOD?*
11:25 AM 71°
RETURN to the MIRACLE AT DAMASCUS
Abelsville, Kansas JILL BENNINGTON
6 ANKS
LIVE
WHAT?
11:25 AM 71°
RETURN to the MIRACLE AT DAMASCUS
Abelsville, Kansas JILL BENNINGTON

Damascus, Kansas. Six months earlier.

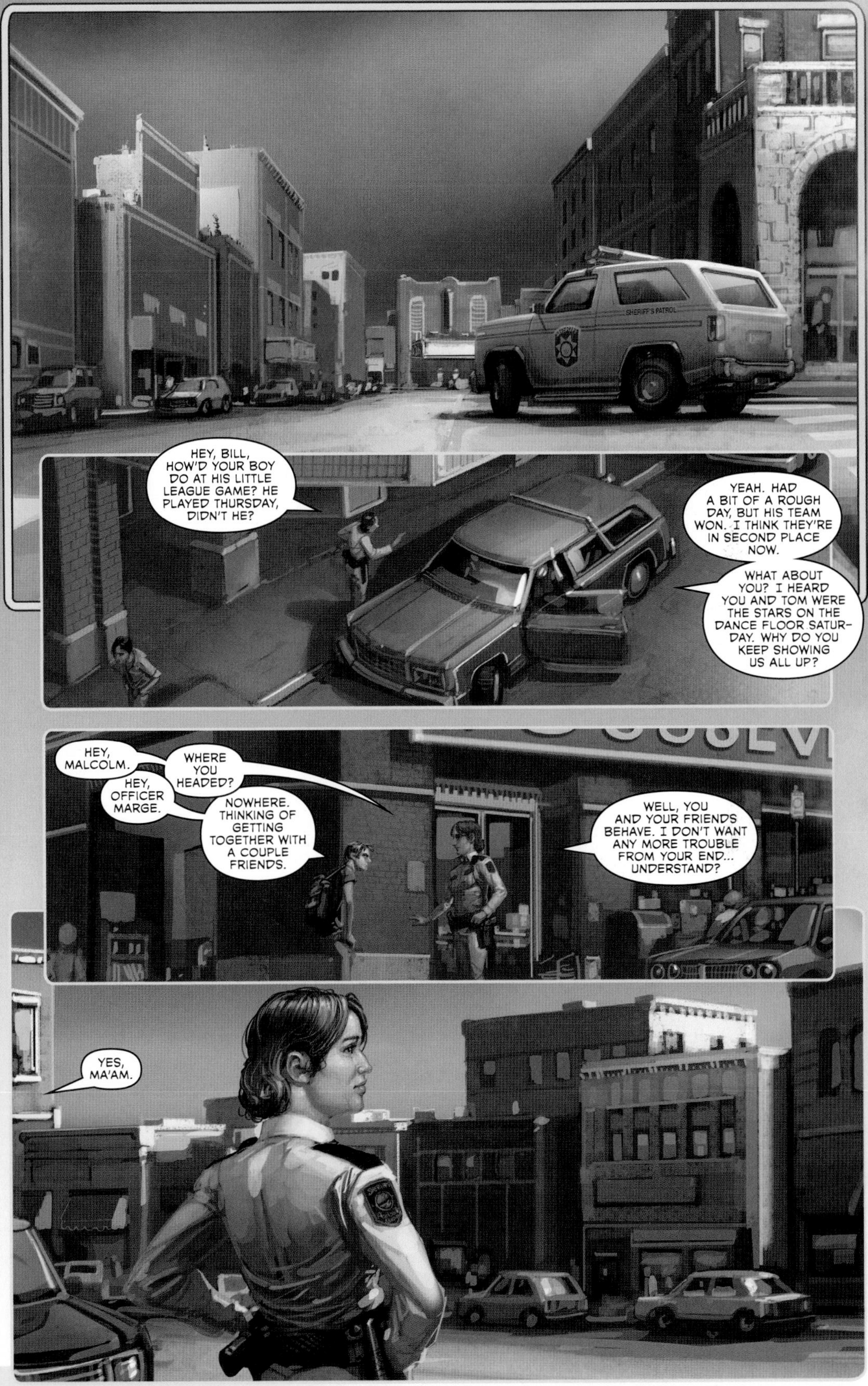

SHERIFF'S PATROL
HEY, BILL, HOW'D YOUR BOY DO AT HIS LITTLE LEAGUE GAME? HE PLAYED THURSDAY, DIDN'T HE?
YEAH. HAD A BIT OF A ROUGH DAY, BUT HIS TEAM WON. I THINK THEY'RE IN SECOND PLACE NOW.
WHAT ABOUT YOU? I HEARD YOU AND TOM WERE THE STARS ON THE DANCE FLOOR SATURDAY. WHY DO YOU KEEP SHOWING US ALL UP?
HEY, MALCOLM.
HEY, OFFICER MARGE.
WHERE YOU HEADED?
NOWHERE. THINKING OF GETTING TOGETHER WITH A COUPLE FRIENDS.
WELL, YOU AND YOUR FRIENDS BEHAVE. I DON'T WANT ANY MORE TROUBLE FROM YOUR END... UNDERSTAND?
YES, MA'AM.

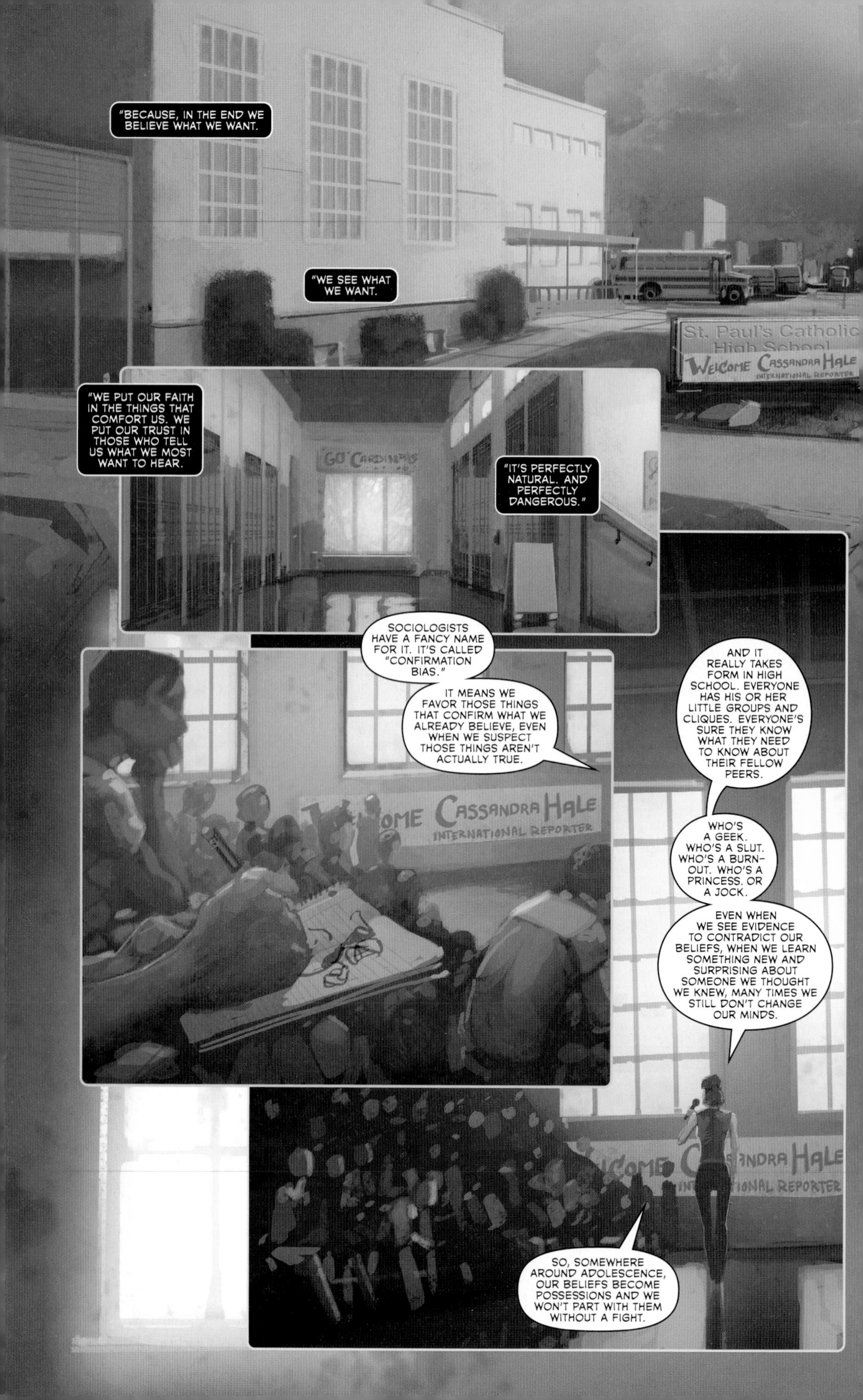
"BECAUSE, IN THE END WE BELIEVE WHAT WE WANT.
"WE SEE WHAT WE WANT.
St. Paul's Catholic High School
WELCOME CASSANDRA HALE INTERNATIONAL REPORTER
"WE PUT OUR FAITH IN THE THINGS THAT COMFORT US. WE PUT OUR TRUST IN THOSE WHO TELL US WHAT WE MOST WANT TO HEAR.
GO CARDINALS
"IT'S PERFECTLY NATURAL. AND PERFECTLY DANGEROUS."
SOCIOLOGISTS HAVE A FANCY NAME FOR IT. IT'S CALLED "CONFIRMATION BIAS."
IT MEANS WE FAVOR THOSE THINGS THAT CONFIRM WHAT WE ALREADY BELIEVE, EVEN WHEN WE SUSPECT THOSE THINGS AREN'T ACTUALLY TRUE.
CASSANDRA HALE INTERNATIONAL REPORTER
AND IT REALLY TAKES FORM IN HIGH SCHOOL. EVERYONE HAS HIS OR HER LITTLE GROUPS AND CLIQUES. EVERYONE'S SURE THEY KNOW WHAT THEY NEED TO KNOW ABOUT THEIR FELLOW PEERS.
WHO'S A GEEK. WHO'S A SLUT. WHO'S A BURN-OUT. WHO'S A PRINCESS. OR A JOCK.
EVEN WHEN WE SEE EVIDENCE TO CONTRADICT OUR BELIEFS, WHEN WE LEARN SOMETHING NEW AND SURPRISING ABOUT SOMEONE WE THOUGHT WE KNEW, MANY TIMES WE STILL DON'T CHANGE OUR MINDS.
SO, SOMEWHERE AROUND ADOLESCENCE, OUR BELIEFS BECOME POSSESSIONS AND WE WON'T PART WITH THEM WITHOUT A FIGHT.

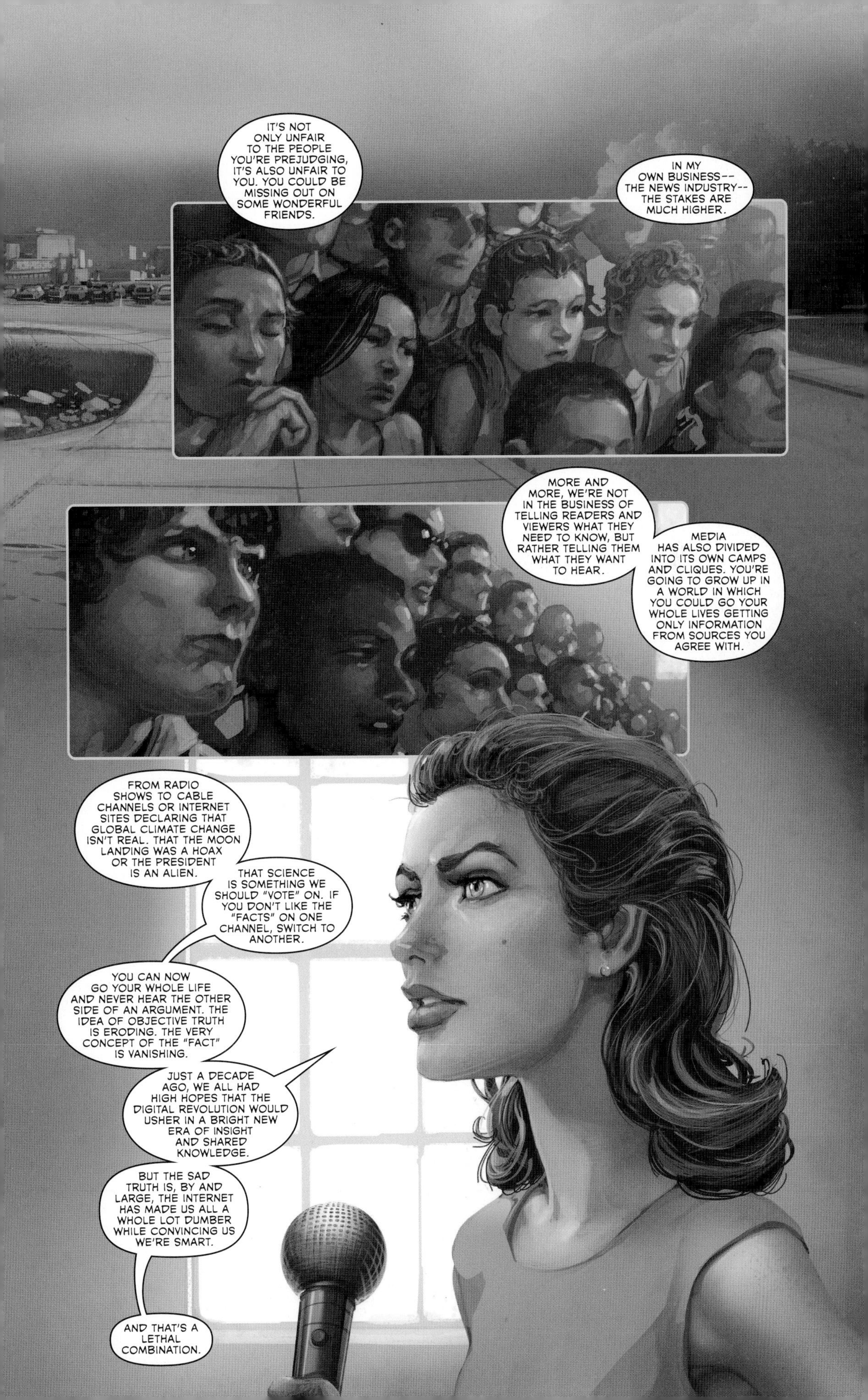
IT'S NOT ONLY UNFAIR TO THE PEOPLE YOU'RE PREJUDGING, IT'S ALSO UNFAIR TO YOU. YOU COULD BE MISSING OUT ON SOME WONDERFUL FRIENDS.
IN MY OWN BUSINESS-- THE NEWS INDUSTRY-- THE STAKES ARE MUCH HIGHER.
MORE AND MORE, WE'RE NOT IN THE BUSINESS OF TELLING READERS AND VIEWERS WHAT THEY NEED TO KNOW, BUT RATHER TELLING THEM WHAT THEY WANT TO HEAR.
MEDIA HAS ALSO DIVIDED INTO ITS OWN CAMPS AND CLIQUES. YOU'RE GOING TO GROW UP IN A WORLD IN WHICH YOU COULD GO YOUR WHOLE LIVES GETTING ONLY INFORMATION FROM SOURCES YOU AGREE WITH.
FROM RADIO SHOWS TO CABLE CHANNELS OR INTERNET SITES DECLARING THAT GLOBAL CLIMATE CHANGE ISN'T REAL. THAT THE MOON LANDING WAS A HOAX OR THE PRESIDENT IS AN ALIEN.
THAT SCIENCE IS SOMETHING WE SHOULD "VOTE" ON. IF YOU DON'T LIKE THE "FACTS" ON ONE CHANNEL, SWITCH TO ANOTHER.
YOU CAN NOW GO YOUR WHOLE LIFE AND NEVER HEAR THE OTHER SIDE OF AN ARGUMENT. THE IDEA OF OBJECTIVE TRUTH IS ERODING. THE VERY CONCEPT OF THE "FACT" IS VANISHING.
JUST A DECADE AGO, WE ALL HAD HIGH HOPES THAT THE DIGITAL REVOLUTION WOULD USHER IN A BRIGHT NEW ERA OF INSIGHT AND SHARED KNOWLEDGE.
BUT THE SAD TRUTH IS, BY AND LARGE, THE INTERNET HAS MADE US ALL A WHOLE LOT DUMBER WHILE CONVINCING US WE'RE SMART.
AND THAT'S A LETHAL COMBINATION.

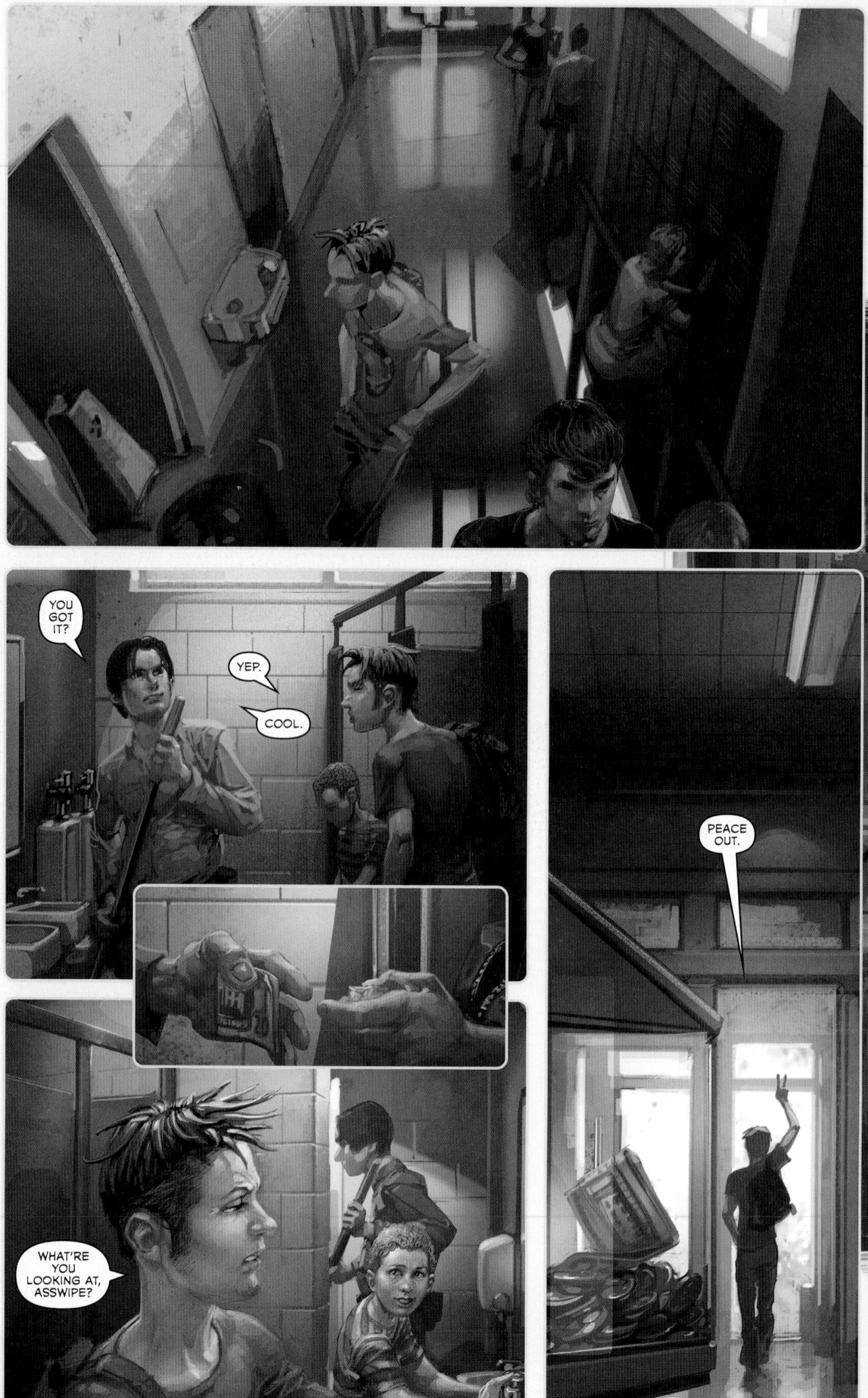
YOU GOT IT?
YEP.
COOL.
WHAT'RE YOU LOOKING AT, ASSWIPE?
PEACE OUT.

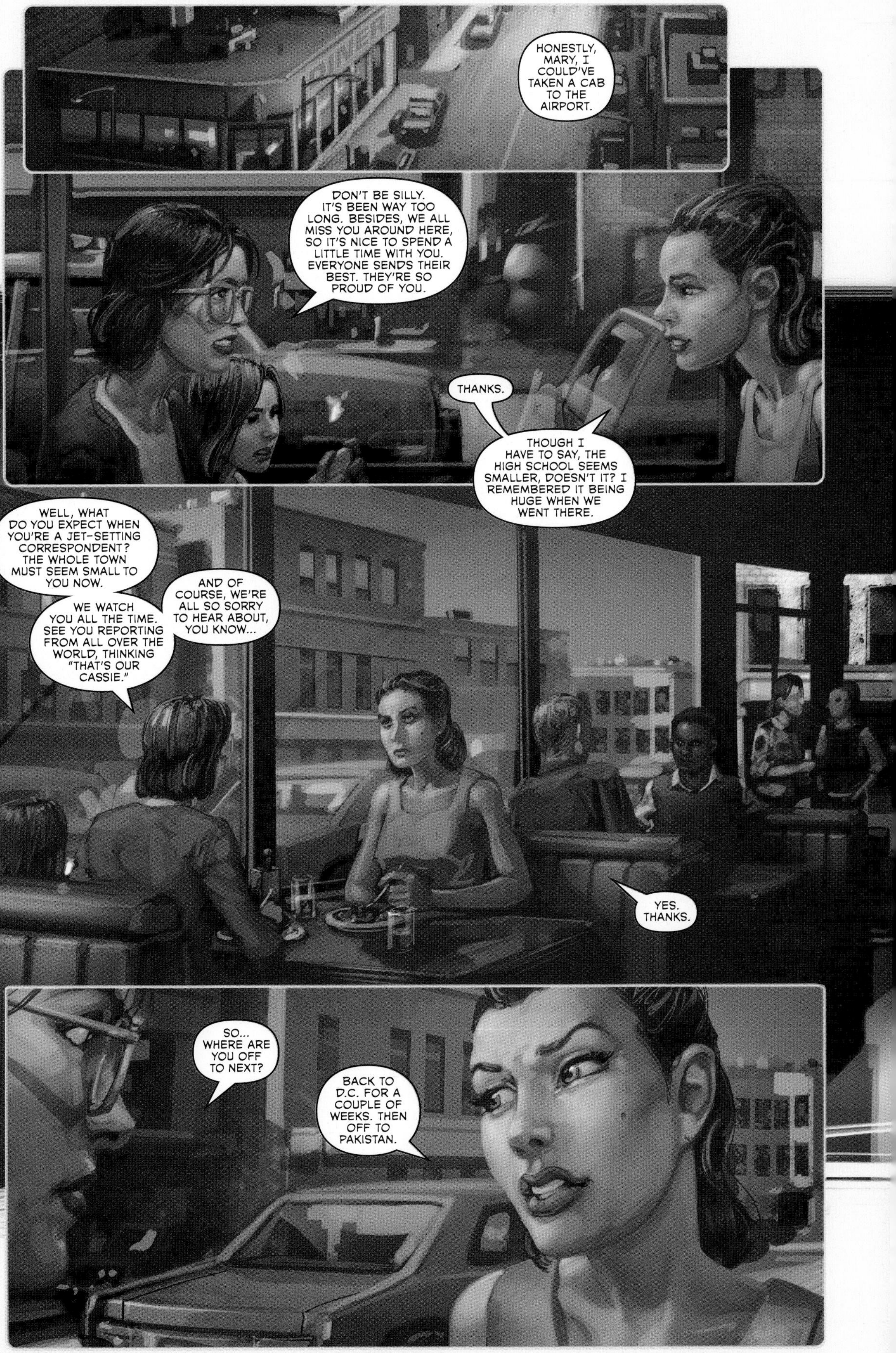
HONESTLY, MARY, I COULD'VE TAKEN A CAB TO THE AIRPORT.
DON'T BE SILLY. IT'S BEEN WAY TOO LONG. BESIDES, WE ALL MISS YOU AROUND HERE, SO IT'S NICE TO SPEND A LITTLE TIME WITH YOU. EVERYONE SENDS THEIR BEST. THEY'RE SO PROUD OF YOU.
THANKS.
THOUGH I HAVE TO SAY, THE HIGH SCHOOL SEEMS SMALLER, DOESN'T IT? I REMEMBERED IT BEING HUGE WHEN WE WENT THERE.
WELL, WHAT DO YOU EXPECT WHEN YOU'RE A JET-SETTING CORRESPONDENT? THE WHOLE TOWN MUST SEEM SMALL TO YOU NOW.
WE WATCH YOU ALL THE TIME. SEE YOU REPORTING FROM ALL OVER THE WORLD, THINKING "THAT'S OUR CASSIE."
AND OF COURSE, WE'RE ALL SO SORRY TO HEAR ABOUT, YOU KNOW...
YES. THANKS.
SO... WHERE ARE YOU OFF TO NEXT?
BACK TO D.C. FOR A COUPLE OF WEEKS. THEN OFF TO PAKISTAN.

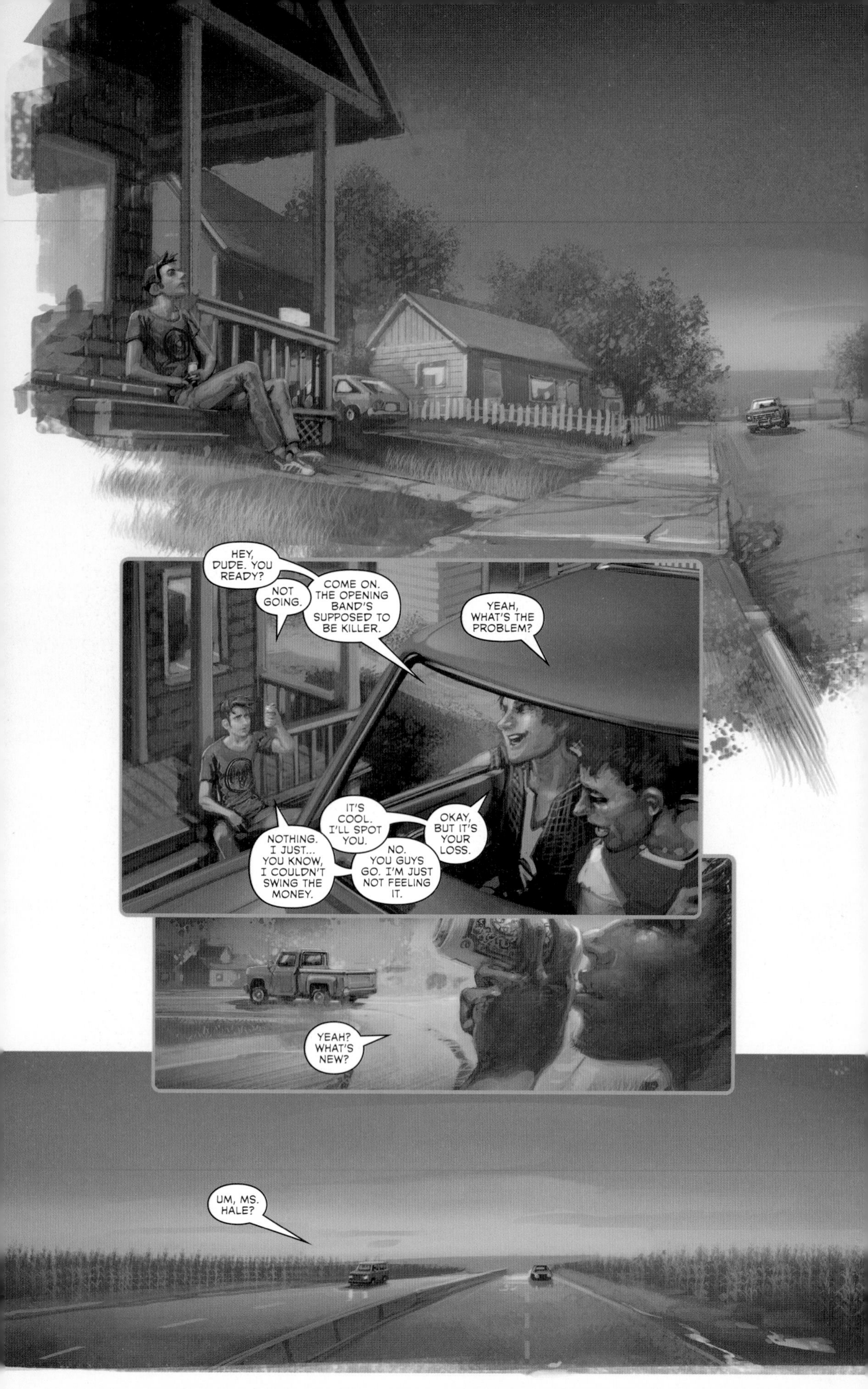
HEY, DUDE. YOU READY?
NOT GOING.
COME ON. THE OPENING BAND'S SUPPOSED TO BE KILLER.
YEAH, WHAT'S THE PROBLEM?
NOTHING. I JUST... YOU KNOW, I COULDN'T SWING THE MONEY.
IT'S COOL. I'LL SPOT YOU.
NO. YOU GUYS GO. I'M JUST NOT FEELING IT.
OKAY, BUT IT'S YOUR LOSS.
YEAH? WHAT'S NEW?
UM, MS. HALE?

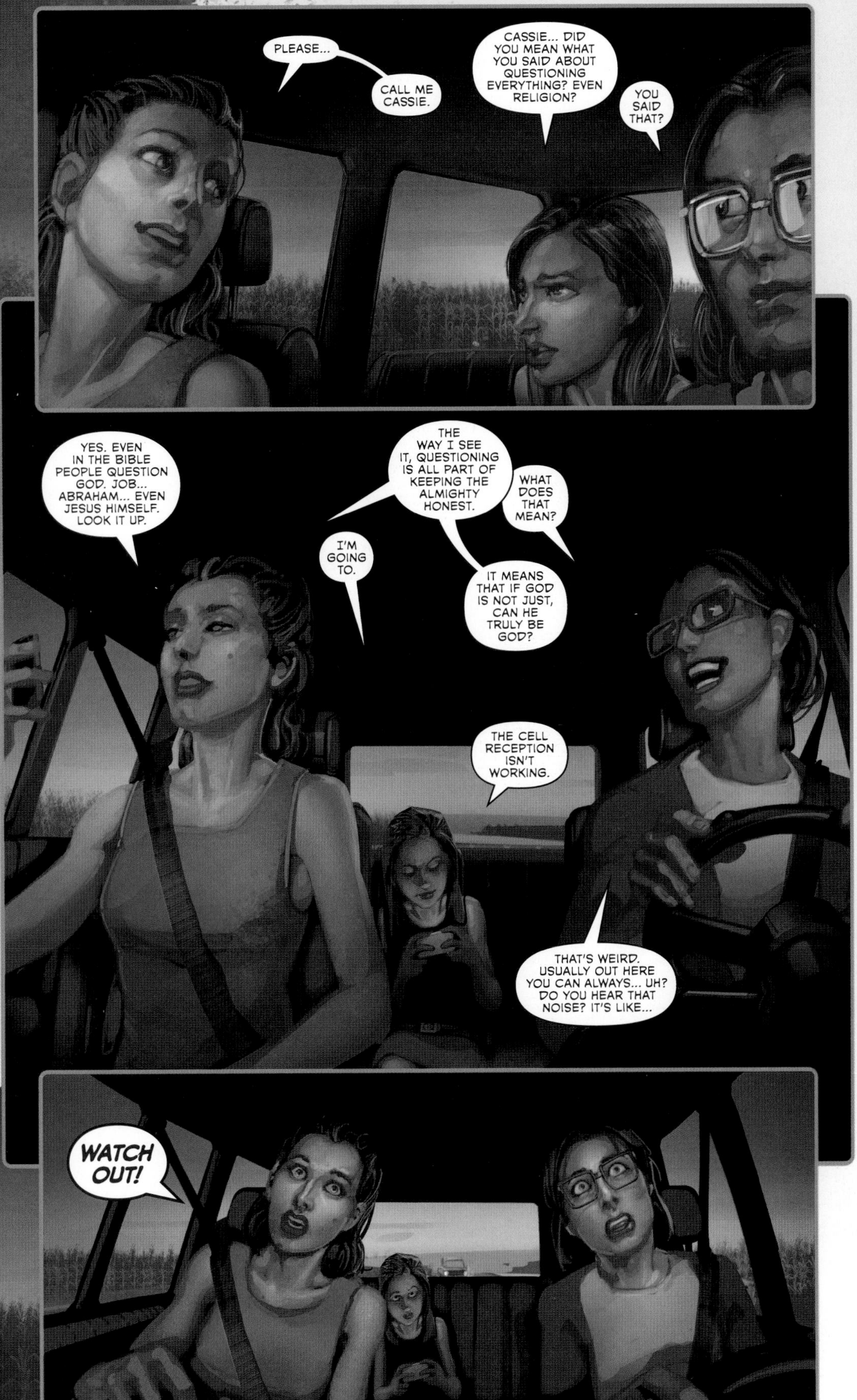
PLEASE...
CALL ME CASSIE.
CASSIE... DID YOU MEAN WHAT YOU SAID ABOUT QUESTIONING EVERYTHING? EVEN RELIGION?
YOU SAID THAT?
YES. EVEN IN THE BIBLE PEOPLE QUESTION GOD. JOB... ABRAHAM... EVEN JESUS HIMSELF. LOOK IT UP.
I'M GOING TO.
THE WAY I SEE IT, QUESTIONING IS ALL PART OF KEEPING THE ALMIGHTY HONEST.
WHAT DOES THAT MEAN?
IT MEANS THAT IF GOD IS NOT JUST, CAN HE TRULY BE GOD?
THE CELL RECEPTION ISN'T WORKING.
THAT'S WEIRD. USUALLY OUT HERE YOU CAN ALWAYS... UH? DO YOU HEAR THAT NOISE? IT'S LIKE...
WATCH OUT!

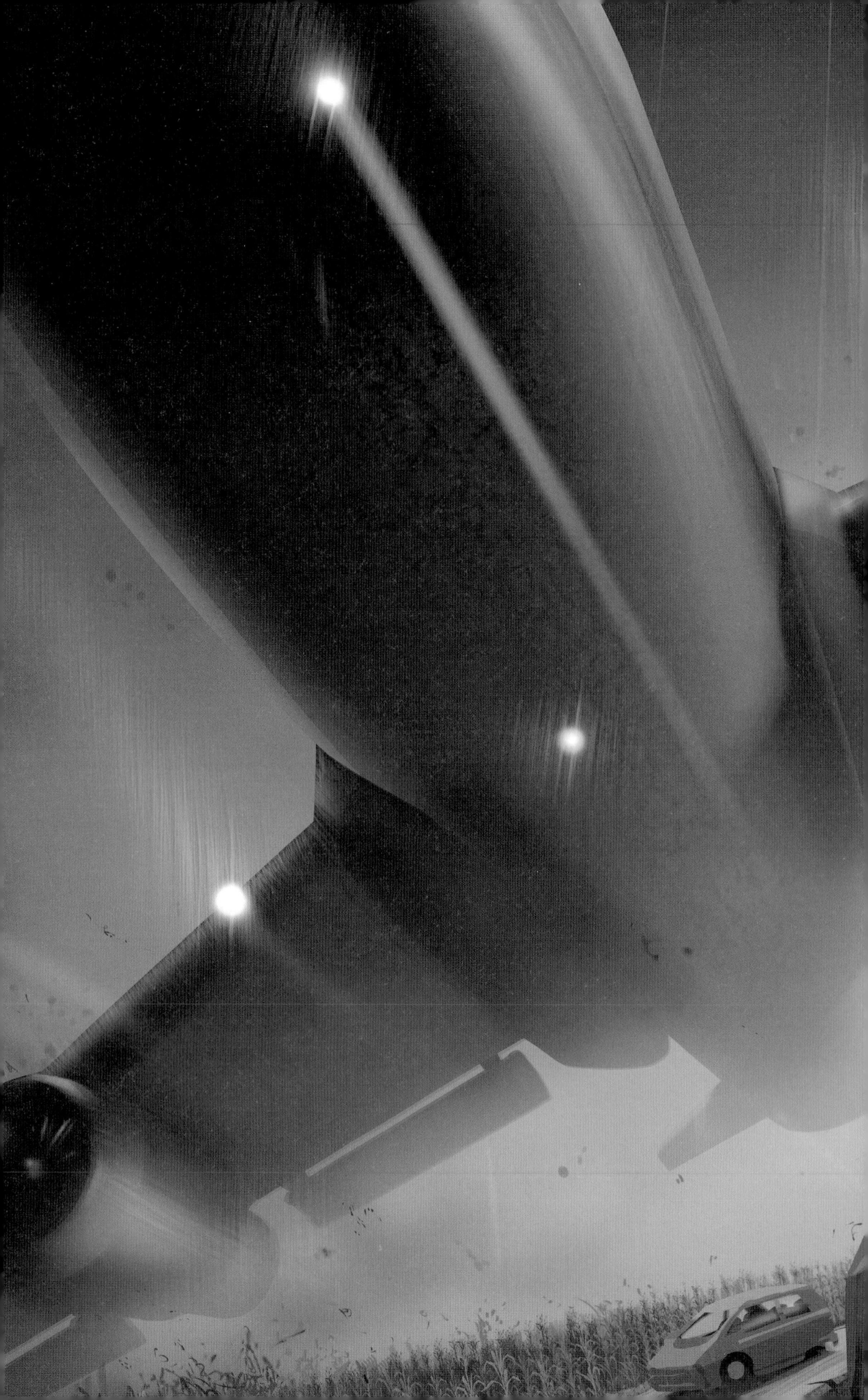

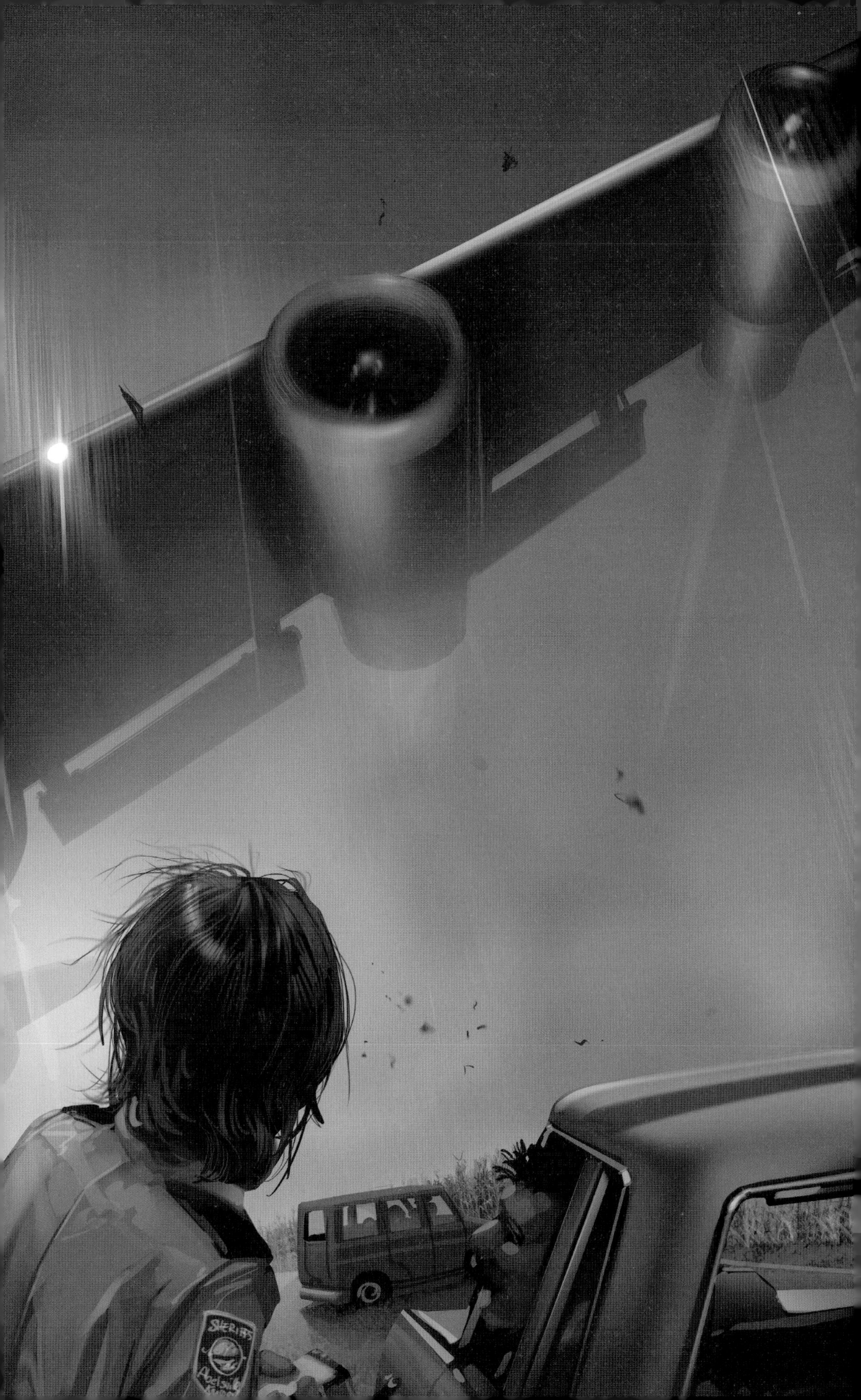
SHERIFFS

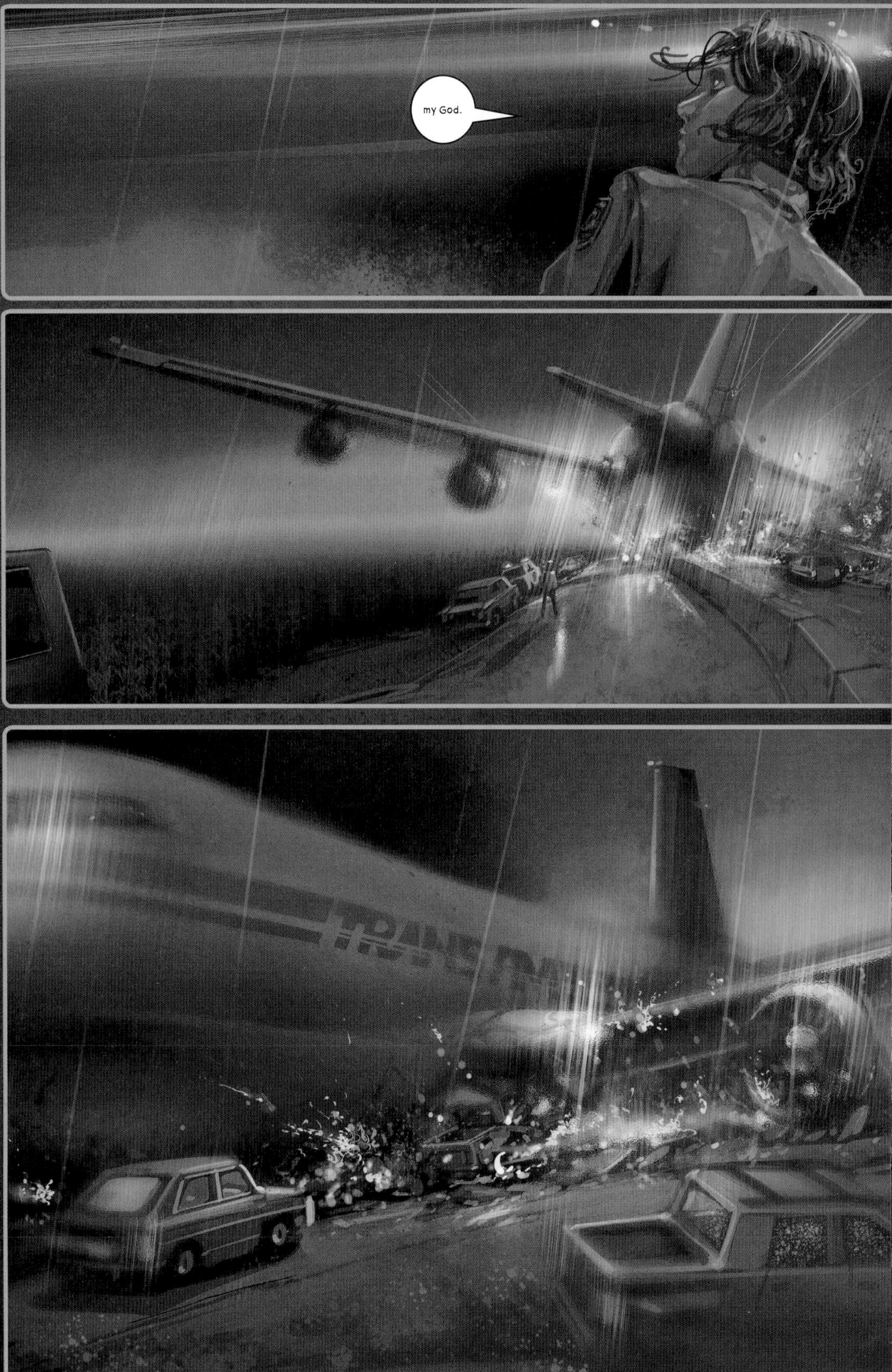
my God.

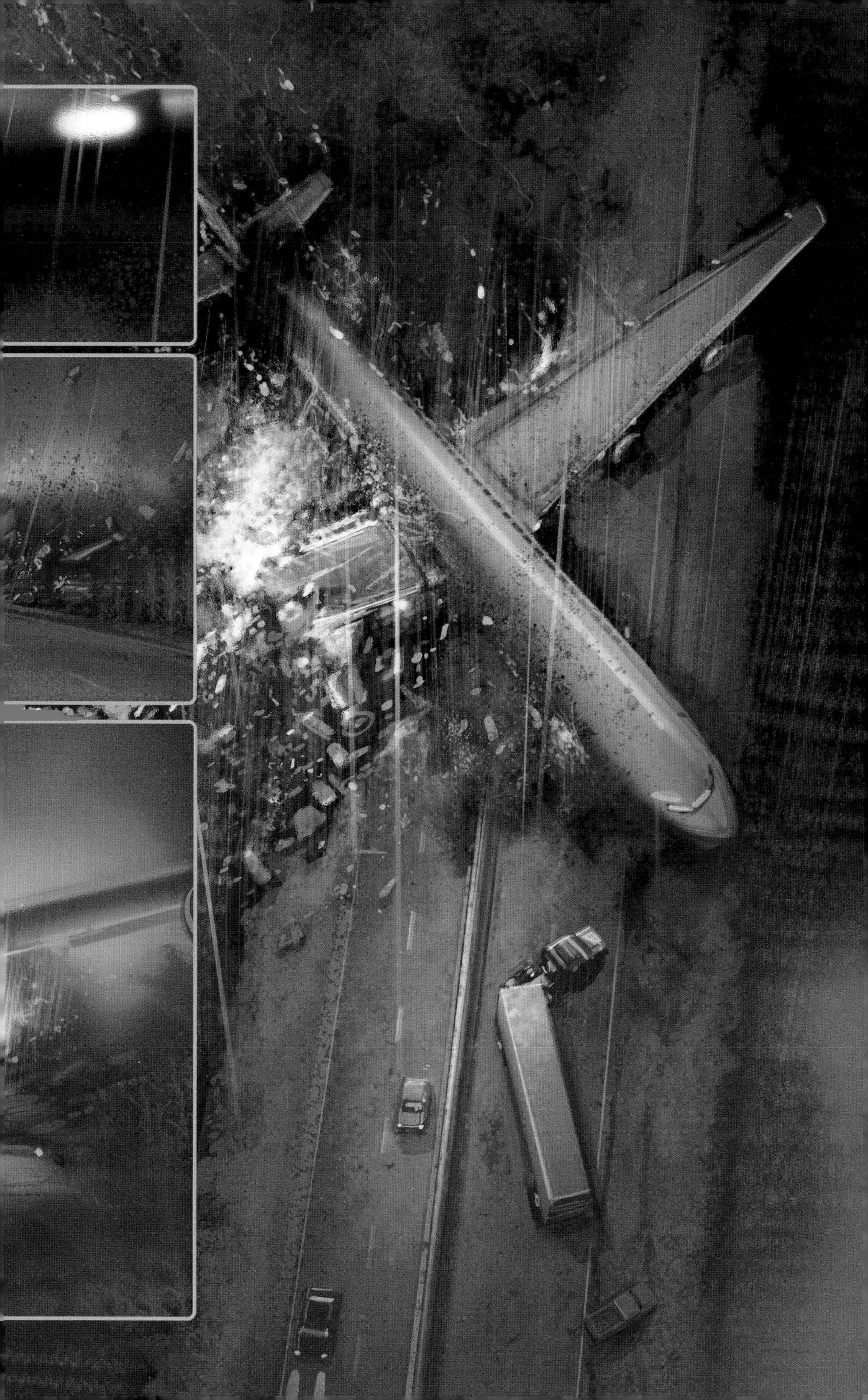

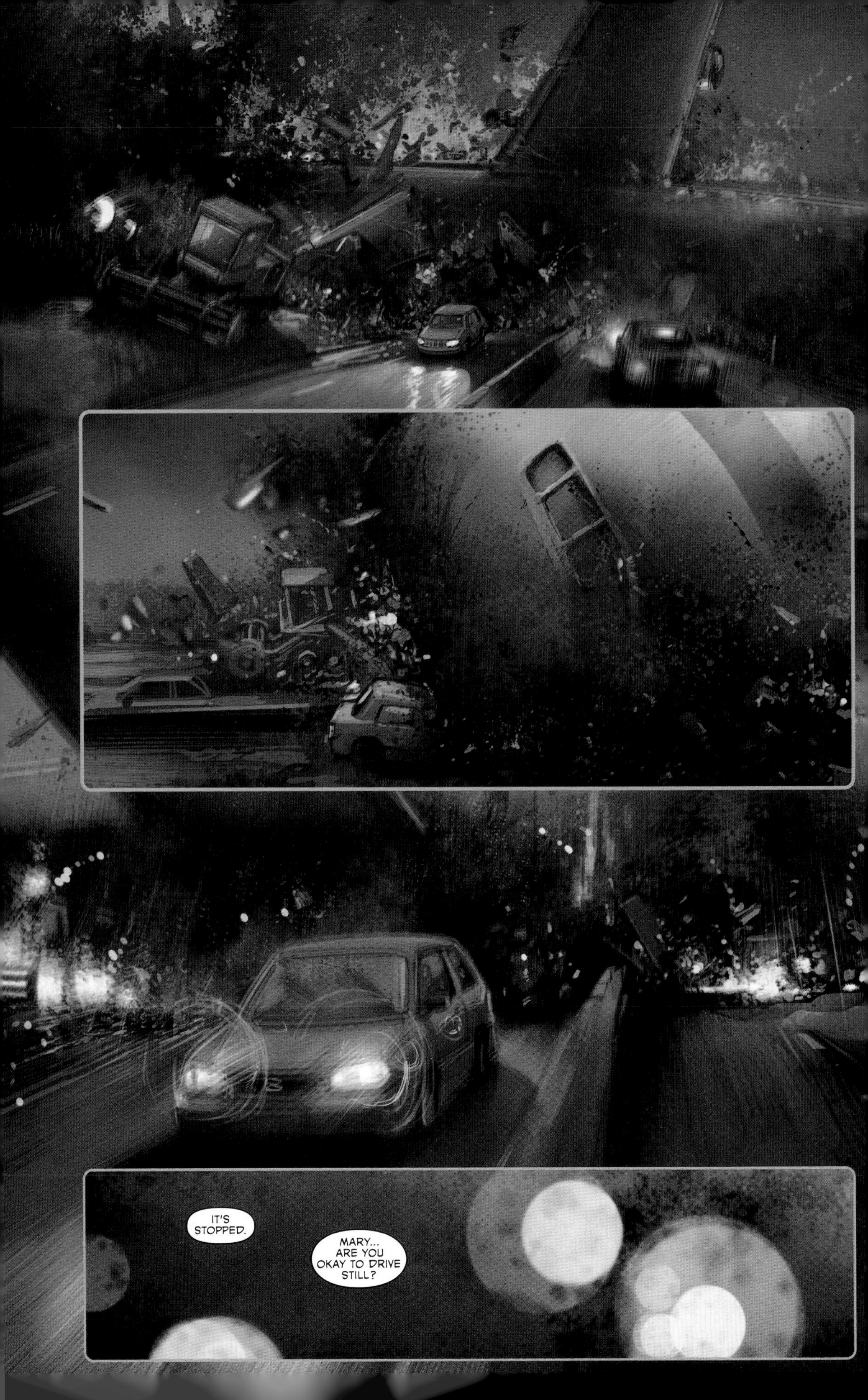
IT'S STOPPED.
MARY... ARE YOU OKAY TO DRIVE STILL?

I THINK SO.

GOOD. THEN DON'T STOP! DRIVE UP ON THE SHOULDER. GET AS CLOSE AS YOU CAN.

DO YOU HAVE A FIRST-AID KIT?

WHY?

IN THE BACK, I THINK.

I'M GOING TO RECORD THIS, BUT I'M GOING TO NEED YOUR HELP.

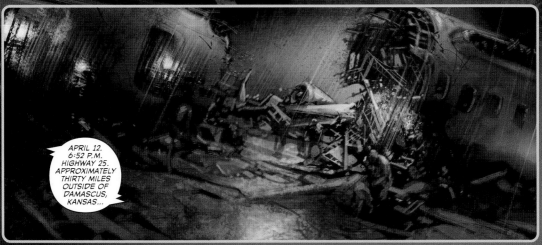

APRIL 12. 6:52 P.M. HIGHWAY 25. APPROXIMATELY THIRTY MILES OUTSIDE OF DAMASCUS, KANSAS...

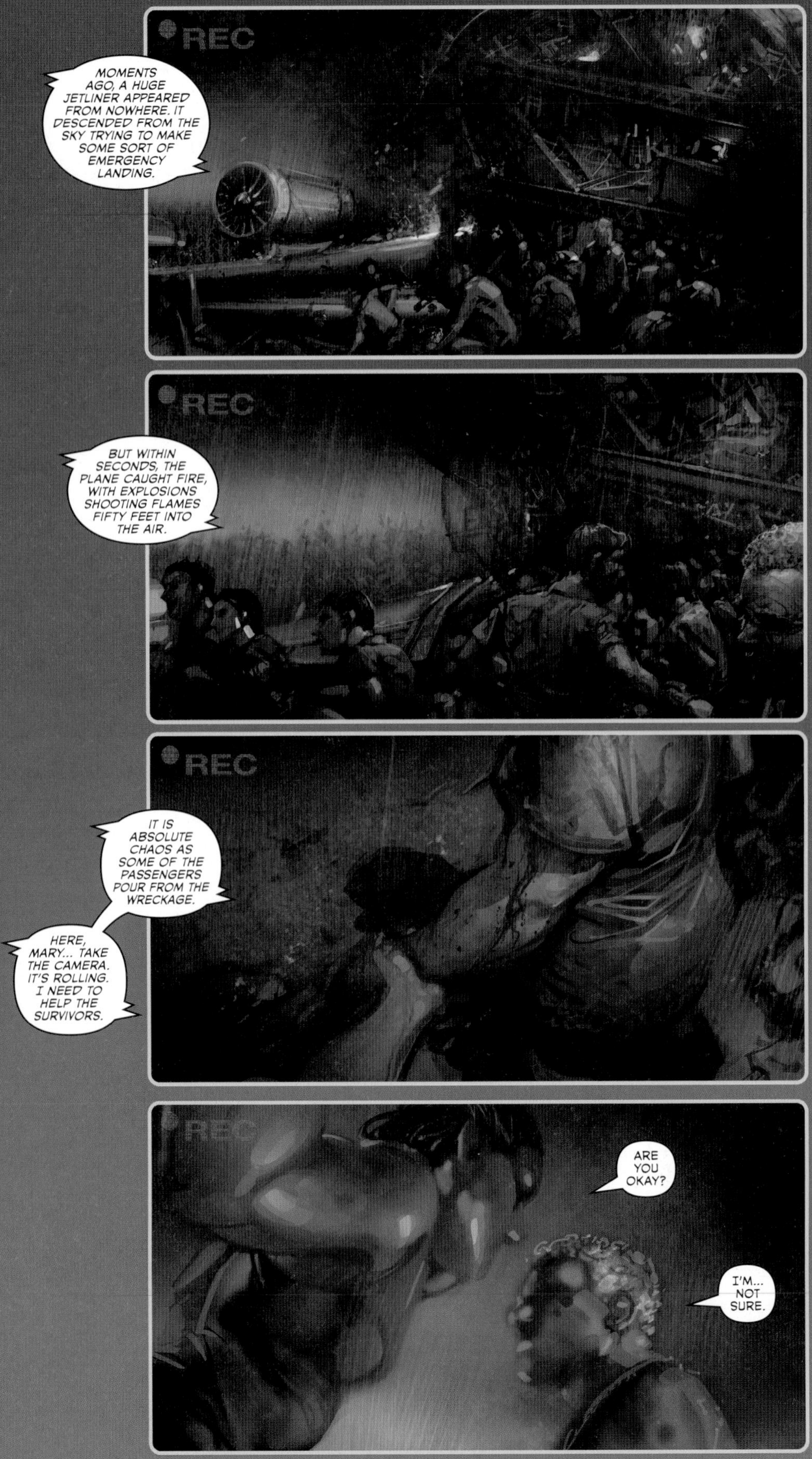
REC
MOMENTS AGO, A HUGE JETLINER APPEARED FROM NOWHERE. IT DESCENDED FROM THE SKY TRYING TO MAKE SOME SORT OF EMERGENCY LANDING.
REC
BUT WITHIN SECONDS, THE PLANE CAUGHT FIRE, WITH EXPLOSIONS SHOOTING FLAMES FIFTY FEET INTO THE AIR.
REC
IT IS ABSOLUTE CHAOS AS SOME OF THE PASSENGERS POUR FROM THE WRECKAGE.
HERE, MARY... TAKE THE CAMERA. IT'S ROLLING. I NEED TO HELP THE SURVIVORS.
REC
ARE YOU OKAY?
I'M... NOT SURE.

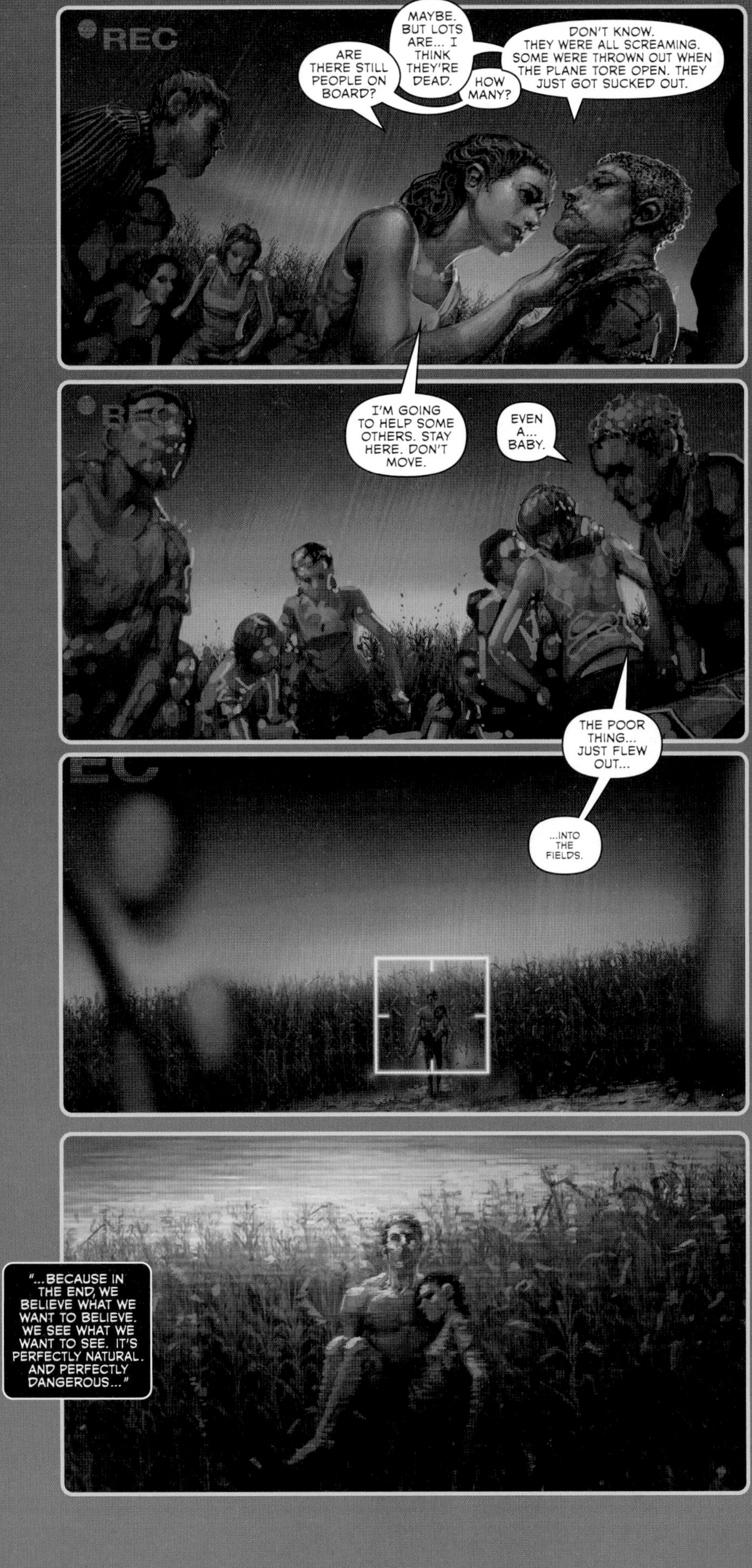
REC
ARE THERE STILL PEOPLE ON BOARD?
MAYBE. BUT LOTS ARE... I THINK THEY'RE DEAD.
HOW MANY?
DON'T KNOW. THEY WERE ALL SCREAMING. SOME WERE THROWN OUT WHEN THE PLANE TORE OPEN. THEY JUST GOT SUCKED OUT.
I'M GOING TO HELP SOME OTHERS. STAY HERE. DON'T MOVE.
EVEN A... BABY.
THE POOR THING... JUST FLEW OUT...
...INTO THE FIELDS.
"...BECAUSE IN THE END, WE BELIEVE WHAT WE WANT TO BELIEVE. WE SEE WHAT WE WANT TO SEE. IT'S PERFECTLY NATURAL. AND PERFECTLY DANGEROUS..."

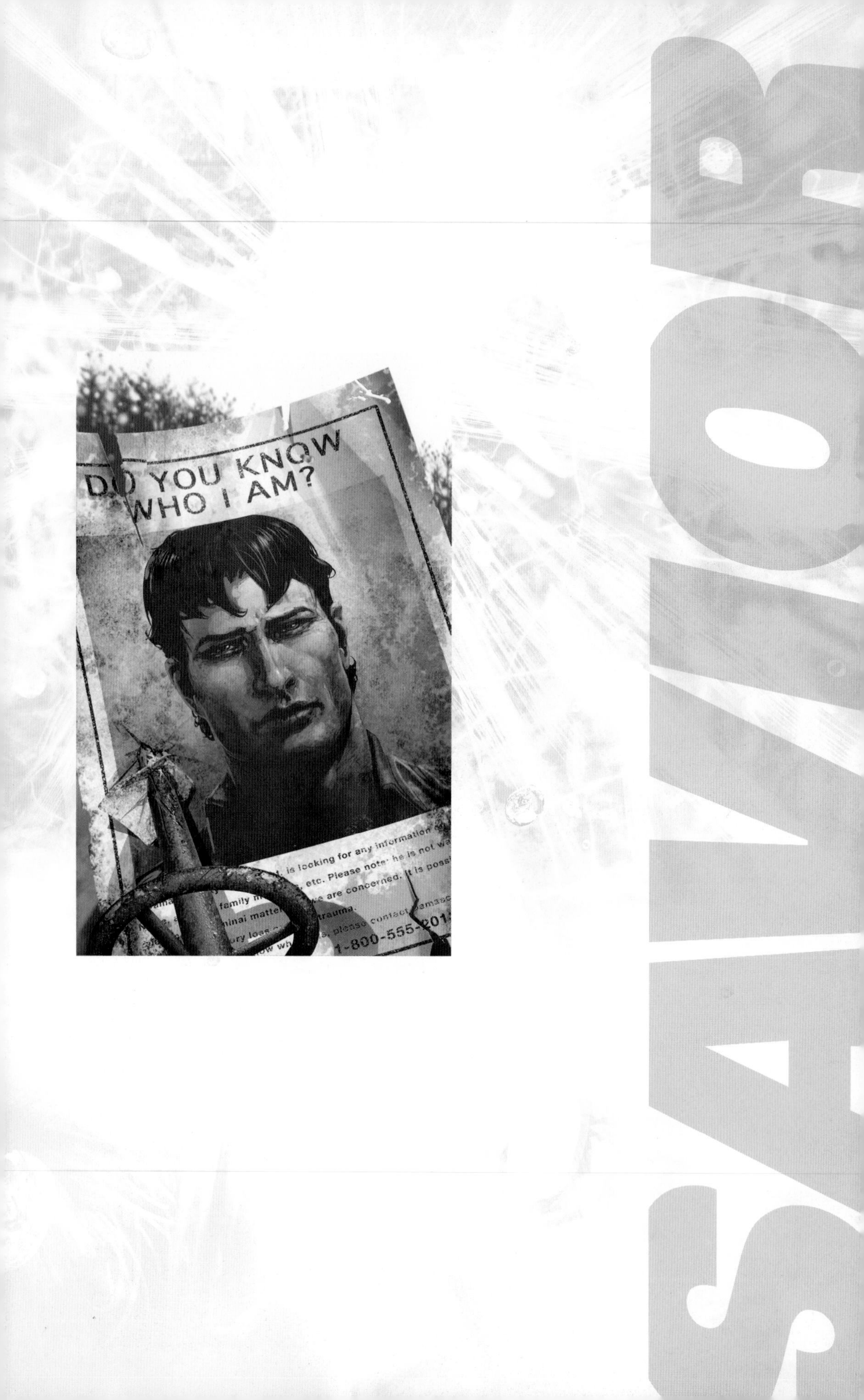
DO YOU KNOW
WHO I AM?
SAVIOR

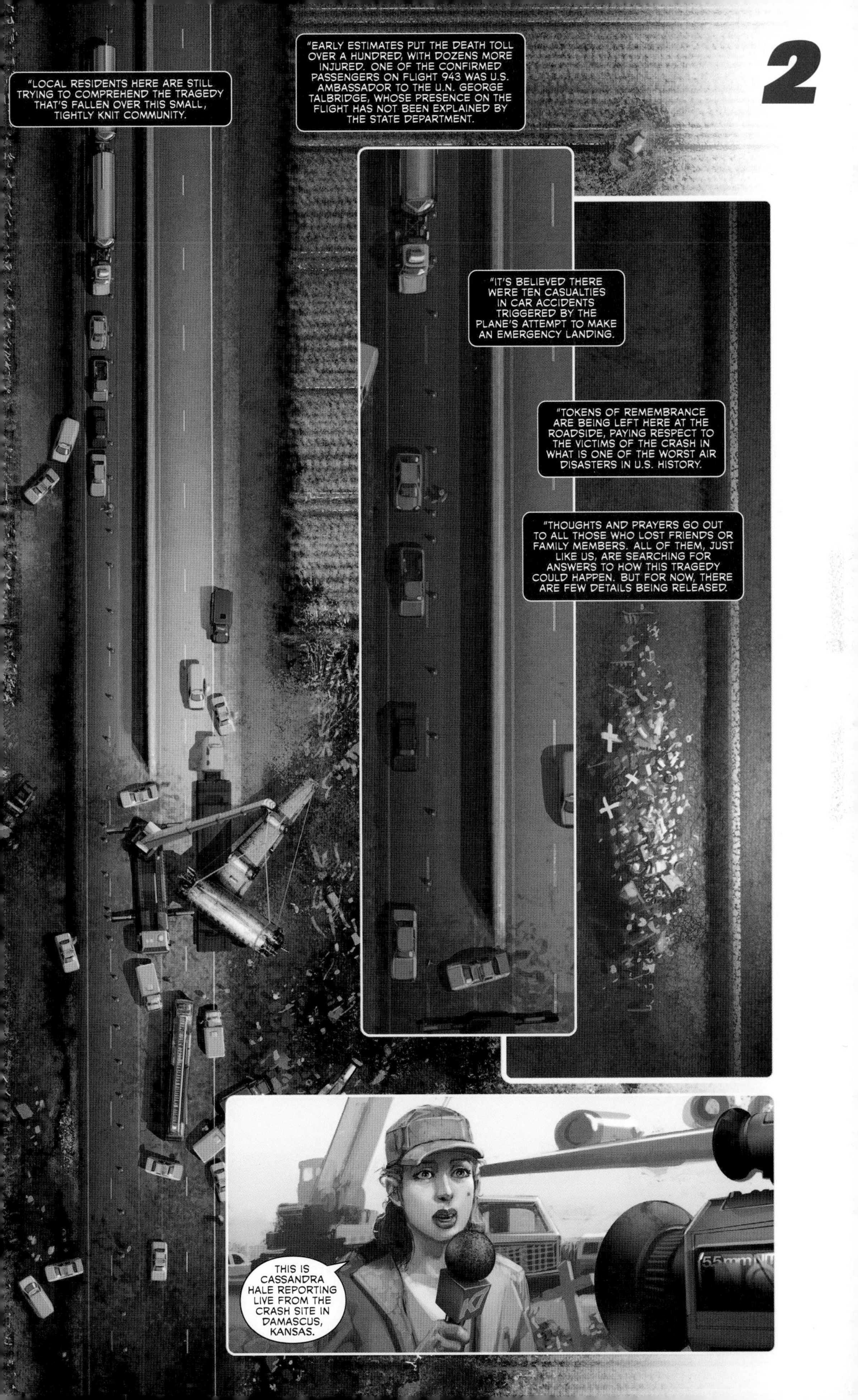
"LOCAL RESIDENTS HERE ARE STILL TRYING TO COMPREHEND THE TRAGEDY THAT'S FALLEN OVER THIS SMALL, TIGHTLY KNIT COMMUNITY.
"EARLY ESTIMATES PUT THE DEATH TOLL OVER A HUNDRED, WITH DOZENS MORE INJURED. ONE OF THE CONFIRMED PASSENGERS ON FLIGHT 943 WAS U.S. AMBASSADOR TO THE U.N. GEORGE TALBRIDGE, WHOSE PRESENCE ON THE FLIGHT HAS NOT BEEN EXPLAINED BY THE STATE DEPARTMENT.
"IT'S BELIEVED THERE WERE TEN CASUALTIES IN CAR ACCIDENTS TRIGGERED BY THE PLANE'S ATTEMPT TO MAKE AN EMERGENCY LANDING.
"TOKENS OF REMEMBRANCE ARE BEING LEFT HERE AT THE ROADSIDE, PAYING RESPECT TO THE VICTIMS OF THE CRASH IN WHAT IS ONE OF THE WORST AIR DISASTERS IN U.S. HISTORY.
"THOUGHTS AND PRAYERS GO OUT TO ALL THOSE WHO LOST FRIENDS OR FAMILY MEMBERS. ALL OF THEM, JUST LIKE US, ARE SEARCHING FOR ANSWERS TO HOW THIS TRAGEDY COULD HAPPEN. BUT FOR NOW, THERE ARE FEW DETAILS BEING RELEASED.
THIS IS CASSANDRA HALE REPORTING LIVE FROM THE CRASH SITE IN DAMASCUS, KANSAS.
55mm

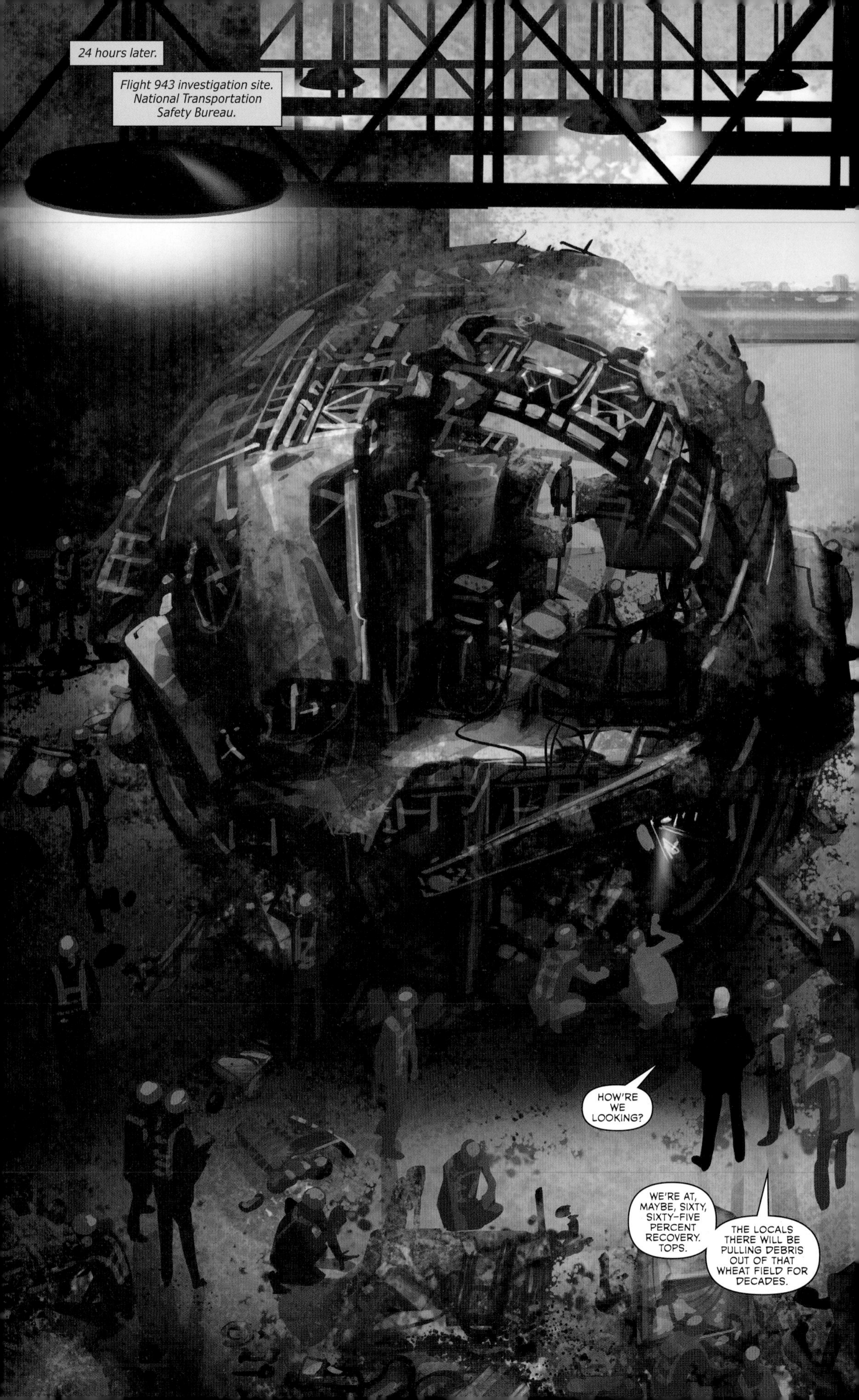
24 hours later.
Flight 943 investigation site. National Transportation Safety Bureau.
HOW'RE WE LOOKING?
WE'RE AT, MAYBE, SIXTY, SIXTY-FIVE PERCENT RECOVERY. TOPS.
THE LOCALS THERE WILL BE PULLING DEBRIS OUT OF THAT WHEAT FIELD FOR DECADES.

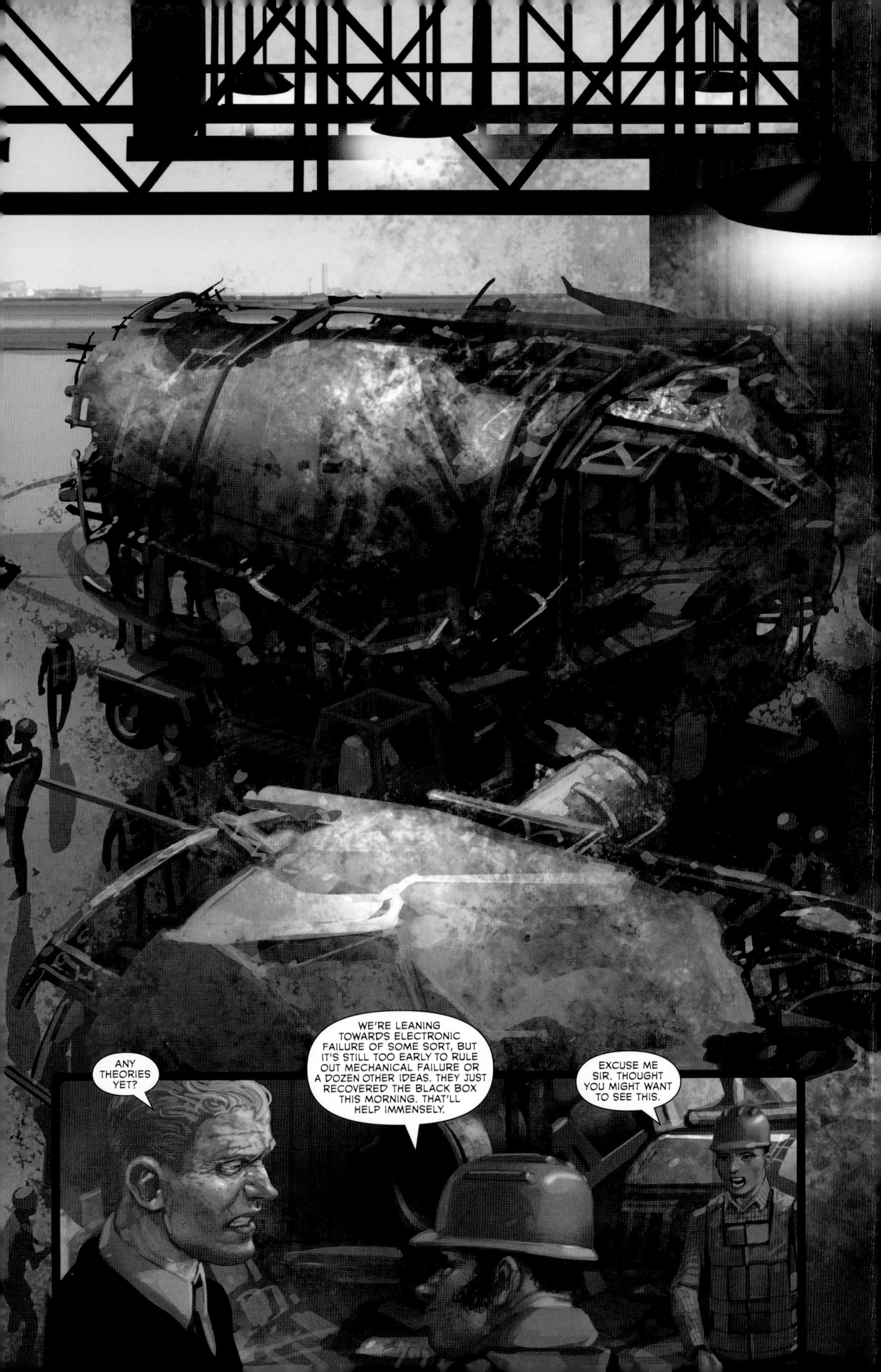
ANY THEORIES YET?
WE'RE LEANING TOWARDS ELECTRONIC FAILURE OF SOME SORT, BUT IT'S STILL TOO EARLY TO RULE OUT MECHANICAL FAILURE OR A DOZEN OTHER IDEAS. THEY JUST RECOVERED THE BLACK BOX THIS MORNING. THAT'LL HELP IMMENSELY.
EXCUSE ME SIR. THOUGHT YOU MIGHT WANT TO SEE THIS.

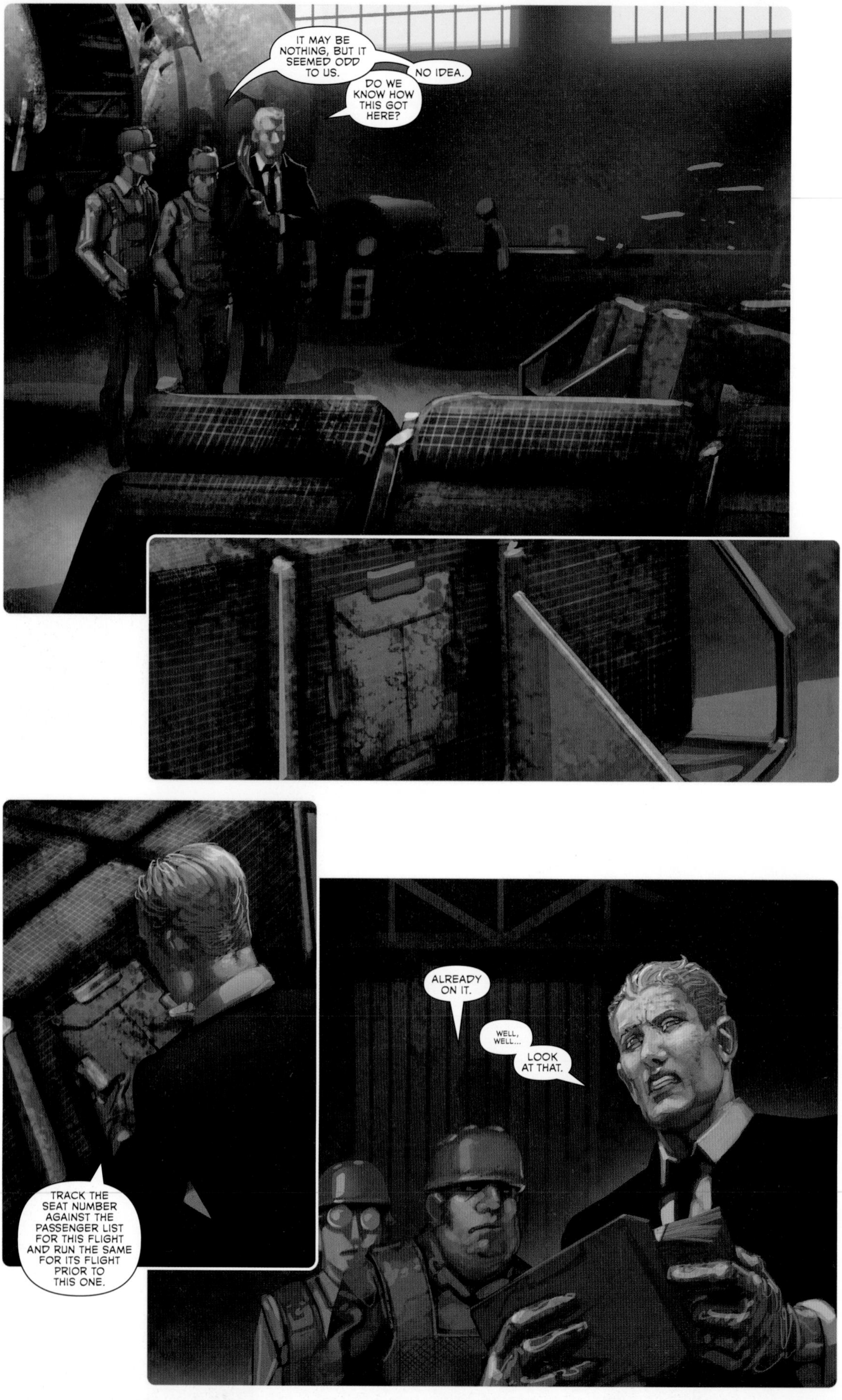
IT MAY BE NOTHING, BUT IT SEEMED ODD TO US.
NO IDEA.
DO WE KNOW HOW THIS GOT HERE?
TRACK THE SEAT NUMBER AGAINST THE PASSENGER LIST FOR THIS FLIGHT AND RUN THE SAME FOR ITS FLIGHT PRIOR TO THIS ONE.
ALREADY ON IT.
WELL, WELL...
LOOK AT THAT.

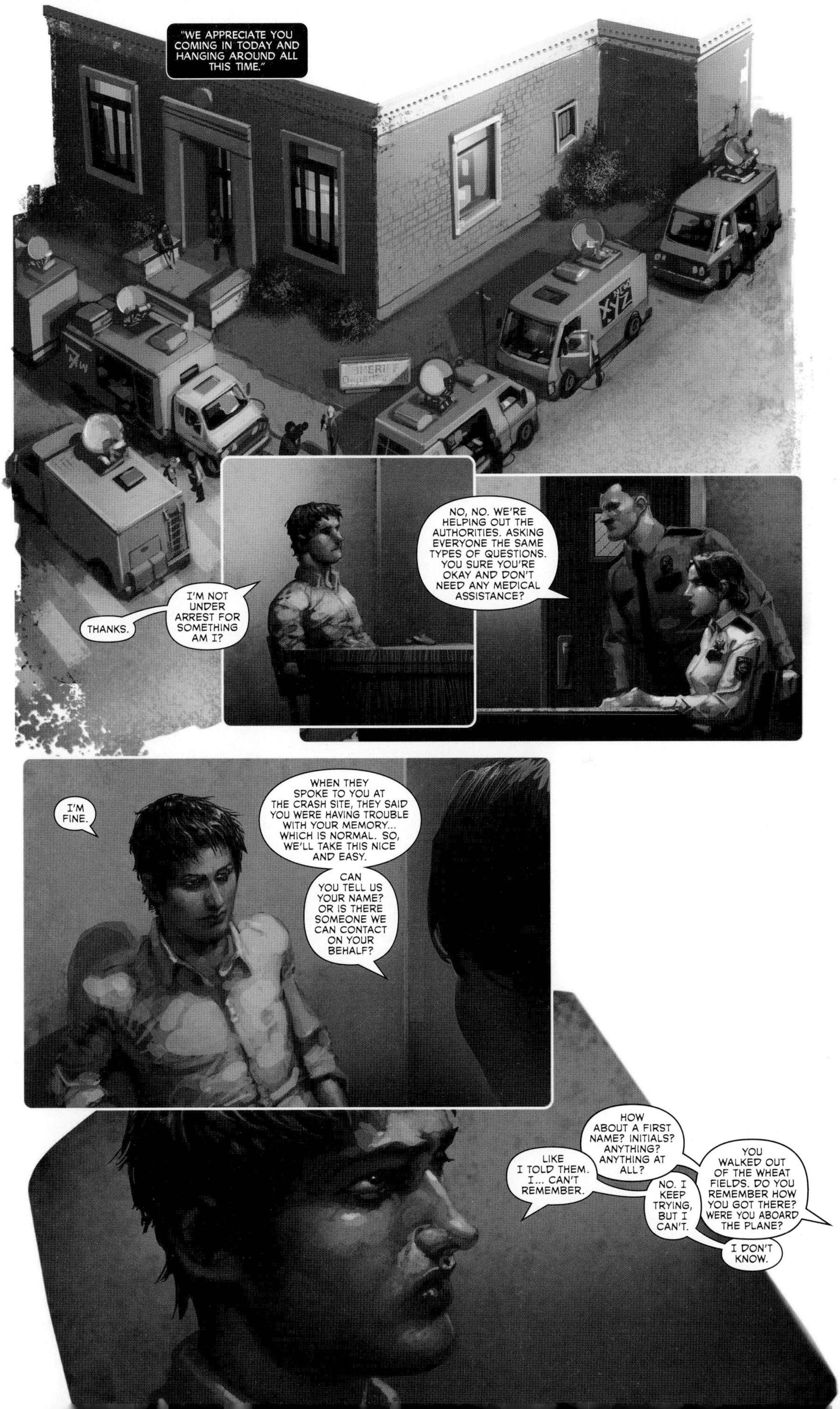
"WE APPRECIATE YOU COMING IN TODAY AND HANGING AROUND ALL THIS TIME."
THANKS.
I'M NOT UNDER ARREST FOR SOMETHING AM I?
NO, NO. WE'RE HELPING OUT THE AUTHORITIES. ASKING EVERYONE THE SAME TYPES OF QUESTIONS. YOU SURE YOU'RE OKAY AND DON'T NEED ANY MEDICAL ASSISTANCE?
I'M FINE.
WHEN THEY SPOKE TO YOU AT THE CRASH SITE, THEY SAID YOU WERE HAVING TROUBLE WITH YOUR MEMORY... WHICH IS NORMAL. SO, WE'LL TAKE THIS NICE AND EASY.
CAN YOU TELL US YOUR NAME? OR IS THERE SOMEONE WE CAN CONTACT ON YOUR BEHALF?
LIKE I TOLD THEM. I... CAN'T REMEMBER.
HOW ABOUT A FIRST NAME? INITIALS? ANYTHING? ANYTHING AT ALL?
NO. I KEEP TRYING, BUT I CAN'T.
YOU WALKED OUT OF THE WHEAT FIELDS. DO YOU REMEMBER HOW YOU GOT THERE? WERE YOU ABOARD THE PLANE?
I DON'T KNOW.

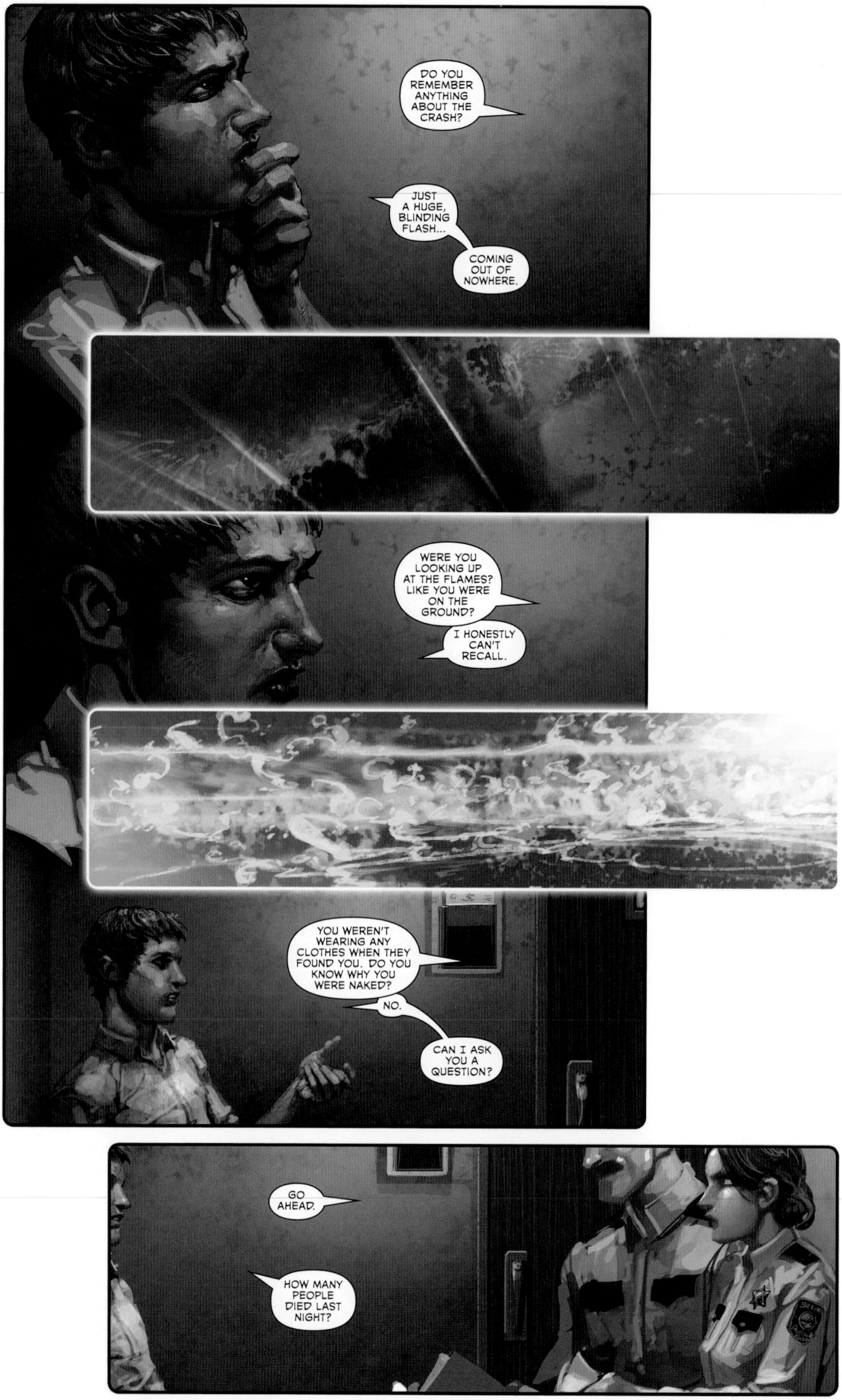
DO YOU REMEMBER ANYTHING ABOUT THE CRASH?
JUST A HUGE, BLINDING FLASH...
COMING OUT OF NOWHERE.
WERE YOU LOOKING UP AT THE FLAMES? LIKE YOU WERE ON THE GROUND?
I HONESTLY CAN'T RECALL.
YOU WEREN'T WEARING ANY CLOTHES WHEN THEY FOUND YOU. DO YOU KNOW WHY YOU WERE NAKED?
NO.
CAN I ASK YOU A QUESTION?
GO AHEAD.
HOW MANY PEOPLE DIED LAST NIGHT?

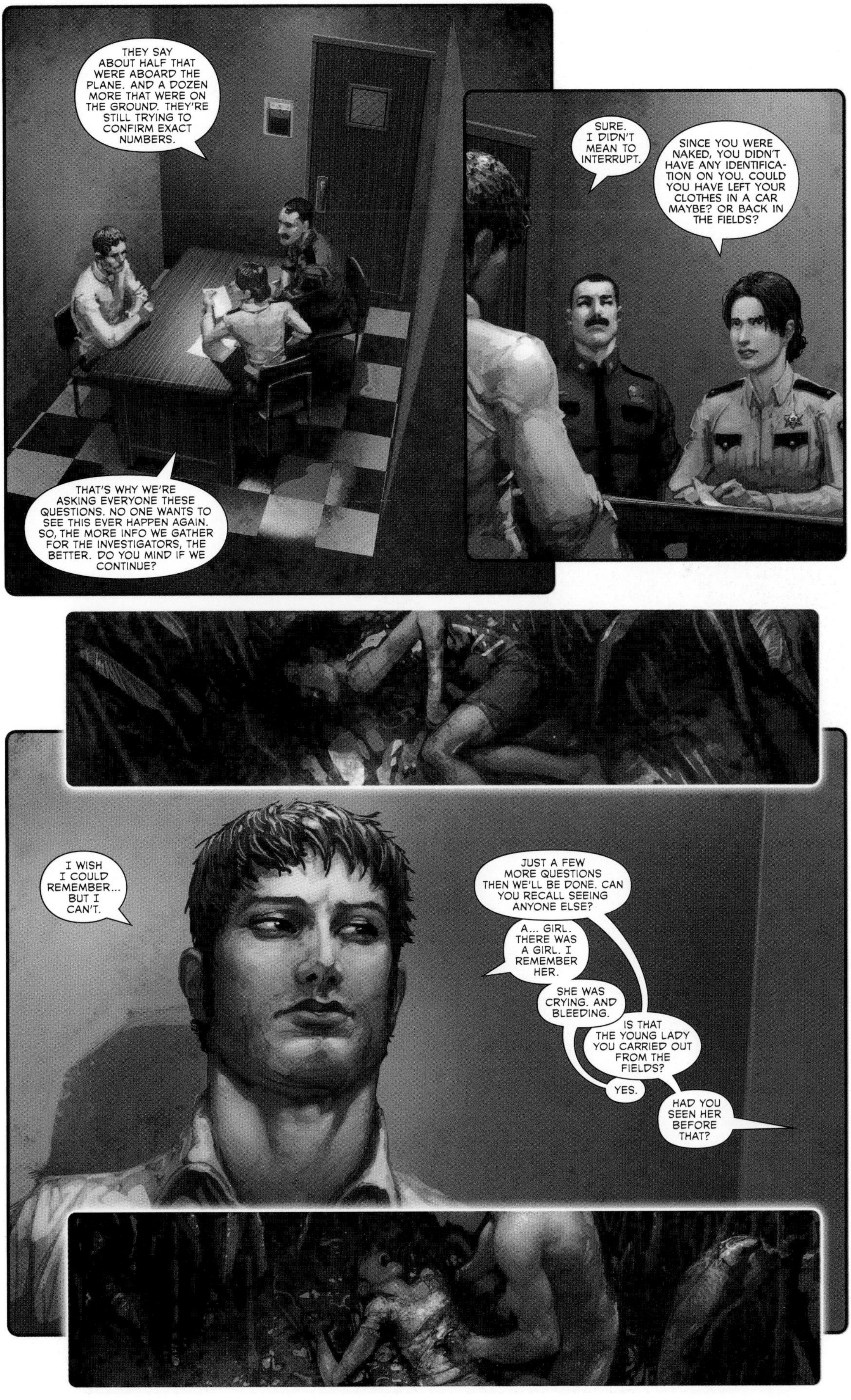
THEY SAY ABOUT HALF THAT WERE ABOARD THE PLANE. AND A DOZEN MORE THAT WERE ON THE GROUND. THEY'RE STILL TRYING TO CONFIRM EXACT NUMBERS.
THAT'S WHY WE'RE ASKING EVERYONE THESE QUESTIONS. NO ONE WANTS TO SEE THIS EVER HAPPEN AGAIN. SO, THE MORE INFO WE GATHER FOR THE INVESTIGATORS, THE BETTER. DO YOU MIND IF WE CONTINUE?
SURE. I DIDN'T MEAN TO INTERRUPT.
SINCE YOU WERE NAKED, YOU DIDN'T HAVE ANY IDENTIFICATION ON YOU. COULD YOU HAVE LEFT YOUR CLOTHES IN A CAR MAYBE? OR BACK IN THE FIELDS?
I WISH I COULD REMEMBER... BUT I CAN'T.
JUST A FEW MORE QUESTIONS THEN WE'LL BE DONE. CAN YOU RECALL SEEING ANYONE ELSE?
A... GIRL. THERE WAS A GIRL. I REMEMBER HER.
SHE WAS CRYING. AND BLEEDING.
IS THAT THE YOUNG LADY YOU CARRIED OUT FROM THE FIELDS?
YES.
HAD YOU SEEN HER BEFORE THAT?

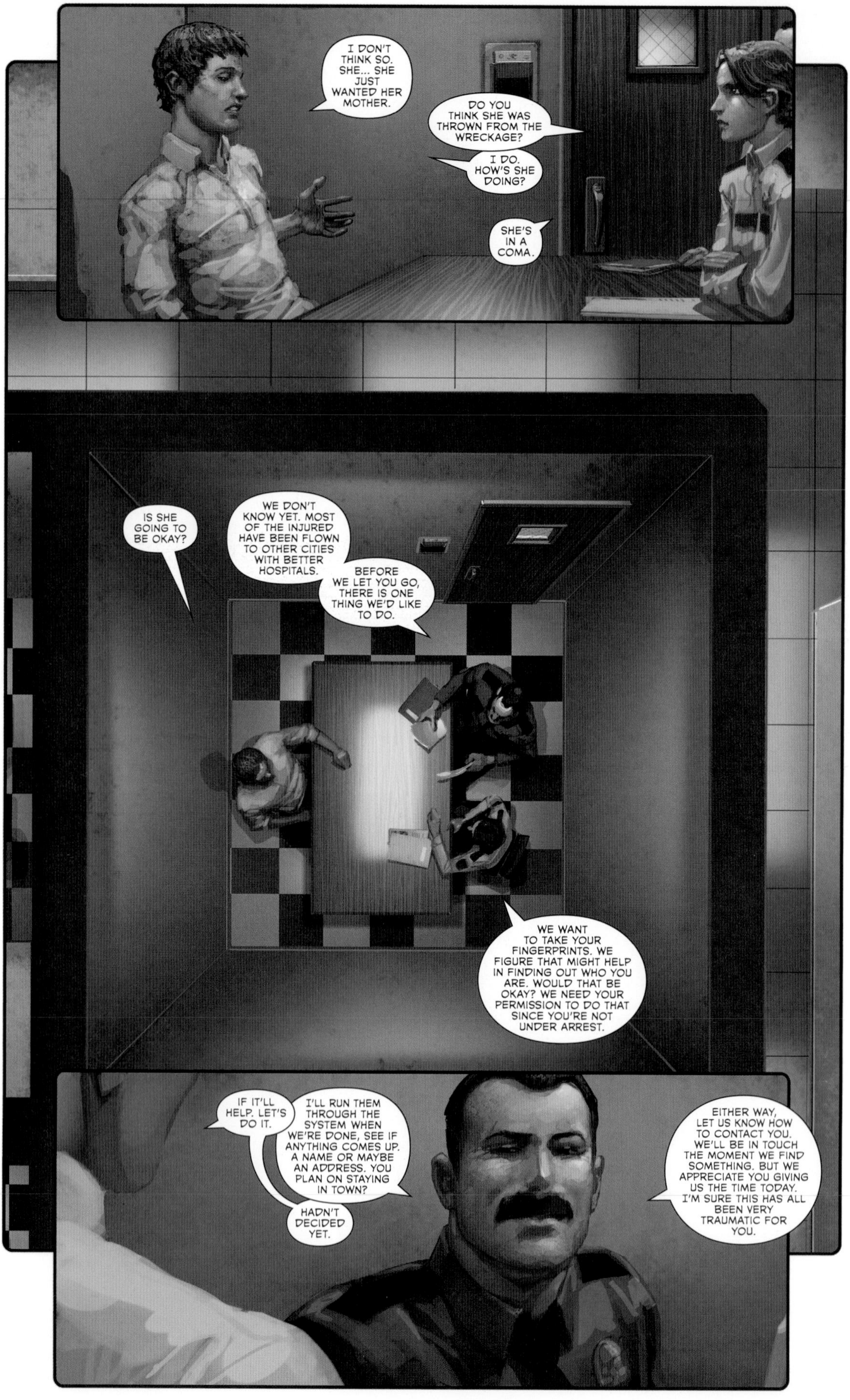
I DON'T THINK SO. SHE... SHE JUST WANTED HER MOTHER.
DO YOU THINK SHE WAS THROWN FROM THE WRECKAGE?
I DO. HOW'S SHE DOING?
SHE'S IN A COMA.
IS SHE GOING TO BE OKAY?
WE DON'T KNOW YET. MOST OF THE INJURED HAVE BEEN FLOWN TO OTHER CITIES WITH BETTER HOSPITALS.
BEFORE WE LET YOU GO, THERE IS ONE THING WE'D LIKE TO DO.
WE WANT TO TAKE YOUR FINGERPRINTS. WE FIGURE THAT MIGHT HELP IN FINDING OUT WHO YOU ARE. WOULD THAT BE OKAY? WE NEED YOUR PERMISSION TO DO THAT SINCE YOU'RE NOT UNDER ARREST.
IF IT'LL HELP. LET'S DO IT.
I'LL RUN THEM THROUGH THE SYSTEM WHEN WE'RE DONE, SEE IF ANYTHING COMES UP. A NAME OR MAYBE AN ADDRESS. YOU PLAN ON STAYING IN TOWN?
HADN'T DECIDED YET.
EITHER WAY, LET US KNOW HOW TO CONTACT YOU. WE'LL BE IN TOUCH THE MOMENT WE FIND SOMETHING. BUT WE APPRECIATE YOU GIVING US THE TIME TODAY. I'M SURE THIS HAS ALL BEEN VERY TRAUMATIC FOR YOU.

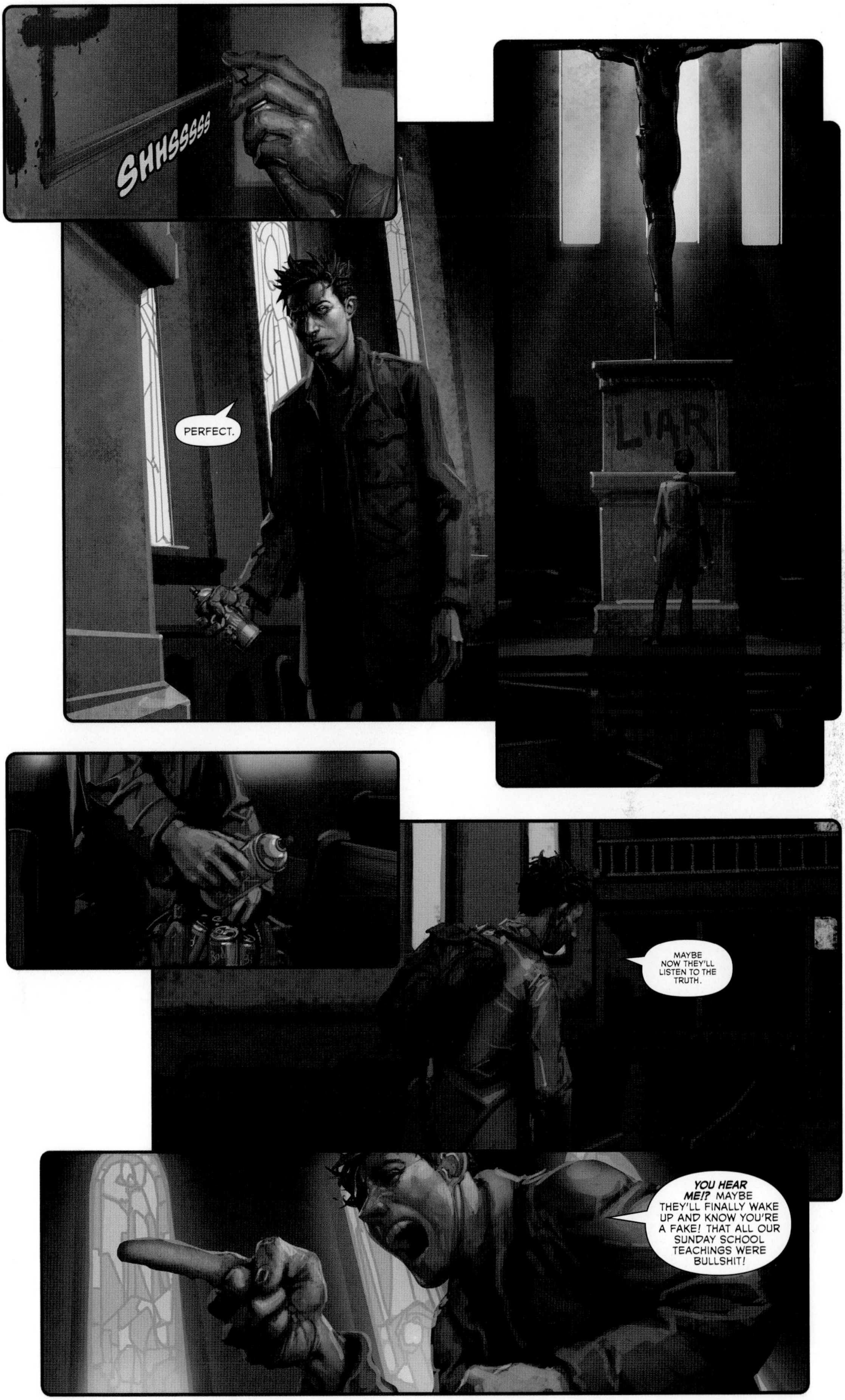
SHHSSSSS
PERFECT.
LIAR
MAYBE NOW THEY'LL LISTEN TO THE TRUTH.
YOU HEAR ME!? MAYBE THEY'LL FINALLY WAKE UP AND KNOW YOU'RE A FAKE! THAT ALL OUR SUNDAY SCHOOL TEACHINGS WERE BULLSHIT!

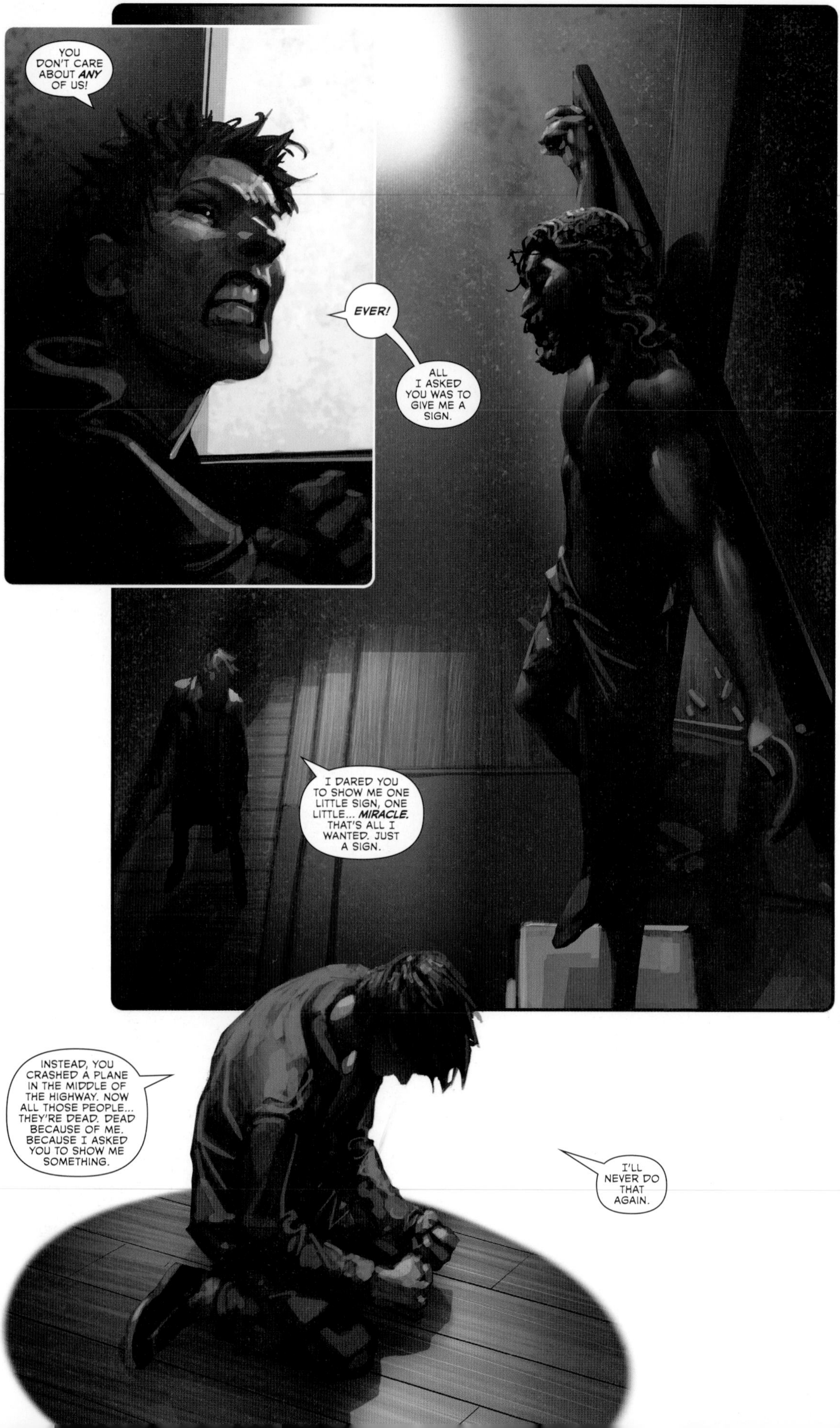
YOU DON'T CARE ABOUT ***ANY*** OF US!
EVER!
ALL I ASKED YOU WAS TO GIVE ME A SIGN.
I DARED YOU TO SHOW ME ONE LITTLE SIGN, ONE LITTLE... ***MIRACLE.*** THAT'S ALL I WANTED. JUST A SIGN.
INSTEAD, YOU CRASHED A PLANE IN THE MIDDLE OF THE HIGHWAY. NOW ALL THOSE PEOPLE... THEY'RE DEAD. DEAD BECAUSE OF ME. BECAUSE I ASKED YOU TO SHOW ME SOMETHING.
I'LL NEVER DO THAT AGAIN.

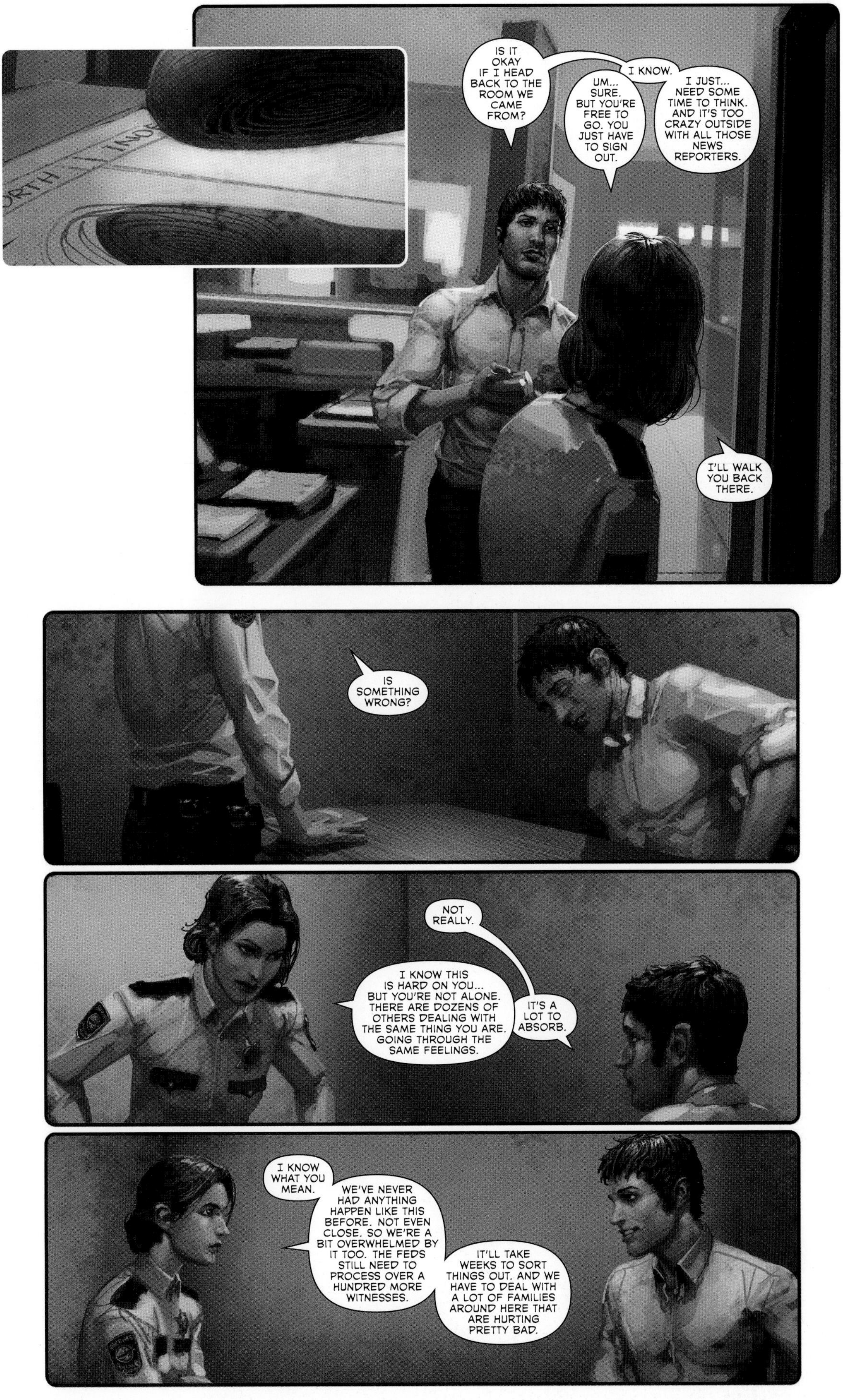
IS IT OKAY IF I HEAD BACK TO THE ROOM WE CAME FROM?
UM... SURE. BUT YOU'RE FREE TO GO. YOU JUST HAVE TO SIGN OUT.
I KNOW.
I JUST... NEED SOME TIME TO THINK. AND IT'S TOO CRAZY OUTSIDE WITH ALL THOSE NEWS REPORTERS.
I'LL WALK YOU BACK THERE.
IS SOMETHING WRONG?
NOT REALLY.
IT'S A LOT TO ABSORB.
I KNOW THIS IS HARD ON YOU... BUT YOU'RE NOT ALONE. THERE ARE DOZENS OF OTHERS DEALING WITH THE SAME THING YOU ARE. GOING THROUGH THE SAME FEELINGS.
I KNOW WHAT YOU MEAN.
WE'VE NEVER HAD ANYTHING HAPPEN LIKE THIS BEFORE. NOT EVEN CLOSE. SO WE'RE A BIT OVERWHELMED BY IT TOO. THE FEDS STILL NEED TO PROCESS OVER A HUNDRED MORE WITNESSES.
IT'LL TAKE WEEKS TO SORT THINGS OUT. AND WE HAVE TO DEAL WITH A LOT OF FAMILIES AROUND HERE THAT ARE HURTING PRETTY BAD.

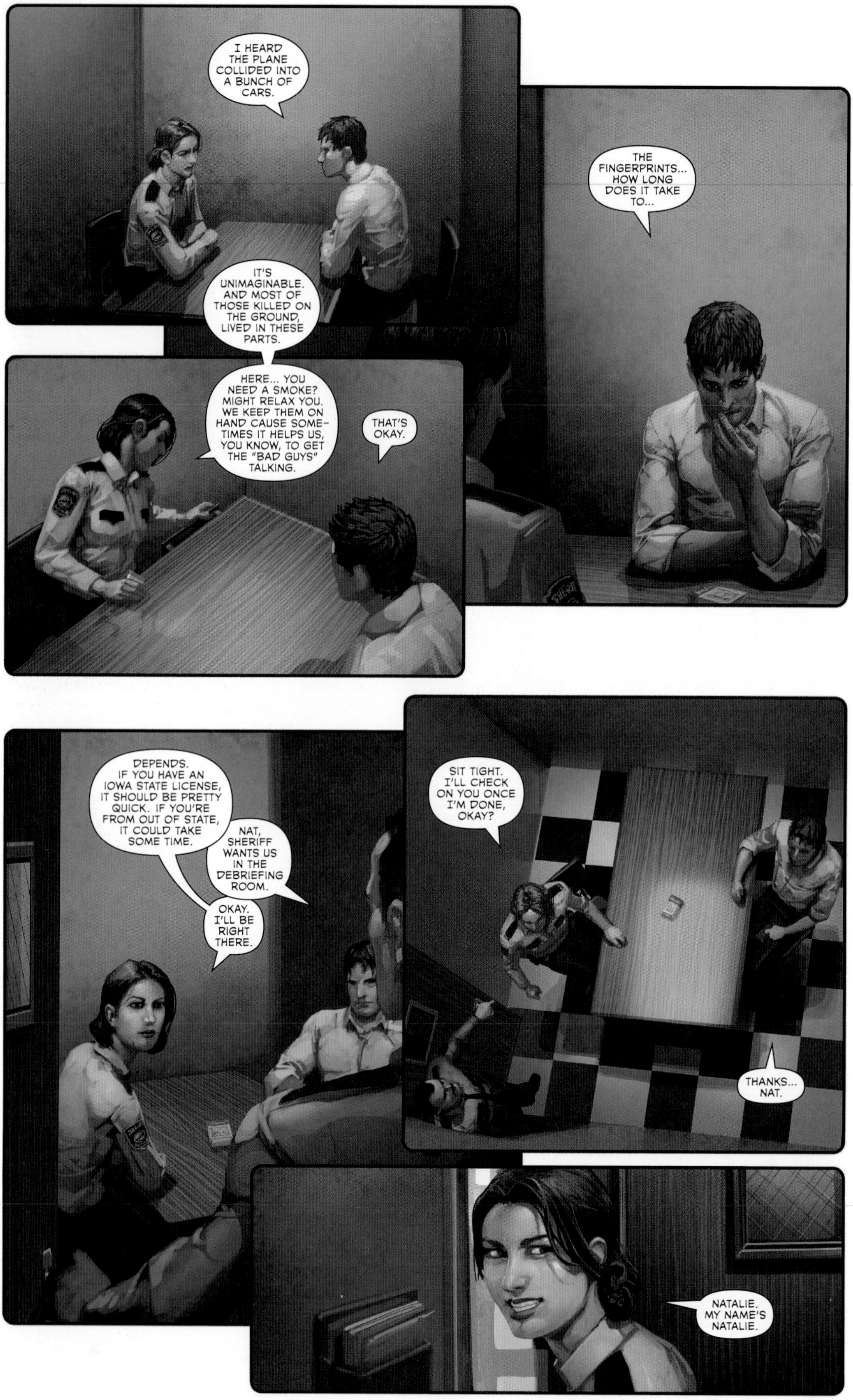
I HEARD THE PLANE COLLIDED INTO A BUNCH OF CARS.
IT'S UNIMAGINABLE. AND MOST OF THOSE KILLED ON THE GROUND, LIVED IN THESE PARTS.
THE FINGERPRINTS... HOW LONG DOES IT TAKE TO...
HERE... YOU NEED A SMOKE? MIGHT RELAX YOU. WE KEEP THEM ON HAND CAUSE SOMETIMES IT HELPS US, YOU KNOW, TO GET THE "BAD GUYS" TALKING.
THAT'S OKAY.
DEPENDS. IF YOU HAVE AN IOWA STATE LICENSE, IT SHOULD BE PRETTY QUICK. IF YOU'RE FROM OUT OF STATE, IT COULD TAKE SOME TIME.
NAT, SHERIFF WANTS US IN THE DEBRIEFING ROOM.
OKAY. I'LL BE RIGHT THERE.
SIT TIGHT. I'LL CHECK ON YOU ONCE I'M DONE, OKAY?
THANKS... NAT.
NATALIE. MY NAME'S NATALIE.

Twenty minutes later.

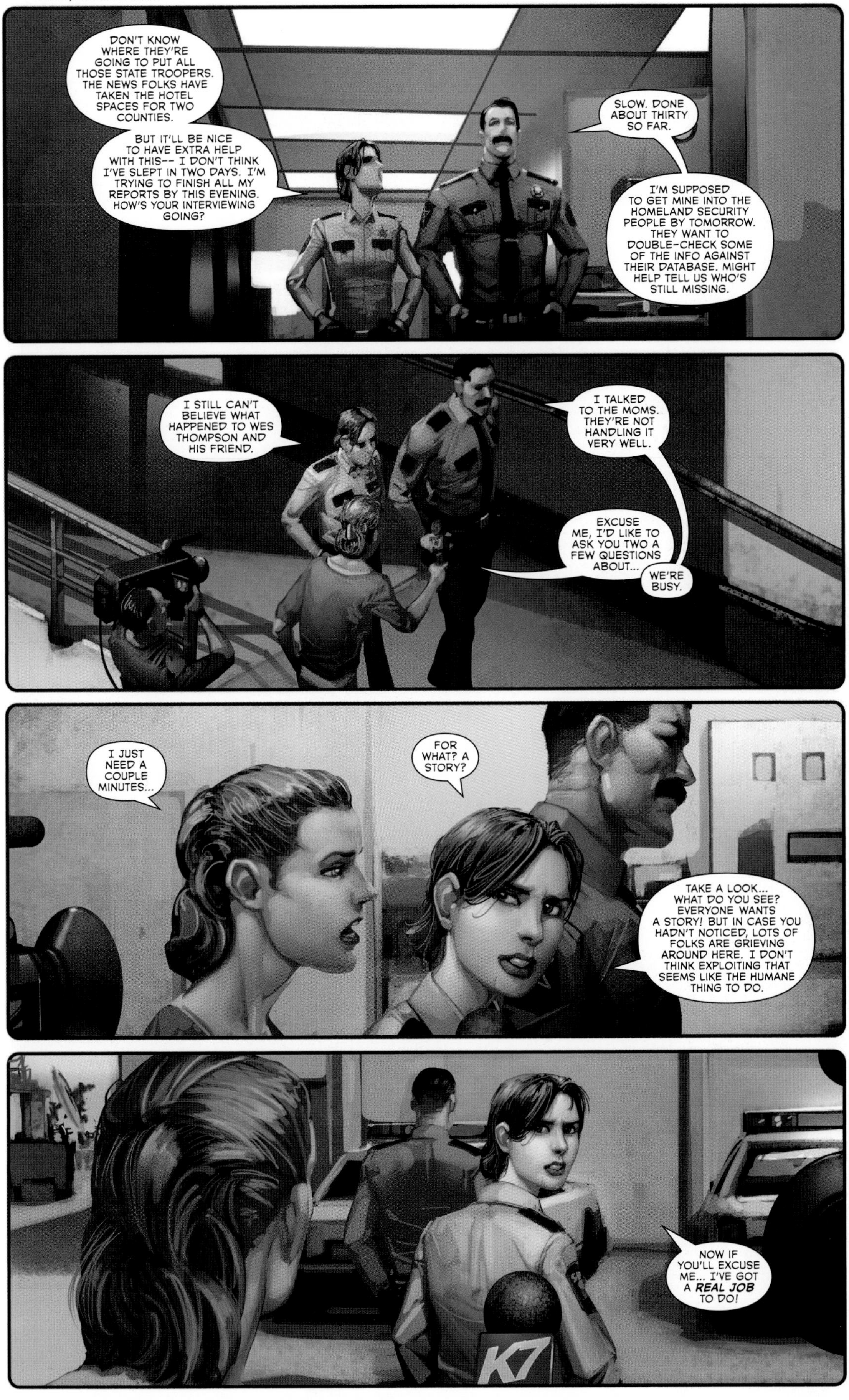
DON'T KNOW WHERE THEY'RE GOING TO PUT ALL THOSE STATE TROOPERS. THE NEWS FOLKS HAVE TAKEN THE HOTEL SPACES FOR TWO COUNTIES.
BUT IT'LL BE NICE TO HAVE EXTRA HELP WITH THIS-- I DON'T THINK I'VE SLEPT IN TWO DAYS. I'M TRYING TO FINISH ALL MY REPORTS BY THIS EVENING. HOW'S YOUR INTERVIEWING GOING?
SLOW. DONE ABOUT THIRTY SO FAR.
I'M SUPPOSED TO GET MINE INTO THE HOMELAND SECURITY PEOPLE BY TOMORROW. THEY WANT TO DOUBLE-CHECK SOME OF THE INFO AGAINST THEIR DATABASE. MIGHT HELP TELL US WHO'S STILL MISSING.
I STILL CAN'T BELIEVE WHAT HAPPENED TO WES THOMPSON AND HIS FRIEND.
I TALKED TO THE MOMS. THEY'RE NOT HANDLING IT VERY WELL.
EXCUSE ME, I'D LIKE TO ASK YOU TWO A FEW QUESTIONS ABOUT...
WE'RE BUSY.
I JUST NEED A COUPLE MINUTES...
FOR WHAT? A STORY?
TAKE A LOOK... WHAT DO YOU SEE? EVERYONE WANTS A STORY! BUT IN CASE YOU HADN'T NOTICED, LOTS OF FOLKS ARE GRIEVING AROUND HERE. I DON'T THINK EXPLOITING THAT SEEMS LIKE THE HUMANE THING TO DO.
NOW IF YOU'LL EXCUSE ME... I'VE GOT A ***REAL JOB*** TO DO!
K7

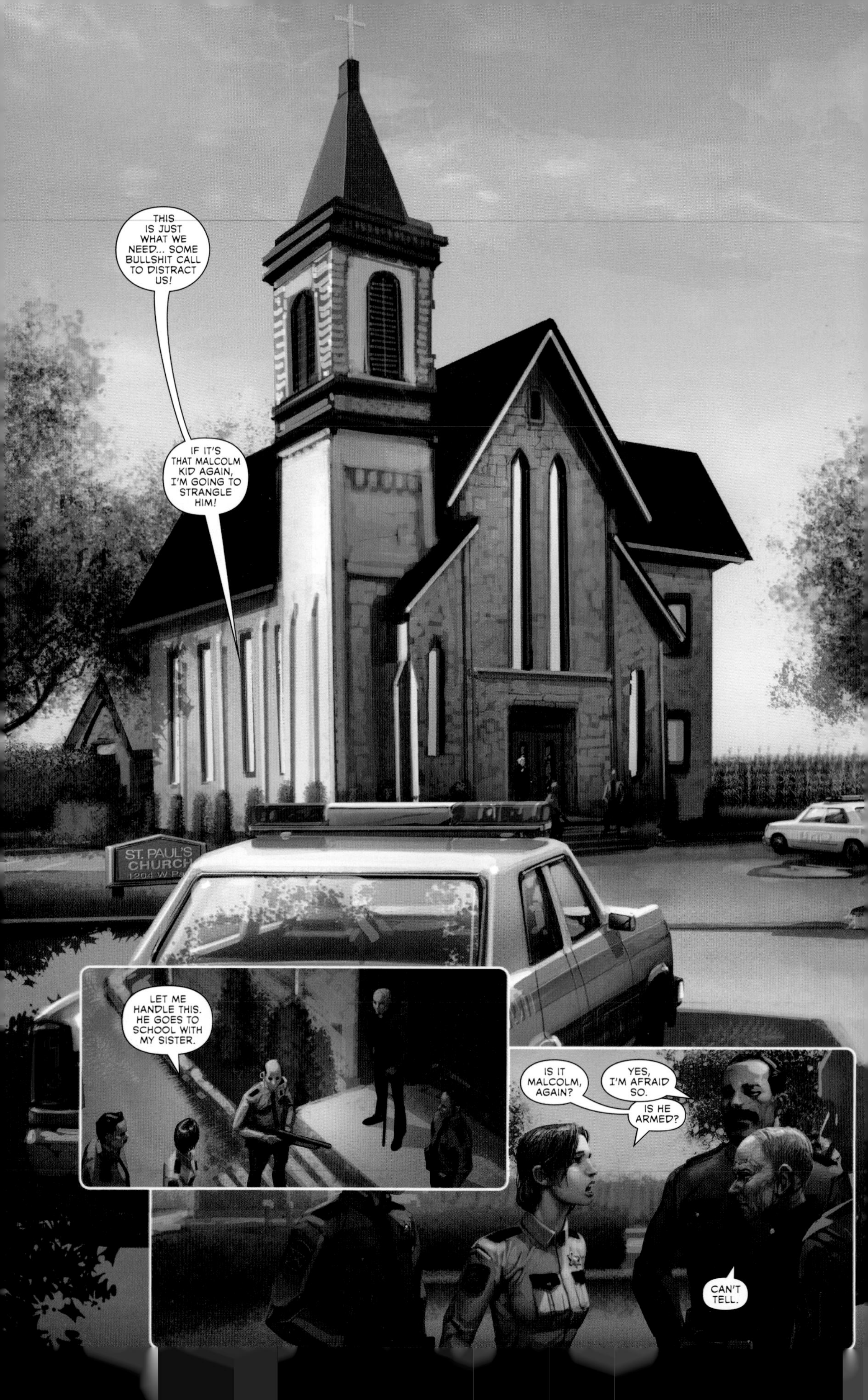
THIS IS JUST WHAT WE NEED... SOME BULLSHIT CALL TO DISTRACT US!
IF IT'S THAT MALCOLM KID AGAIN, I'M GOING TO STRANGLE HIM!
ST. PAUL'S CHURCH
LET ME HANDLE THIS. HE GOES TO SCHOOL WITH MY SISTER.
IS IT MALCOLM, AGAIN?
YES, I'M AFRAID SO.
IS HE ARMED?
CAN'T TELL.

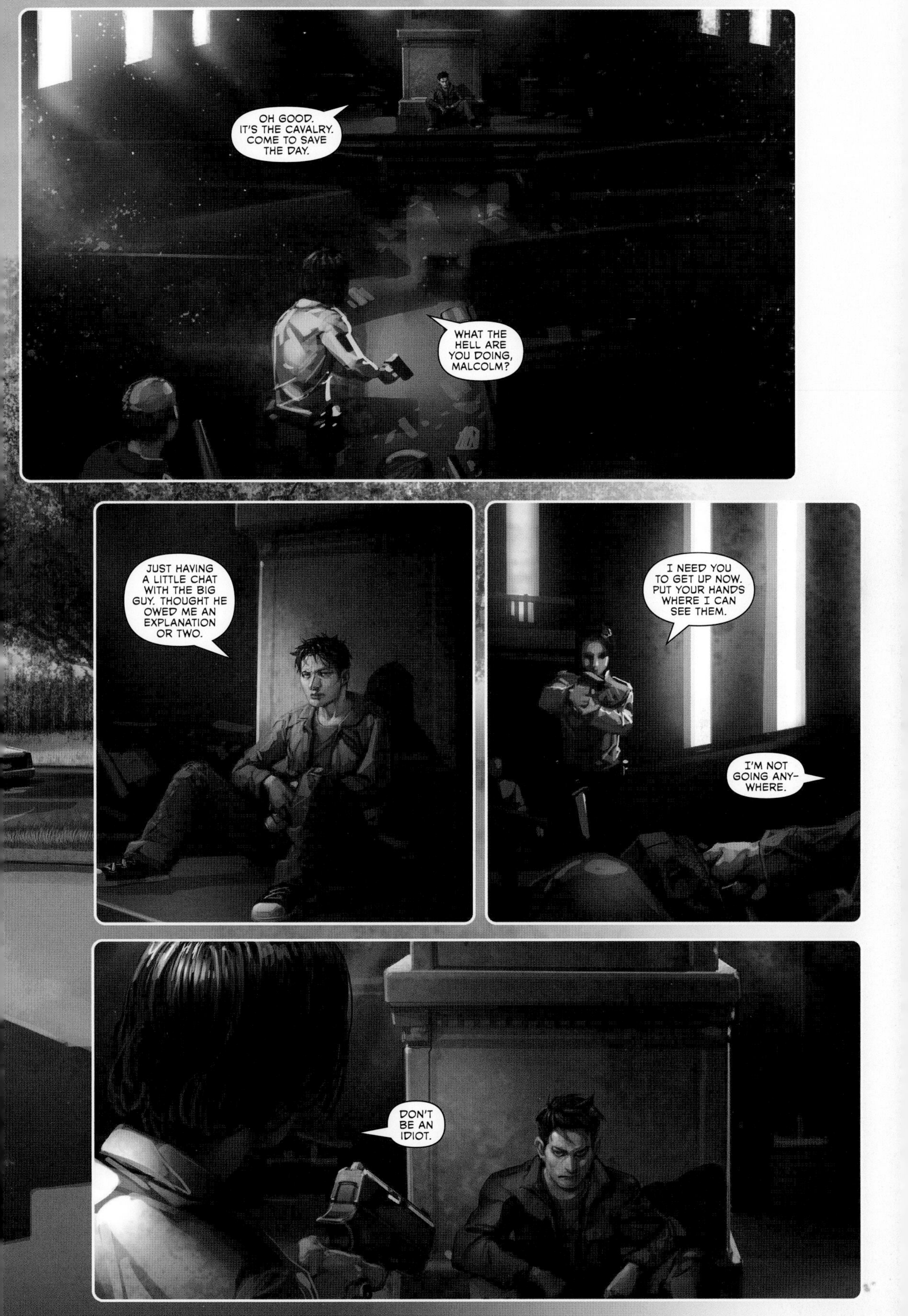
OH GOOD. IT'S THE CAVALRY. COME TO SAVE THE DAY.
WHAT THE HELL ARE YOU DOING, MALCOLM?
JUST HAVING A LITTLE CHAT WITH THE BIG GUY. THOUGHT HE OWED ME AN EXPLANATION OR TWO.
I NEED YOU TO GET UP NOW. PUT YOUR HANDS WHERE I CAN SEE THEM.
I'M NOT GOING ANY-WHERE.
DON'T BE AN IDIOT.

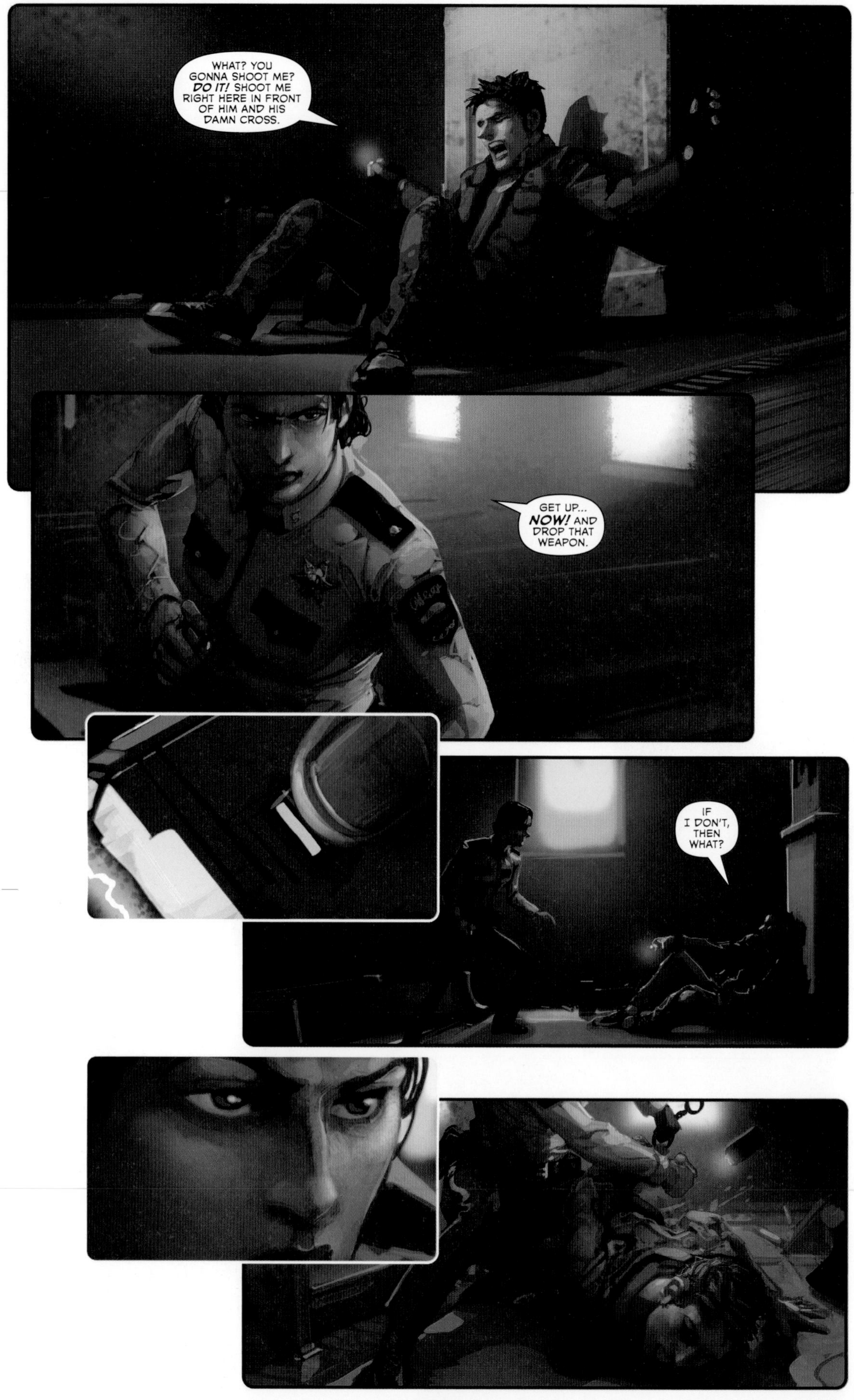
WHAT? YOU GONNA SHOOT ME? *DO IT!* SHOOT ME RIGHT HERE IN FRONT OF HIM AND HIS DAMN CROSS.
GET UP... *NOW!* AND DROP THAT WEAPON.
IF I DON'T, THEN WHAT?

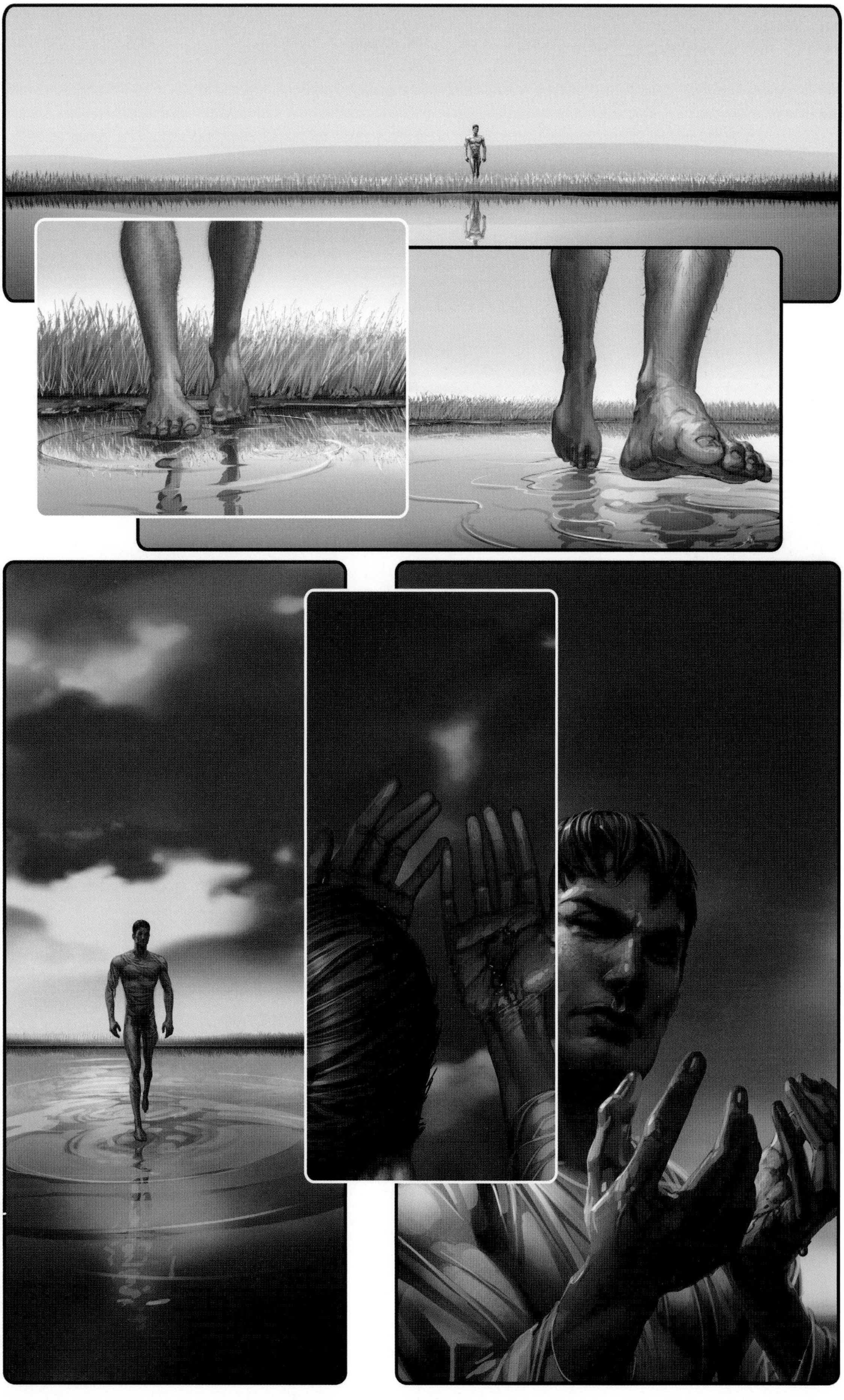

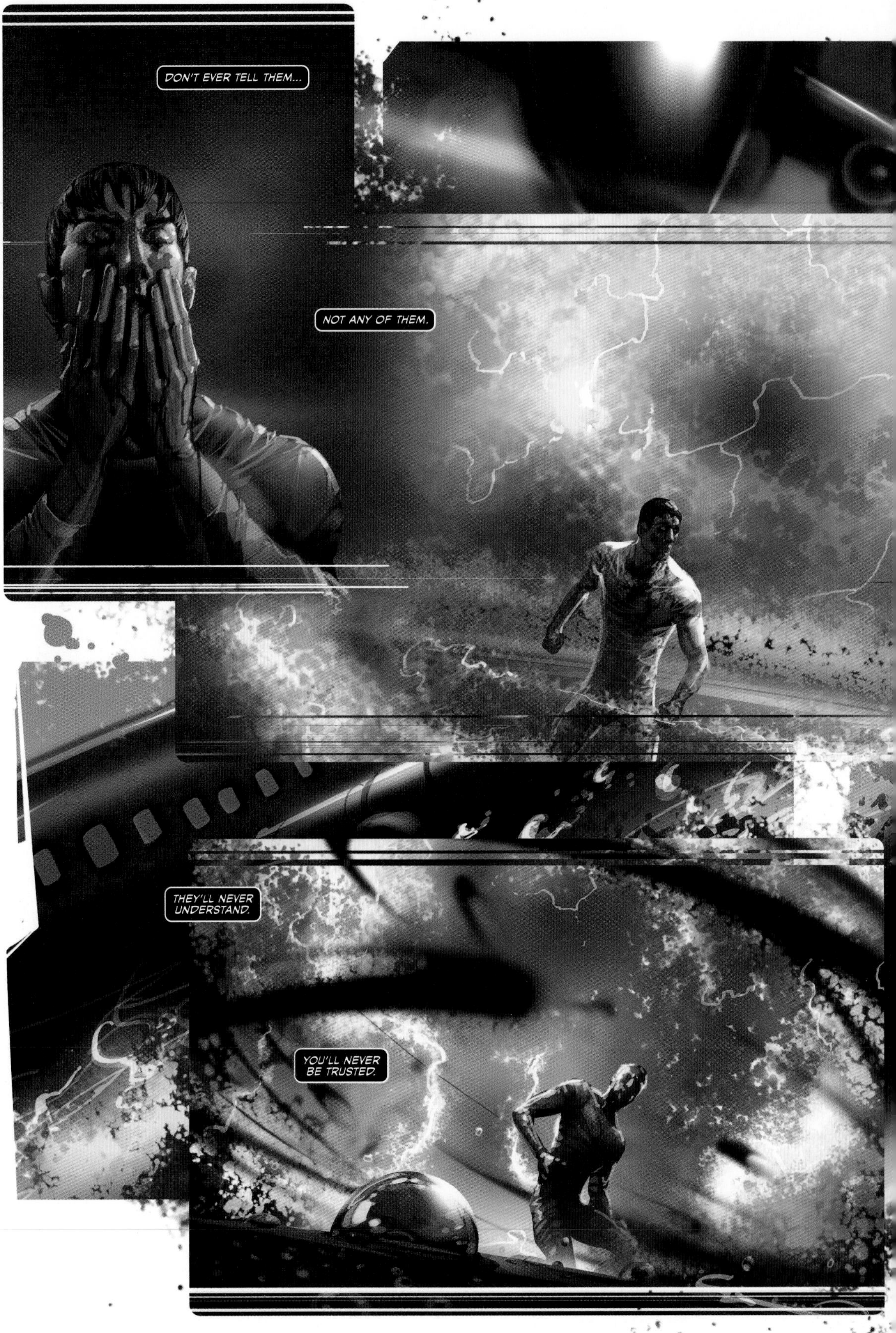
DON'T EVER TELL THEM...
NOT ANY OF THEM.
THEY'LL NEVER UNDERSTAND.
YOU'LL NEVER BE TRUSTED.

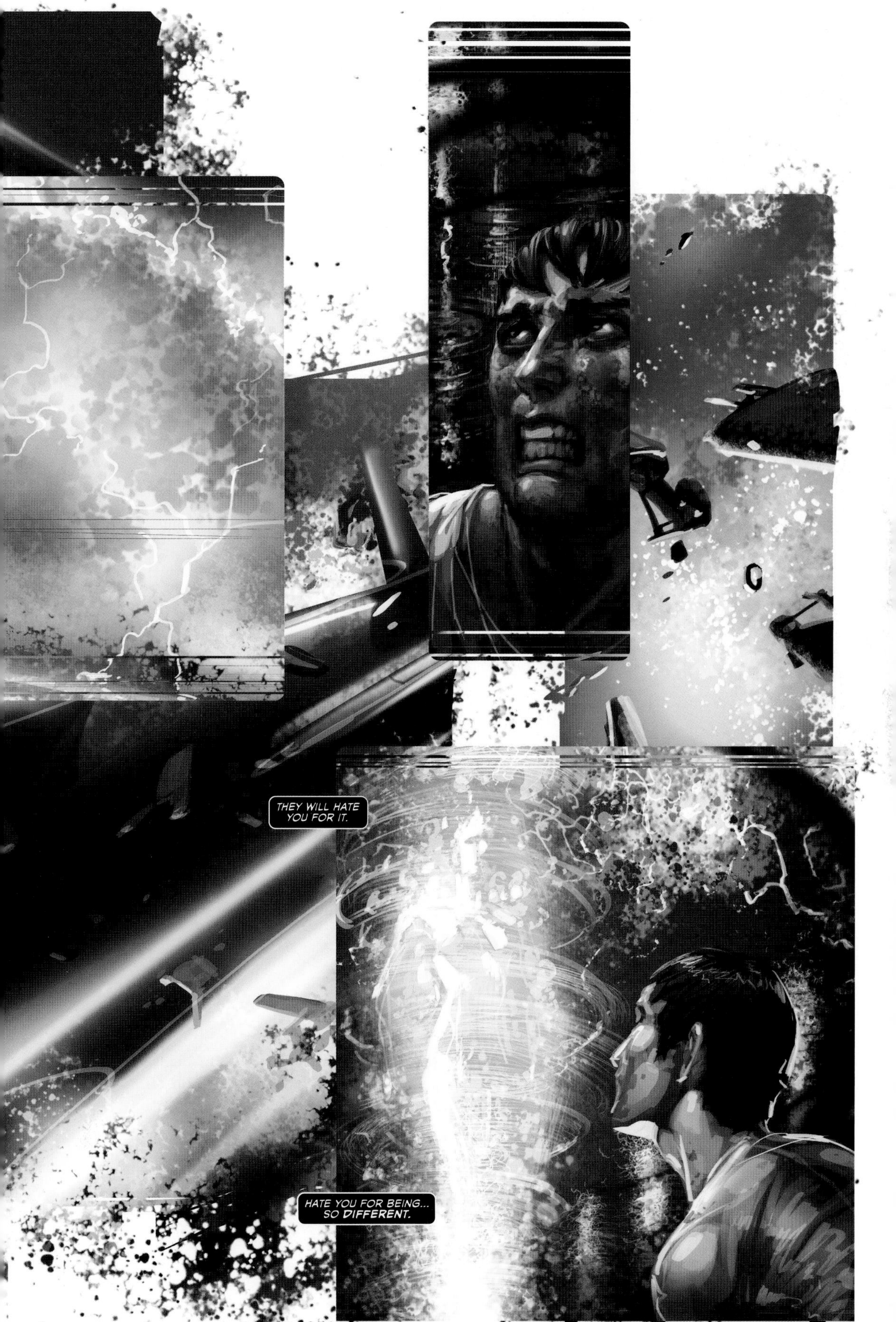
THEY WILL HATE YOU FOR IT.
HATE YOU FOR BEING... SO DIFFERENT.

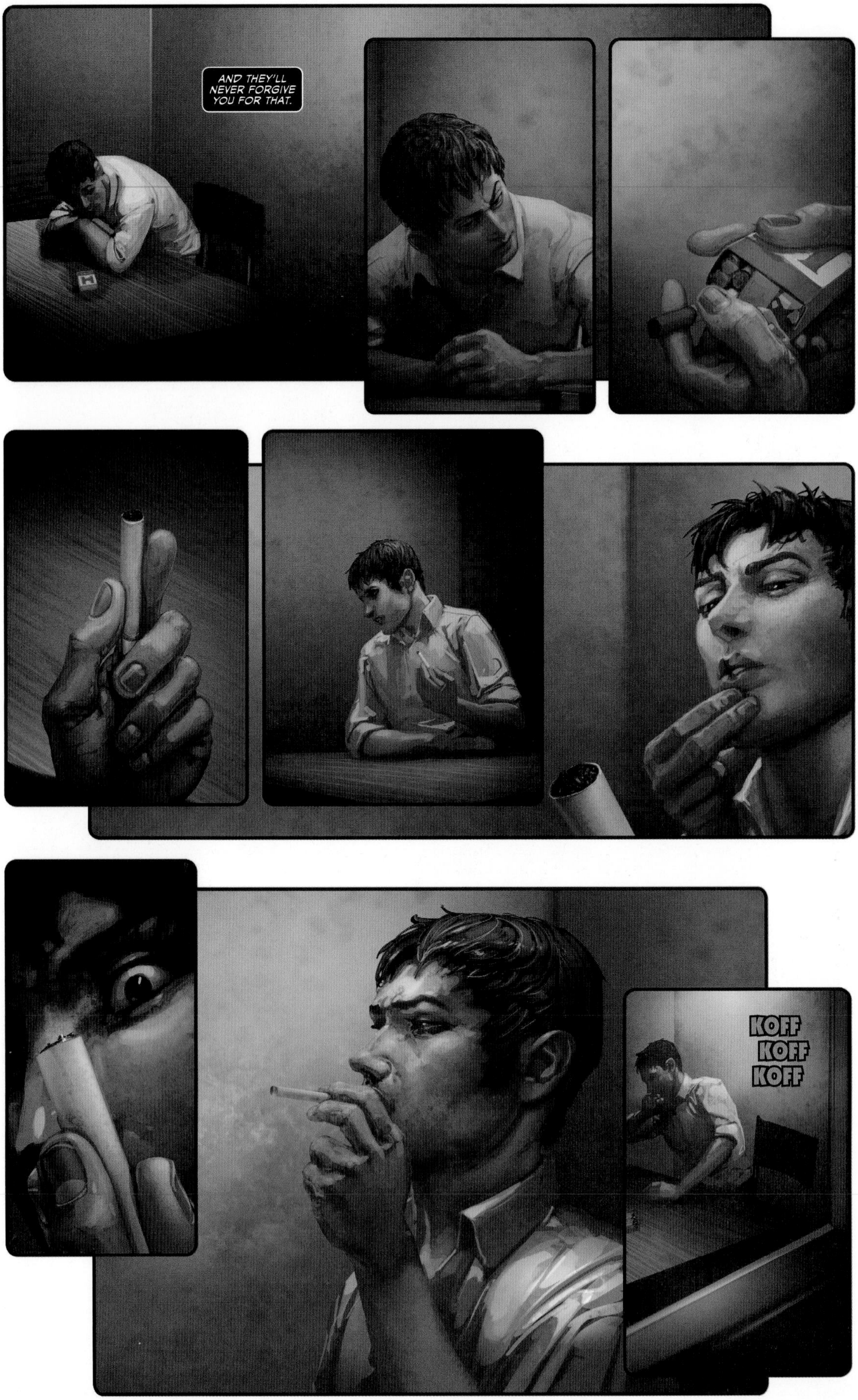
AND THEY'LL NEVER FORGIVE YOU FOR THAT.
KOFF KOFF KOFF

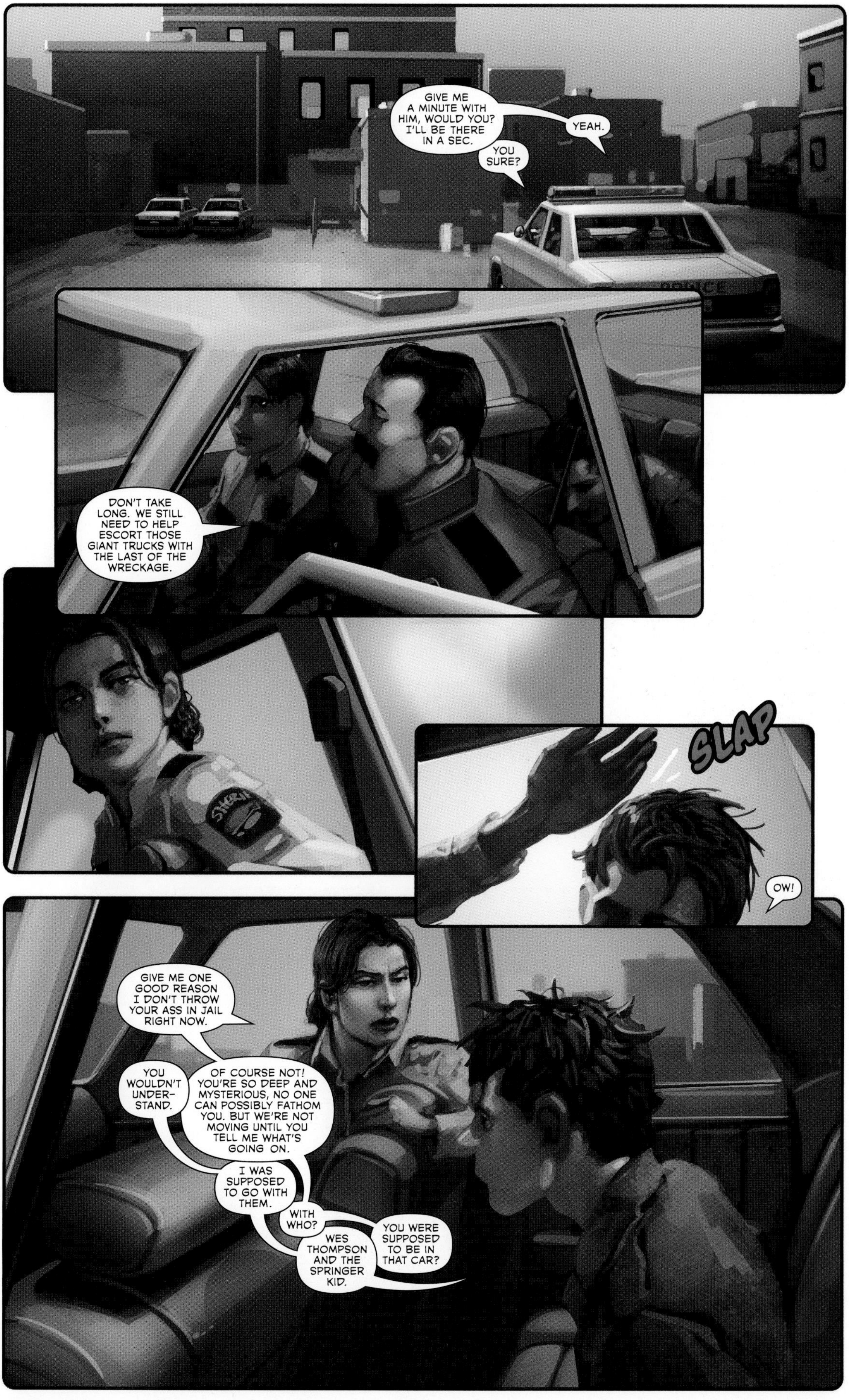
GIVE ME A MINUTE WITH HIM, WOULD YOU? I'LL BE THERE IN A SEC.
YEAH.
YOU SURE?
POLICE
DON'T TAKE LONG. WE STILL NEED TO HELP ESCORT THOSE GIANT TRUCKS WITH THE LAST OF THE WRECKAGE.
SLAP
OW!
GIVE ME ONE GOOD REASON I DON'T THROW YOUR ASS IN JAIL RIGHT NOW.
YOU WOULDN'T UNDER-STAND.
OF COURSE NOT! YOU'RE SO DEEP AND MYSTERIOUS, NO ONE CAN POSSIBLY FATHOM YOU. BUT WE'RE NOT MOVING UNTIL YOU TELL ME WHAT'S GOING ON.
I WAS SUPPOSED TO GO WITH THEM.
WITH WHO?
WES THOMPSON AND THE SPRINGER KID.
YOU WERE SUPPOSED TO BE IN THAT CAR?

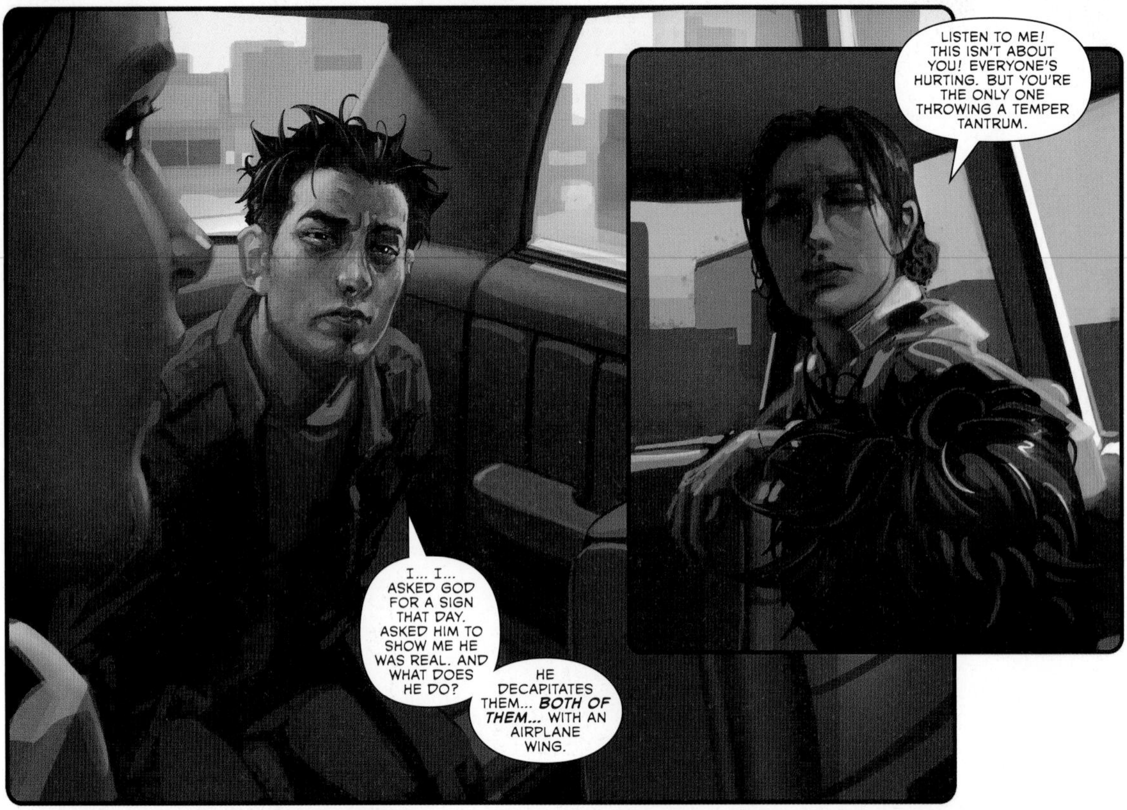
I... I... ASKED GOD FOR A SIGN THAT DAY. ASKED HIM TO SHOW ME HE WAS REAL. AND WHAT DOES HE DO?
HE DECAPITATES THEM... BOTH OF THEM... WITH AN AIRPLANE WING.
LISTEN TO ME! THIS ISN'T ABOUT YOU! EVERYONE'S HURTING. BUT YOU'RE THE ONLY ONE THROWING A TEMPER TANTRUM.

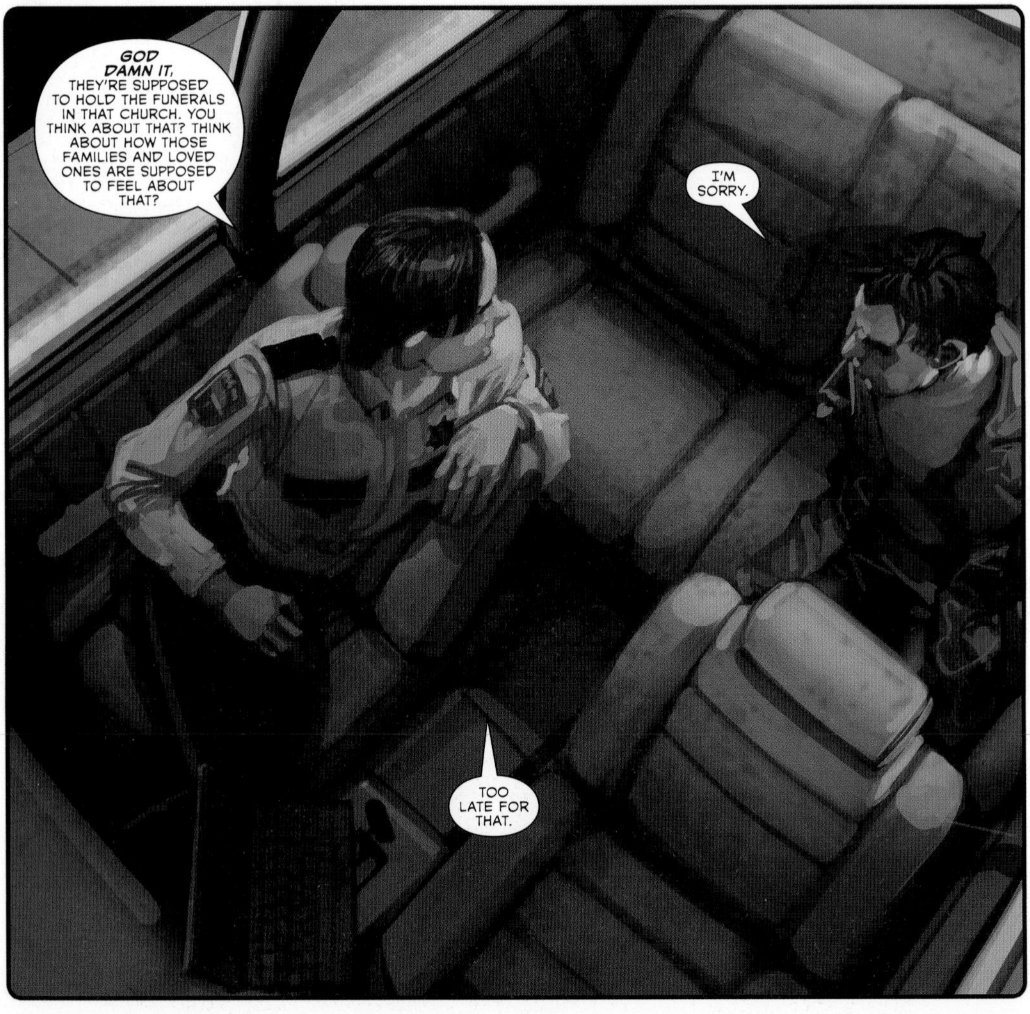
GOD DAMN IT, THEY'RE SUPPOSED TO HOLD THE FUNERALS IN THAT CHURCH. YOU THINK ABOUT THAT? THINK ABOUT HOW THOSE FAMILIES AND LOVED ONES ARE SUPPOSED TO FEEL ABOUT THAT?
I'M SORRY.
TOO LATE FOR THAT.

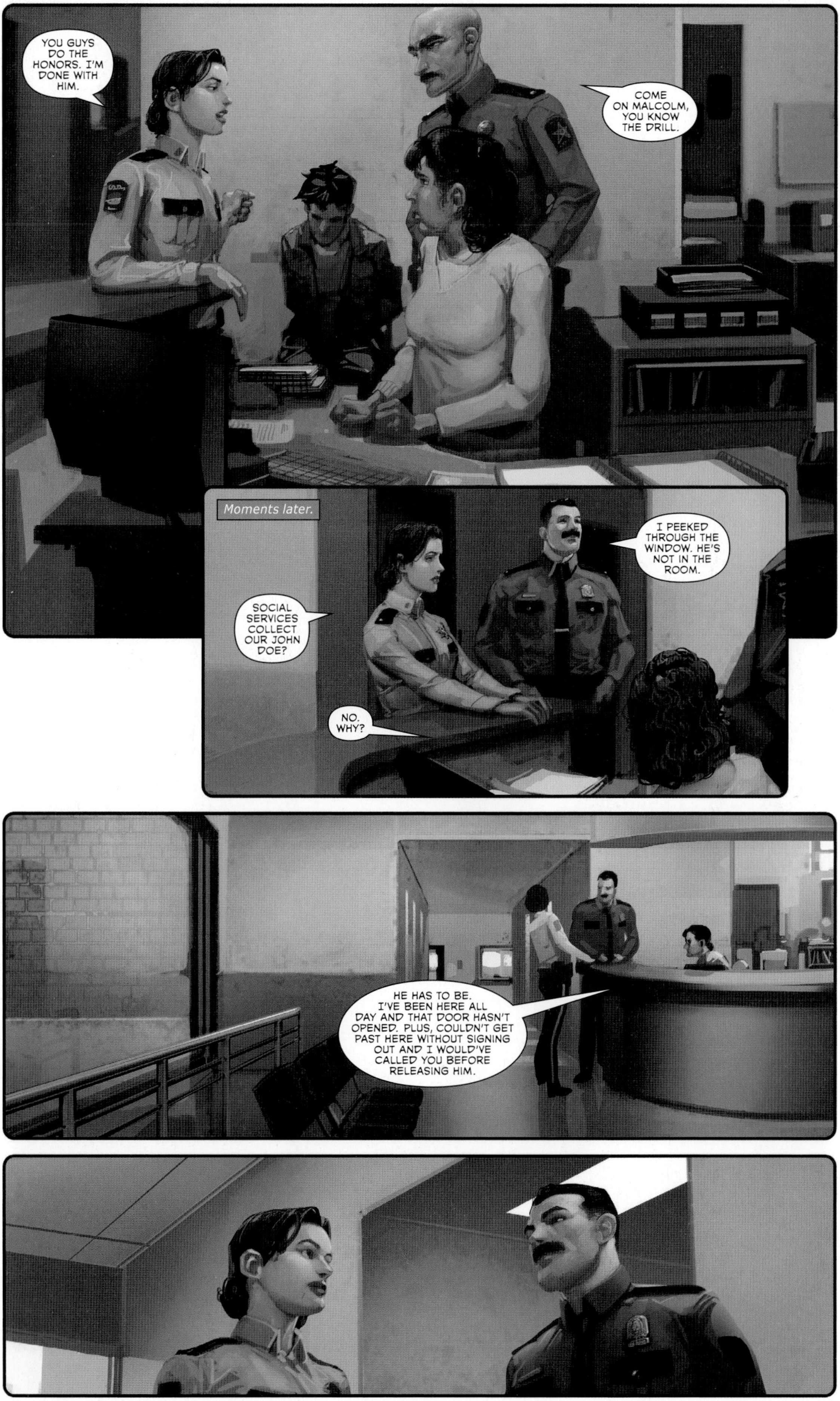
YOU GUYS DO THE HONORS. I'M DONE WITH HIM.
COME ON MALCOLM, YOU KNOW THE DRILL.
Moments later.
I PEEKED THROUGH THE WINDOW. HE'S NOT IN THE ROOM.
SOCIAL SERVICES COLLECT OUR JOHN DOE?
NO. WHY?
HE HAS TO BE. I'VE BEEN HERE ALL DAY AND THAT DOOR HASN'T OPENED. PLUS, COULDN'T GET PAST HERE WITHOUT SIGNING OUT AND I WOULD'VE CALLED YOU BEFORE RELEASING HIM.

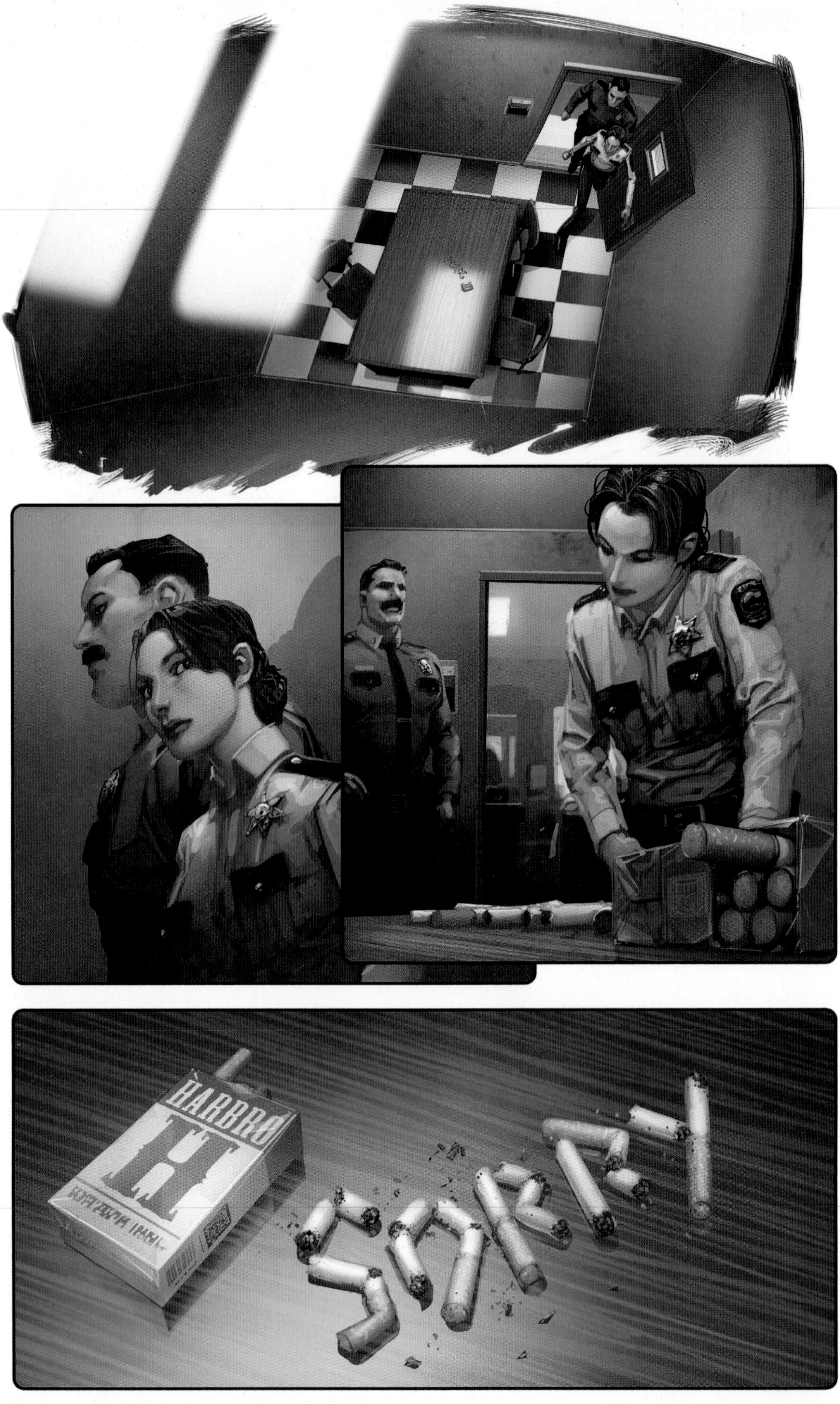
HARBRO

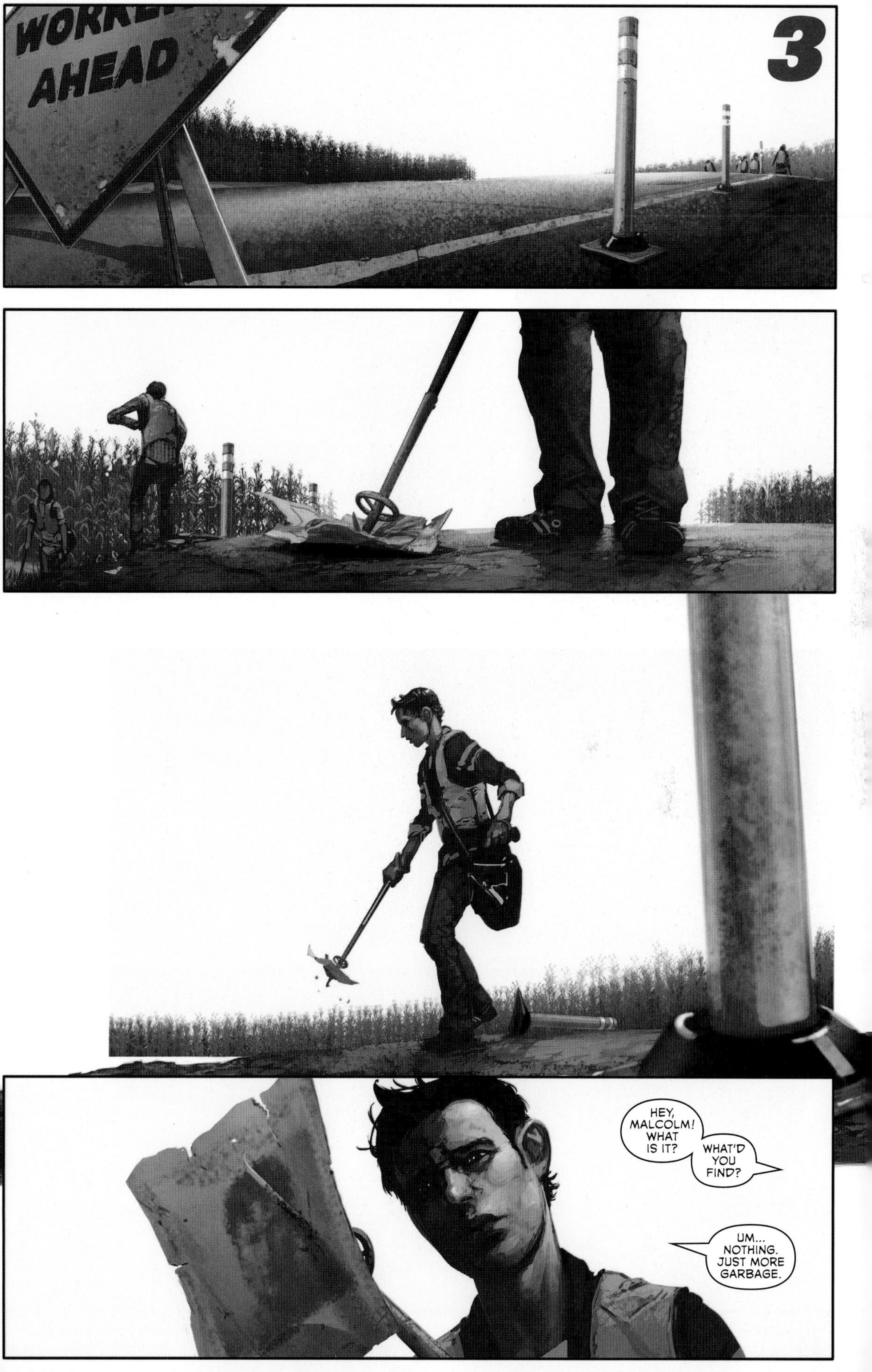
WORKERS
AHEAD
3
HEY, MALCOLM! WHAT IS IT?
WHAT'D YOU FIND?
UM... NOTHING. JUST MORE GARBAGE.

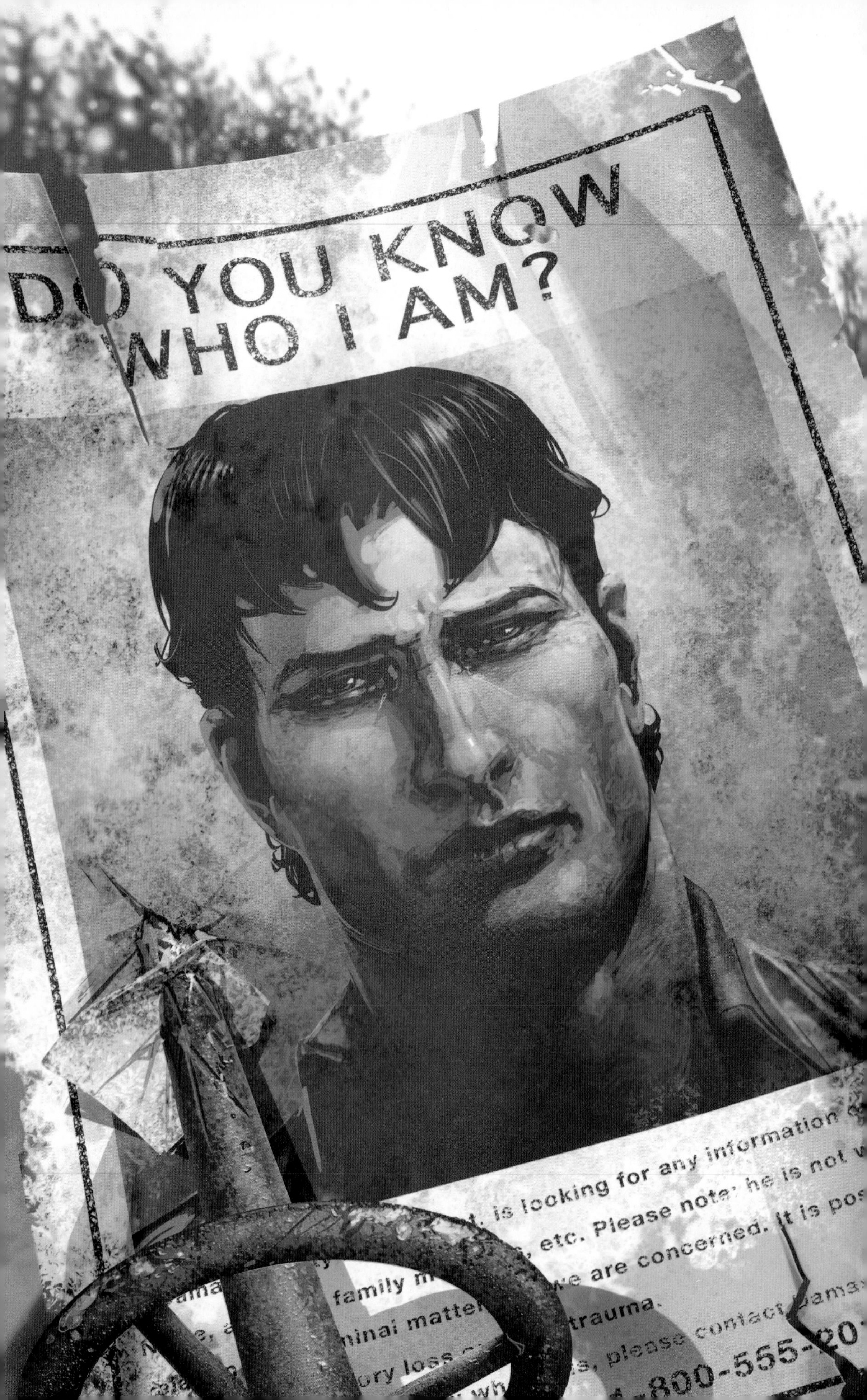

DO YOU KNOW WHO I AM?
is looking for any information
etc. Please note: he is not
we are concerned. It is
family
trauma.
please contact
800-555-

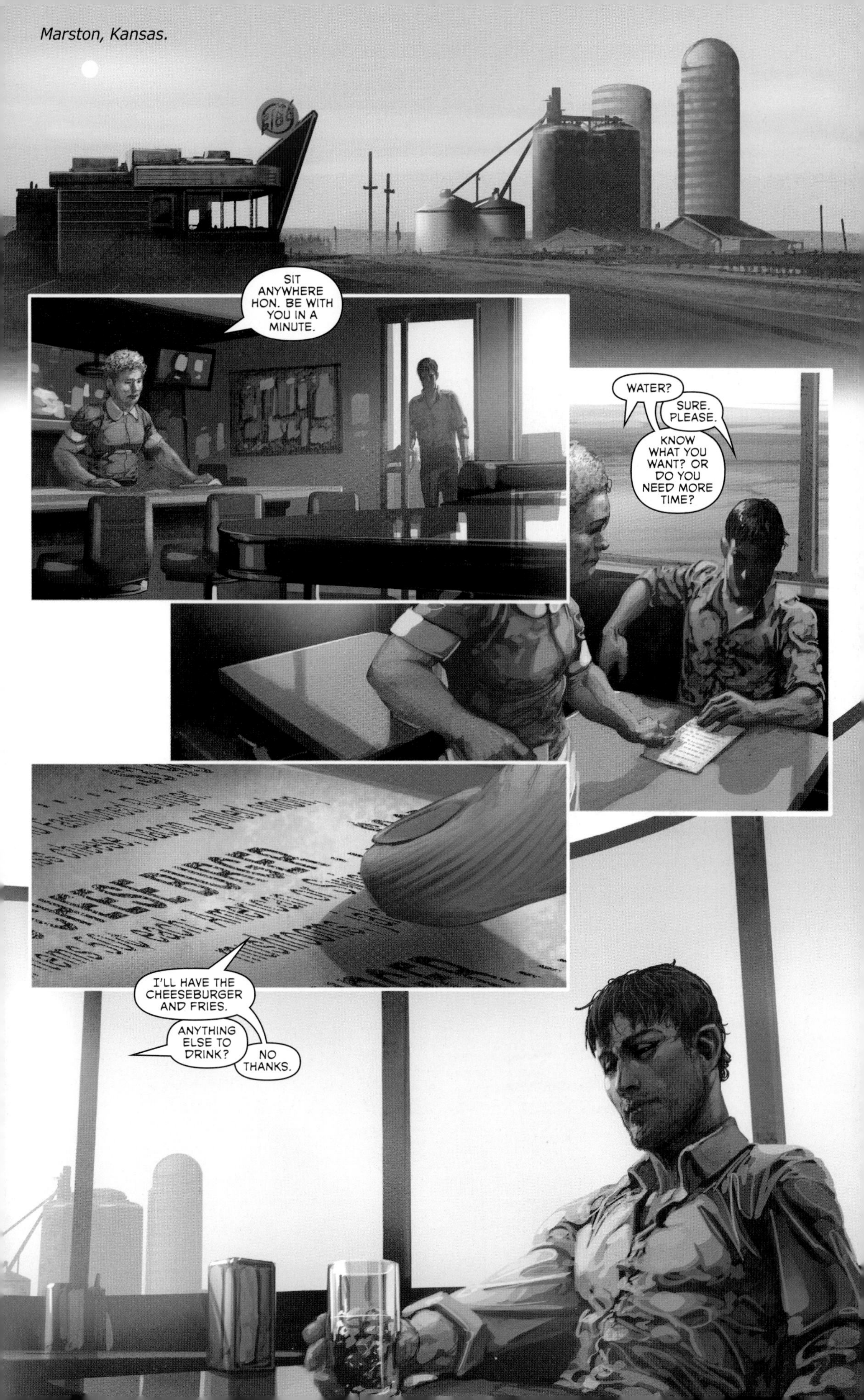
Marston, Kansas.
SIT ANYWHERE HON. BE WITH YOU IN A MINUTE.
WATER?
SURE. PLEASE.
KNOW WHAT YOU WANT? OR DO YOU NEED MORE TIME?
CHEESE BURGER
I'LL HAVE THE CHEESEBURGER AND FRIES.
ANYTHING ELSE TO DRINK?
NO THANKS.

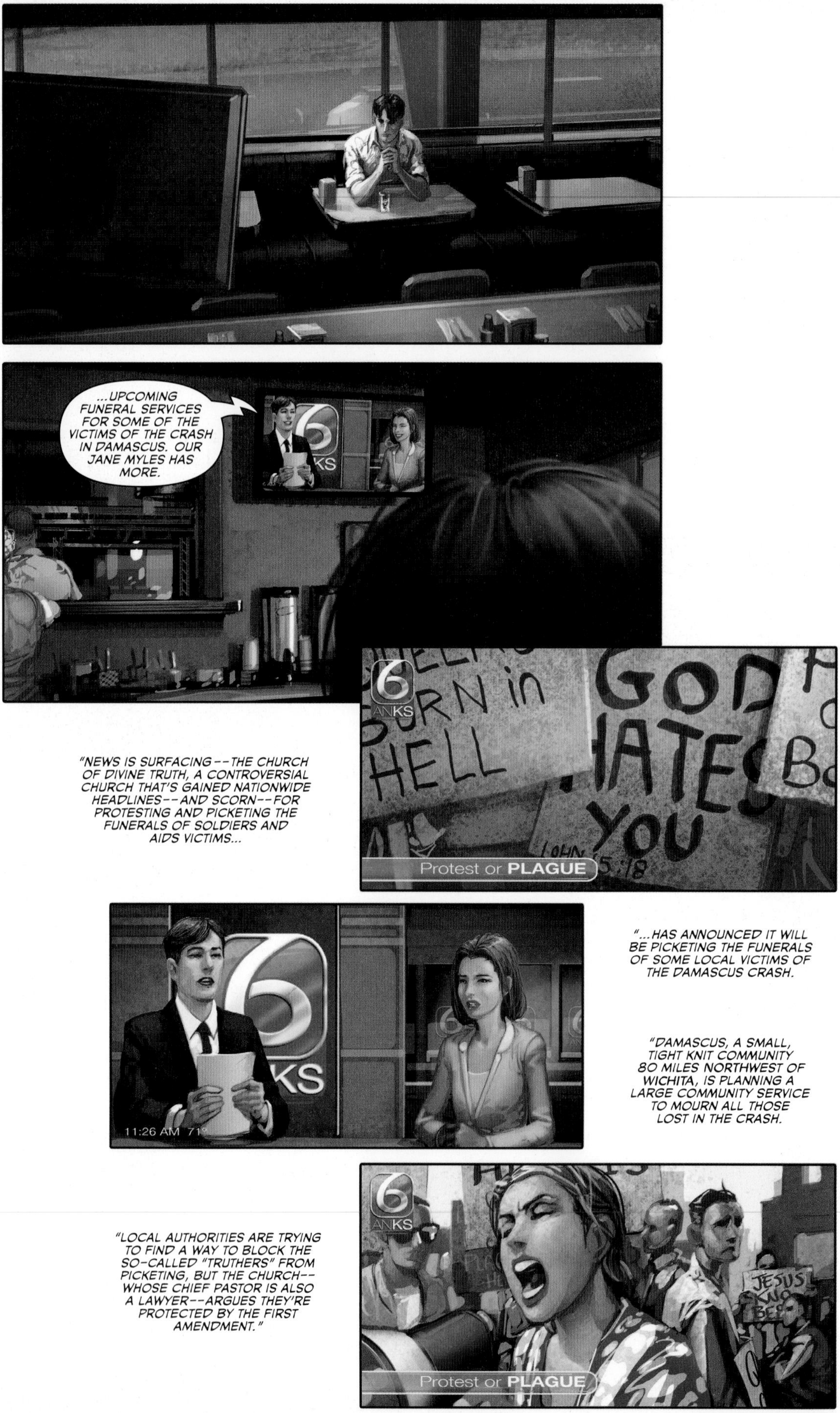
...UPCOMING FUNERAL SERVICES FOR SOME OF THE VICTIMS OF THE CRASH IN DAMASCUS. OUR JANE MYLES HAS MORE.
"NEWS IS SURFACING--THE CHURCH OF DIVINE TRUTH, A CONTROVERSIAL CHURCH THAT'S GAINED NATIONWIDE HEADLINES--AND SCORN--FOR PROTESTING AND PICKETING THE FUNERALS OF SOLDIERS AND AIDS VICTIMS...
GOD
HELL
YOU
Protest or PLAGUE
"...HAS ANNOUNCED IT WILL BE PICKETING THE FUNERALS OF SOME LOCAL VICTIMS OF THE DAMASCUS CRASH.
11:26 AM 71°
"DAMASCUS, A SMALL, TIGHT KNIT COMMUNITY 80 MILES NORTHWEST OF WICHITA, IS PLANNING A LARGE COMMUNITY SERVICE TO MOURN ALL THOSE LOST IN THE CRASH.
"LOCAL AUTHORITIES ARE TRYING TO FIND A WAY TO BLOCK THE SO-CALLED "TRUTHERS" FROM PICKETING, BUT THE CHURCH--WHOSE CHIEF PASTOR IS ALSO A LAWYER--ARGUES THEY'RE PROTECTED BY THE FIRST AMENDMENT."
Protest or PLAGUE

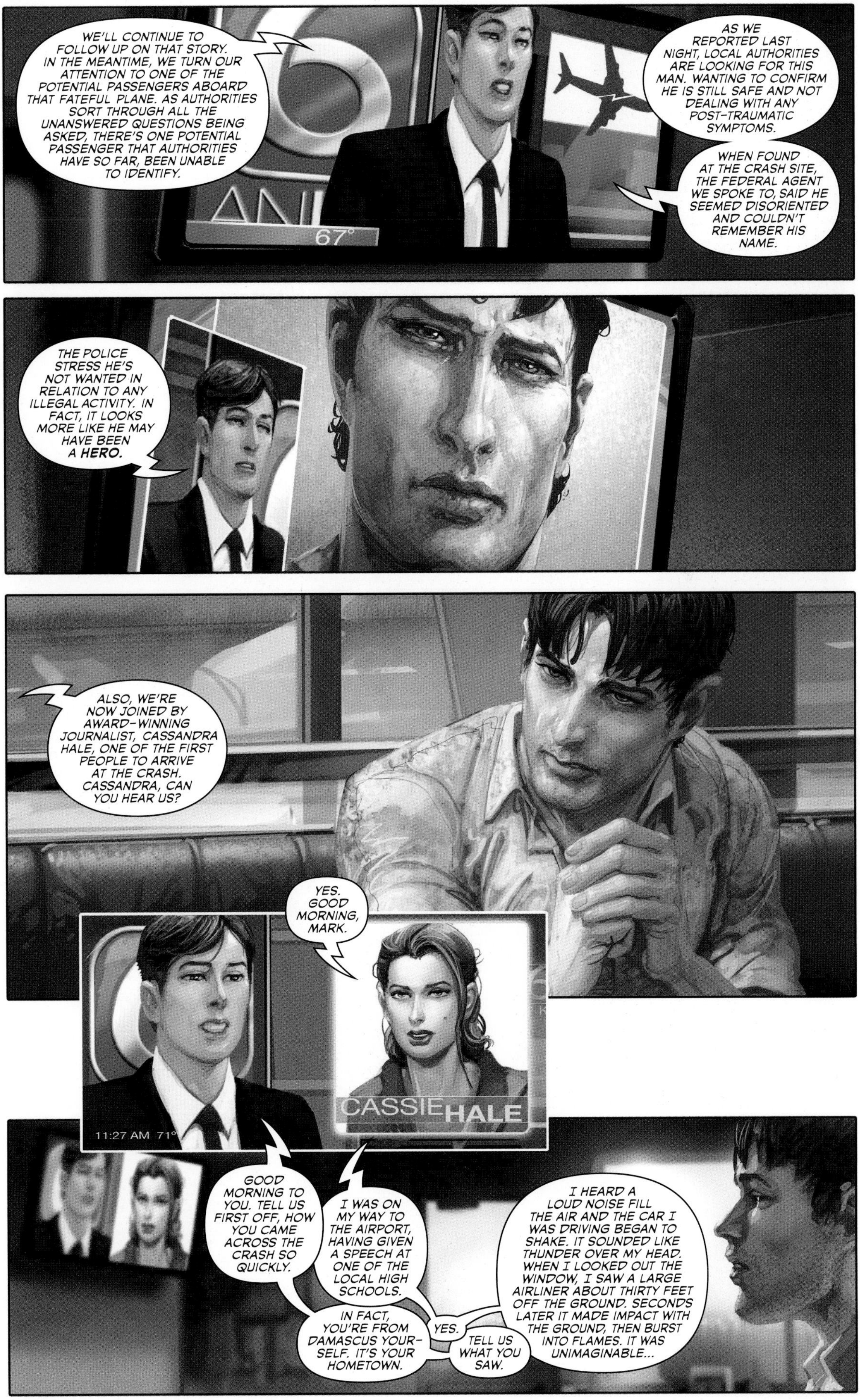

WE'LL CONTINUE TO FOLLOW UP ON THAT STORY. IN THE MEANTIME, WE TURN OUR ATTENTION TO ONE OF THE POTENTIAL PASSENGERS ABOARD THAT FATEFUL PLANE. AS AUTHORITIES SORT THROUGH ALL THE UNANSWERED QUESTIONS BEING ASKED, THERE'S ONE POTENTIAL PASSENGER THAT AUTHORITIES HAVE SO FAR, BEEN UNABLE TO IDENTIFY.
67°
AS WE REPORTED LAST NIGHT, LOCAL AUTHORITIES ARE LOOKING FOR THIS MAN. WANTING TO CONFIRM HE IS STILL SAFE AND NOT DEALING WITH ANY POST-TRAUMATIC SYMPTOMS.
WHEN FOUND AT THE CRASH SITE, THE FEDERAL AGENT WE SPOKE TO, SAID HE SEEMED DISORIENTED AND COULDN'T REMEMBER HIS NAME.
THE POLICE STRESS HE'S NOT WANTED IN RELATION TO ANY ILLEGAL ACTIVITY. IN FACT, IT LOOKS MORE LIKE HE MAY HAVE BEEN A **HERO.**
ALSO, WE'RE NOW JOINED BY AWARD-WINNING JOURNALIST, CASSANDRA HALE, ONE OF THE FIRST PEOPLE TO ARRIVE AT THE CRASH. CASSANDRA, CAN YOU HEAR US?
YES. GOOD MORNING, MARK.
11:27 AM 71°
CASSIE HALE
GOOD MORNING TO YOU. TELL US FIRST OFF, HOW YOU CAME ACROSS THE CRASH SO QUICKLY.
I WAS ON MY WAY TO THE AIRPORT, HAVING GIVEN A SPEECH AT ONE OF THE LOCAL HIGH SCHOOLS.
IN FACT, YOU'RE FROM DAMASCUS YOURSELF. IT'S YOUR HOMETOWN.
YES.
TELL US WHAT YOU SAW.
I HEARD A LOUD NOISE FILL THE AIR AND THE CAR I WAS DRIVING BEGAN TO SHAKE. IT SOUNDED LIKE THUNDER OVER MY HEAD. WHEN I LOOKED OUT THE WINDOW, I SAW A LARGE AIRLINER ABOUT THIRTY FEET OFF THE GROUND. SECONDS LATER IT MADE IMPACT WITH THE GROUND, THEN BURST INTO FLAMES. IT WAS UNIMAGINABLE...

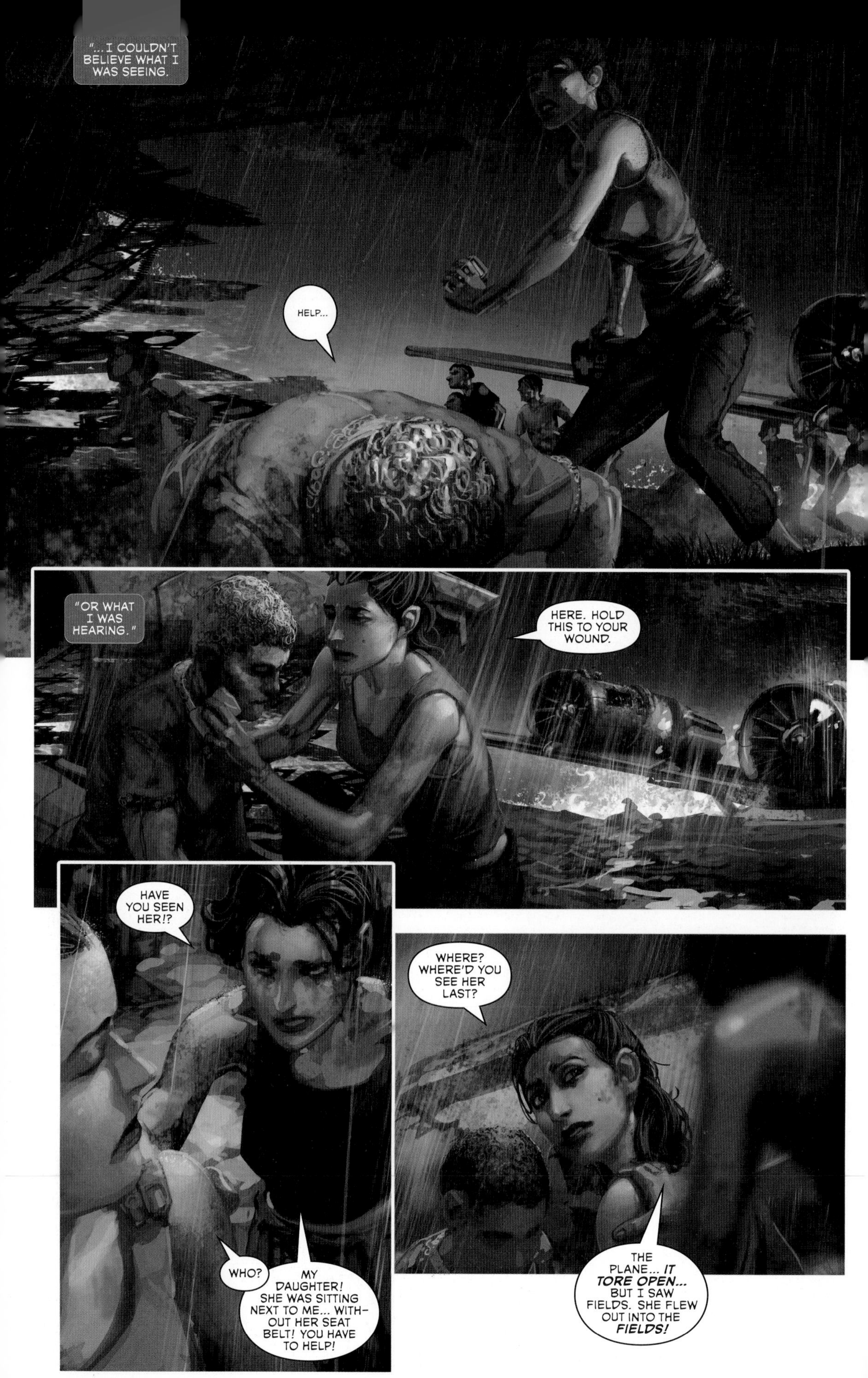
"...I COULDN'T BELIEVE WHAT I WAS SEEING.
HELP...
"OR WHAT I WAS HEARING."
HERE. HOLD THIS TO YOUR WOUND.
HAVE YOU SEEN HER!?
WHO?
MY DAUGHTER! SHE WAS SITTING NEXT TO ME... WITH-OUT HER SEAT BELT! YOU HAVE TO HELP!
WHERE? WHERE'D YOU SEE HER LAST?
THE PLANE... *IT TORE OPEN...* BUT I SAW FIELDS. SHE FLEW OUT INTO THE *FIELDS!*

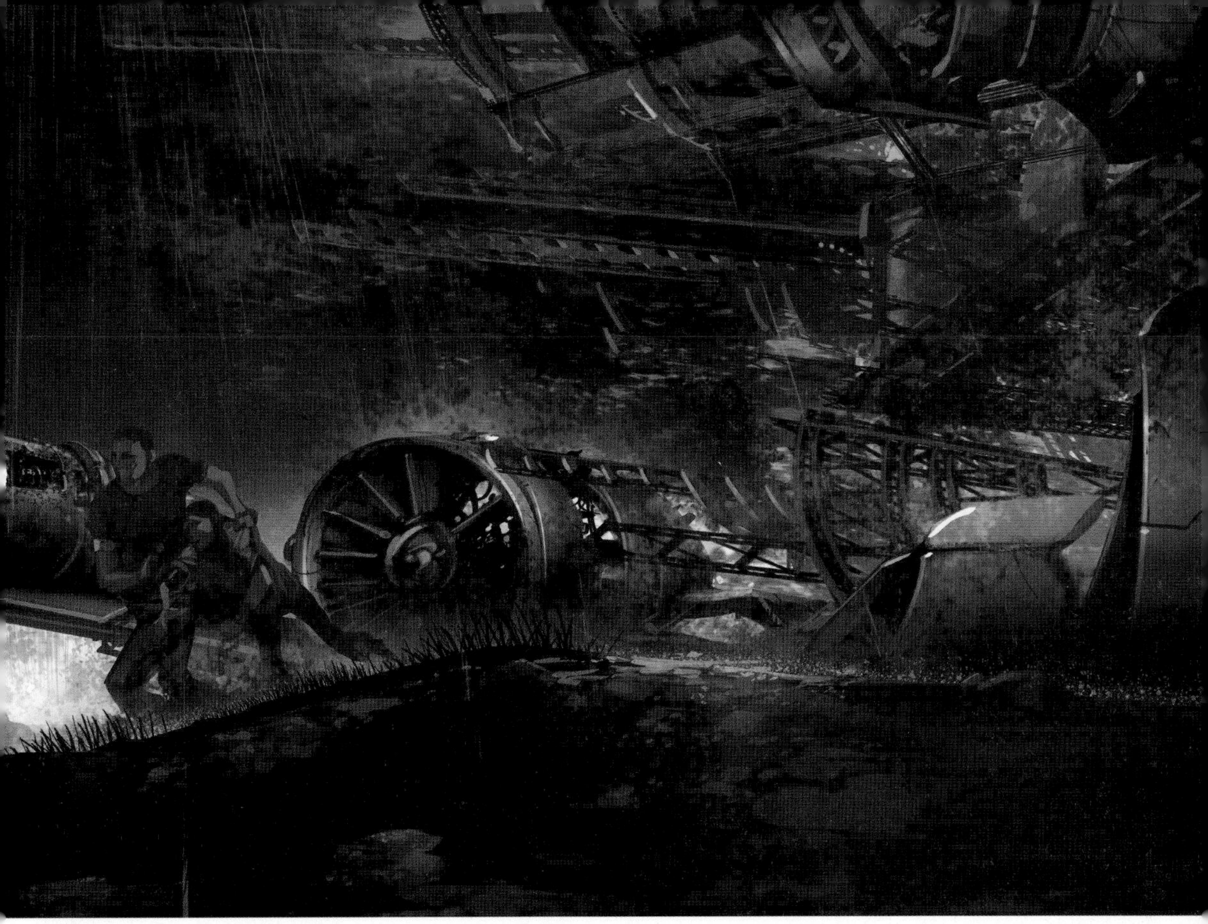

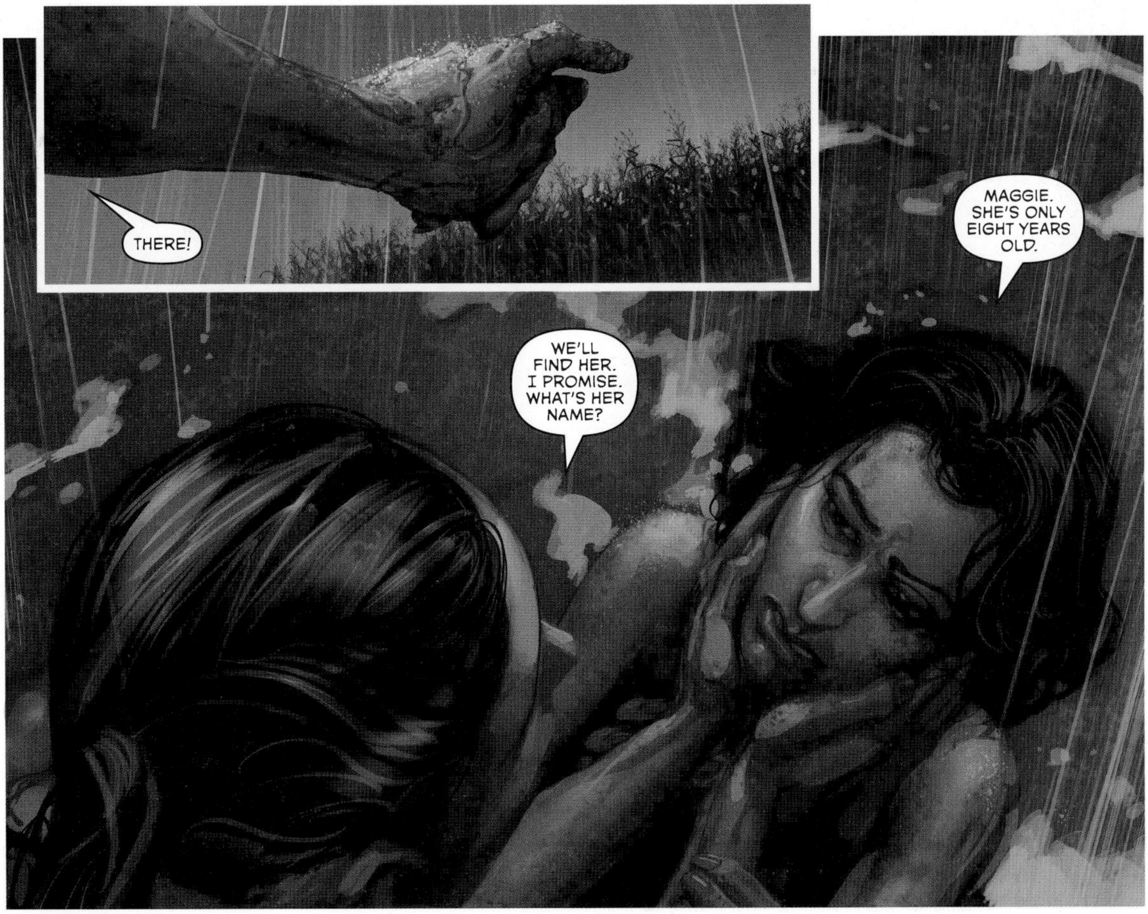
THERE!
WE'LL FIND HER. I PROMISE. WHAT'S HER NAME?
MAGGIE. SHE'S ONLY EIGHT YEARS OLD.

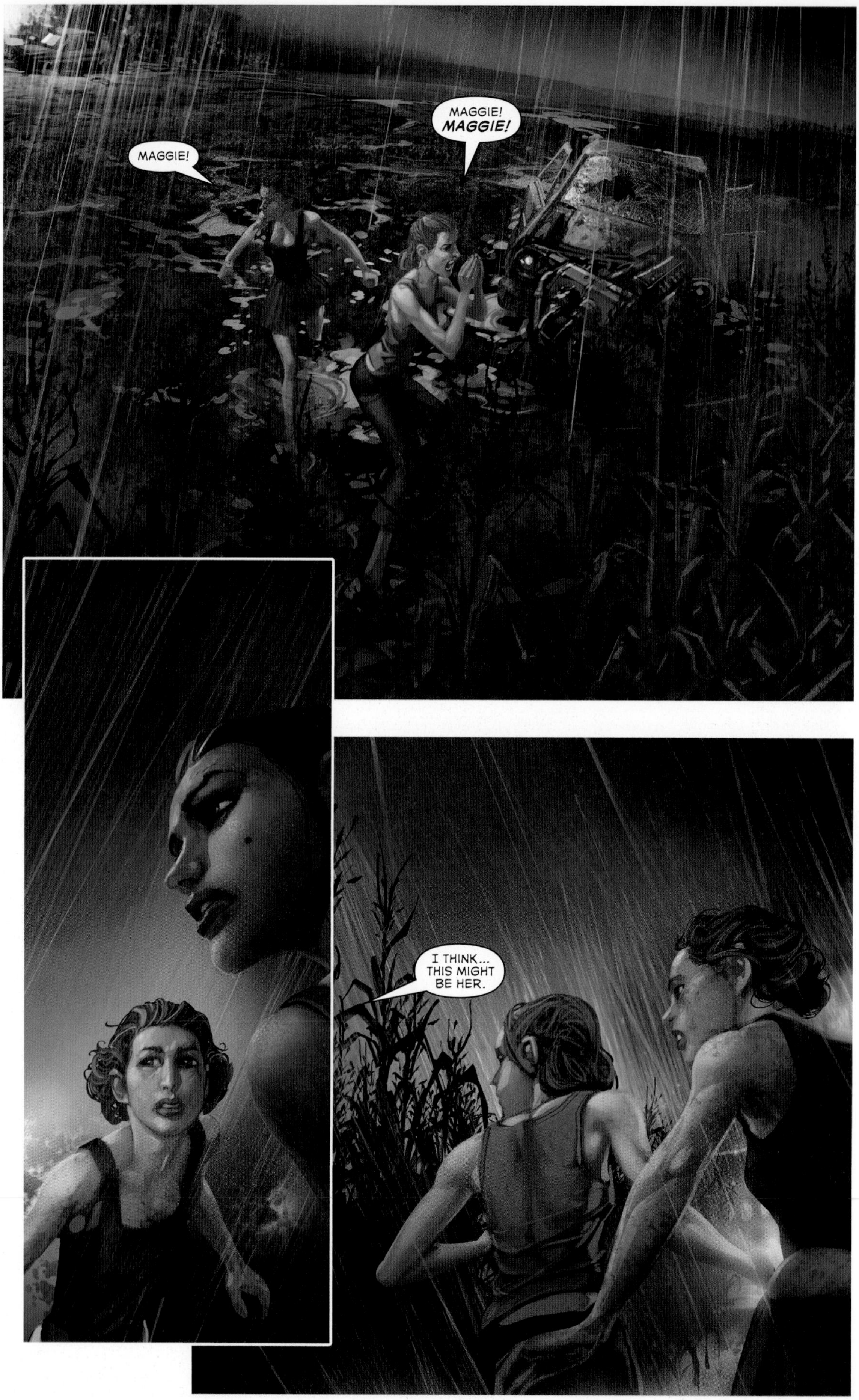

MAGGIE!
MAGGIE! MAGGIE!
I THINK... THIS MIGHT BE HER.

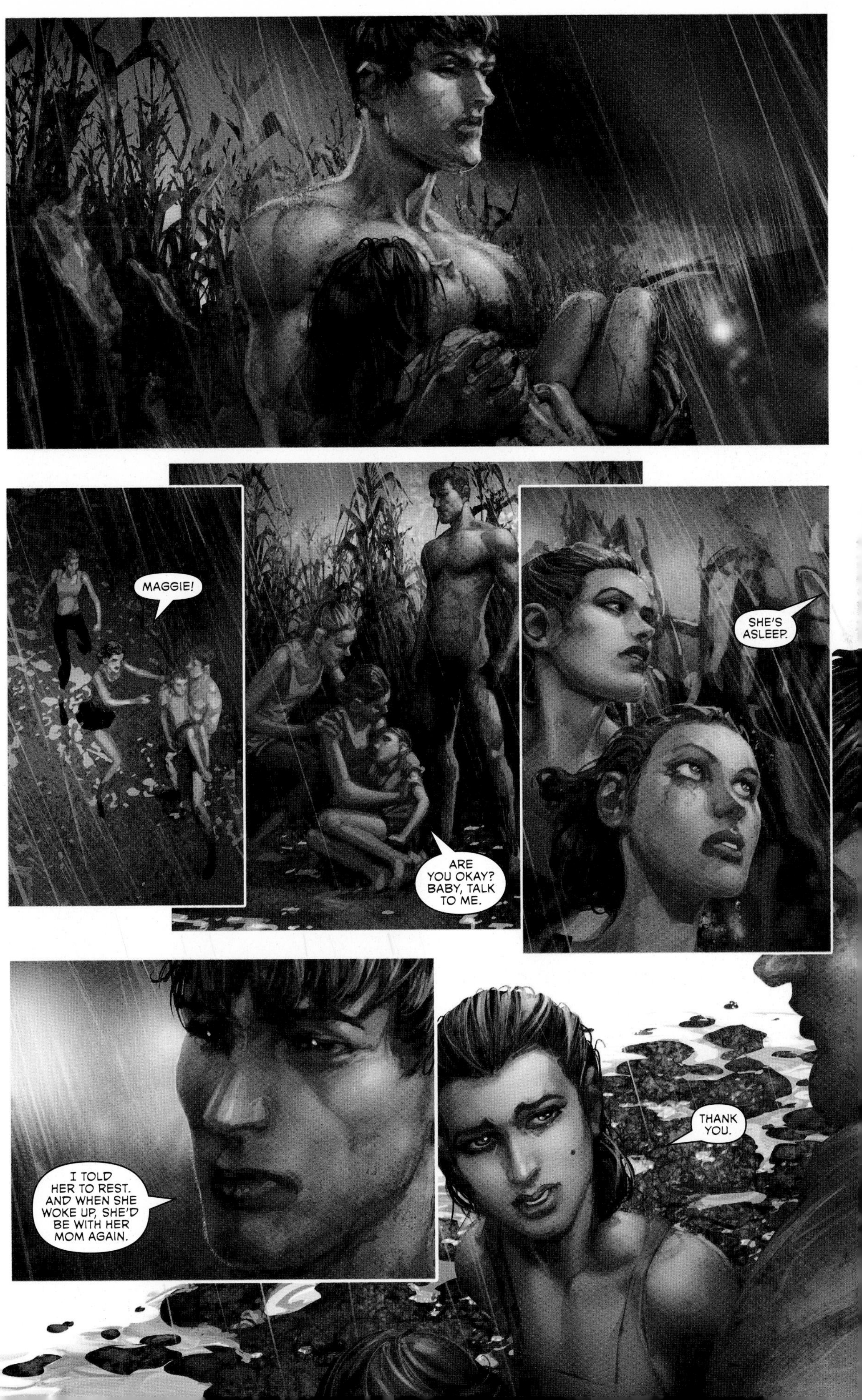
MAGGIE!
ARE YOU OKAY? BABY, TALK TO ME.
SHE'S ASLEEP.
I TOLD HER TO REST. AND WHEN SHE WOKE UP, SHE'D BE WITH HER MOM AGAIN.
THANK YOU.

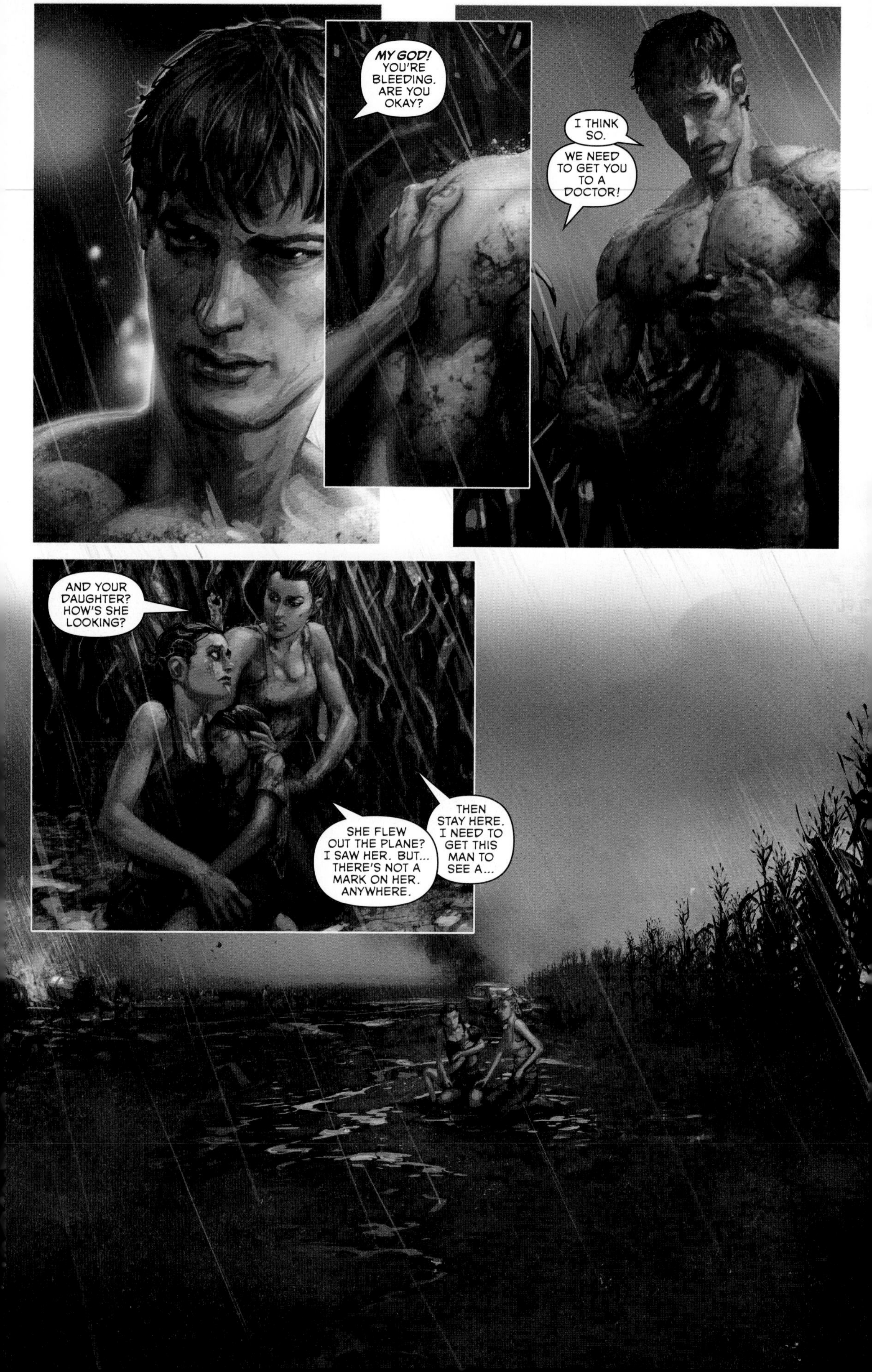
MY GOD! YOU'RE BLEEDING. ARE YOU OKAY?
I THINK SO.
WE NEED TO GET YOU TO A DOCTOR!
AND YOUR DAUGHTER? HOW'S SHE LOOKING?
SHE FLEW OUT THE PLANE? I SAW HER. BUT... THERE'S NOT A MARK ON HER. ANYWHERE.
THEN STAY HERE. I NEED TO GET THIS MAN TO SEE A...

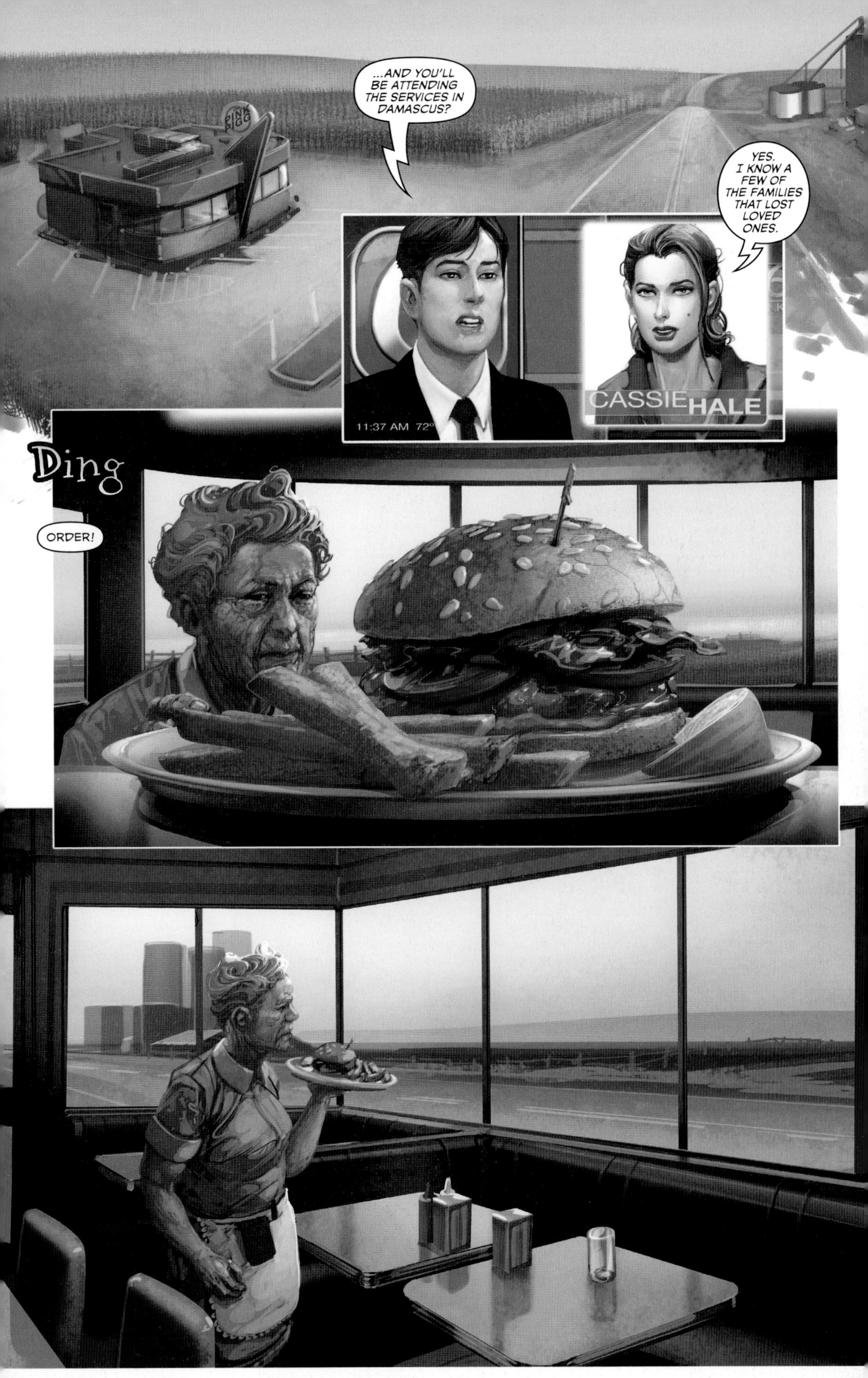
PINK PIGG
...AND YOU'LL BE ATTENDING THE SERVICES IN DAMASCUS?
YES. I KNOW A FEW OF THE FAMILIES THAT LOST LOVED ONES.
11:37 AM 72°
CASSIE HALE
Ding
ORDER!

Two days later.

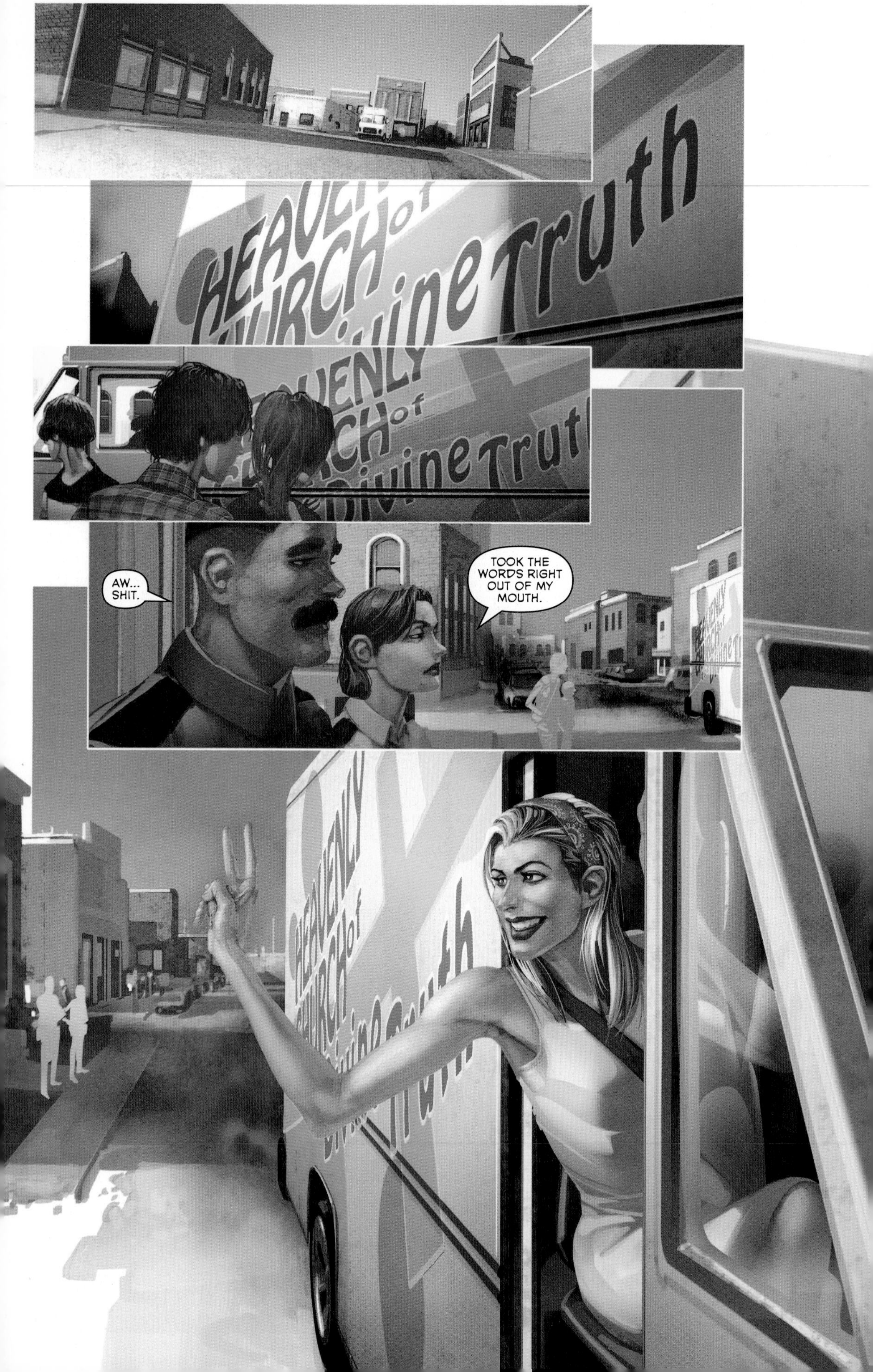

HEAVENLY CHURCH of DIVINE Truth
AW... SHIT.
TOOK THE WORDS RIGHT OUT OF MY MOUTH.

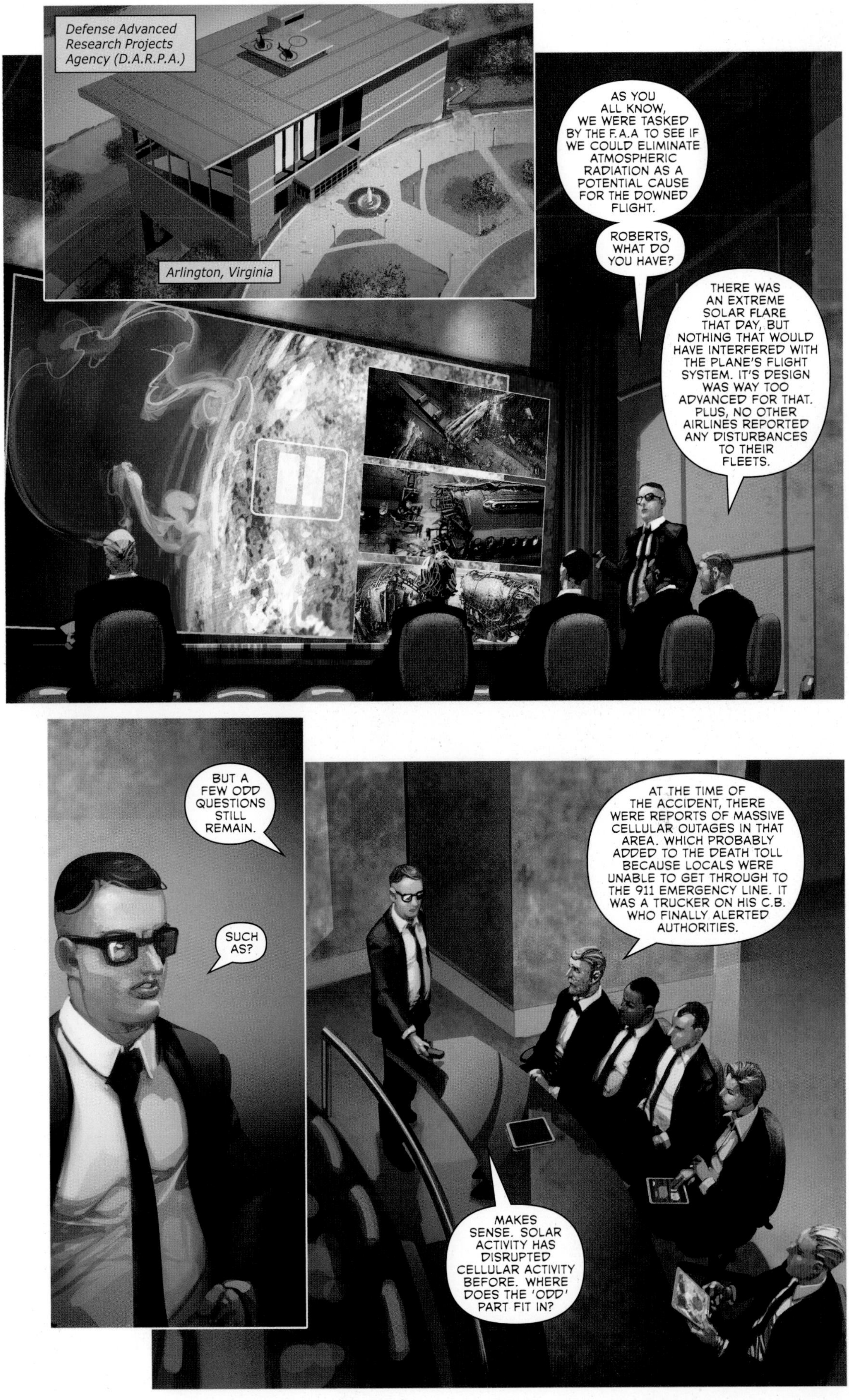
Defense Advanced Research Projects Agency (D.A.R.P.A.)
Arlington, Virginia
AS YOU ALL KNOW, WE WERE TASKED BY THE F.A.A TO SEE IF WE COULD ELIMINATE ATMOSPHERIC RADIATION AS A POTENTIAL CAUSE FOR THE DOWNED FLIGHT.
ROBERTS, WHAT DO YOU HAVE?
THERE WAS AN EXTREME SOLAR FLARE THAT DAY, BUT NOTHING THAT WOULD HAVE INTERFERED WITH THE PLANE'S FLIGHT SYSTEM. IT'S DESIGN WAS WAY TOO ADVANCED FOR THAT. PLUS, NO OTHER AIRLINES REPORTED ANY DISTURBANCES TO THEIR FLEETS.
BUT A FEW ODD QUESTIONS STILL REMAIN.
SUCH AS?
AT THE TIME OF THE ACCIDENT, THERE WERE REPORTS OF MASSIVE CELLULAR OUTAGES IN THAT AREA. WHICH PROBABLY ADDED TO THE DEATH TOLL BECAUSE LOCALS WERE UNABLE TO GET THROUGH TO THE 911 EMERGENCY LINE. IT WAS A TRUCKER ON HIS C.B. WHO FINALLY ALERTED AUTHORITIES.
MAKES SENSE. SOLAR ACTIVITY HAS DISRUPTED CELLULAR ACTIVITY BEFORE. WHERE DOES THE 'ODD' PART FIT IN?

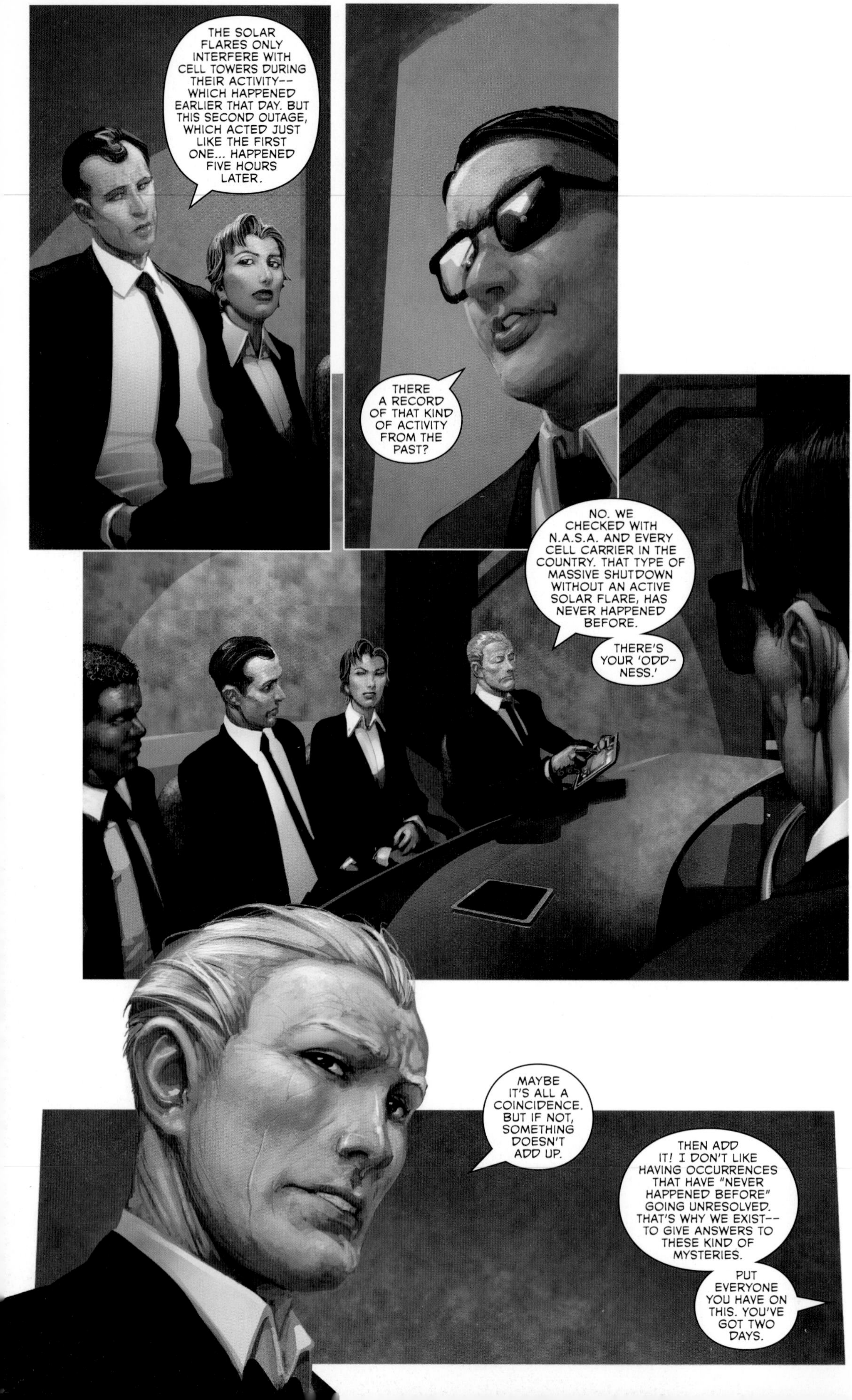
THE SOLAR FLARES ONLY INTERFERE WITH CELL TOWERS DURING THEIR ACTIVITY-- WHICH HAPPENED EARLIER THAT DAY. BUT THIS SECOND OUTAGE, WHICH ACTED JUST LIKE THE FIRST ONE... HAPPENED FIVE HOURS LATER.
THERE A RECORD OF THAT KIND OF ACTIVITY FROM THE PAST?
NO. WE CHECKED WITH N.A.S.A. AND EVERY CELL CARRIER IN THE COUNTRY. THAT TYPE OF MASSIVE SHUTDOWN WITHOUT AN ACTIVE SOLAR FLARE, HAS NEVER HAPPENED BEFORE.
THERE'S YOUR 'ODD-NESS.'
MAYBE IT'S ALL A COINCIDENCE. BUT IF NOT, SOMETHING DOESN'T ADD UP.
THEN ADD IT! I DON'T LIKE HAVING OCCURRENCES THAT HAVE "NEVER HAPPENED BEFORE" GOING UNRESOLVED. THAT'S WHY WE EXIST-- TO GIVE ANSWERS TO THESE KIND OF MYSTERIES.
PUT EVERYONE YOU HAVE ON THIS. YOU'VE GOT TWO DAYS.

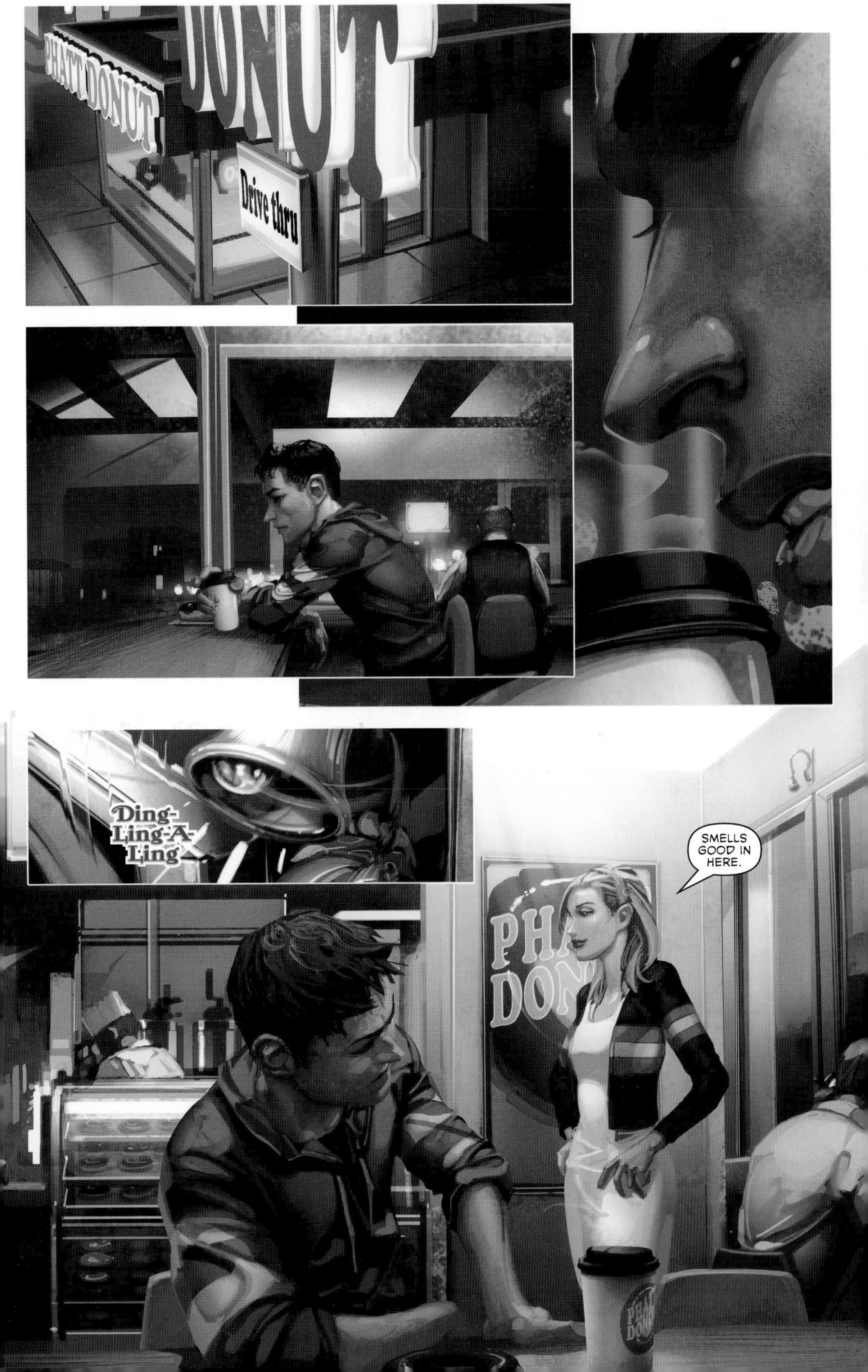
PHATT DONUT
DONUT
Drive thru
Ding-Ling-A-Ling
SMELLS GOOD IN HERE.

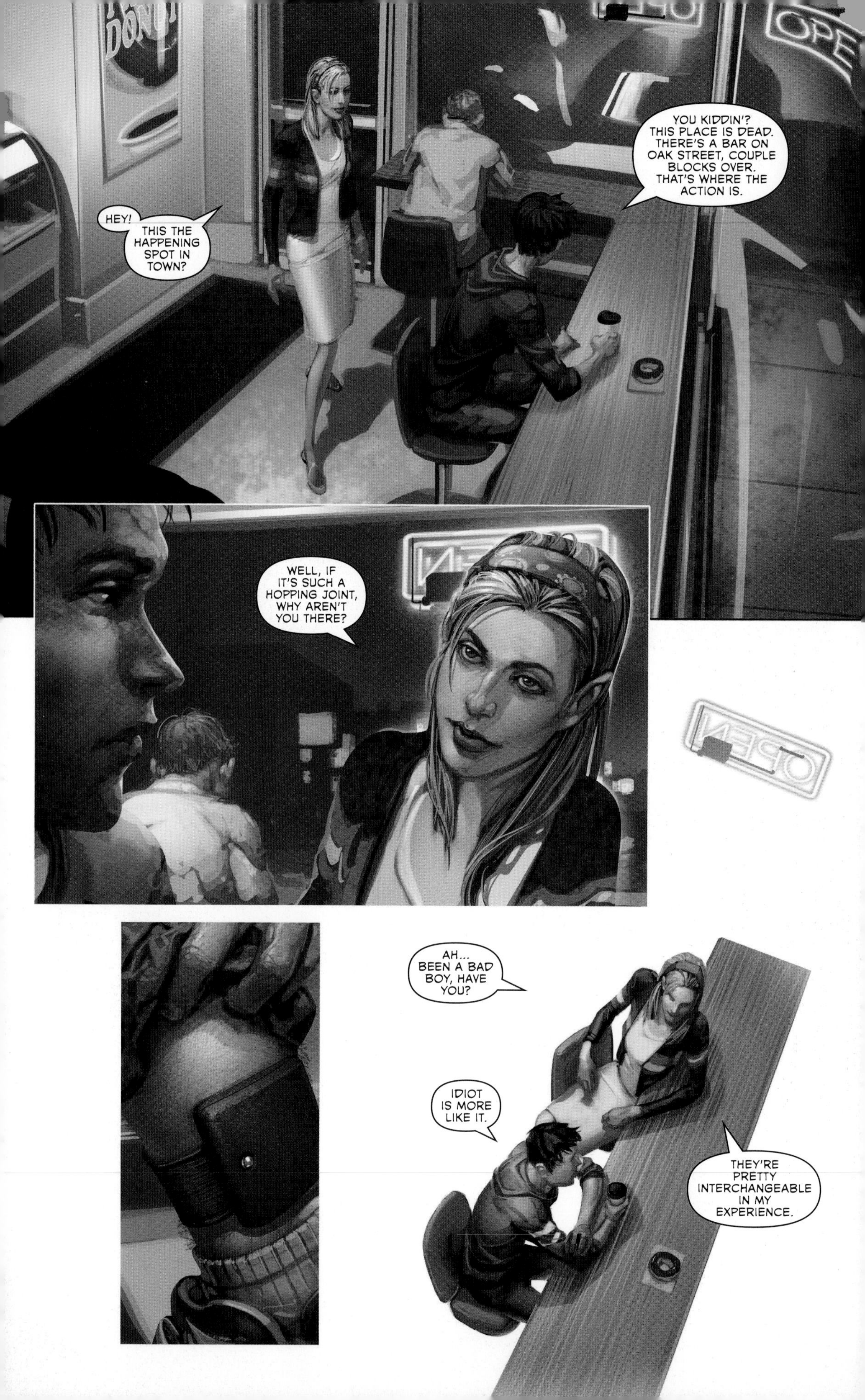
HEY!
THIS THE HAPPENING SPOT IN TOWN?
YOU KIDDIN'? THIS PLACE IS DEAD. THERE'S A BAR ON OAK STREET, COUPLE BLOCKS OVER. THAT'S WHERE THE ACTION IS.
WELL, IF IT'S SUCH A HOPPING JOINT, WHY AREN'T YOU THERE?
OPEN
AH... BEEN A BAD BOY, HAVE YOU?
IDIOT IS MORE LIKE IT.
THEY'RE PRETTY INTERCHANGEABLE IN MY EXPERIENCE.

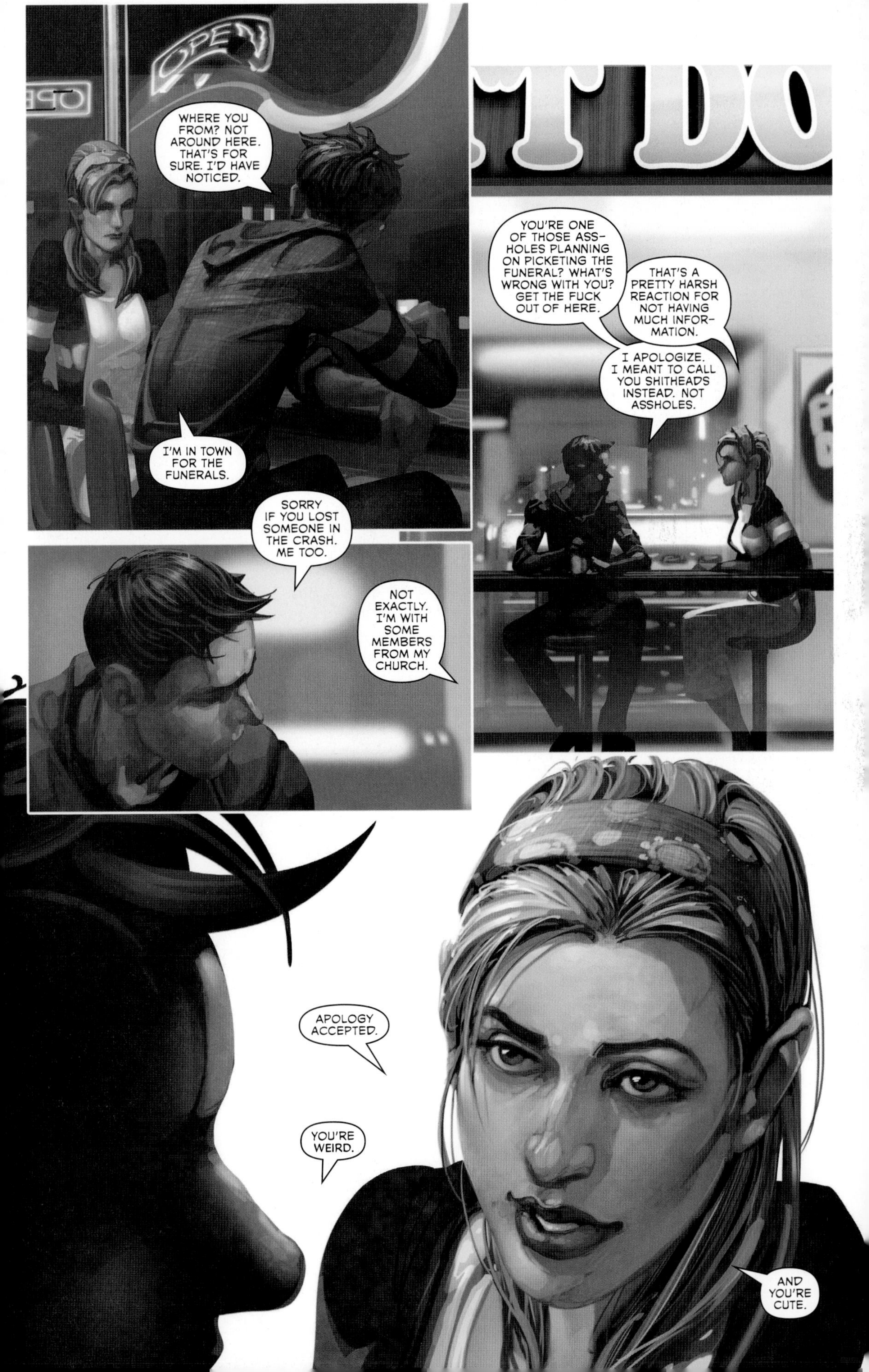
WHERE YOU FROM? NOT AROUND HERE. THAT'S FOR SURE. I'D HAVE NOTICED.
I'M IN TOWN FOR THE FUNERALS.
SORRY IF YOU LOST SOMEONE IN THE CRASH. ME TOO.
NOT EXACTLY. I'M WITH SOME MEMBERS FROM MY CHURCH.
YOU'RE ONE OF THOSE ASS-HOLES PLANNING ON PICKETING THE FUNERAL? WHAT'S WRONG WITH YOU? GET THE FUCK OUT OF HERE.
THAT'S A PRETTY HARSH REACTION FOR NOT HAVING MUCH INFOR-MATION.
I APOLOGIZE. I MEANT TO CALL YOU SHITHEADS INSTEAD. NOT ASSHOLES.
APOLOGY ACCEPTED.
YOU'RE WEIRD.
AND YOU'RE CUTE.

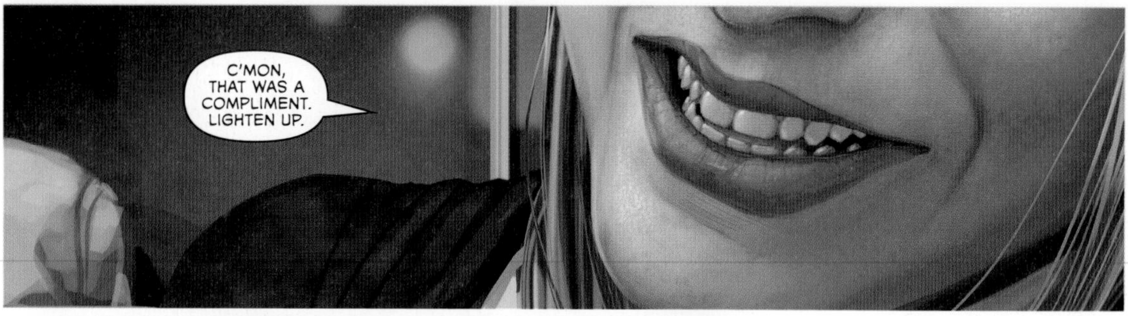
C'MON, THAT WAS A COMPLIMENT. LIGHTEN UP.

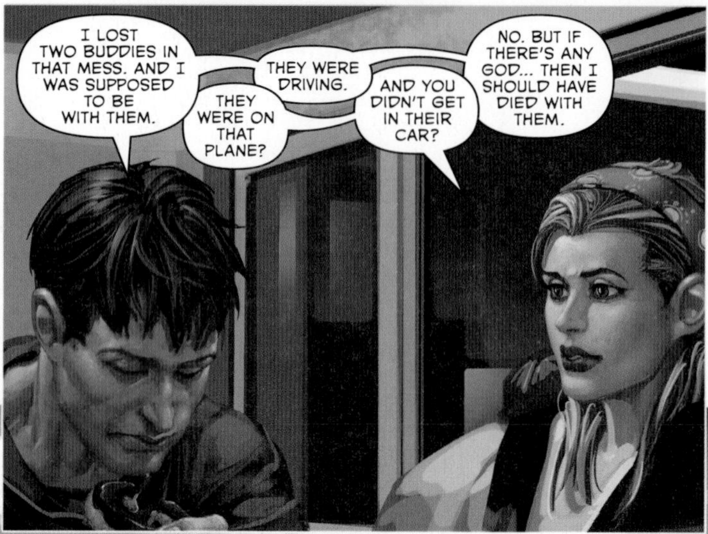
I LOST TWO BUDDIES IN THAT MESS. AND I WAS SUPPOSED TO BE WITH THEM.
THEY WERE ON THAT PLANE?
THEY WERE DRIVING.
AND YOU DIDN'T GET IN THEIR CAR?
NO. BUT IF THERE'S ANY GOD... THEN I SHOULD HAVE DIED WITH THEM.

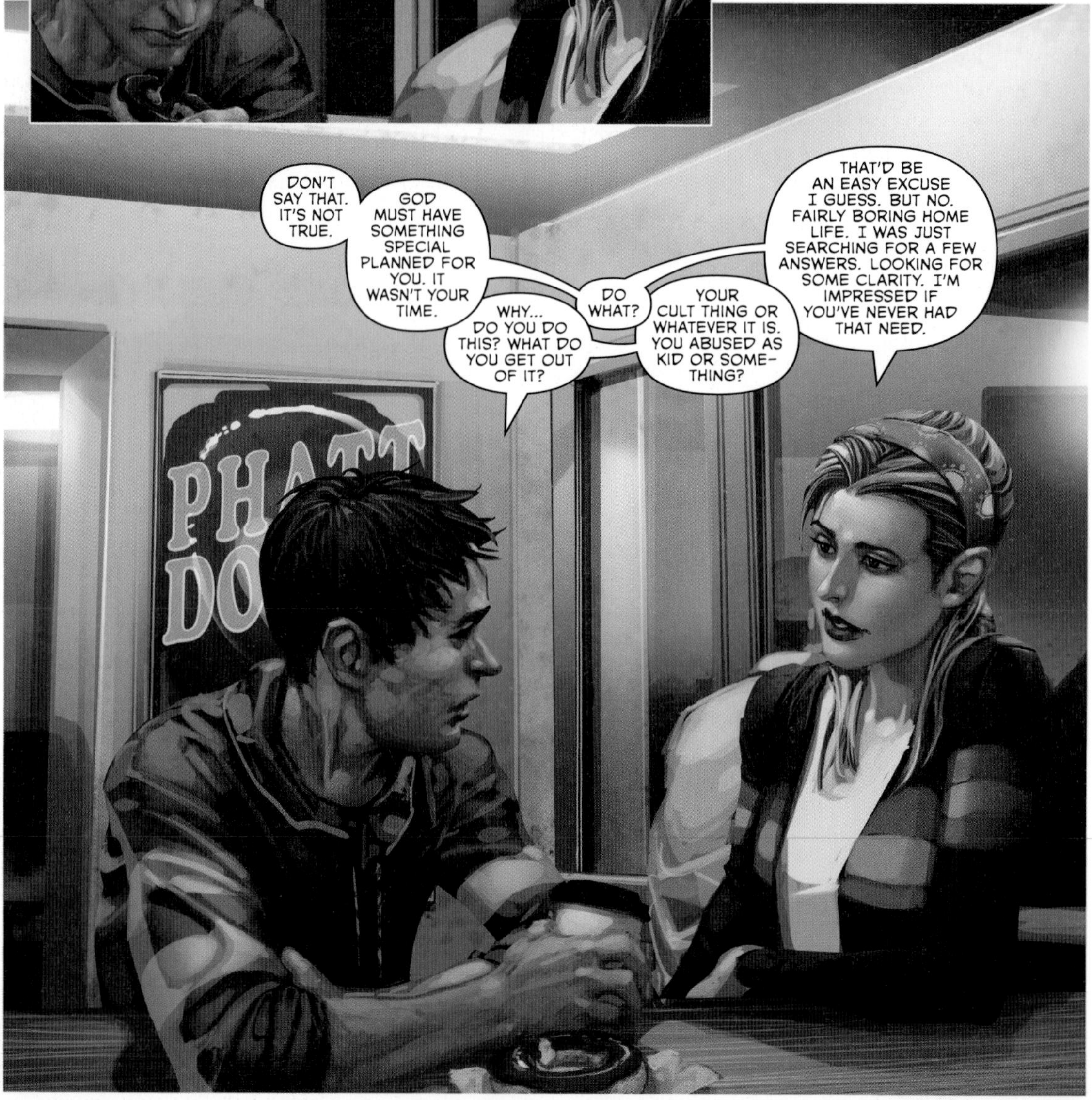
DON'T SAY THAT. IT'S NOT TRUE.
GOD MUST HAVE SOMETHING SPECIAL PLANNED FOR YOU. IT WASN'T YOUR TIME.
DO WHAT?
WHY... DO YOU DO THIS? WHAT DO YOU GET OUT OF IT?
YOUR CULT THING OR WHATEVER IT IS. YOU ABUSED AS KID OR SOME-THING?
THAT'D BE AN EASY EXCUSE I GUESS. BUT NO. FAIRLY BORING HOME LIFE. I WAS JUST SEARCHING FOR A FEW ANSWERS. LOOKING FOR SOME CLARITY. I'M IMPRESSED IF YOU'VE NEVER HAD THAT NEED.
PHATT DO

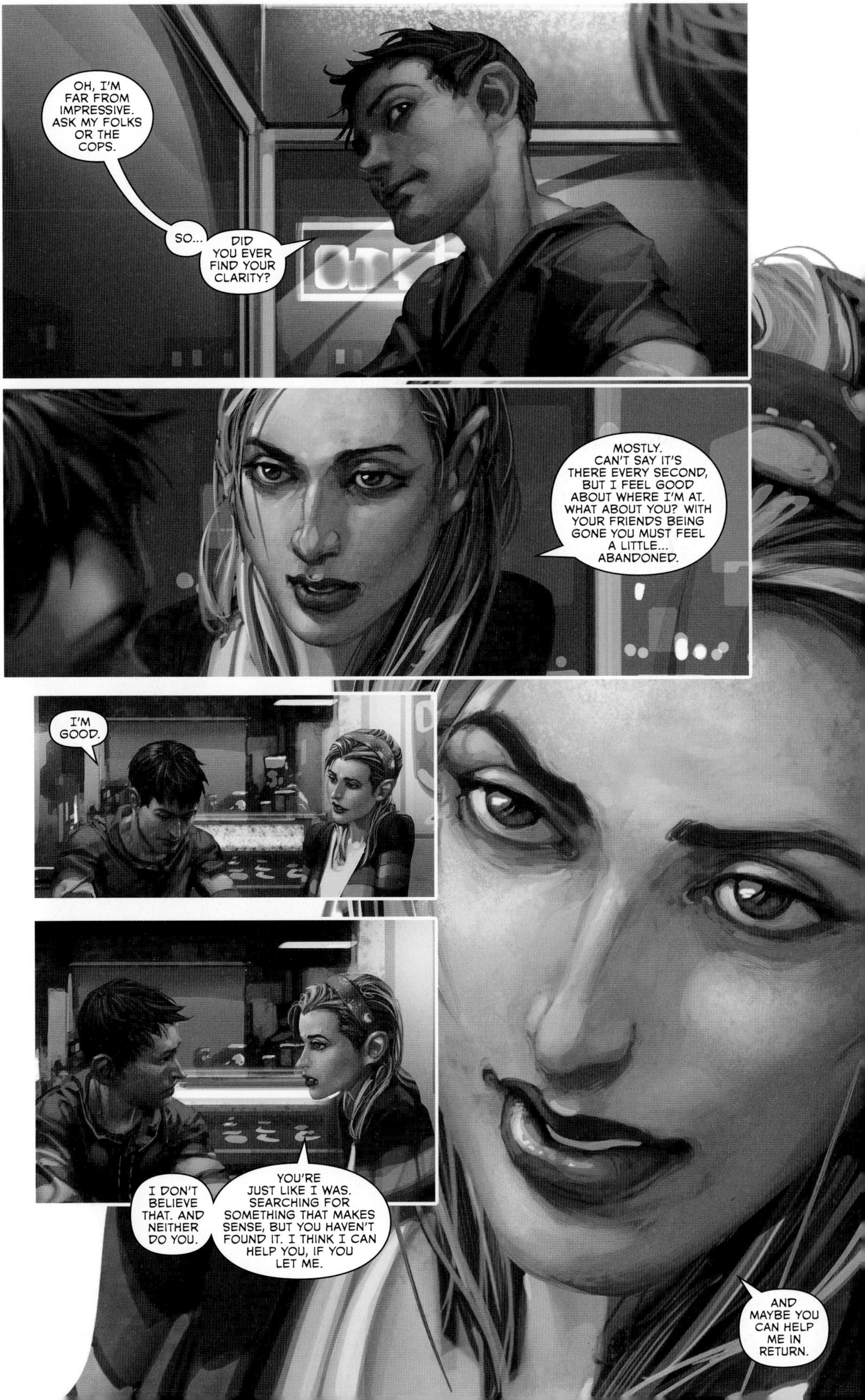
OH, I'M FAR FROM IMPRESSIVE. ASK MY FOLKS OR THE COPS.
SO...
DID YOU EVER FIND YOUR CLARITY?
MOSTLY. CAN'T SAY IT'S THERE EVERY SECOND, BUT I FEEL GOOD ABOUT WHERE I'M AT. WHAT ABOUT YOU? WITH YOUR FRIENDS BEING GONE YOU MUST FEEL A LITTLE... ABANDONED.
I'M GOOD.
I DON'T BELIEVE THAT. AND NEITHER DO YOU.
YOU'RE JUST LIKE I WAS. SEARCHING FOR SOMETHING THAT MAKES SENSE, BUT YOU HAVEN'T FOUND IT. I THINK I CAN HELP YOU, IF YOU LET ME.
AND MAYBE YOU CAN HELP ME IN RETURN.

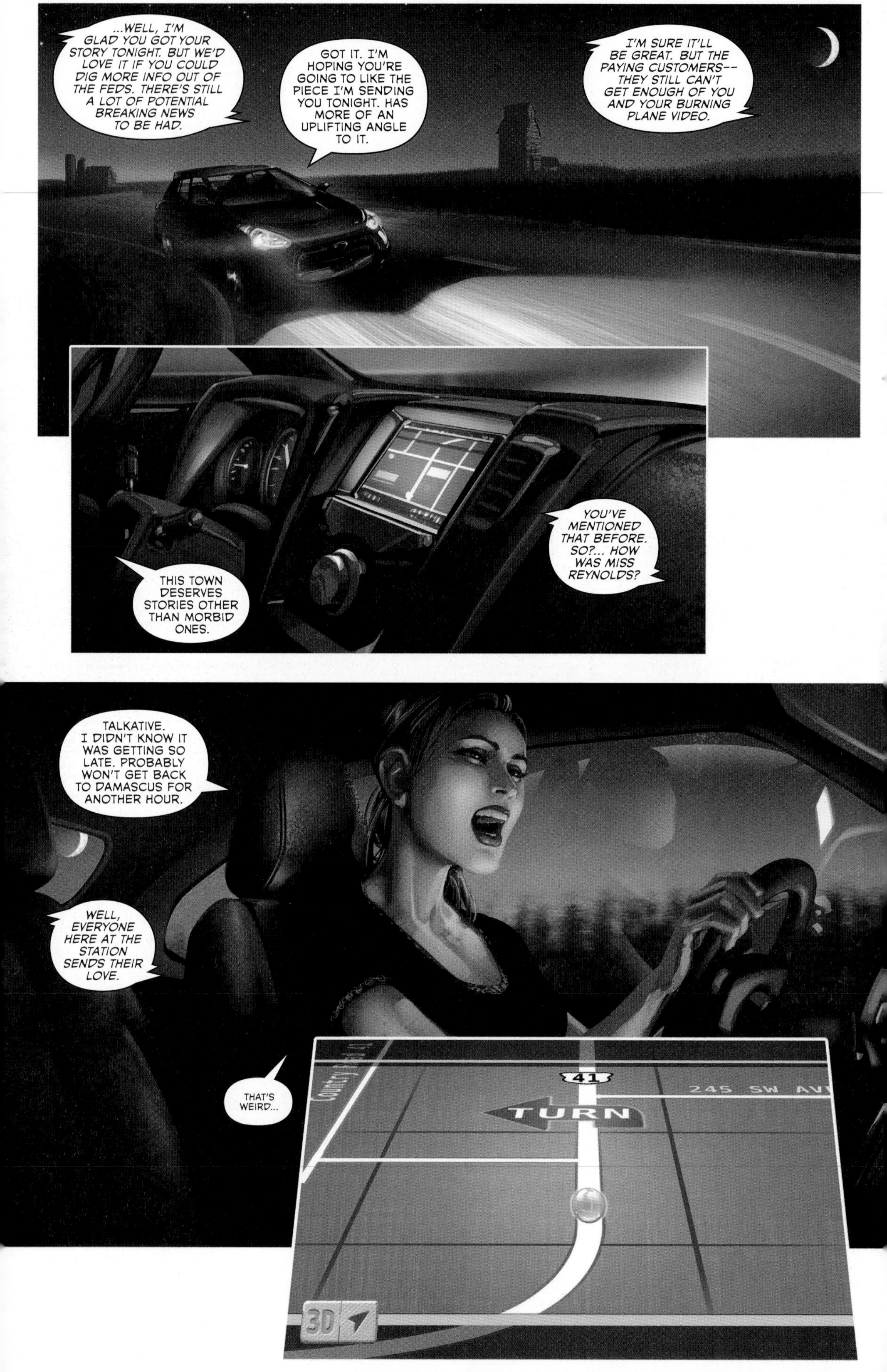
...WELL, I'M GLAD YOU GOT YOUR STORY TONIGHT. BUT WE'D LOVE IT IF YOU COULD DIG MORE INFO OUT OF THE FEDS. THERE'S STILL A LOT OF POTENTIAL BREAKING NEWS TO BE HAD.
GOT IT. I'M HOPING YOU'RE GOING TO LIKE THE PIECE I'M SENDING YOU TONIGHT. HAS MORE OF AN UPLIFTING ANGLE TO IT.
I'M SURE IT'LL BE GREAT. BUT THE PAYING CUSTOMERS-- THEY STILL CAN'T GET ENOUGH OF YOU AND YOUR BURNING PLANE VIDEO.
THIS TOWN DESERVES STORIES OTHER THAN MORBID ONES.
YOU'VE MENTIONED THAT BEFORE. SO?... HOW WAS MISS REYNOLDS?
TALKATIVE. I DIDN'T KNOW IT WAS GETTING SO LATE. PROBABLY WON'T GET BACK TO DAMASCUS FOR ANOTHER HOUR.
WELL, EVERYONE HERE AT THE STATION SENDS THEIR LOVE.
THAT'S WEIRD...
41
245 SW AV
TURN
3D

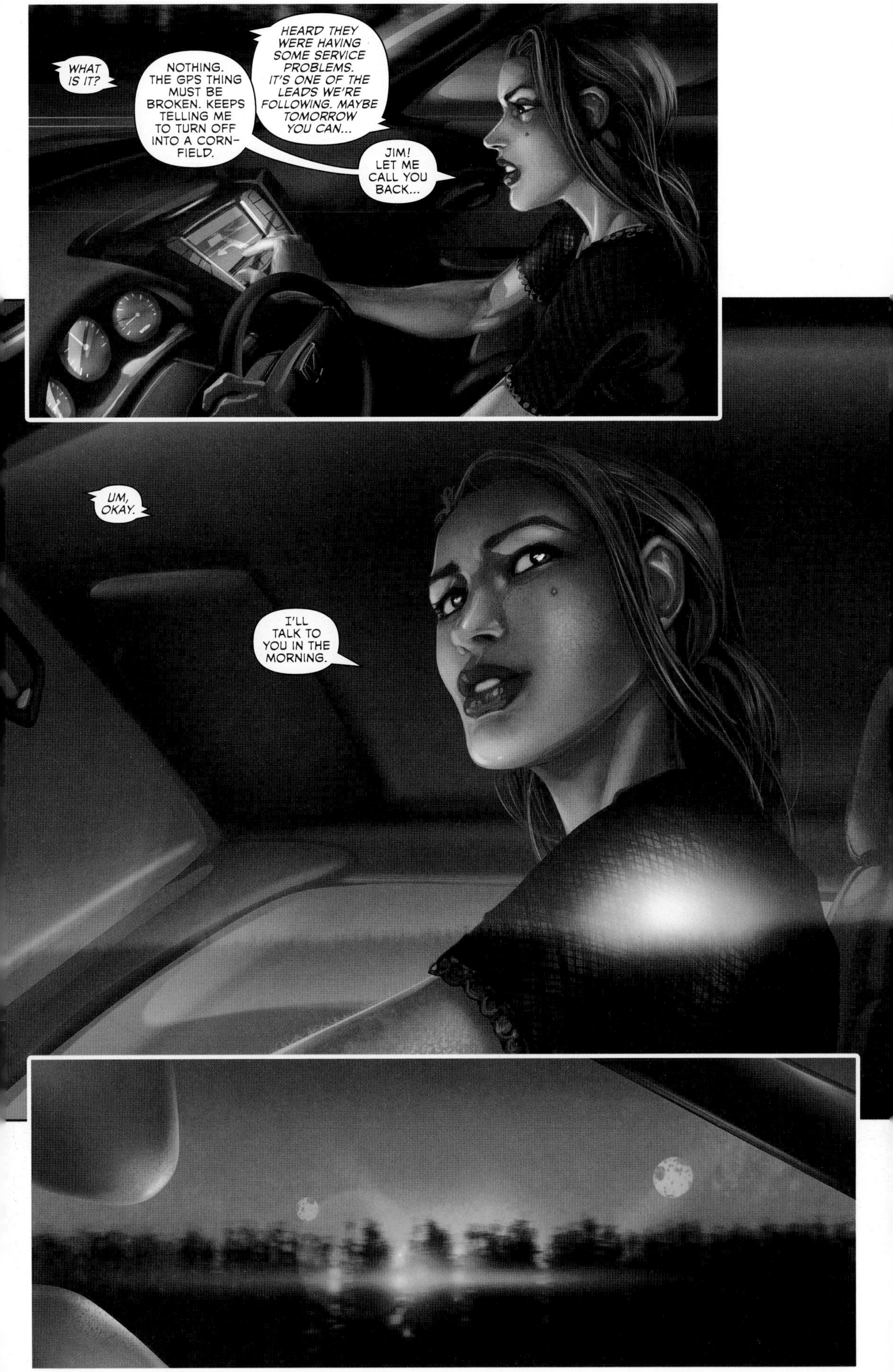
WHAT IS IT?
NOTHING. THE GPS THING MUST BE BROKEN. KEEPS TELLING ME TO TURN OFF INTO A CORN-FIELD.
HEARD THEY WERE HAVING SOME SERVICE PROBLEMS. IT'S ONE OF THE LEADS WE'RE FOLLOWING. MAYBE TOMORROW YOU CAN...
JIM! LET ME CALL YOU BACK...
UM, OKAY.
I'LL TALK TO YOU IN THE MORNING.

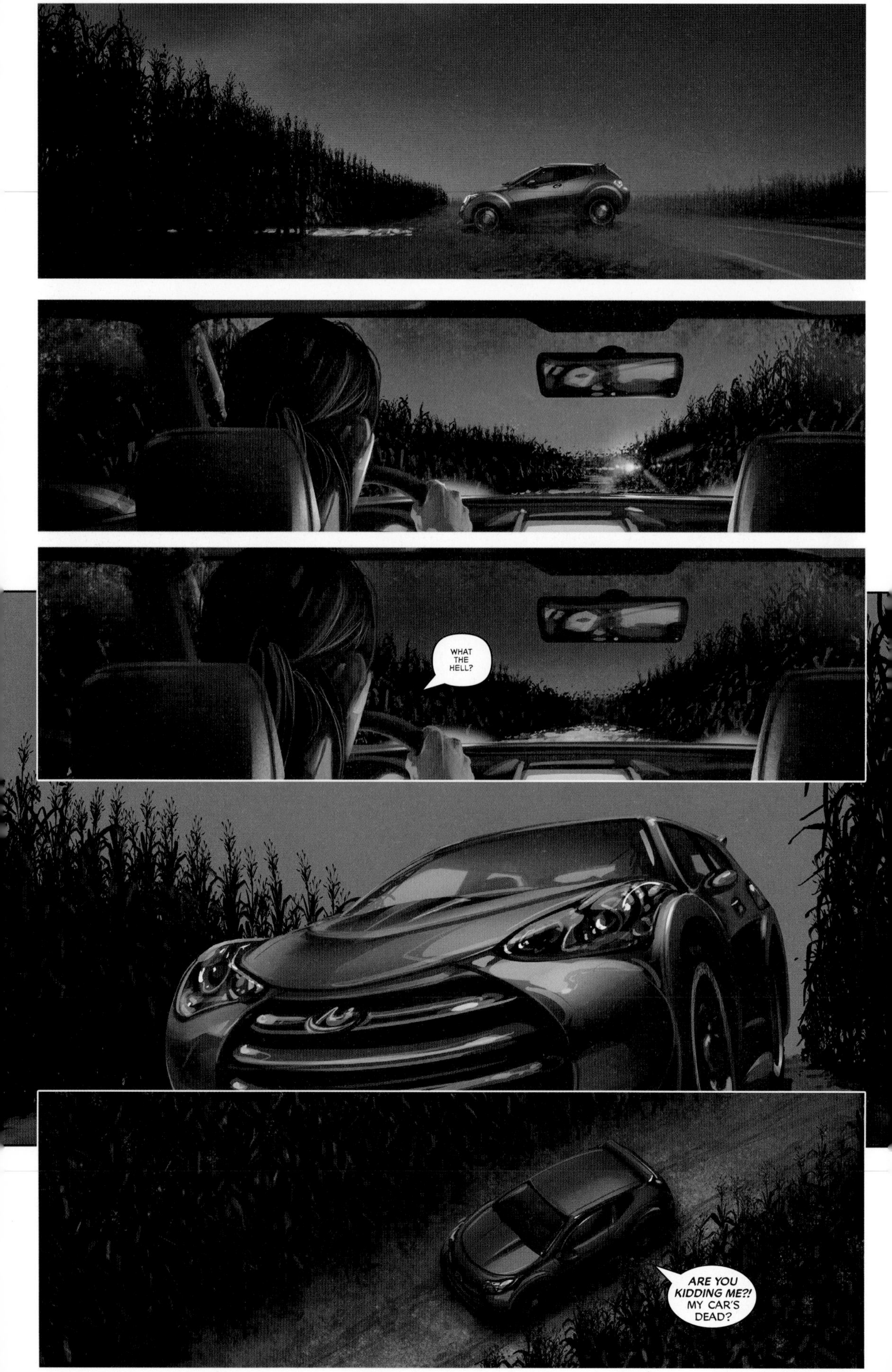
WHAT THE HELL?
ARE YOU KIDDING ME?! MY CAR'S DEAD?

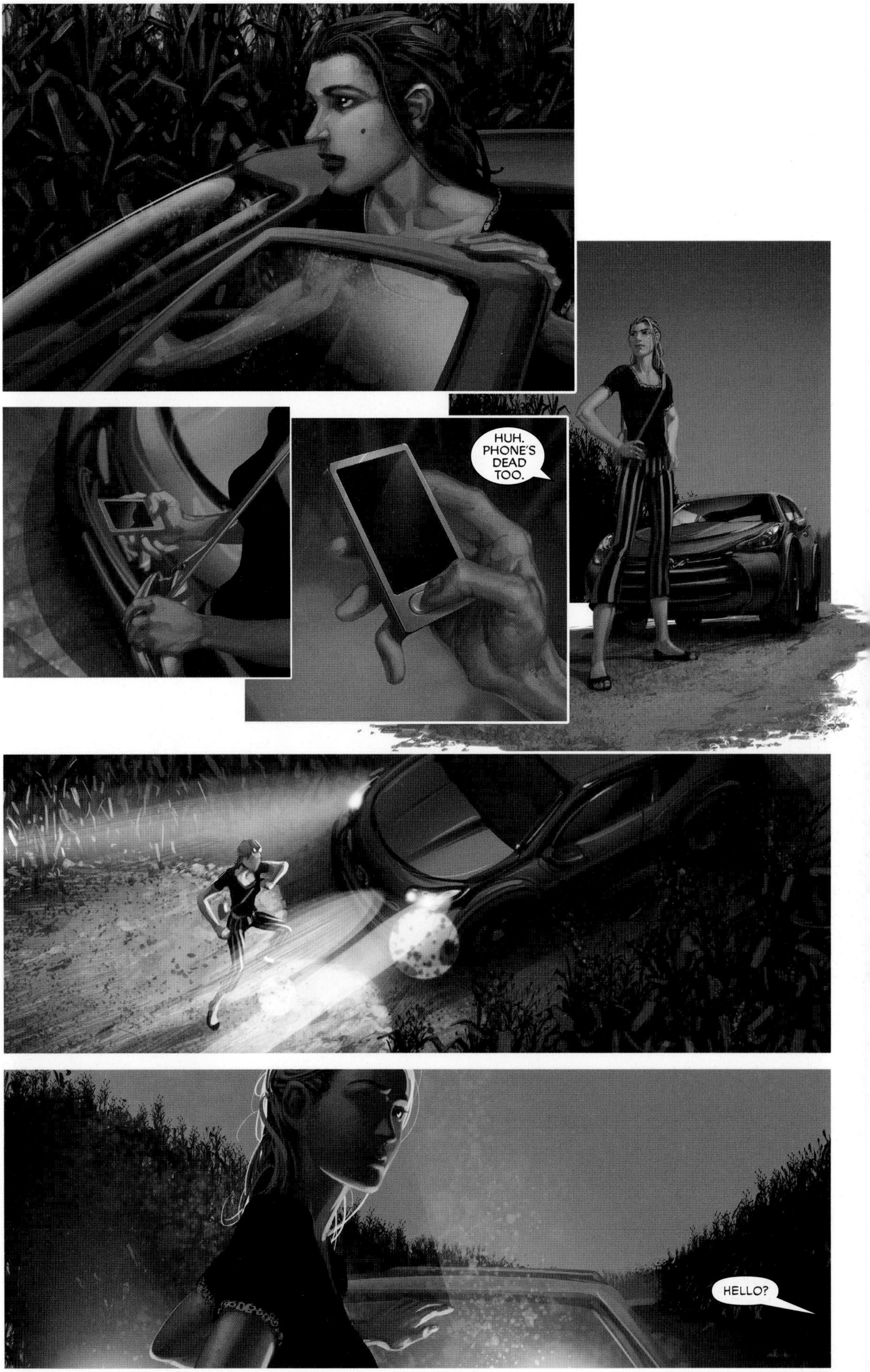
HUH. PHONE'S DEAD TOO.
HELLO?

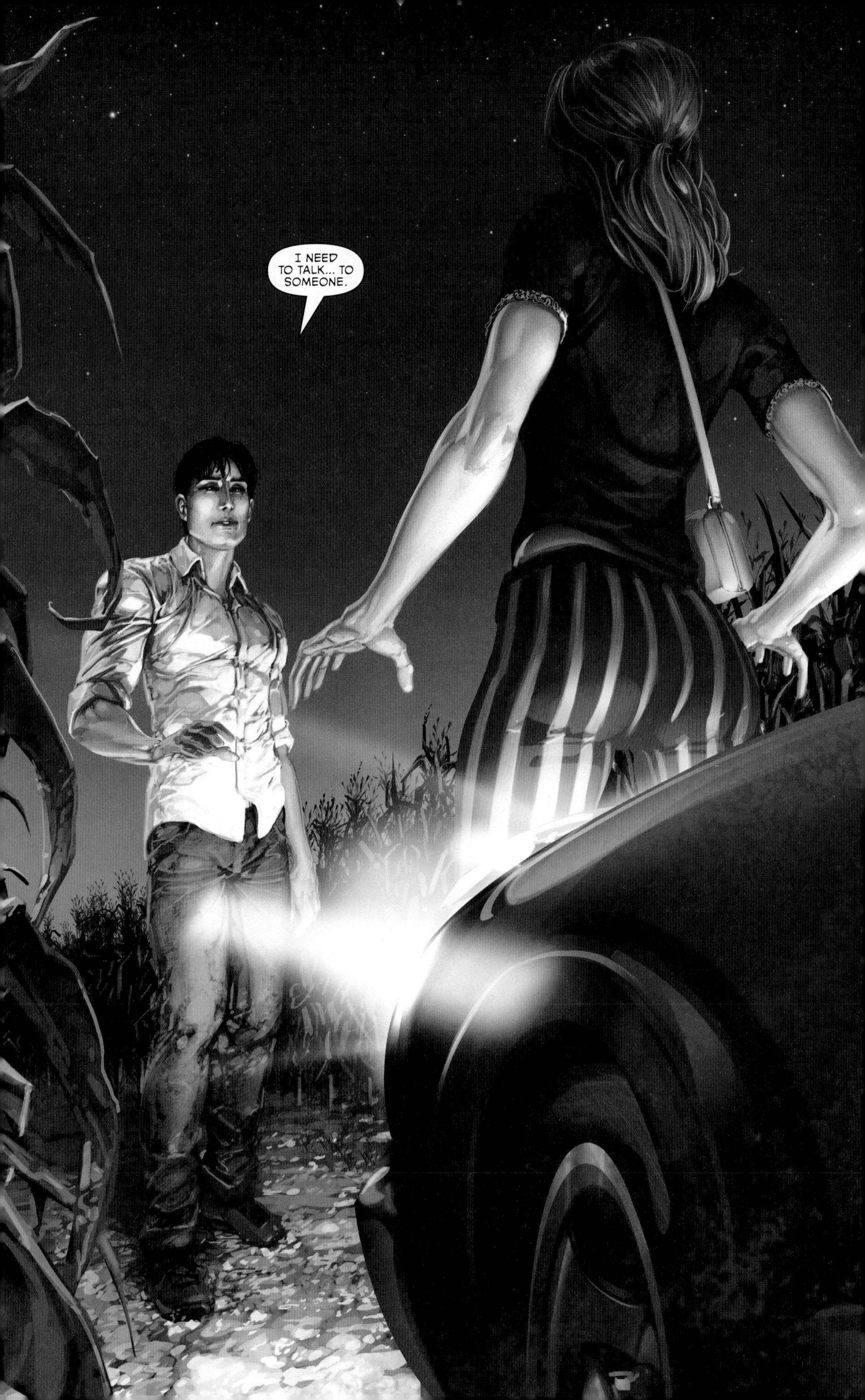
I NEED TO TALK... TO SOMEONE.

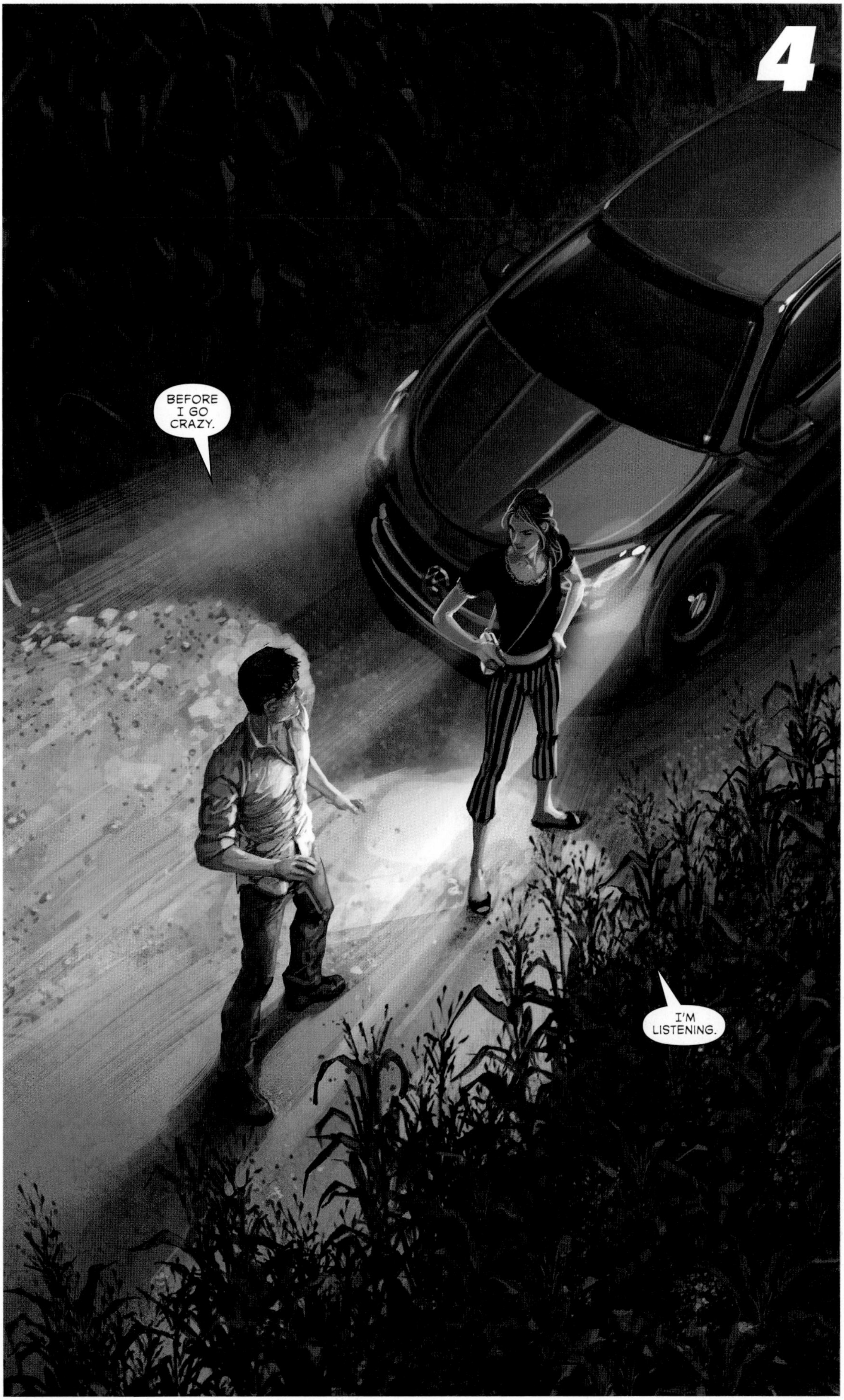
4
BEFORE I GO CRAZY.
I'M LISTENING.

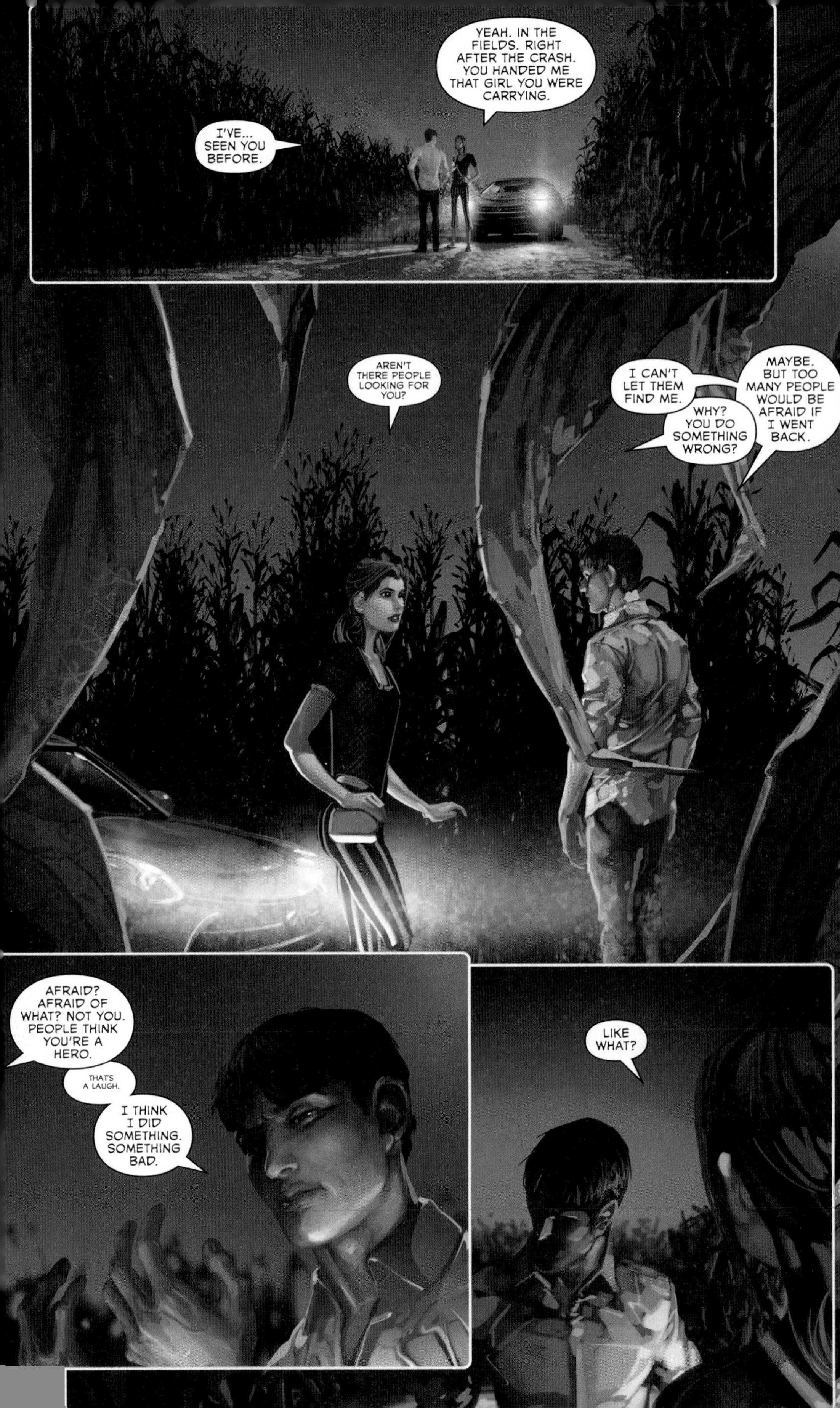
YEAH. IN THE FIELDS. RIGHT AFTER THE CRASH. YOU HANDED ME THAT GIRL YOU WERE CARRYING.
I'VE... SEEN YOU BEFORE.
AREN'T THERE PEOPLE LOOKING FOR YOU?
I CAN'T LET THEM FIND ME.
WHY? YOU DO SOMETHING WRONG?
MAYBE. BUT TOO MANY PEOPLE WOULD BE AFRAID IF I WENT BACK.
AFRAID? AFRAID OF WHAT? NOT YOU. PEOPLE THINK YOU'RE A HERO.
THAT'S A LAUGH.
I THINK I DID SOMETHING. SOMETHING BAD.
LIKE WHAT?

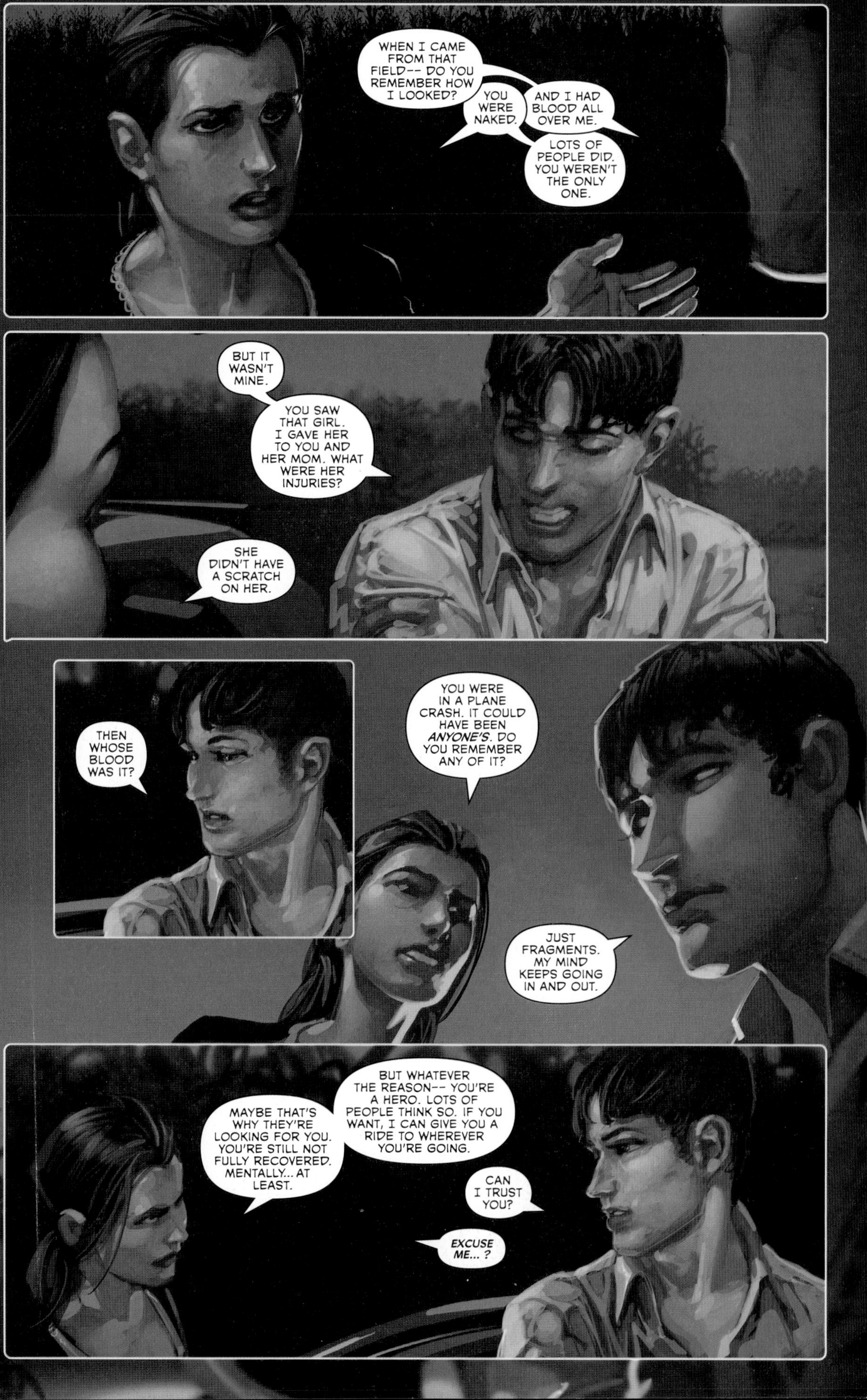

WHEN I CAME FROM THAT FIELD-- DO YOU REMEMBER HOW I LOOKED?
YOU WERE NAKED.
AND I HAD BLOOD ALL OVER ME.
LOTS OF PEOPLE DID. YOU WEREN'T THE ONLY ONE.
BUT IT WASN'T MINE.
YOU SAW THAT GIRL. I GAVE HER TO YOU AND HER MOM. WHAT WERE HER INJURIES?
SHE DIDN'T HAVE A SCRATCH ON HER.
THEN WHOSE BLOOD WAS IT?
YOU WERE IN A PLANE CRASH. IT COULD HAVE BEEN *ANYONE'S*. DO YOU REMEMBER ANY OF IT?
JUST FRAGMENTS. MY MIND KEEPS GOING IN AND OUT.
MAYBE THAT'S WHY THEY'RE LOOKING FOR YOU. YOU'RE STILL NOT FULLY RECOVERED. MENTALLY... AT LEAST.
BUT WHATEVER THE REASON-- YOU'RE A HERO. LOTS OF PEOPLE THINK SO. IF YOU WANT, I CAN GIVE YOU A RIDE TO WHEREVER YOU'RE GOING.
CAN I TRUST YOU?
EXCUSE ME... ?

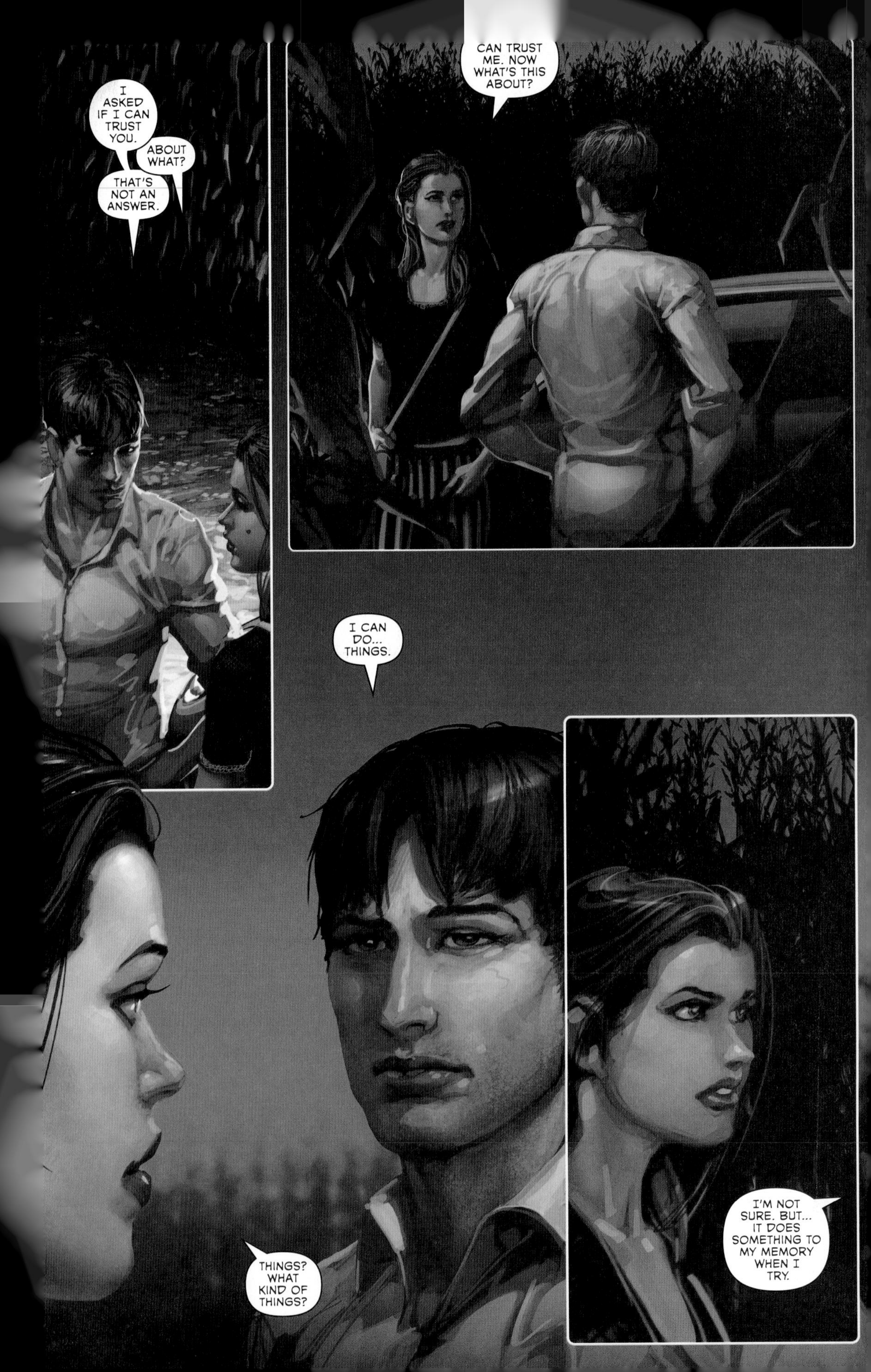
I ASKED IF I CAN TRUST YOU.
ABOUT WHAT?
THAT'S NOT AN ANSWER.
CAN TRUST ME. NOW WHAT'S THIS ABOUT?
I CAN DO... THINGS.
THINGS? WHAT KIND OF THINGS?
I'M NOT SURE. BUT... IT DOES SOMETHING TO MY MEMORY WHEN I TRY.

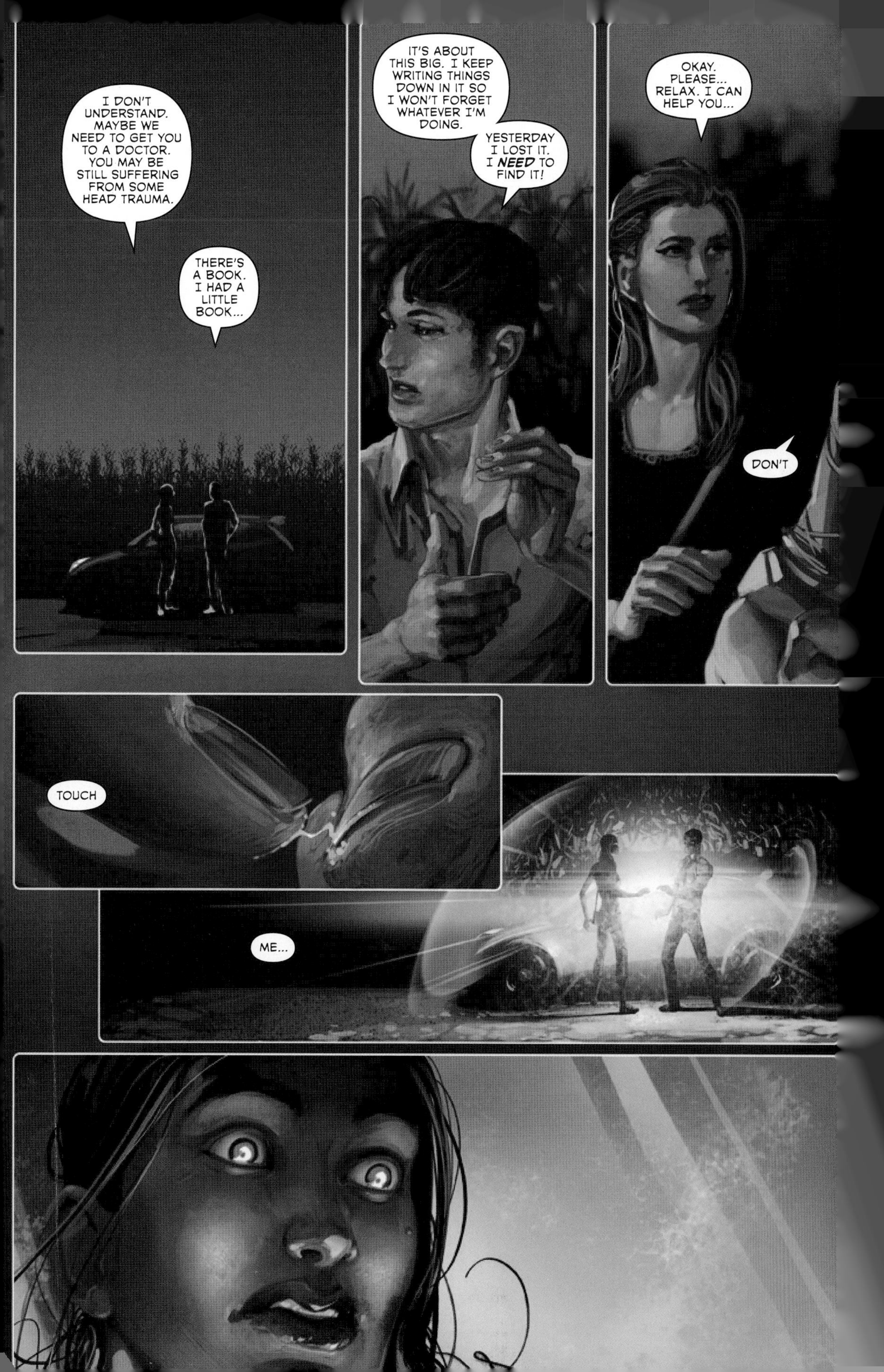
I DON'T UNDERSTAND. MAYBE WE NEED TO GET YOU TO A DOCTOR. YOU MAY BE STILL SUFFERING FROM SOME HEAD TRAUMA.
THERE'S A BOOK. I HAD A LITTLE BOOK...
IT'S ABOUT THIS BIG. I KEEP WRITING THINGS DOWN IN IT SO I WON'T FORGET WHATEVER I'M DOING.
YESTERDAY I LOST IT. I *NEED* TO FIND IT!
OKAY. PLEASE... RELAX. I CAN HELP YOU...
DON'T
TOUCH
ME...

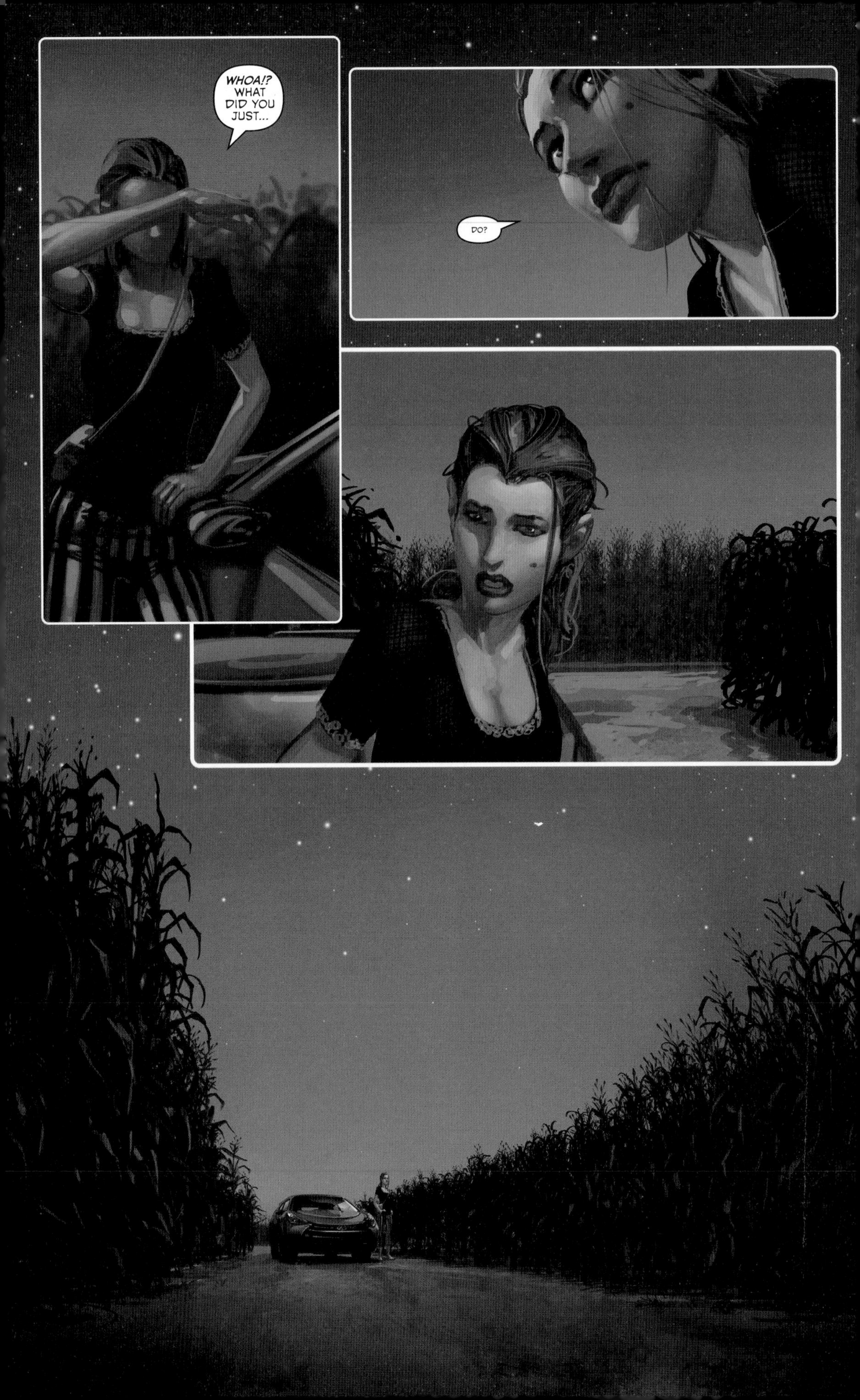
WHOA!? WHAT DID YOU JUST...
DO?

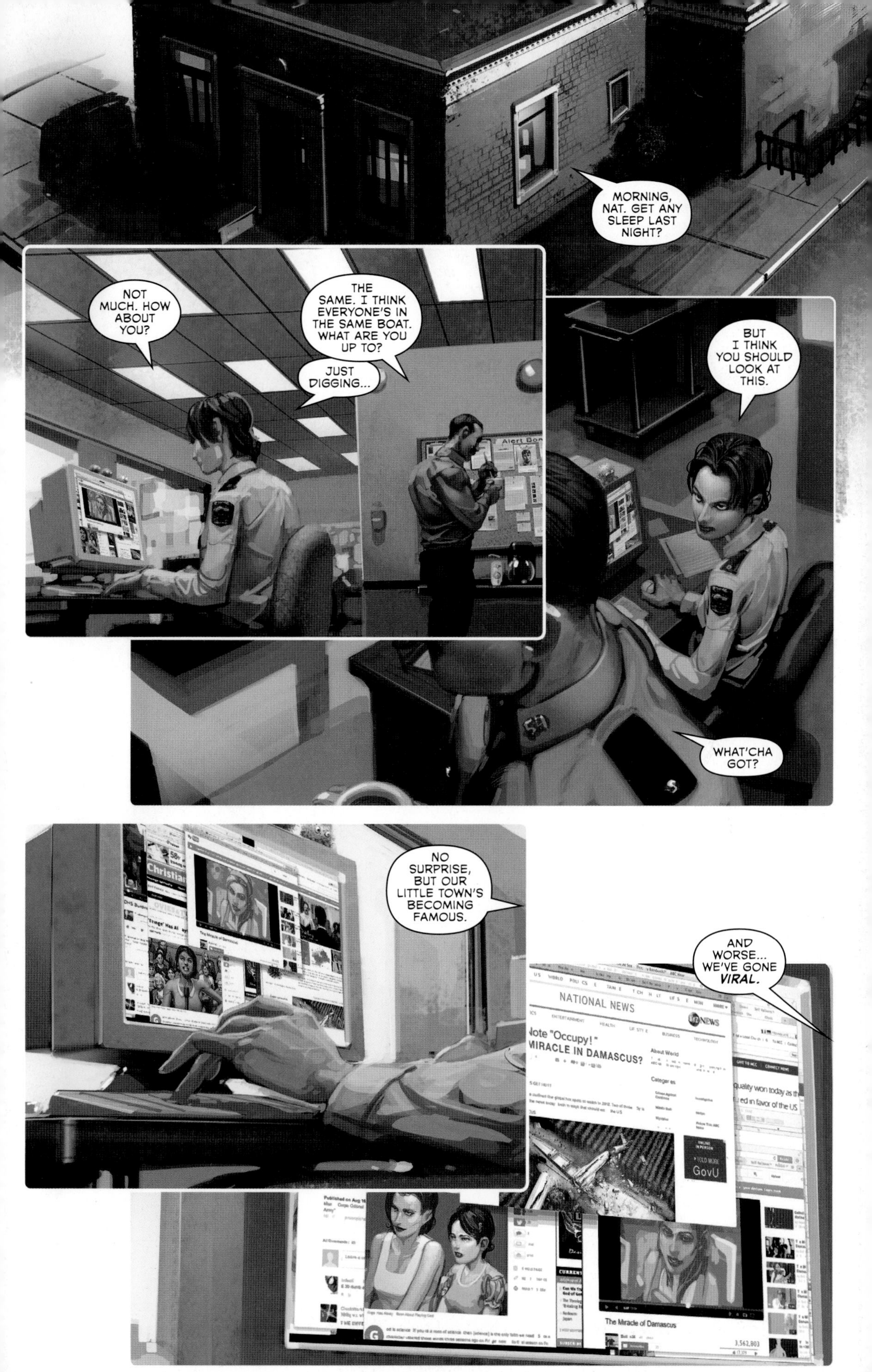
MORNING, NAT. GET ANY SLEEP LAST NIGHT?
NOT MUCH. HOW ABOUT YOU?
THE SAME. I THINK EVERYONE'S IN THE SAME BOAT. WHAT ARE YOU UP TO?
JUST DIGGING...
BUT I THINK YOU SHOULD LOOK AT THIS.
WHAT'CHA GOT?
NO SURPRISE, BUT OUR LITTLE TOWN'S BECOMING FAMOUS.
AND WORSE... WE'VE GONE *VIRAL.*
NATIONAL NEWS
MIRACLE IN DAMASCUS?
The Miracle of Damascus

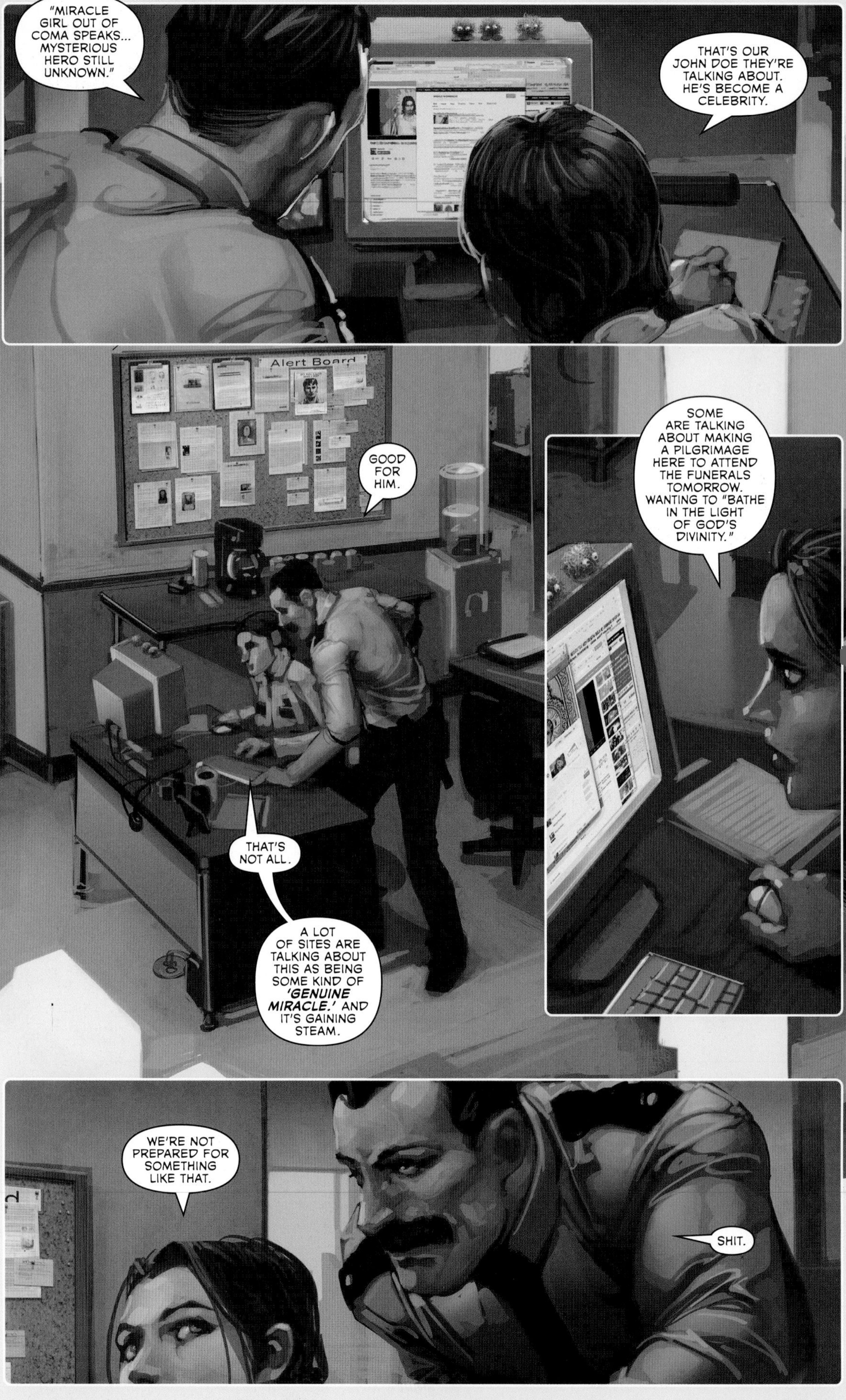
"MIRACLE GIRL OUT OF COMA SPEAKS... MYSTERIOUS HERO STILL UNKNOWN."
THAT'S OUR JOHN DOE THEY'RE TALKING ABOUT. HE'S BECOME A CELEBRITY.
Alert Board
GOOD FOR HIM.
THAT'S NOT ALL.
A LOT OF SITES ARE TALKING ABOUT THIS AS BEING SOME KIND OF *'GENUINE MIRACLE.'* AND IT'S GAINING STEAM.
SOME ARE TALKING ABOUT MAKING A PILGRIMAGE HERE TO ATTEND THE FUNERALS TOMORROW. WANTING TO "BATHE IN THE LIGHT OF GOD'S DIVINITY."
WE'RE NOT PREPARED FOR SOMETHING LIKE THAT.
SHIT.

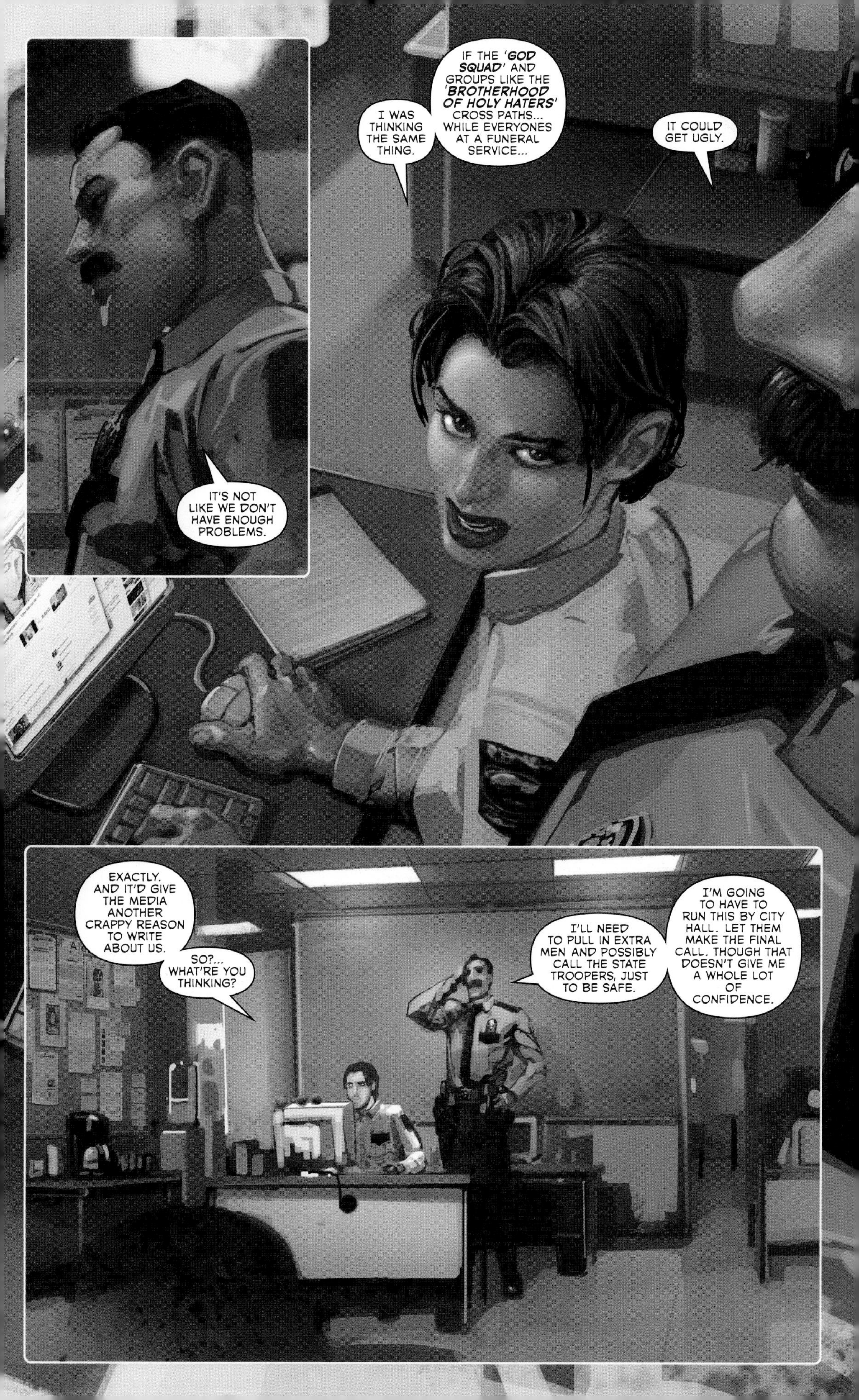
I WAS THINKING THE SAME THING.
IF THE 'GOD SQUAD' AND GROUPS LIKE THE 'BROTHERHOOD OF HOLY HATERS' CROSS PATHS... WHILE EVERYONES AT A FUNERAL SERVICE...
IT COULD GET UGLY.
IT'S NOT LIKE WE DON'T HAVE ENOUGH PROBLEMS.
EXACTLY. AND IT'D GIVE THE MEDIA ANOTHER CRAPPY REASON TO WRITE ABOUT US.
SO?... WHAT'RE YOU THINKING?
I'LL NEED TO PULL IN EXTRA MEN AND POSSIBLY CALL THE STATE TROOPERS, JUST TO BE SAFE.
I'M GOING TO HAVE TO RUN THIS BY CITY HALL. LET THEM MAKE THE FINAL CALL. THOUGH THAT DOESN'T GIVE ME A WHOLE LOT OF CONFIDENCE.

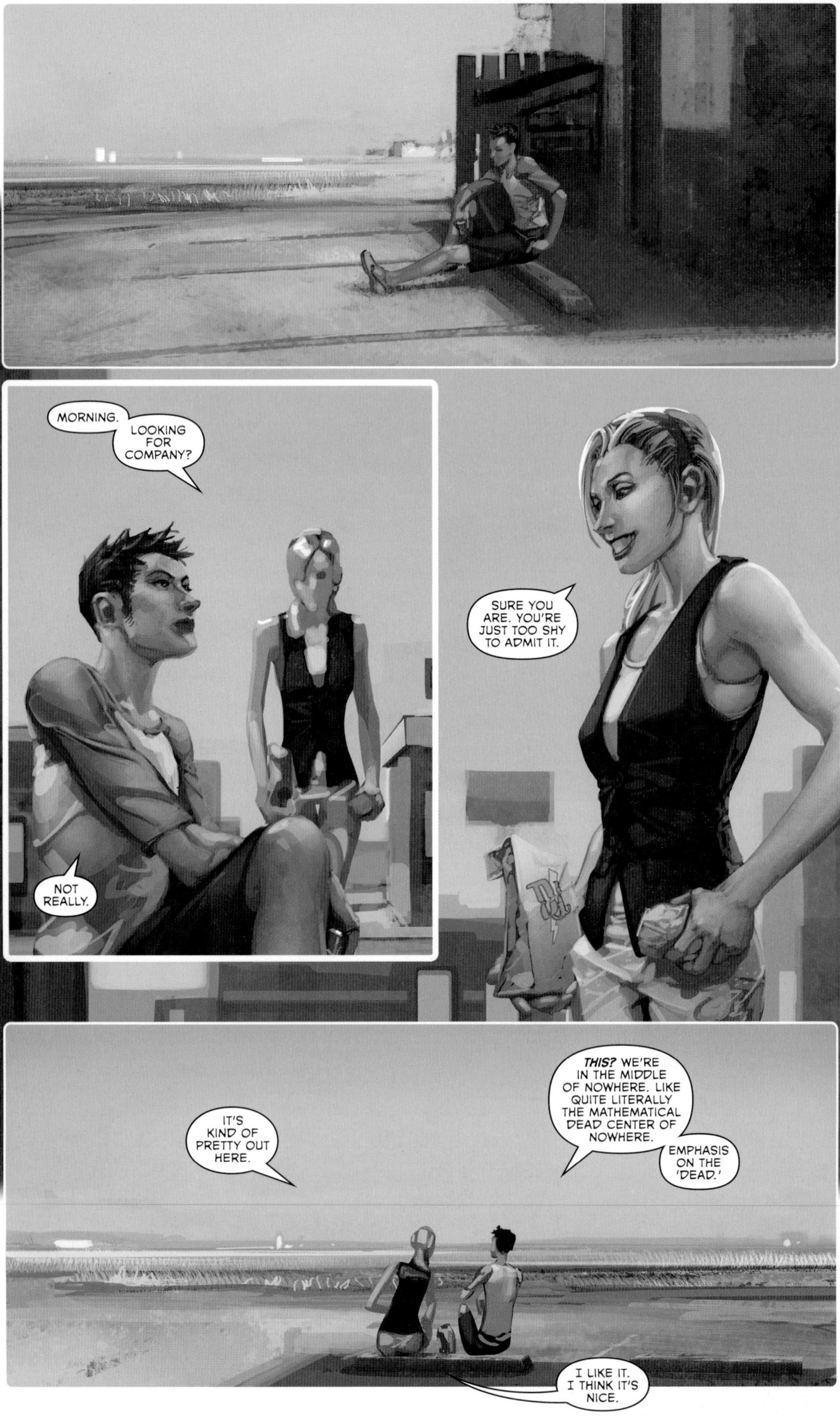

MORNING.
LOOKING FOR COMPANY?
NOT REALLY.
SURE YOU ARE. YOU'RE JUST TOO SHY TO ADMIT IT.
IT'S KIND OF PRETTY OUT HERE.
THIS? WE'RE IN THE MIDDLE OF NOWHERE. LIKE QUITE LITERALLY THE MATHEMATICAL DEAD CENTER OF NOWHERE.
EMPHASIS ON THE 'DEAD.'
I LIKE IT. I THINK IT'S NICE.

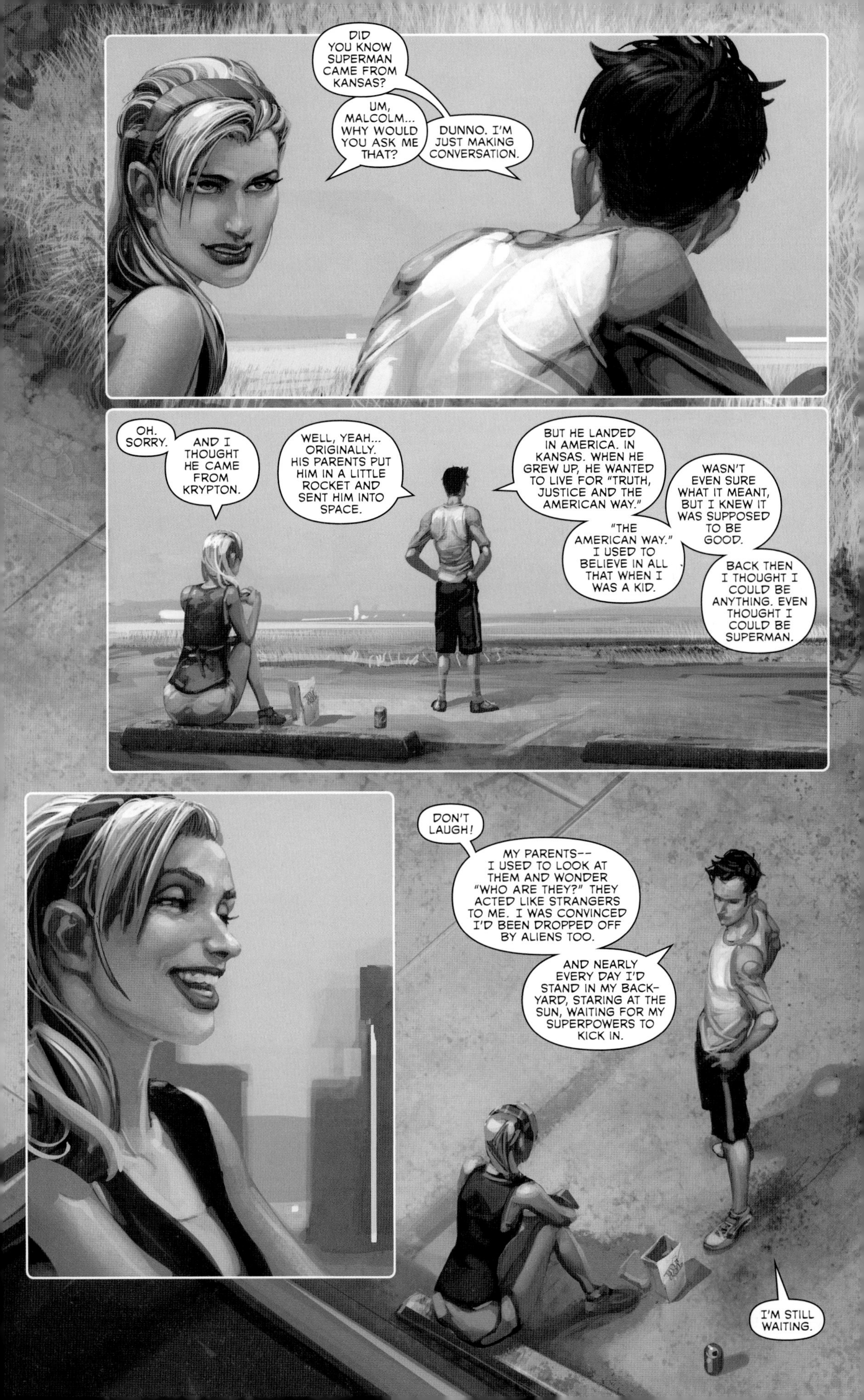
DID YOU KNOW SUPERMAN CAME FROM KANSAS?
UM, MALCOLM... WHY WOULD YOU ASK ME THAT?
DUNNO. I'M JUST MAKING CONVERSATION.
OH. SORRY.
AND I THOUGHT HE CAME FROM KRYPTON.
WELL, YEAH... ORIGINALLY. HIS PARENTS PUT HIM IN A LITTLE ROCKET AND SENT HIM INTO SPACE.
BUT HE LANDED IN AMERICA. IN KANSAS. WHEN HE GREW UP, HE WANTED TO LIVE FOR "TRUTH, JUSTICE AND THE AMERICAN WAY."
"THE AMERICAN WAY." I USED TO BELIEVE IN ALL THAT WHEN I WAS A KID.
WASN'T EVEN SURE WHAT IT MEANT, BUT I KNEW IT WAS SUPPOSED TO BE GOOD.
BACK THEN I THOUGHT I COULD BE ANYTHING. EVEN THOUGHT I COULD BE SUPERMAN.
DON'T LAUGH!
MY PARENTS-- I USED TO LOOK AT THEM AND WONDER "WHO ARE THEY?" THEY ACTED LIKE STRANGERS TO ME. I WAS CONVINCED I'D BEEN DROPPED OFF BY ALIENS TOO.
AND NEARLY EVERY DAY I'D STAND IN MY BACK-YARD, STARING AT THE SUN, WAITING FOR MY SUPERPOWERS TO KICK IN.
I'M STILL WAITING.

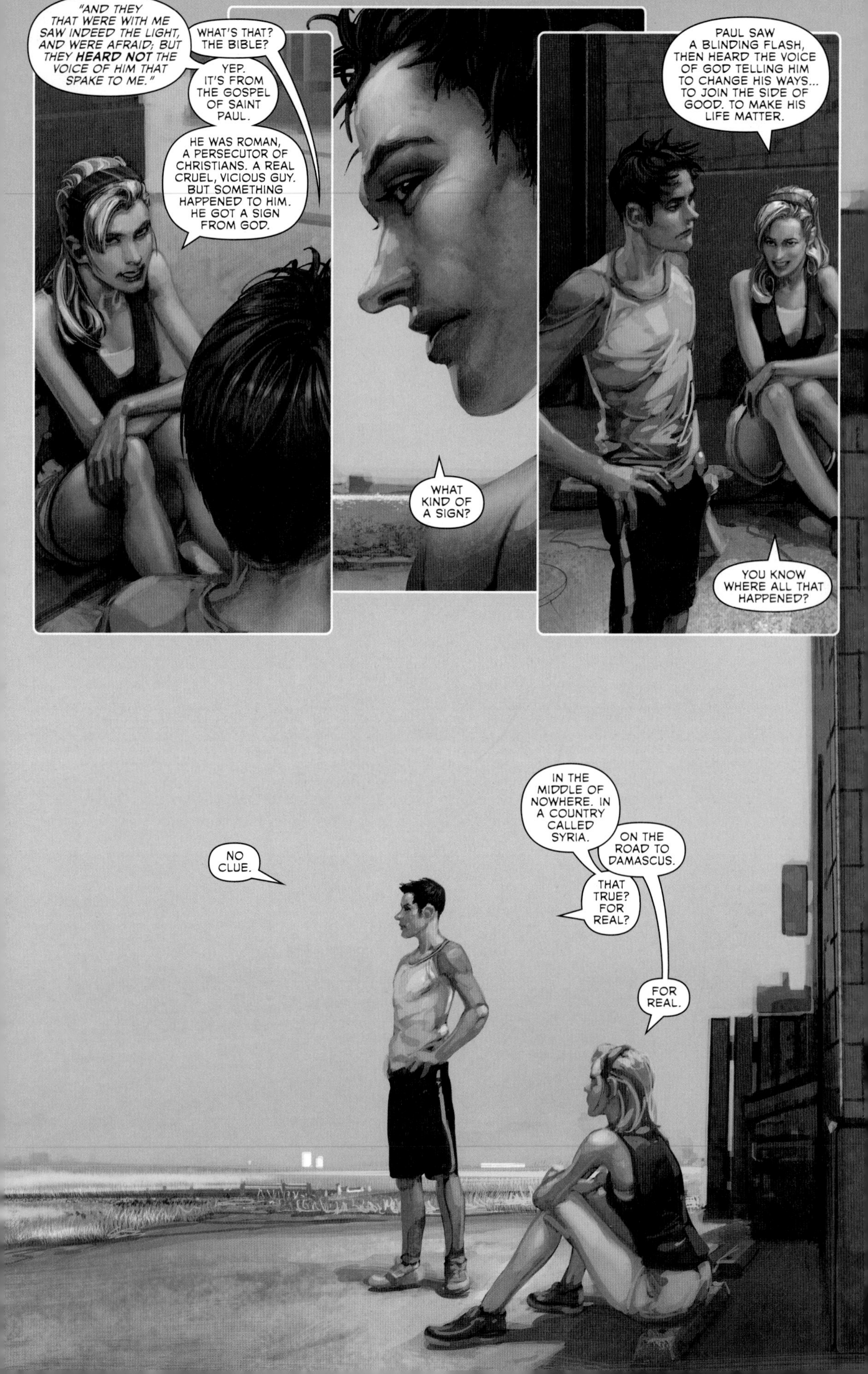

*"AND THEY THAT WERE WITH ME SAW INDEED THE LIGHT, AND WERE AFRAID; BUT THEY **HEARD NOT** THE VOICE OF HIM THAT SPAKE TO ME."*
WHAT'S THAT? THE BIBLE?
YEP. IT'S FROM THE GOSPEL OF SAINT PAUL.
HE WAS ROMAN, A PERSECUTOR OF CHRISTIANS. A REAL CRUEL, VICIOUS GUY. BUT SOMETHING HAPPENED TO HIM. HE GOT A SIGN FROM GOD.
WHAT KIND OF A SIGN?
PAUL SAW A BLINDING FLASH, THEN HEARD THE VOICE OF GOD TELLING HIM TO CHANGE HIS WAYS... TO JOIN THE SIDE OF GOOD. TO MAKE HIS LIFE MATTER.
YOU KNOW WHERE ALL THAT HAPPENED?
NO CLUE.
IN THE MIDDLE OF NOWHERE. IN A COUNTRY CALLED SYRIA.
ON THE ROAD TO DAMASCUS.
THAT TRUE? FOR REAL?
FOR REAL.

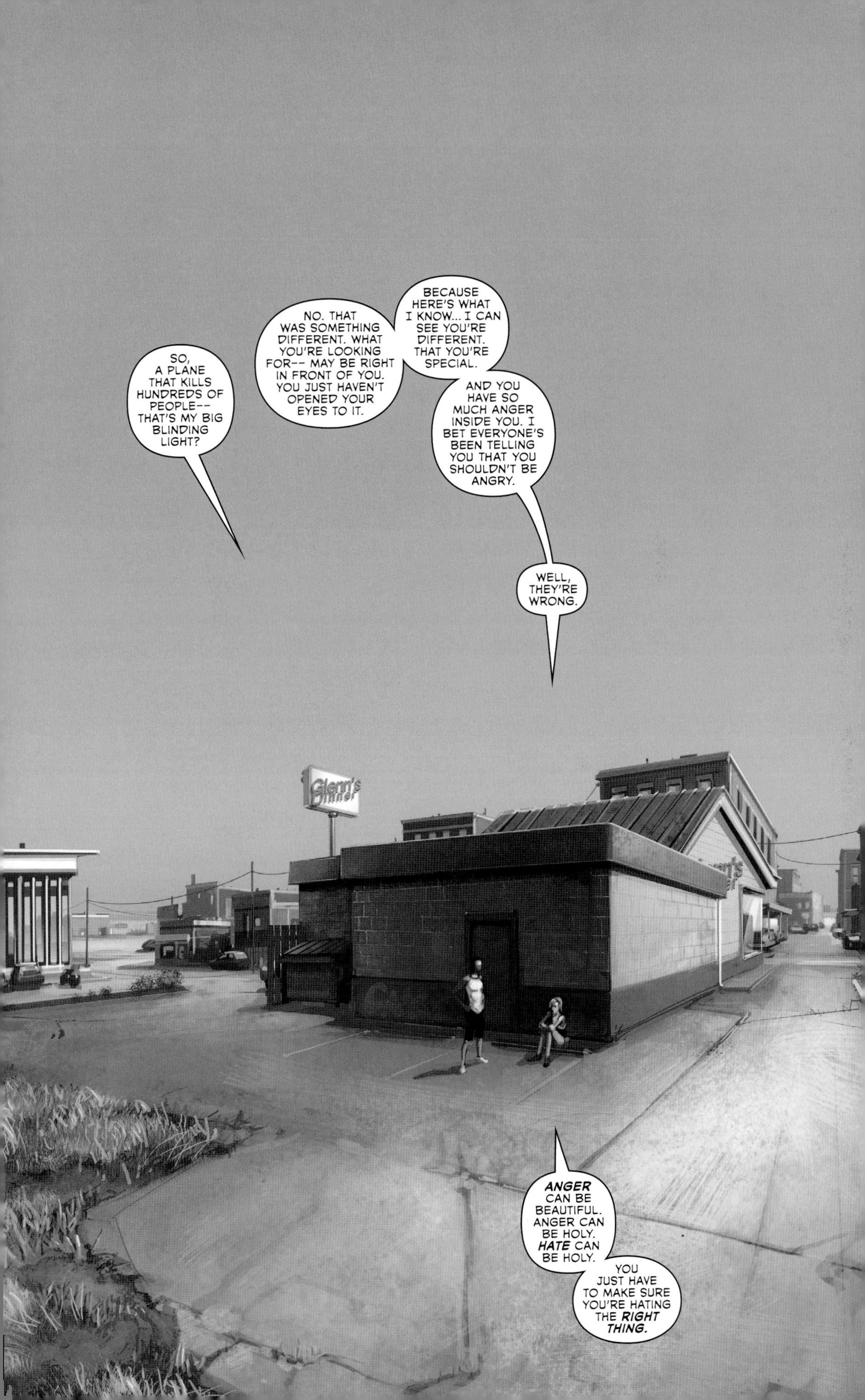
SO, A PLANE THAT KILLS HUNDREDS OF PEOPLE-- THAT'S MY BIG BLINDING LIGHT?
NO. THAT WAS SOMETHING DIFFERENT. WHAT YOU'RE LOOKING FOR-- MAY BE RIGHT IN FRONT OF YOU. YOU JUST HAVEN'T OPENED YOUR EYES TO IT.
BECAUSE HERE'S WHAT I KNOW... I CAN SEE YOU'RE DIFFERENT. THAT YOU'RE SPECIAL.
AND YOU HAVE SO MUCH ANGER INSIDE YOU. I BET EVERYONE'S BEEN TELLING YOU THAT YOU SHOULDN'T BE ANGRY.
WELL, THEY'RE WRONG.
Glenn's Diner
ANGER CAN BE BEAUTIFUL. ANGER CAN BE HOLY. ***HATE*** CAN BE HOLY.
YOU JUST HAVE TO MAKE SURE YOU'RE HATING THE ***RIGHT THING.***

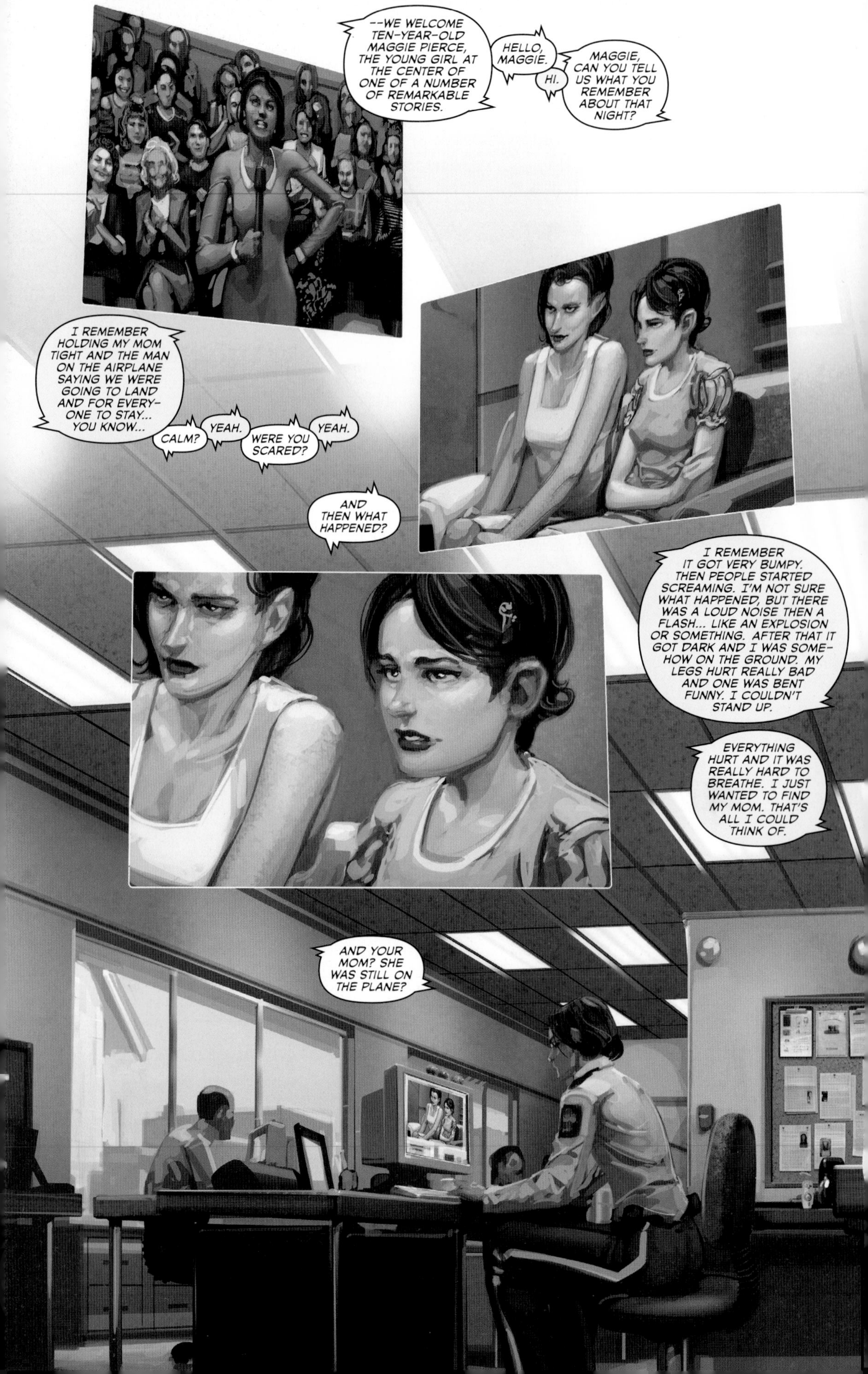
--WE WELCOME TEN-YEAR-OLD MAGGIE PIERCE, THE YOUNG GIRL AT THE CENTER OF ONE OF A NUMBER OF REMARKABLE STORIES.
HELLO, MAGGIE.
HI.
MAGGIE, CAN YOU TELL US WHAT YOU REMEMBER ABOUT THAT NIGHT?
I REMEMBER HOLDING MY MOM TIGHT AND THE MAN ON THE AIRPLANE SAYING WE WERE GOING TO LAND AND FOR EVERY-ONE TO STAY... YOU KNOW...
CALM?
YEAH.
WERE YOU SCARED?
YEAH.
AND THEN WHAT HAPPENED?
I REMEMBER IT GOT VERY BUMPY. THEN PEOPLE STARTED SCREAMING. I'M NOT SURE WHAT HAPPENED, BUT THERE WAS A LOUD NOISE THEN A FLASH... LIKE AN EXPLOSION OR SOMETHING. AFTER THAT IT GOT DARK AND I WAS SOME-HOW ON THE GROUND. MY LEGS HURT REALLY BAD AND ONE WAS BENT FUNNY. I COULDN'T STAND UP.
EVERYTHING HURT AND IT WAS REALLY HARD TO BREATHE. I JUST WANTED TO FIND MY MOM. THAT'S ALL I COULD THINK OF.
AND YOUR MOM? SHE WAS STILL ON THE PLANE?

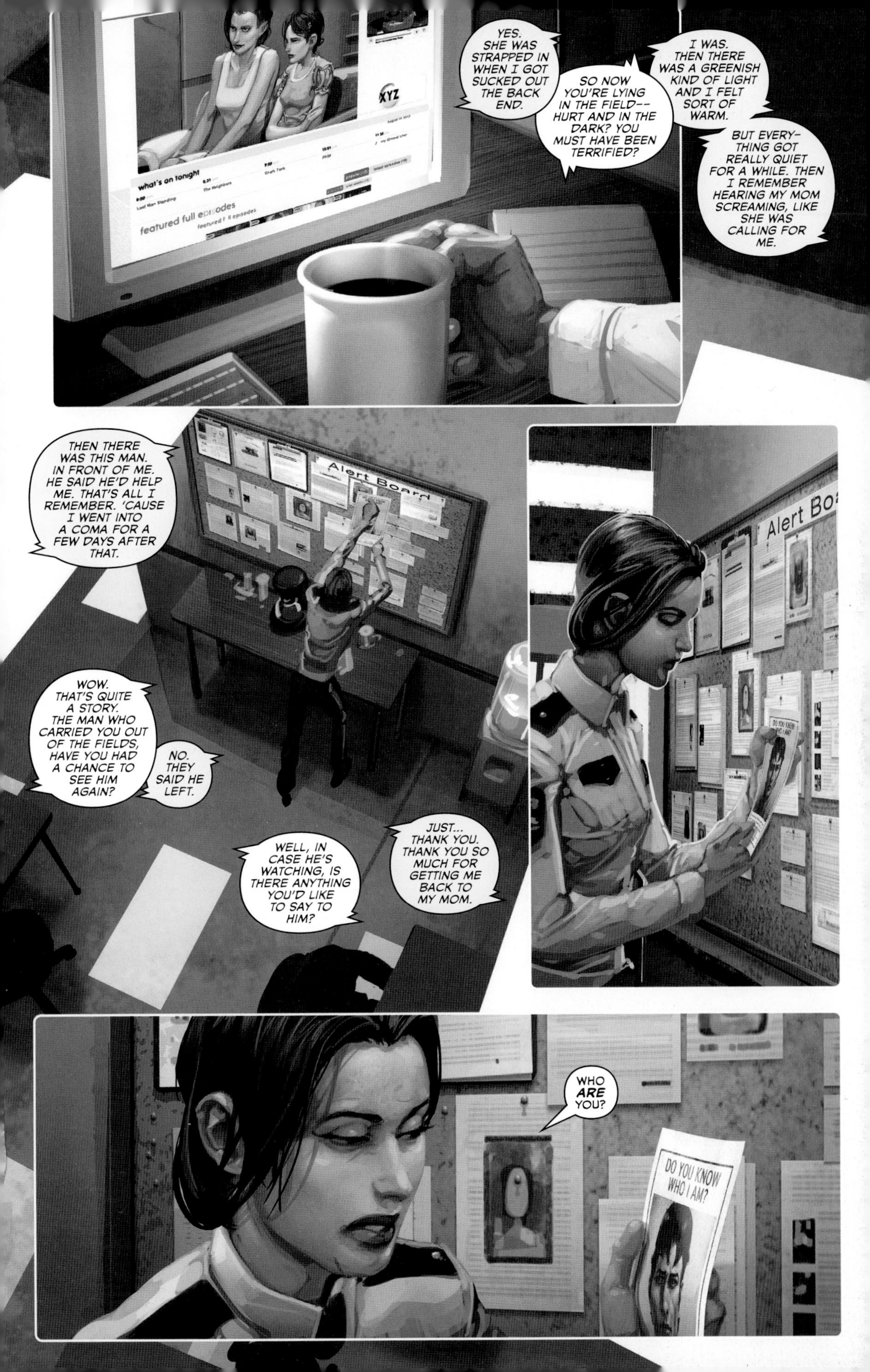
YES. SHE WAS STRAPPED IN WHEN I GOT SUCKED OUT THE BACK END.
SO NOW YOU'RE LYING IN THE FIELD-- HURT AND IN THE DARK? YOU MUST HAVE BEEN TERRIFIED?
I WAS. THEN THERE WAS A GREENISH KIND OF LIGHT AND I FELT SORT OF WARM.
BUT EVERY-THING GOT REALLY QUIET FOR A WHILE. THEN I REMEMBER HEARING MY MOM SCREAMING, LIKE SHE WAS CALLING FOR ME.
what's on tonight
featured full episodes
XYZ
THEN THERE WAS THIS MAN. IN FRONT OF ME. HE SAID HE'D HELP ME. THAT'S ALL I REMEMBER. 'CAUSE I WENT INTO A COMA FOR A FEW DAYS AFTER THAT.
Alert Board
WOW. THAT'S QUITE A STORY. THE MAN WHO CARRIED YOU OUT OF THE FIELDS, HAVE YOU HAD A CHANCE TO SEE HIM AGAIN?
NO. THEY SAID HE LEFT.
WELL, IN CASE HE'S WATCHING, IS THERE ANYTHING YOU'D LIKE TO SAY TO HIM?
JUST... THANK YOU. THANK YOU SO MUCH FOR GETTING ME BACK TO MY MOM.
Alert Bo
WHO *ARE* YOU?
DO YOU KNOW WHO I AM?

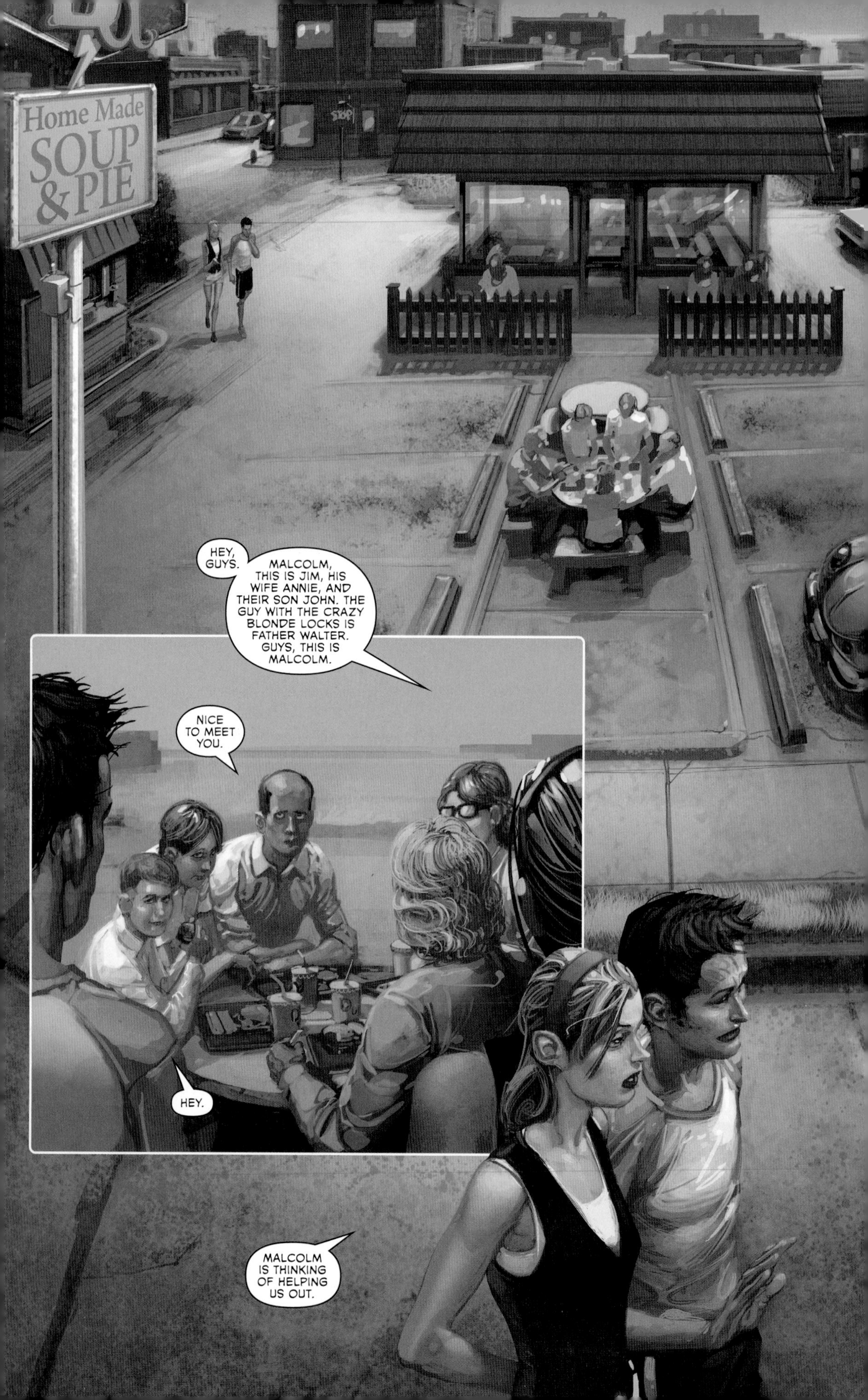
Home Made
SOUP
& PIE
STOP
HEY, GUYS.
MALCOLM, THIS IS JIM, HIS WIFE ANNIE, AND THEIR SON JOHN. THE GUY WITH THE CRAZY BLONDE LOCKS IS FATHER WALTER. GUYS, THIS IS MALCOLM.
NICE TO MEET YOU.
HEY.
MALCOLM IS THINKING OF HELPING US OUT.

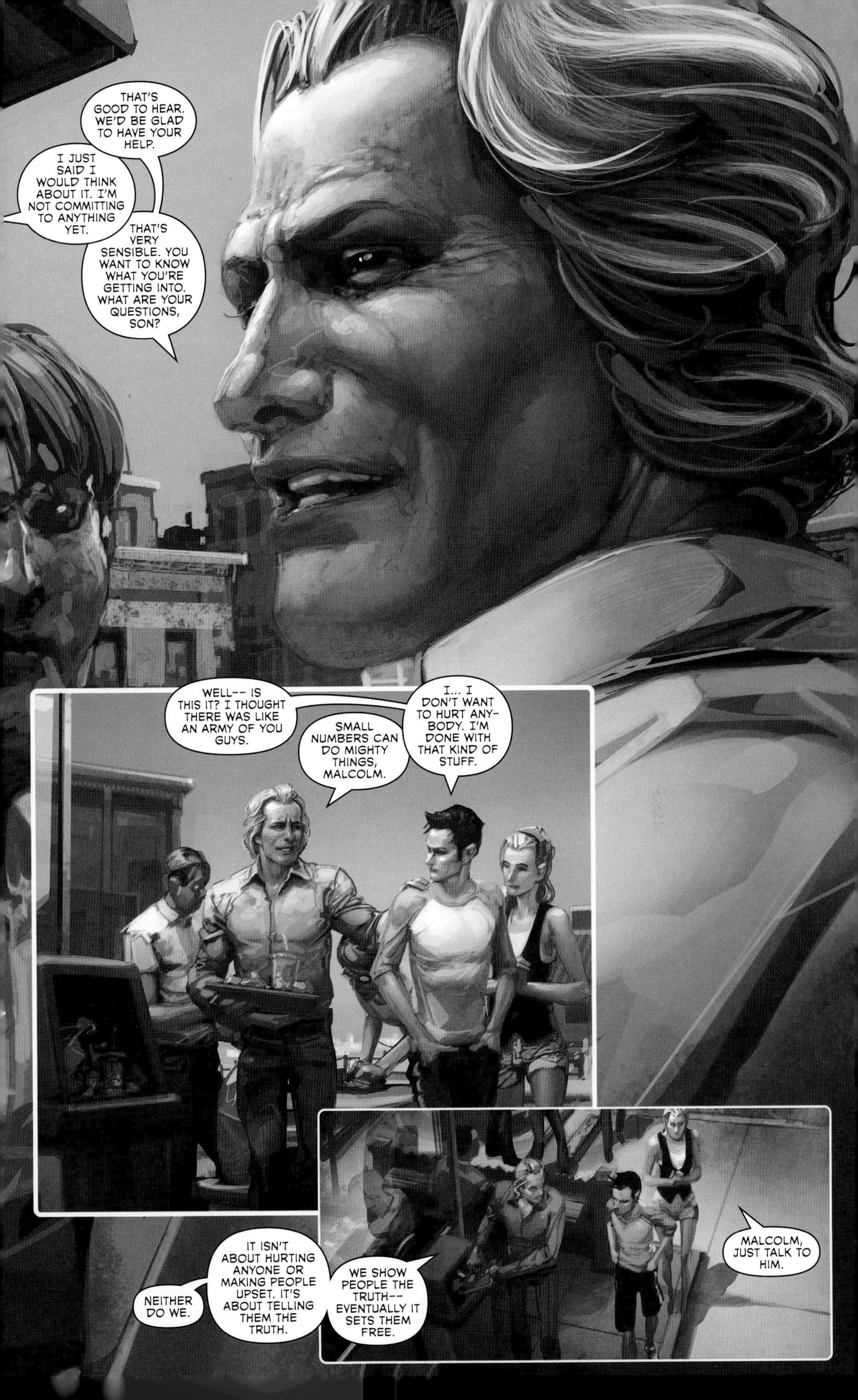
THAT'S GOOD TO HEAR. WE'D BE GLAD TO HAVE YOUR HELP.
I JUST SAID I WOULD THINK ABOUT IT. I'M NOT COMMITTING TO ANYTHING YET.
THAT'S VERY SENSIBLE. YOU WANT TO KNOW WHAT YOU'RE GETTING INTO. WHAT ARE YOUR QUESTIONS, SON?
WELL-- IS THIS IT? I THOUGHT THERE WAS LIKE AN ARMY OF YOU GUYS.
SMALL NUMBERS CAN DO MIGHTY THINGS, MALCOLM.
I... I DON'T WANT TO HURT ANY-BODY. I'M DONE WITH THAT KIND OF STUFF.
NEITHER DO WE.
IT ISN'T ABOUT HURTING ANYONE OR MAKING PEOPLE UPSET. IT'S ABOUT TELLING THEM THE TRUTH.
WE SHOW PEOPLE THE TRUTH-- EVENTUALLY IT SETS THEM FREE.
MALCOLM, JUST TALK TO HIM.

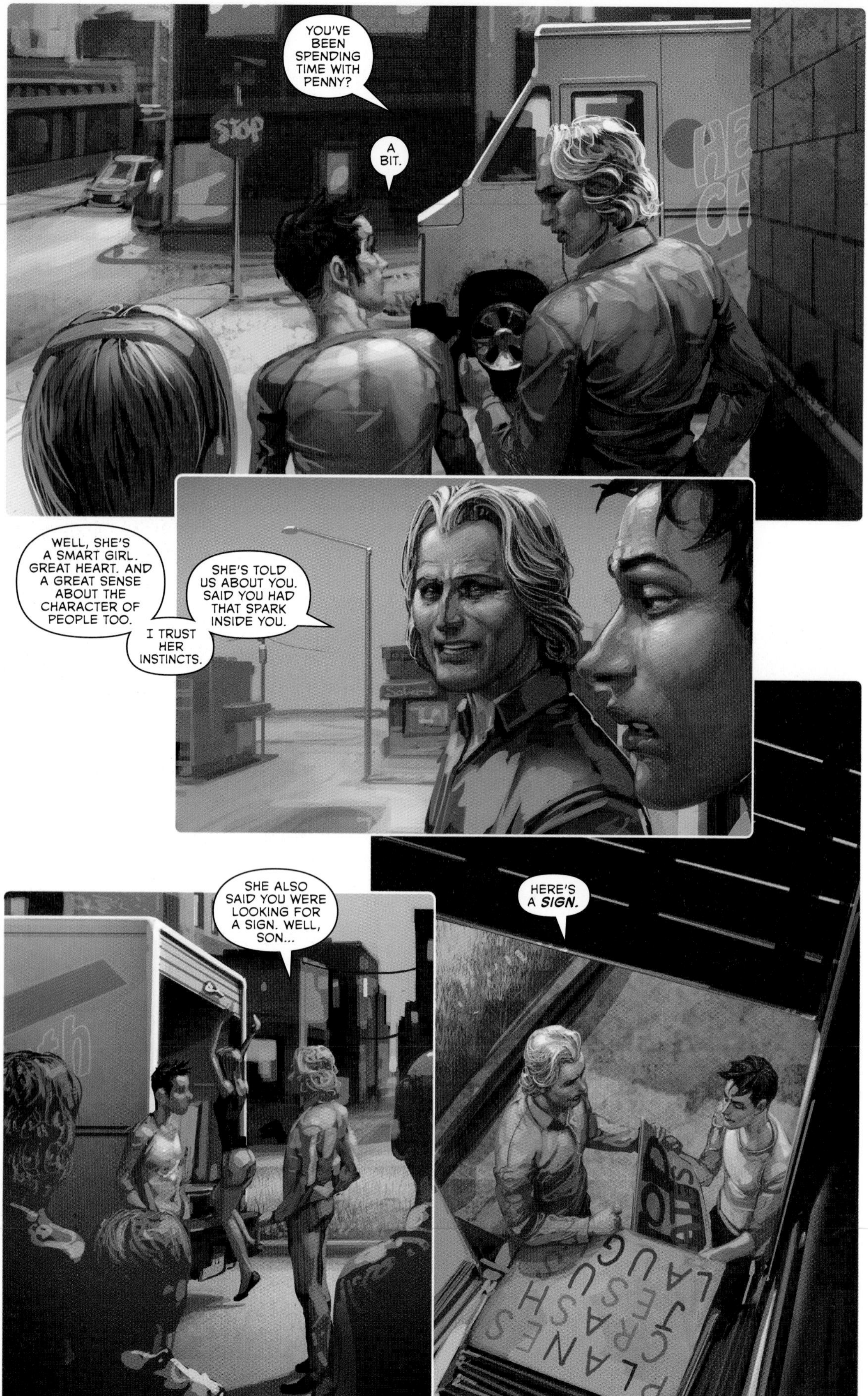
YOU'VE BEEN SPENDING TIME WITH PENNY?
A BIT.
STOP
WELL, SHE'S A SMART GIRL. GREAT HEART. AND A GREAT SENSE ABOUT THE CHARACTER OF PEOPLE TOO.
I TRUST HER INSTINCTS.
SHE'S TOLD US ABOUT YOU. SAID YOU HAD THAT SPARK INSIDE YOU.
SHE ALSO SAID YOU WERE LOOKING FOR A SIGN. WELL, SON...
HERE'S A ***SIGN.***

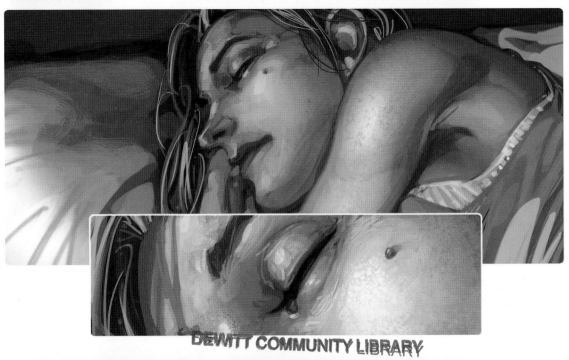

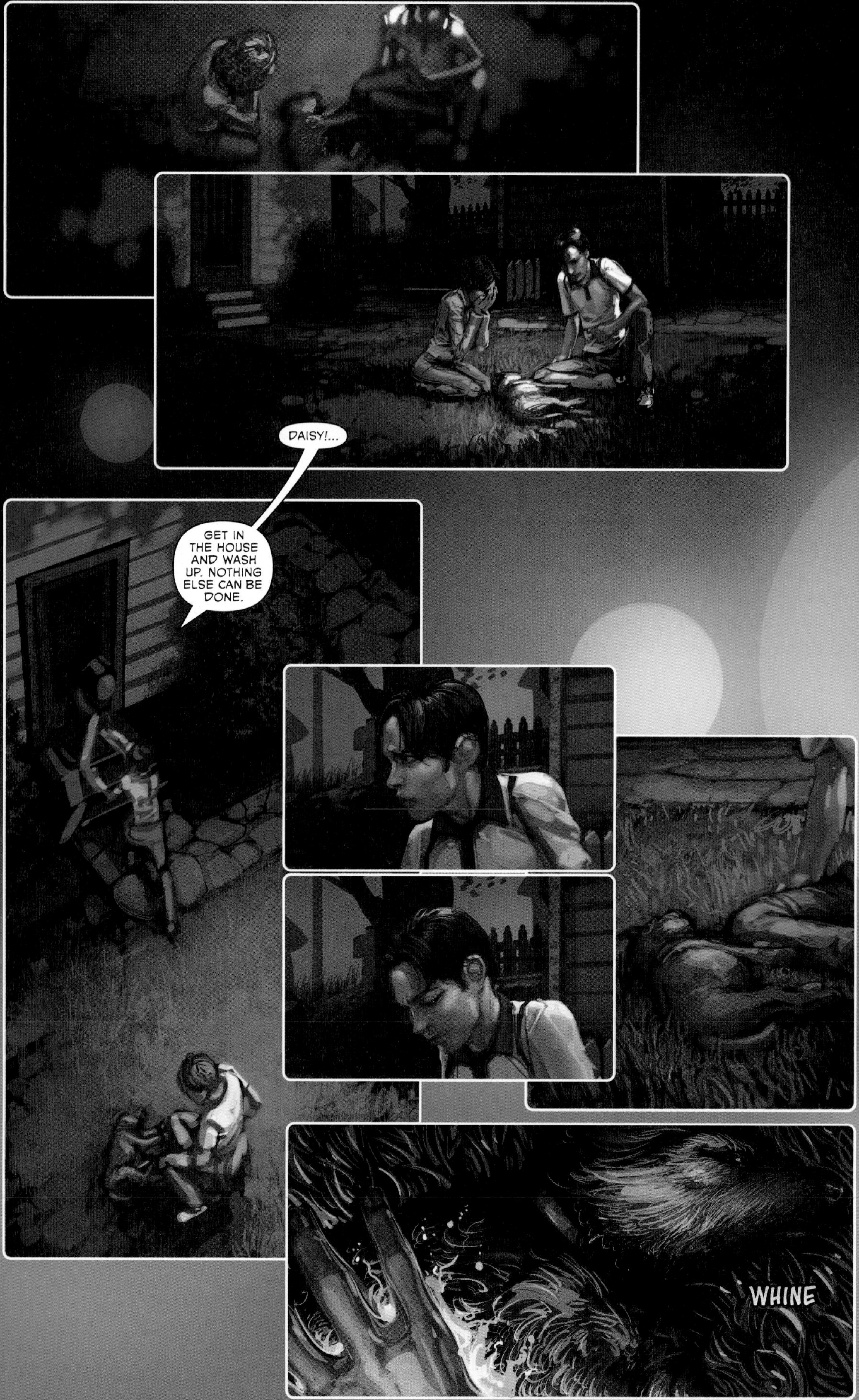
DAISY!...
GET IN THE HOUSE AND WASH UP. NOTHING ELSE CAN BE DONE.
WHINE

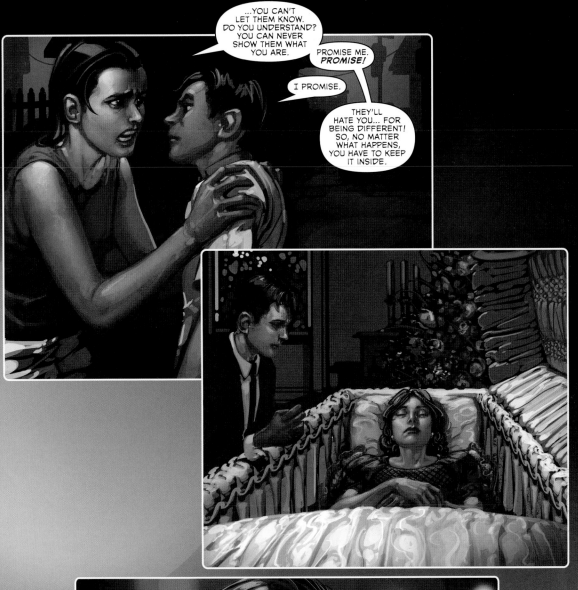

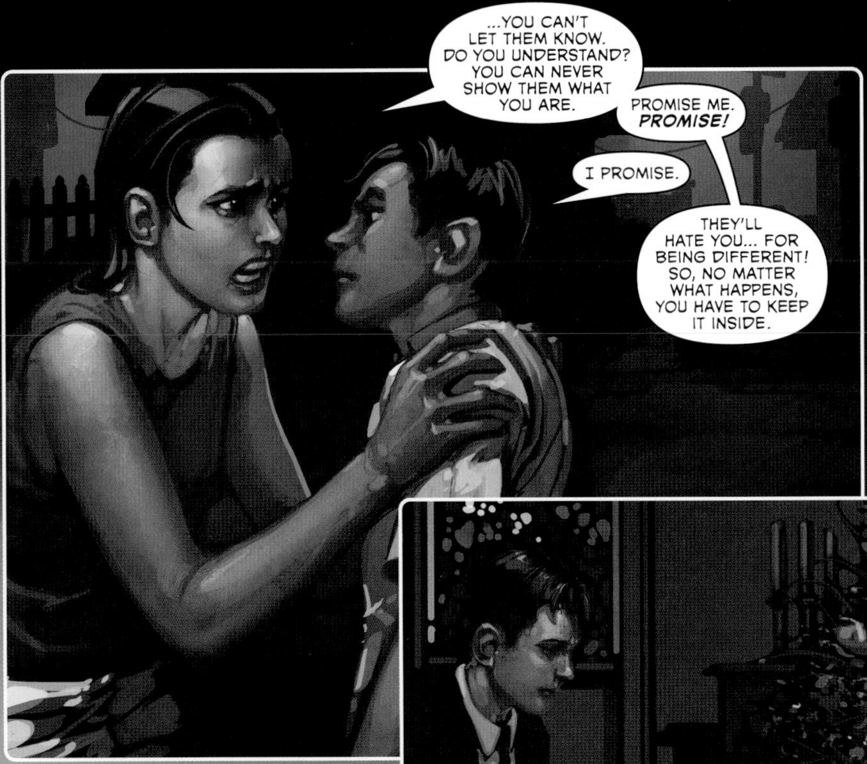
...YOU CAN'T LET THEM KNOW. DO YOU UNDERSTAND? YOU CAN NEVER SHOW THEM WHAT YOU ARE.
PROMISE ME. PROMISE!
I PROMISE.
THEY'LL HATE YOU... FOR BEING DIFFERENT! SO, NO MATTER WHAT HAPPENS, YOU HAVE TO KEEP IT INSIDE.

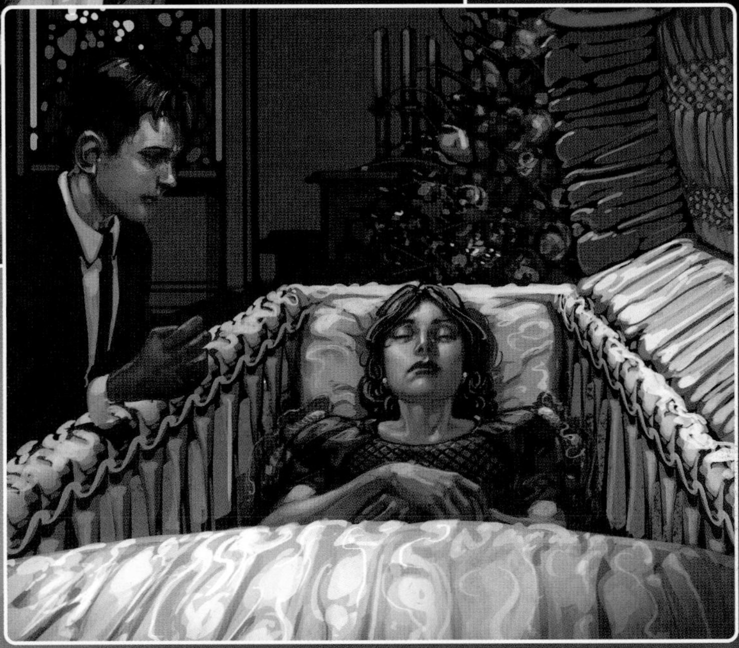

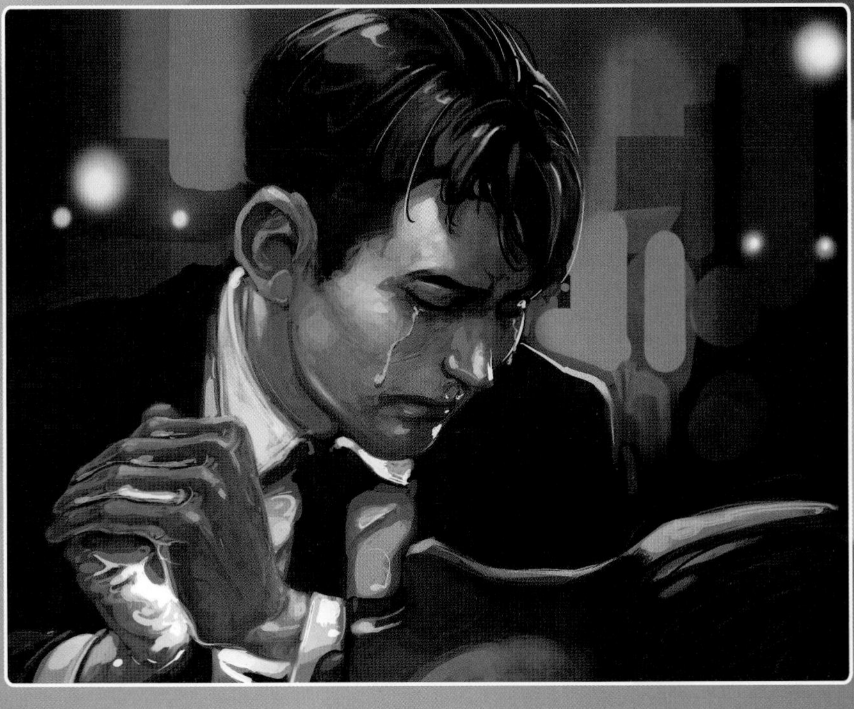

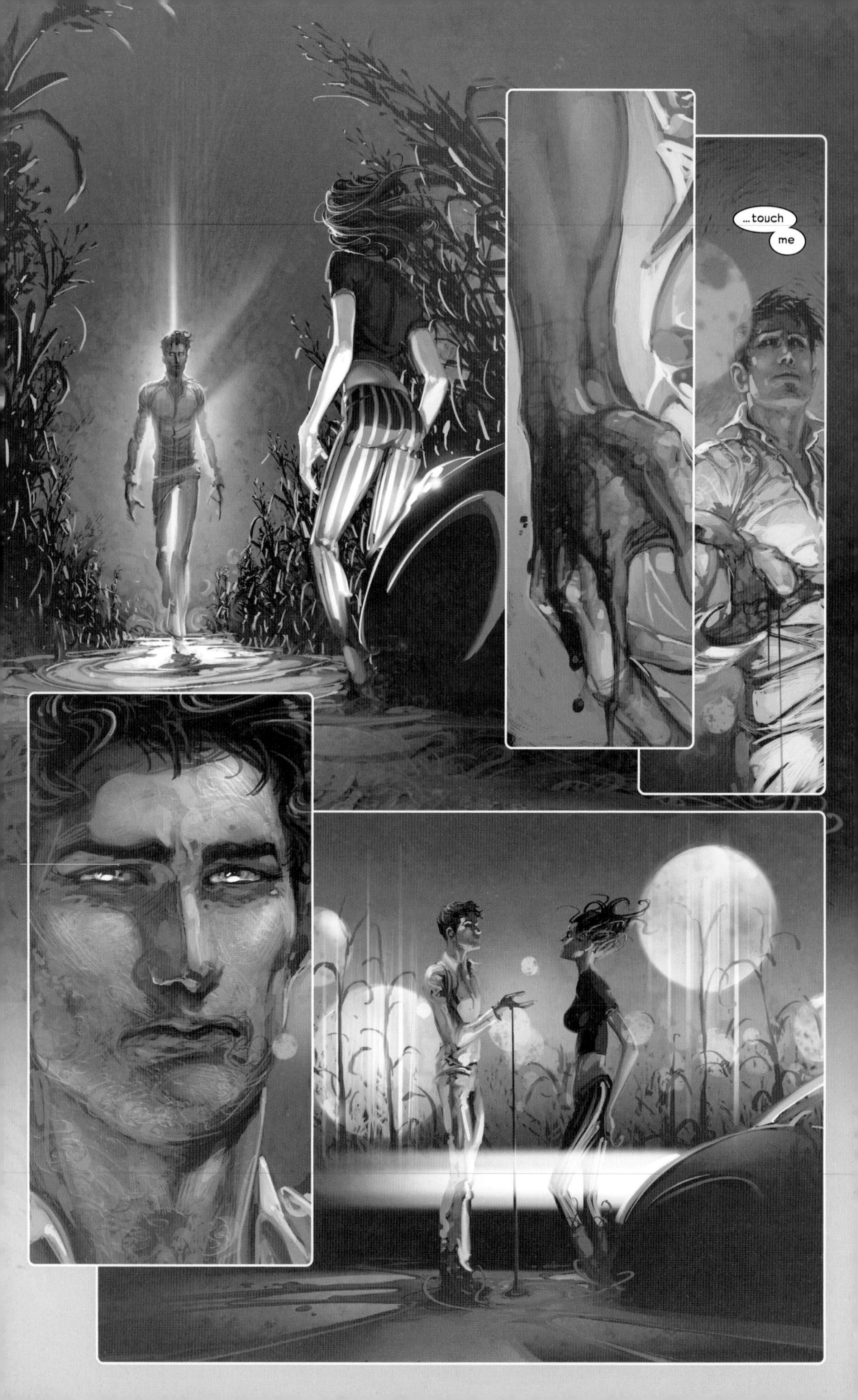
...touch
me

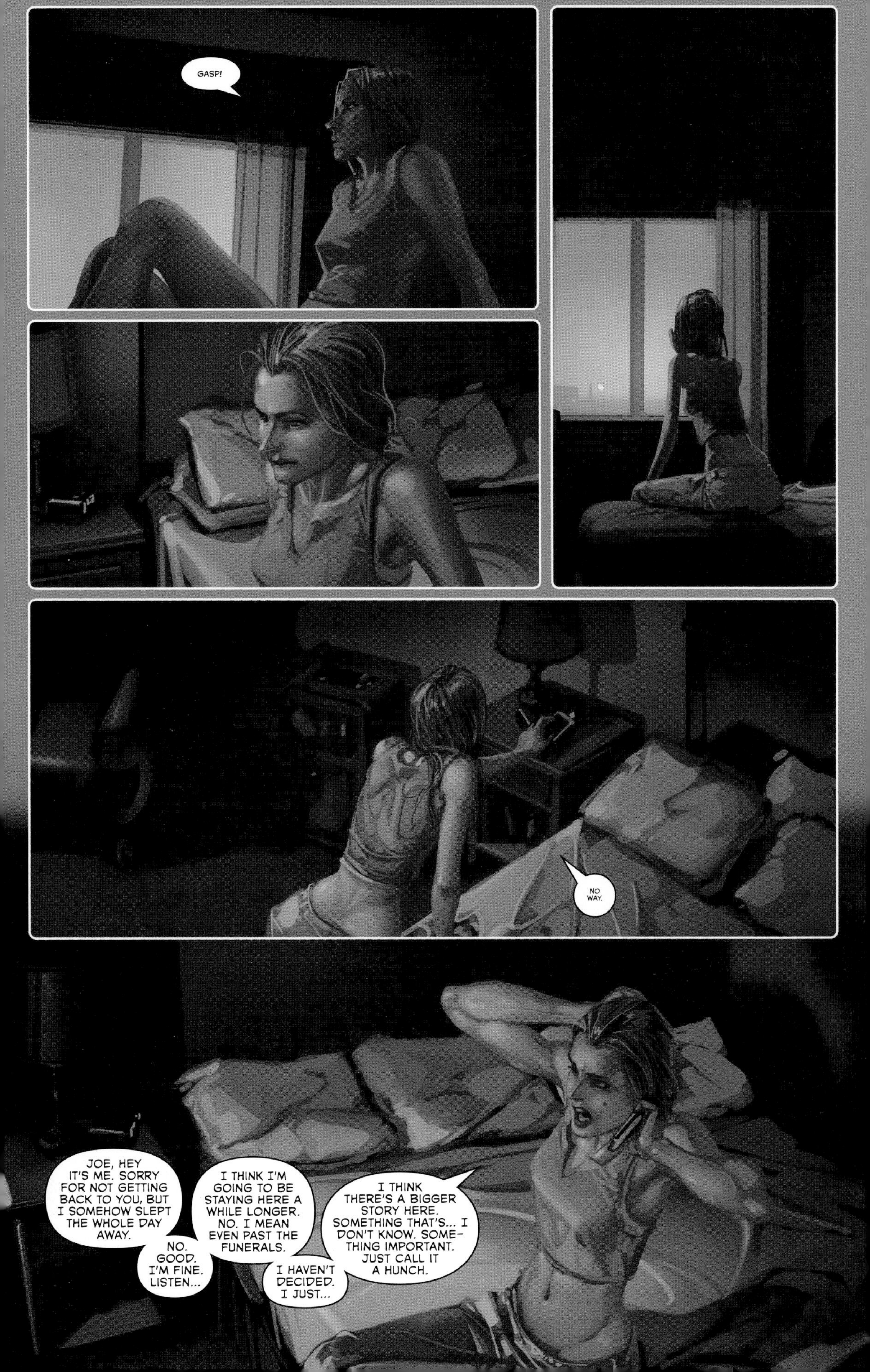
GASP!
NO WAY.
JOE, HEY IT'S ME. SORRY FOR NOT GETTING BACK TO YOU, BUT I SOMEHOW SLEPT THE WHOLE DAY AWAY.
NO. GOOD. I'M FINE. LISTEN...
I THINK I'M GOING TO BE STAYING HERE A WHILE LONGER. NO. I MEAN EVEN PAST THE FUNERALS.
I HAVEN'T DECIDED. I JUST...
I THINK THERE'S A BIGGER STORY HERE. SOMETHING THAT'S... I DON'T KNOW. SOME-THING IMPORTANT. JUST CALL IT A HUNCH.

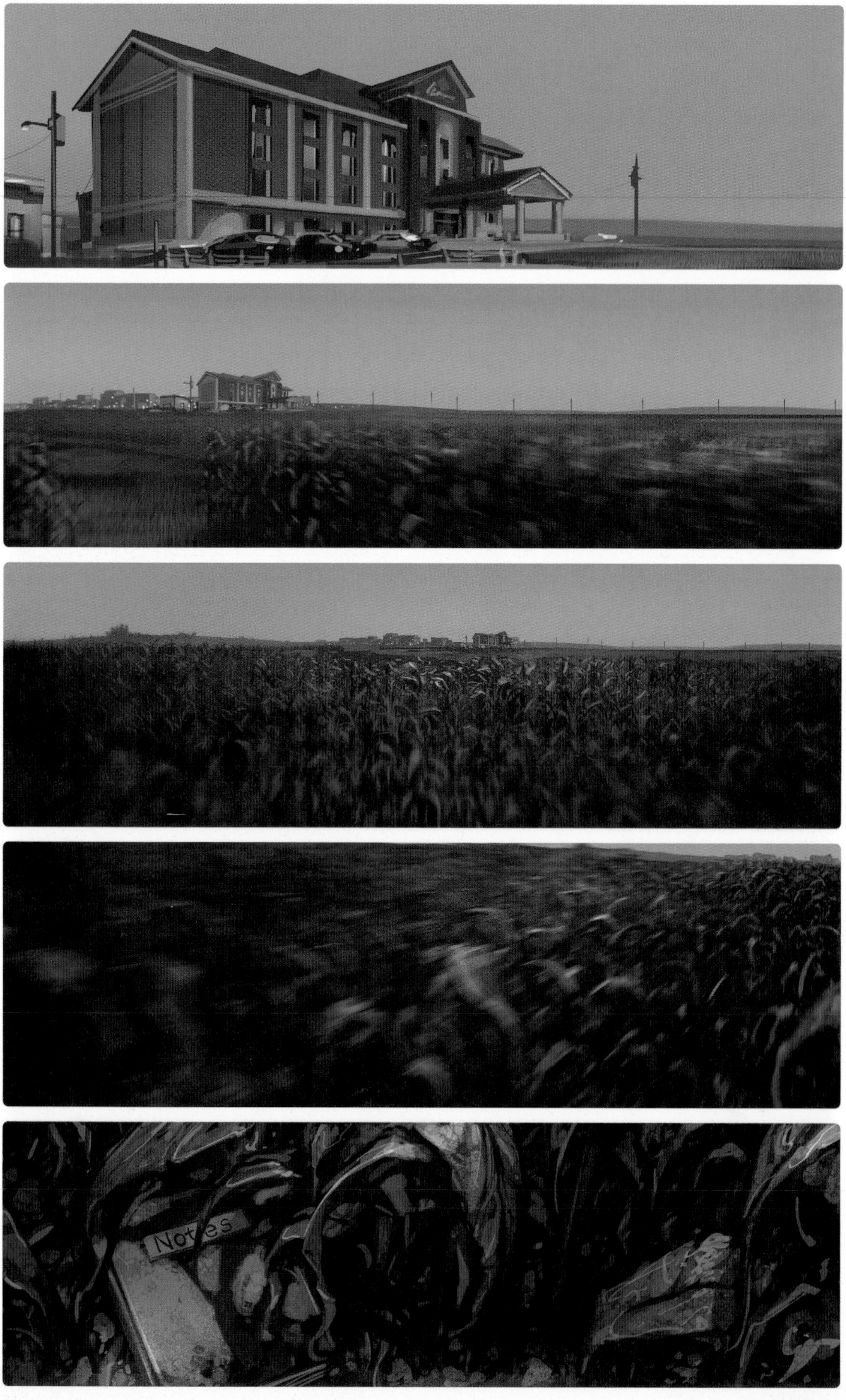
Notes

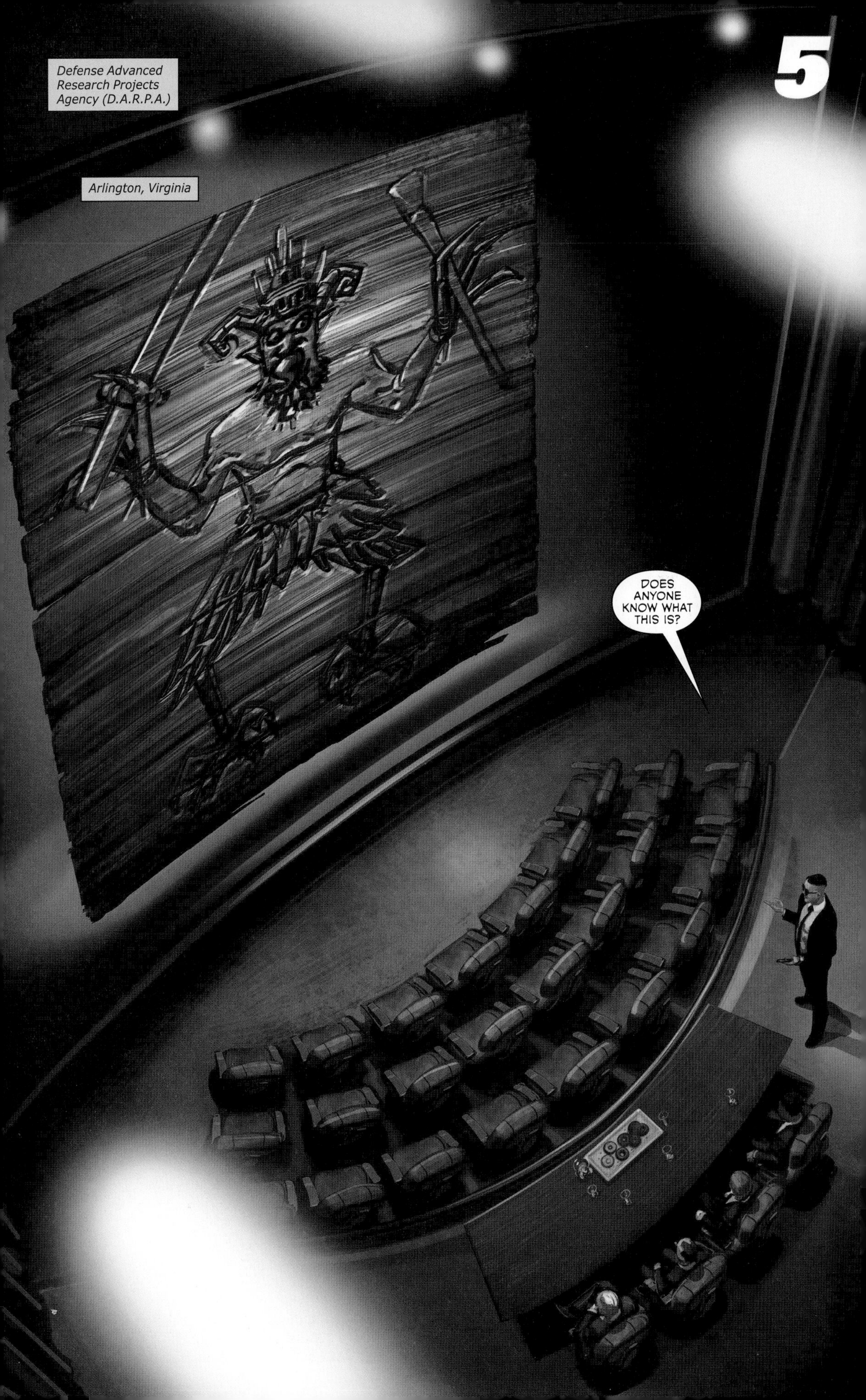
5
Defense Advanced Research Projects Agency (D.A.R.P.A.)
Arlington, Virginia
DOES ANYONE KNOW WHAT THIS IS?

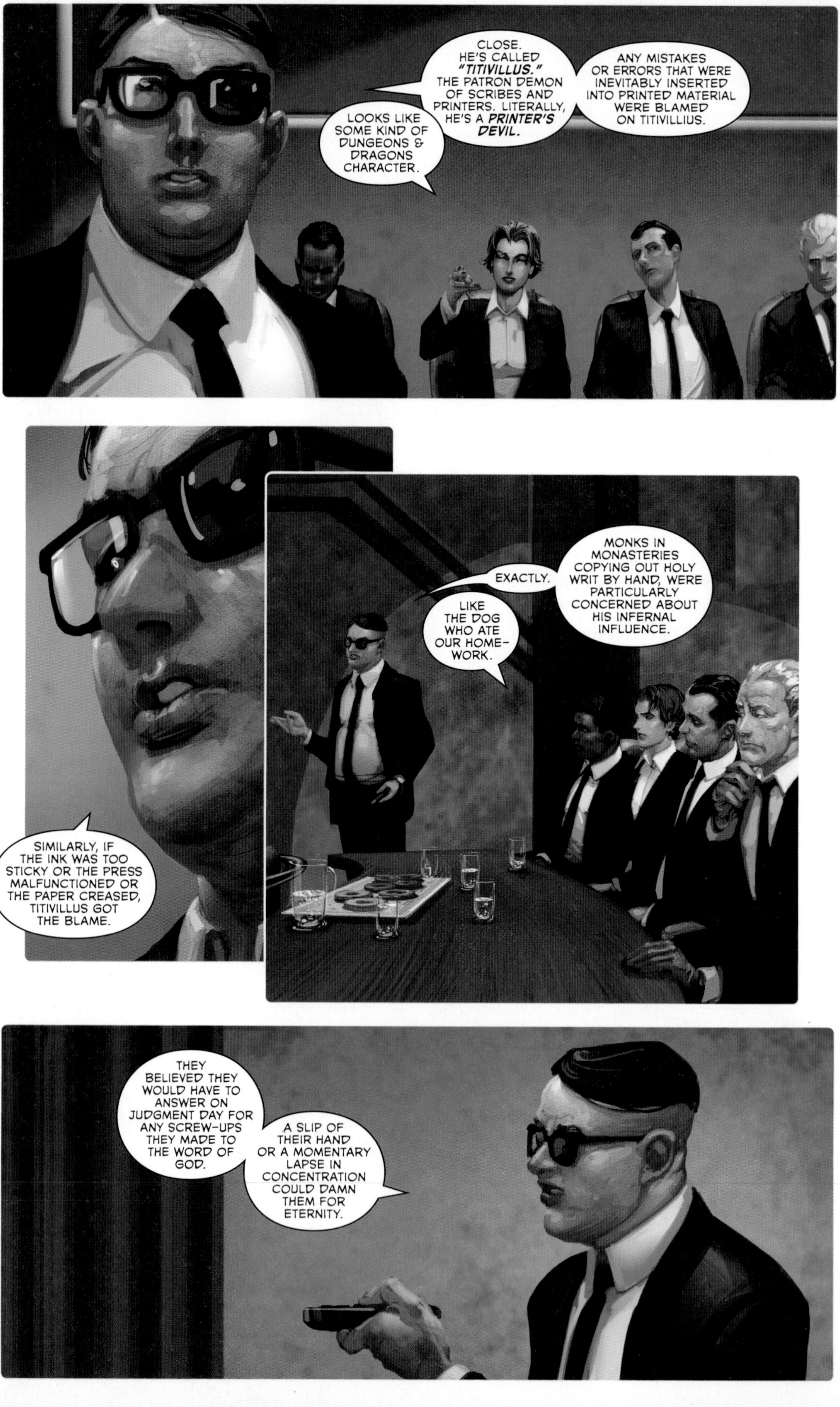
LOOKS LIKE SOME KIND OF DUNGEONS & DRAGONS CHARACTER.
CLOSE. HE'S CALLED *"TITIVILLUS."* THE PATRON DEMON OF SCRIBES AND PRINTERS. LITERALLY, HE'S A *PRINTER'S DEVIL.*
ANY MISTAKES OR ERRORS THAT WERE INEVITABLY INSERTED INTO PRINTED MATERIAL WERE BLAMED ON TITIVILLIUS.
SIMILARLY, IF THE INK WAS TOO STICKY OR THE PRESS MALFUNCTIONED OR THE PAPER CREASED, TITIVILLUS GOT THE BLAME.
LIKE THE DOG WHO ATE OUR HOME-WORK.
EXACTLY.
MONKS IN MONASTERIES COPYING OUT HOLY WRIT BY HAND, WERE PARTICULARLY CONCERNED ABOUT HIS INFERNAL INFLUENCE.
THEY BELIEVED THEY WOULD HAVE TO ANSWER ON JUDGMENT DAY FOR ANY SCREW-UPS THEY MADE TO THE WORD OF GOD.
A SLIP OF THEIR HAND OR A MOMENTARY LAPSE IN CONCENTRATION COULD DAMN THEM FOR ETERNITY.

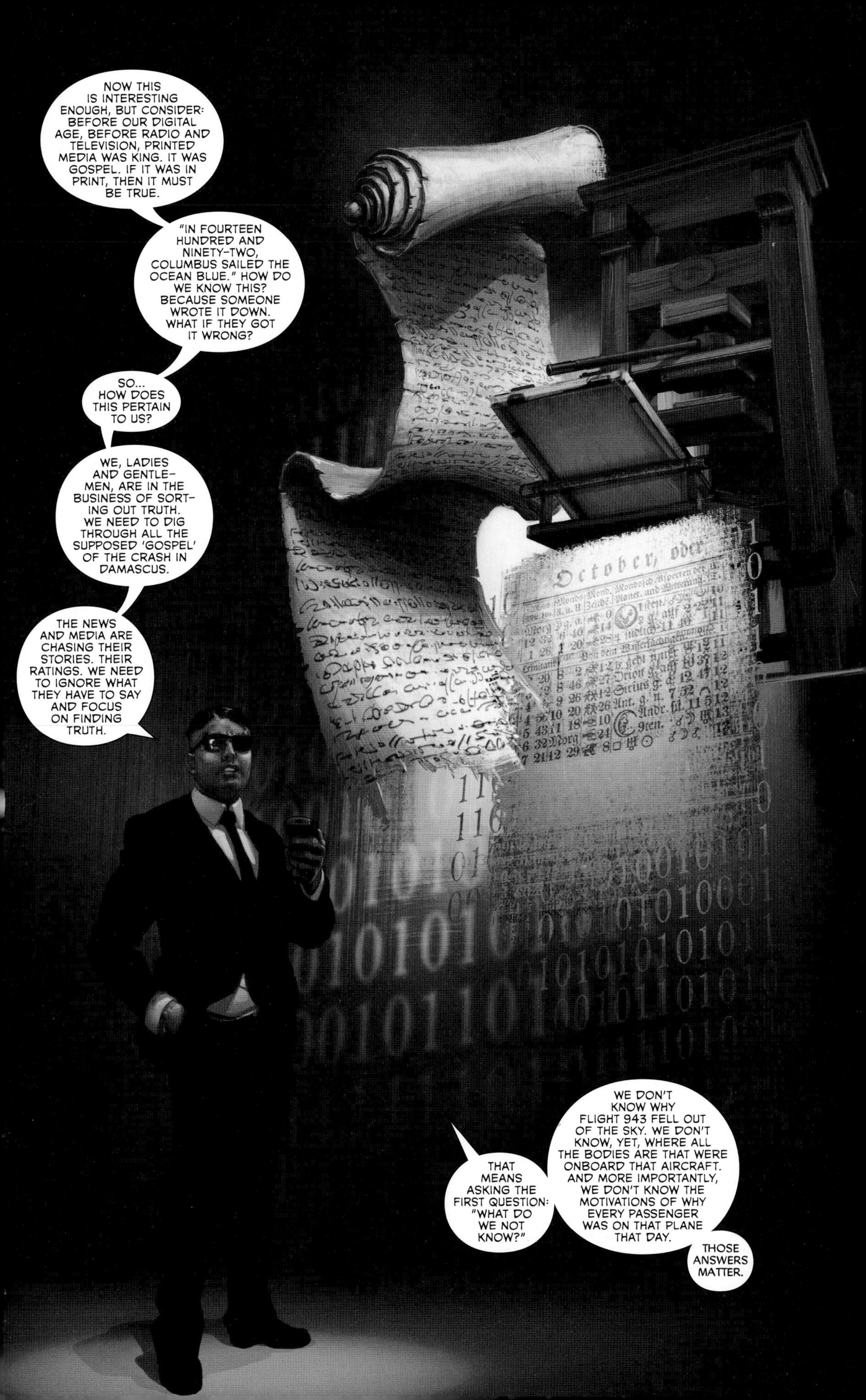
NOW THIS IS INTERESTING ENOUGH, BUT CONSIDER: BEFORE OUR DIGITAL AGE, BEFORE RADIO AND TELEVISION, PRINTED MEDIA WAS KING. IT WAS GOSPEL. IF IT WAS IN PRINT, THEN IT MUST BE TRUE.
"IN FOURTEEN HUNDRED AND NINETY-TWO, COLUMBUS SAILED THE OCEAN BLUE." HOW DO WE KNOW THIS? BECAUSE SOMEONE WROTE IT DOWN. WHAT IF THEY GOT IT WRONG?
SO... HOW DOES THIS PERTAIN TO US?
WE, LADIES AND GENTLE-MEN, ARE IN THE BUSINESS OF SORT-ING OUT TRUTH. WE NEED TO DIG THROUGH ALL THE SUPPOSED 'GOSPEL' OF THE CRASH IN DAMASCUS.
THE NEWS AND MEDIA ARE CHASING THEIR STORIES. THEIR RATINGS. WE NEED TO IGNORE WHAT THEY HAVE TO SAY AND FOCUS ON FINDING TRUTH.
October, oder
THAT MEANS ASKING THE FIRST QUESTION: "WHAT DO WE NOT KNOW?"
WE DON'T KNOW WHY FLIGHT 943 FELL OUT OF THE SKY. WE DON'T KNOW, YET, WHERE ALL THE BODIES ARE THAT WERE ONBOARD THAT AIRCRAFT. AND MORE IMPORTANTLY, WE DON'T KNOW THE MOTIVATIONS OF WHY EVERY PASSENGER WAS ON THAT PLANE THAT DAY.
THOSE ANSWERS MATTER.

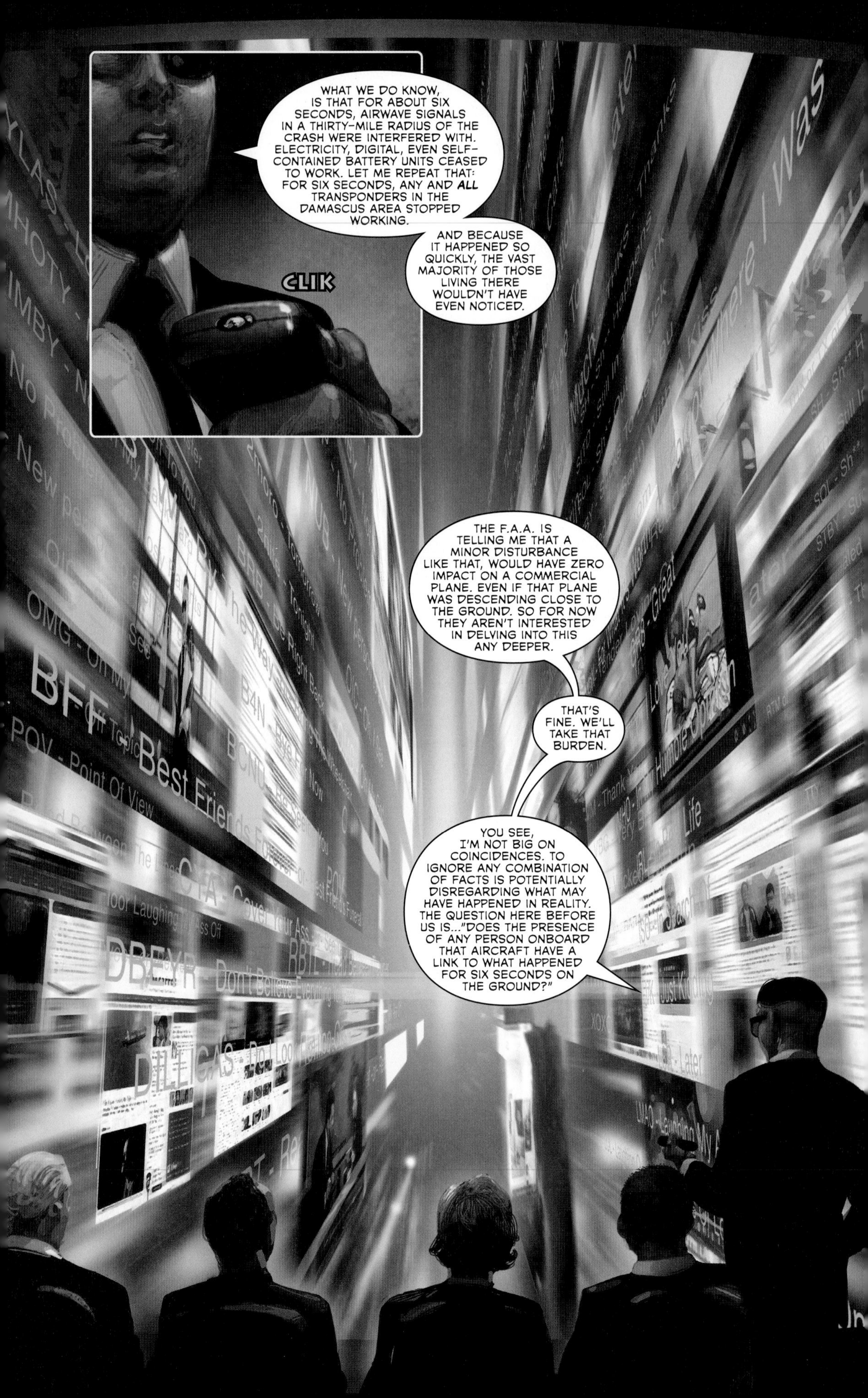
WHAT WE DO KNOW, IS THAT FOR ABOUT SIX SECONDS, AIRWAVE SIGNALS IN A THIRTY-MILE RADIUS OF THE CRASH WERE INTERFERED WITH. ELECTRICITY, DIGITAL, EVEN SELF-CONTAINED BATTERY UNITS CEASED TO WORK. LET ME REPEAT THAT: FOR SIX SECONDS, ANY AND **ALL** TRANSPONDERS IN THE DAMASCUS AREA STOPPED WORKING.
AND BECAUSE IT HAPPENED SO QUICKLY, THE VAST MAJORITY OF THOSE LIVING THERE WOULDN'T HAVE EVEN NOTICED.
CLIK
THE F.A.A. IS TELLING ME THAT A MINOR DISTURBANCE LIKE THAT, WOULD HAVE ZERO IMPACT ON A COMMERCIAL PLANE. EVEN IF THAT PLANE WAS DESCENDING CLOSE TO THE GROUND. SO FOR NOW THEY AREN'T INTERESTED IN DELVING INTO THIS ANY DEEPER.
THAT'S FINE. WE'LL TAKE THAT BURDEN.
YOU SEE, I'M NOT BIG ON COINCIDENCES. TO IGNORE ANY COMBINATION OF FACTS IS POTENTIALLY DISREGARDING WHAT MAY HAVE HAPPENED IN REALITY. THE QUESTION HERE BEFORE US IS..."DOES THE PRESENCE OF ANY PERSON ONBOARD THAT AIRCRAFT HAVE A LINK TO WHAT HAPPENED FOR SIX SECONDS ON THE GROUND?"

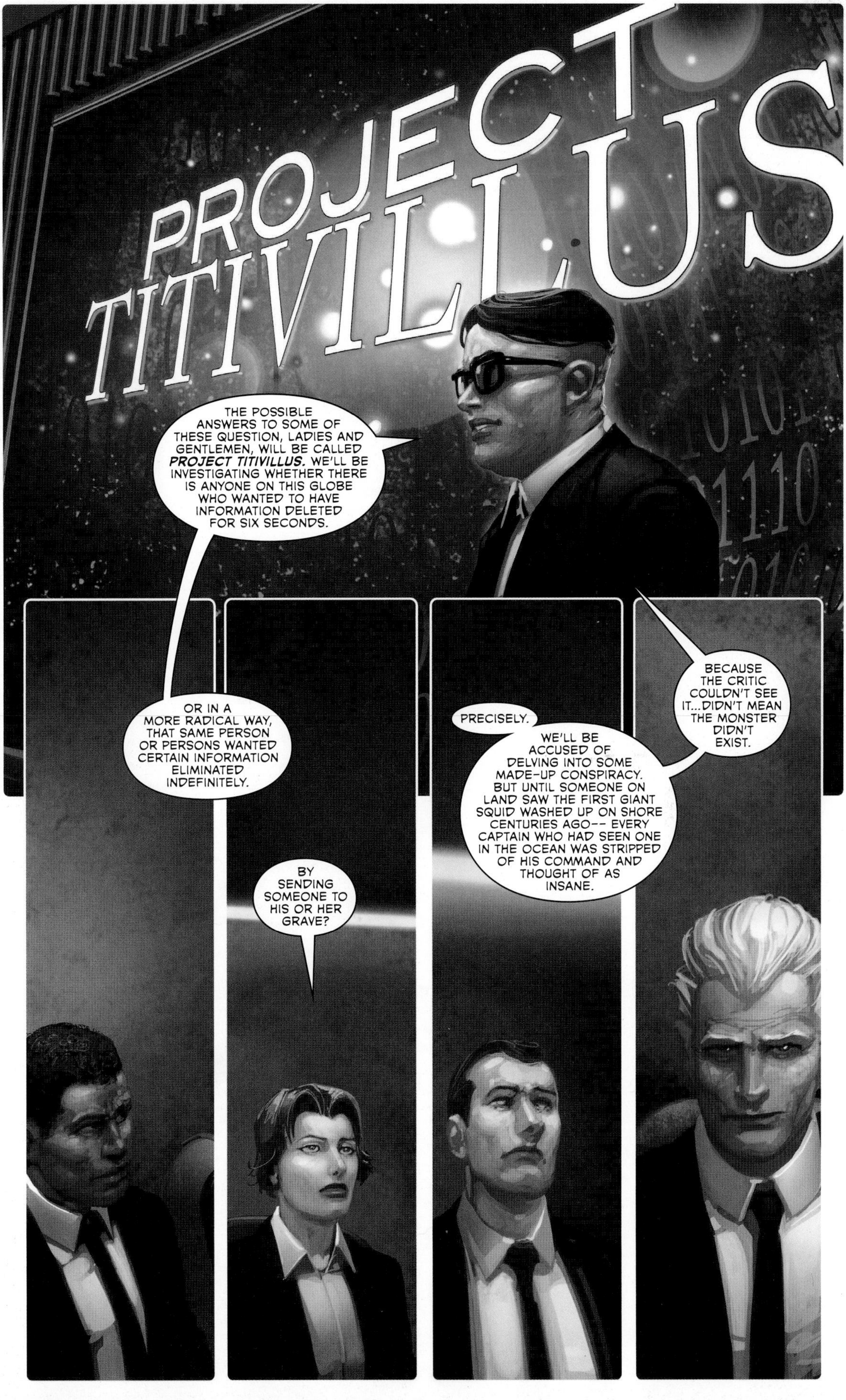
PROJECT TITIVILLUS
THE POSSIBLE ANSWERS TO SOME OF THESE QUESTION, LADIES AND GENTLEMEN, WILL BE CALLED PROJECT TITIVILLUS. WE'LL BE INVESTIGATING WHETHER THERE IS ANYONE ON THIS GLOBE WHO WANTED TO HAVE INFORMATION DELETED FOR SIX SECONDS.
OR IN A MORE RADICAL WAY, THAT SAME PERSON OR PERSONS WANTED CERTAIN INFORMATION ELIMINATED INDEFINITELY.
BY SENDING SOMEONE TO HIS OR HER GRAVE?
PRECISELY.
WE'LL BE ACCUSED OF DELVING INTO SOME MADE-UP CONSPIRACY. BUT UNTIL SOMEONE ON LAND SAW THE FIRST GIANT SQUID WASHED UP ON SHORE CENTURIES AGO-- EVERY CAPTAIN WHO HAD SEEN ONE IN THE OCEAN WAS STRIPPED OF HIS COMMAND AND THOUGHT OF AS INSANE.
BECAUSE THE CRITIC COULDN'T SEE IT...DIDN'T MEAN THE MONSTER DIDN'T EXIST.

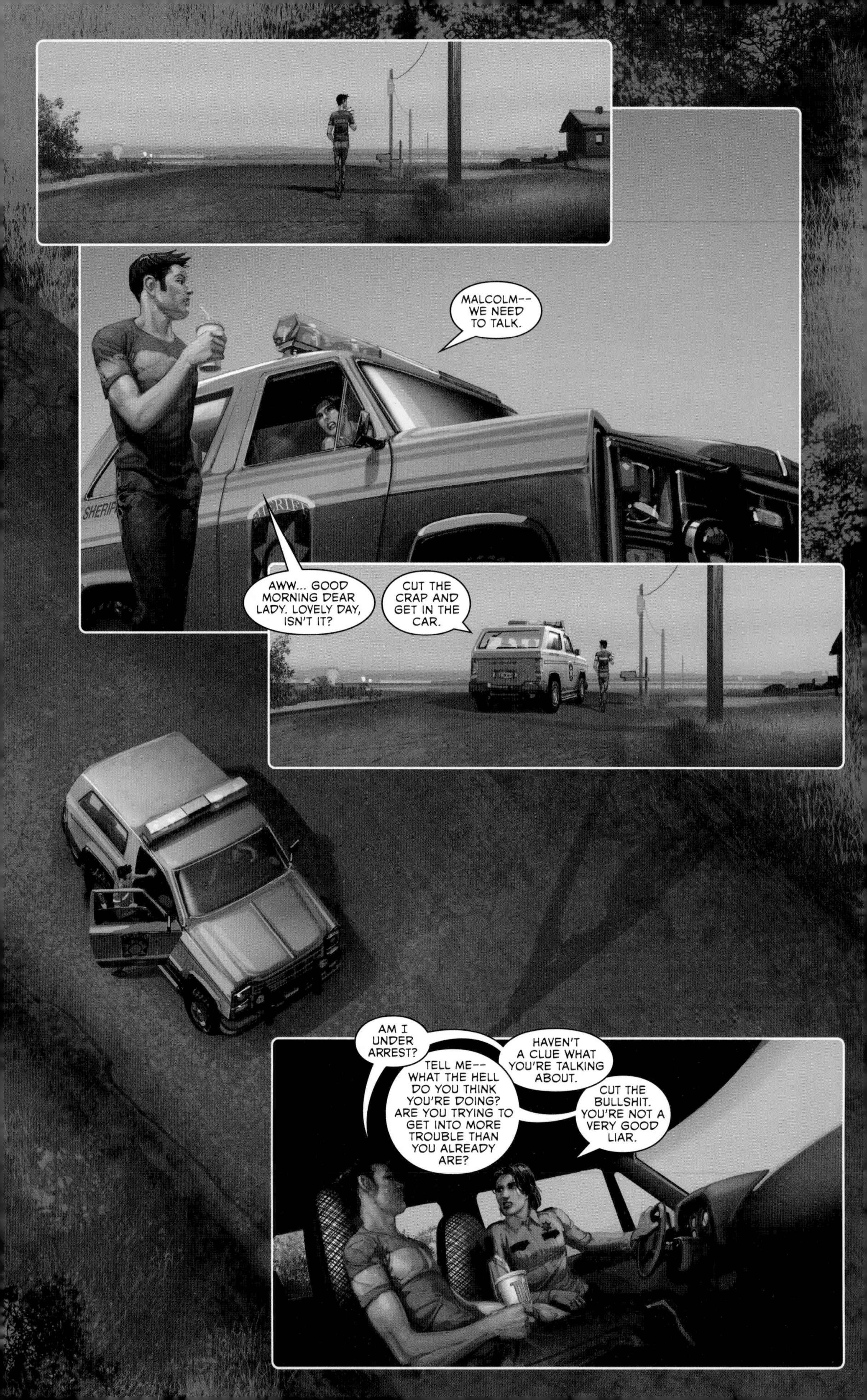
MALCOLM-- WE NEED TO TALK.
SHERIFF
AWW... GOOD MORNING DEAR LADY. LOVELY DAY, ISN'T IT?
CUT THE CRAP AND GET IN THE CAR.
AM I UNDER ARREST?
TELL ME-- WHAT THE HELL DO YOU THINK YOU'RE DOING? ARE YOU TRYING TO GET INTO MORE TROUBLE THAN YOU ALREADY ARE?
HAVEN'T A CLUE WHAT YOU'RE TALKING ABOUT.
CUT THE BULLSHIT. YOU'RE NOT A VERY GOOD LIAR.

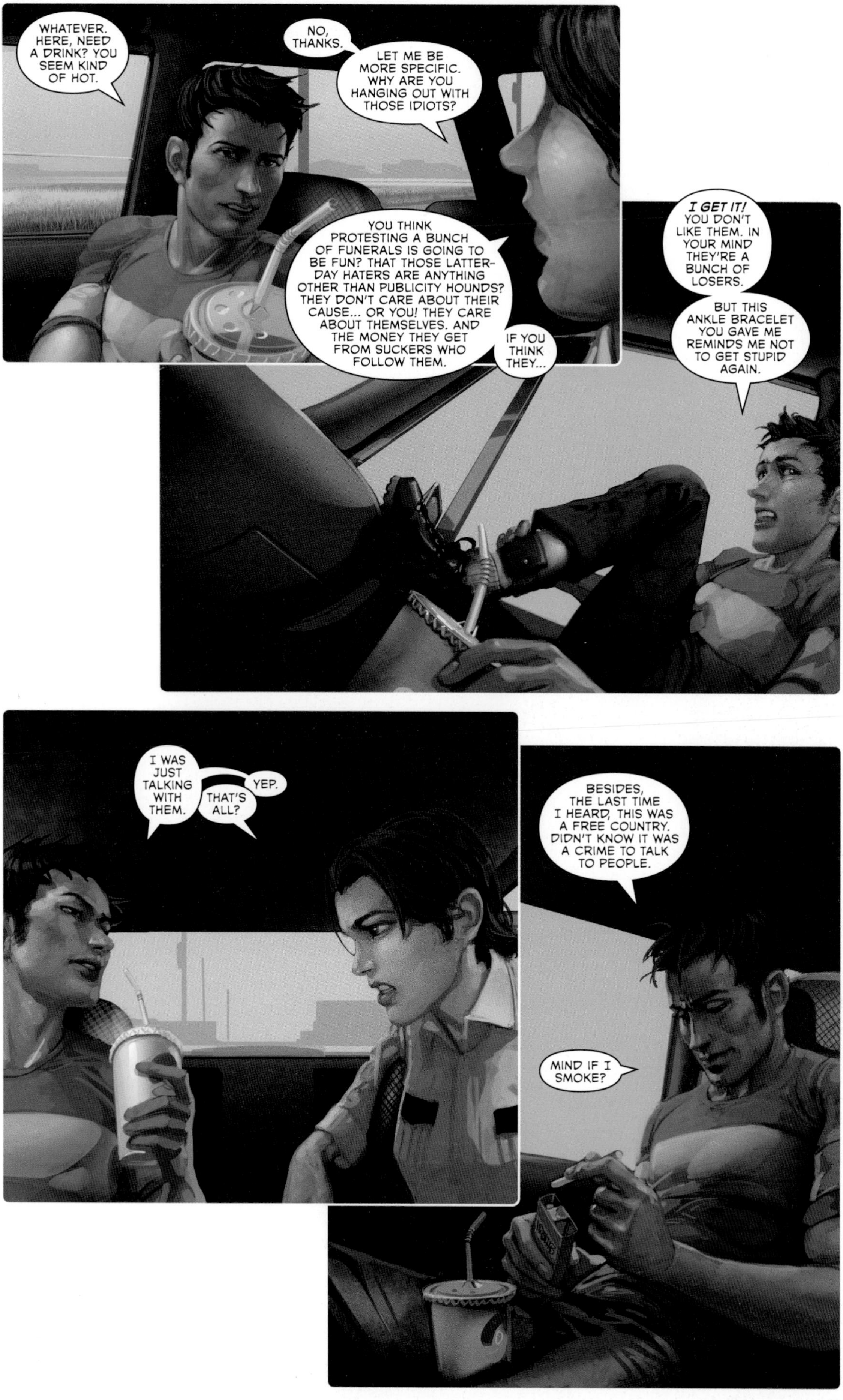
WHATEVER. HERE, NEED A DRINK? YOU SEEM KIND OF HOT.
NO, THANKS.
LET ME BE MORE SPECIFIC. WHY ARE YOU HANGING OUT WITH THOSE IDIOTS?
YOU THINK PROTESTING A BUNCH OF FUNERALS IS GOING TO BE FUN? THAT THOSE LATTER-DAY HATERS ARE ANYTHING OTHER THAN PUBLICITY HOUNDS? THEY DON'T CARE ABOUT THEIR CAUSE... OR YOU! THEY CARE ABOUT THEMSELVES. AND THE MONEY THEY GET FROM SUCKERS WHO FOLLOW THEM.
IF YOU THINK THEY...
I GET IT! YOU DON'T LIKE THEM. IN YOUR MIND THEY'RE A BUNCH OF LOSERS.
BUT THIS ANKLE BRACELET YOU GAVE ME REMINDS ME NOT TO GET STUPID AGAIN.
I WAS JUST TALKING WITH THEM.
THAT'S ALL?
YEP.
BESIDES, THE LAST TIME I HEARD, THIS WAS A FREE COUNTRY. DIDN'T KNOW IT WAS A CRIME TO TALK TO PEOPLE.
MIND IF I SMOKE?

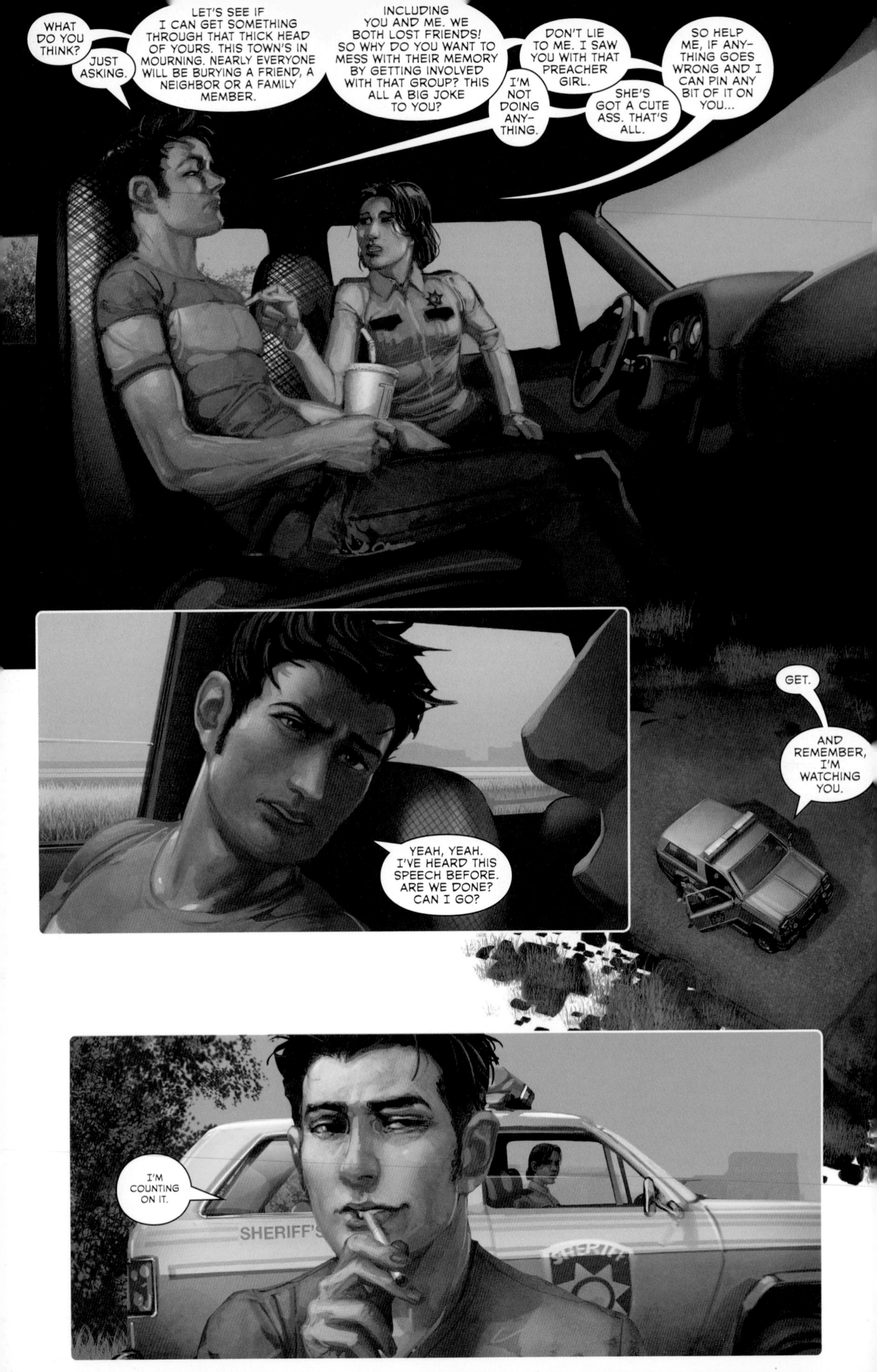
WHAT DO YOU THINK?
JUST ASKING.
LET'S SEE IF I CAN GET SOMETHING THROUGH THAT THICK HEAD OF YOURS. THIS TOWN'S IN MOURNING. NEARLY EVERYONE WILL BE BURYING A FRIEND, A NEIGHBOR OR A FAMILY MEMBER.
INCLUDING YOU AND ME. WE BOTH LOST FRIENDS! SO WHY DO YOU WANT TO MESS WITH THEIR MEMORY BY GETTING INVOLVED WITH THAT GROUP? THIS ALL A BIG JOKE TO YOU?
I'M NOT DOING ANY-THING.
DON'T LIE TO ME. I SAW YOU WITH THAT PREACHER GIRL.
SHE'S GOT A CUTE ASS. THAT'S ALL.
SO HELP ME, IF ANY-THING GOES WRONG AND I CAN PIN ANY BIT OF IT ON YOU...
YEAH, YEAH. I'VE HEARD THIS SPEECH BEFORE. ARE WE DONE? CAN I GO?
GET.
AND REMEMBER, I'M WATCHING YOU.
I'M COUNTING ON IT.
SHERIFF'S
SHERIFF

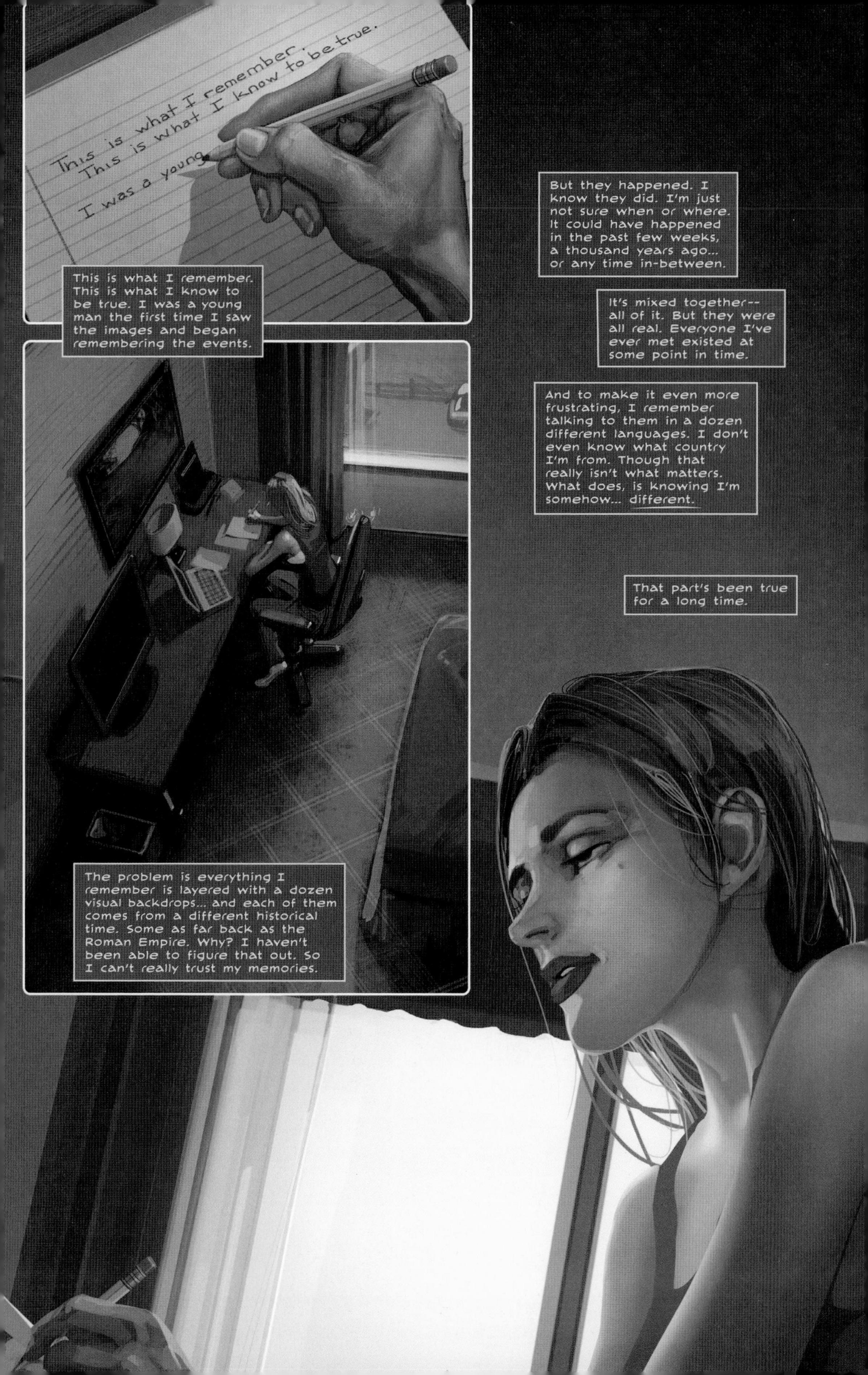
This is what I remember.
This is what I know to be true.
I was a young
This is what I remember. This is what I know to be true. I was a young man the first time I saw the images and began remembering the events.
The problem is everything I remember is layered with a dozen visual backdrops... and each of them comes from a different historical time. Some as far back as the Roman Empire. Why? I haven't been able to figure that out. So I can't really trust my memories.
But they happened. I know they did. I'm just not sure when or where. It could have happened in the past few weeks, a thousand years ago... or any time in-between.
It's mixed together-- all of it. But they were all real. Everyone I've ever met existed at some point in time.
And to make it even more frustrating, I remember talking to them in a dozen different languages. I don't even know what country I'm from. Though that really isn't what matters. What does, is knowing I'm somehow... different.
That part's been true for a long time.

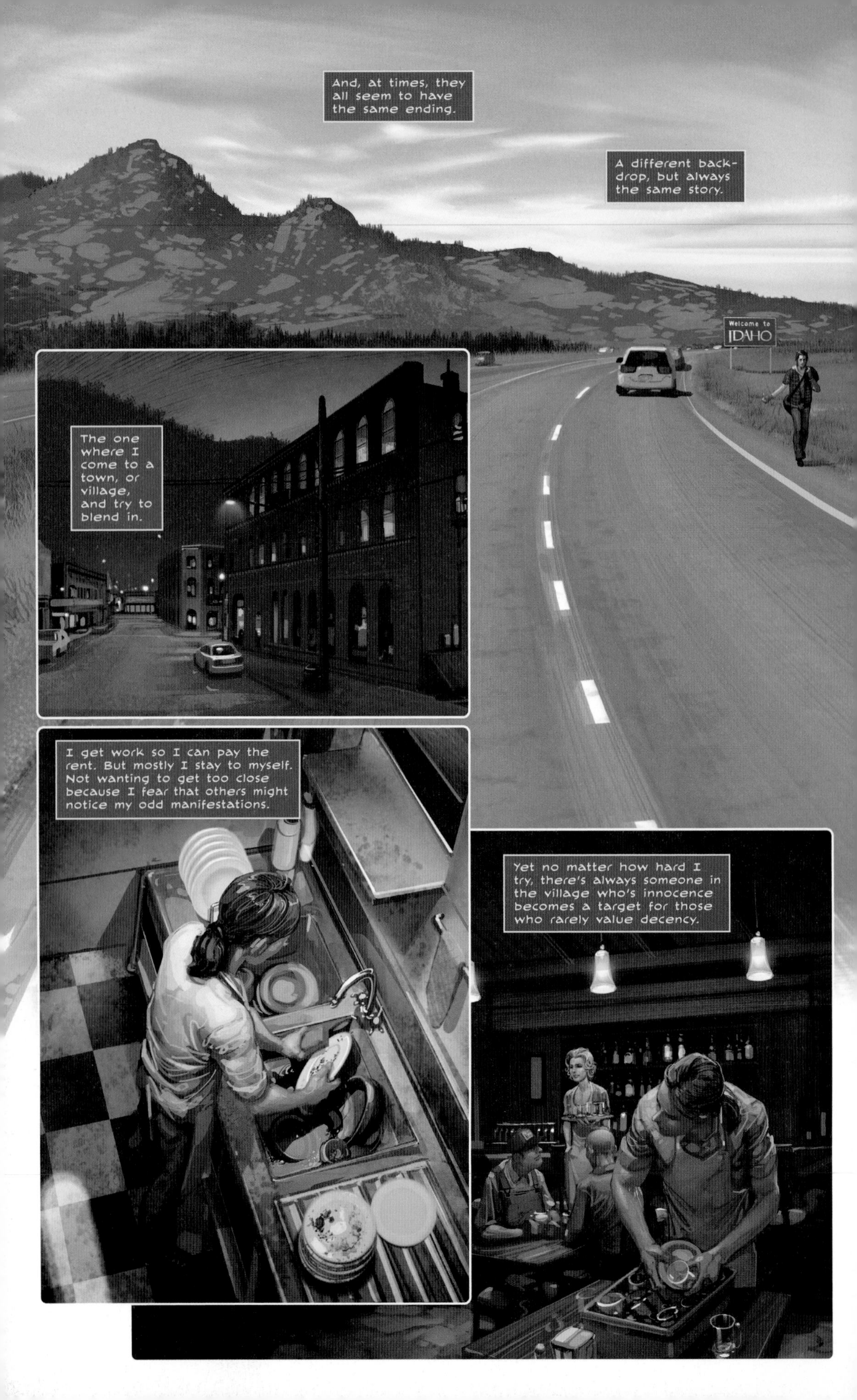

And, at times, they all seem to have the same ending.
A different back-drop, but always the same story.
Welcome to IDAHO
The one where I come to a town, or village, and try to blend in.
I get work so I can pay the rent. But mostly I stay to myself. Not wanting to get too close because I fear that others might notice my odd manifestations.
Yet no matter how hard I try, there's always someone in the village who's innocence becomes a target for those who rarely value decency.

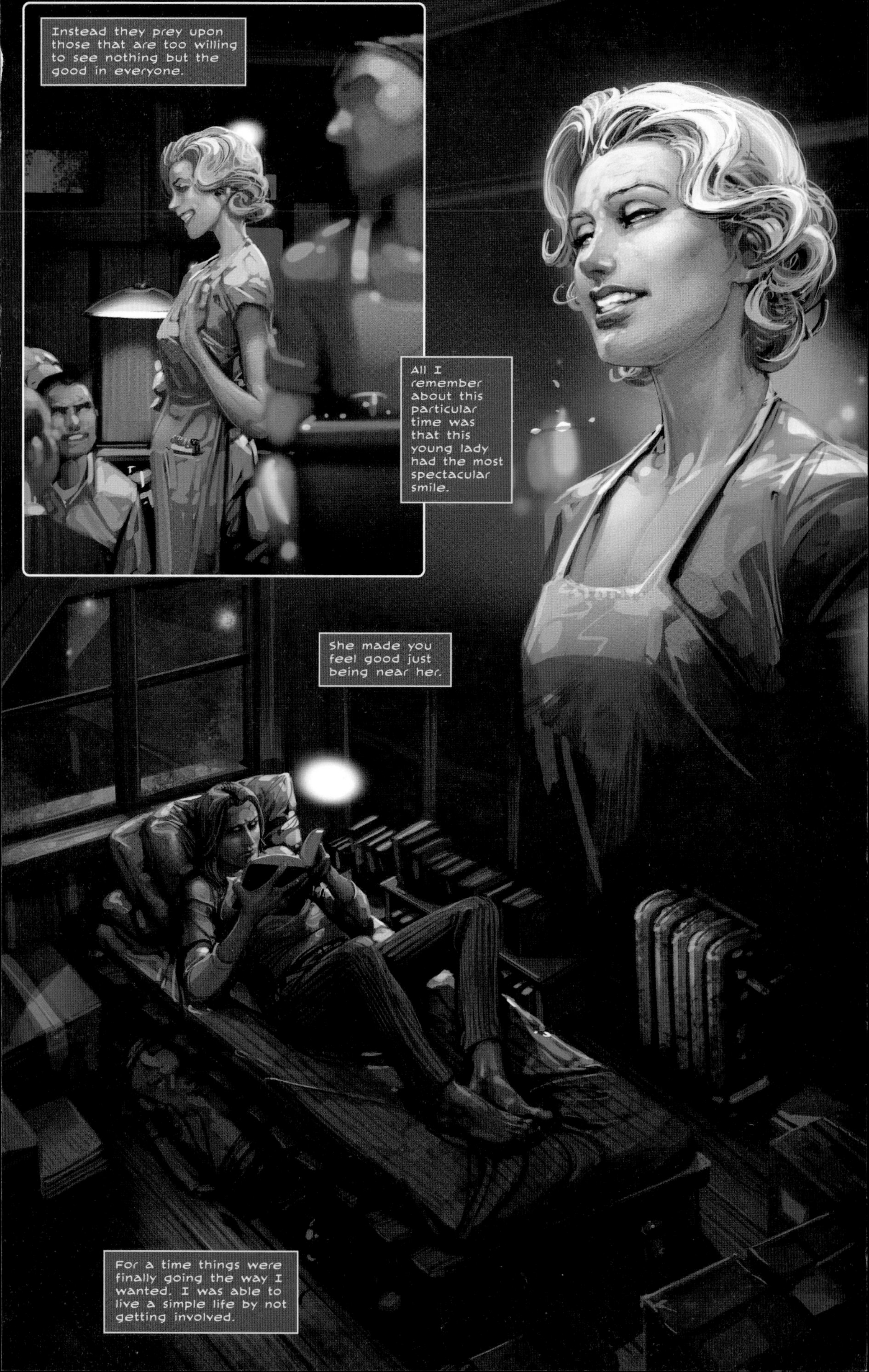
Instead they prey upon those that are too willing to see nothing but the good in everyone.
All I remember about this particular time was that this young lady had the most spectacular smile.
She made you feel good just being near her.
For a time things were finally going the way I wanted. I was able to live a simple life by not getting involved.

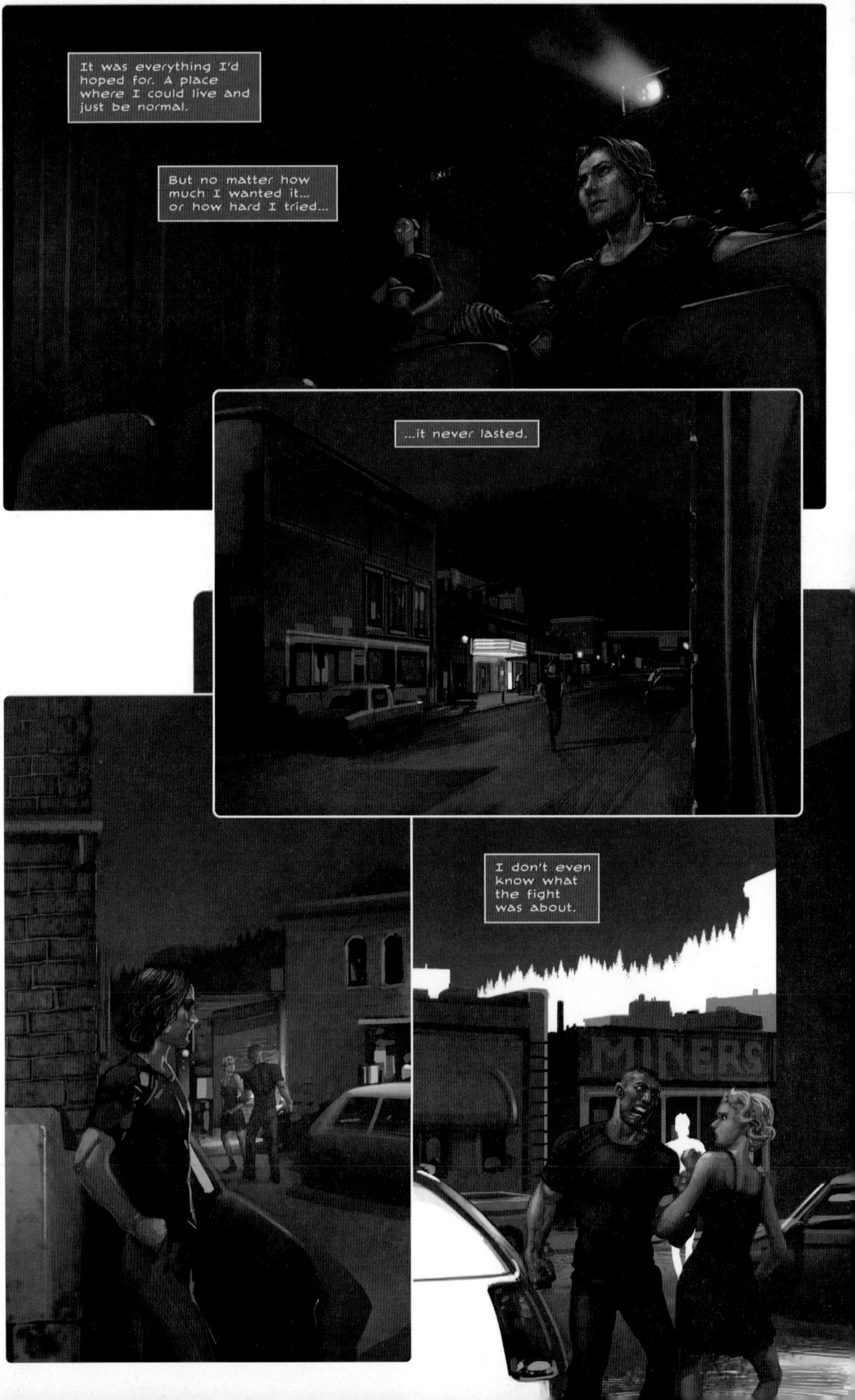
It was everything I'd hoped for. A place where I could live and just be normal.
But no matter how much I wanted it... or how hard I tried...
...it never lasted.
I don't even know what the fight was about.
MINERS

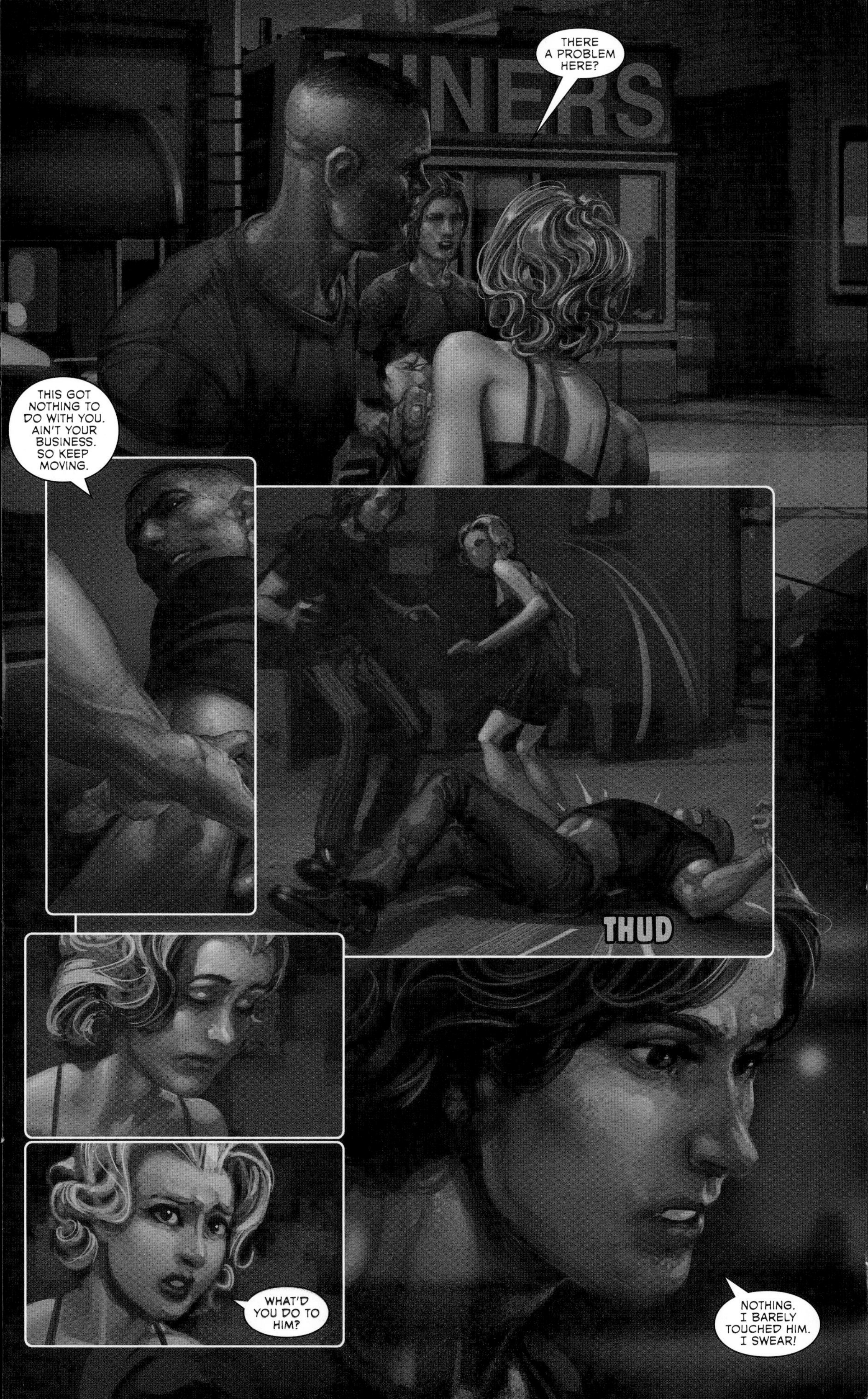
THERE A PROBLEM HERE?
THIS GOT NOTHING TO DO WITH YOU. AIN'T YOUR BUSINESS. SO KEEP MOVING.
THUD
WHAT'D YOU DO TO HIM?
NOTHING. I BARELY TOUCHED HIM. I SWEAR!

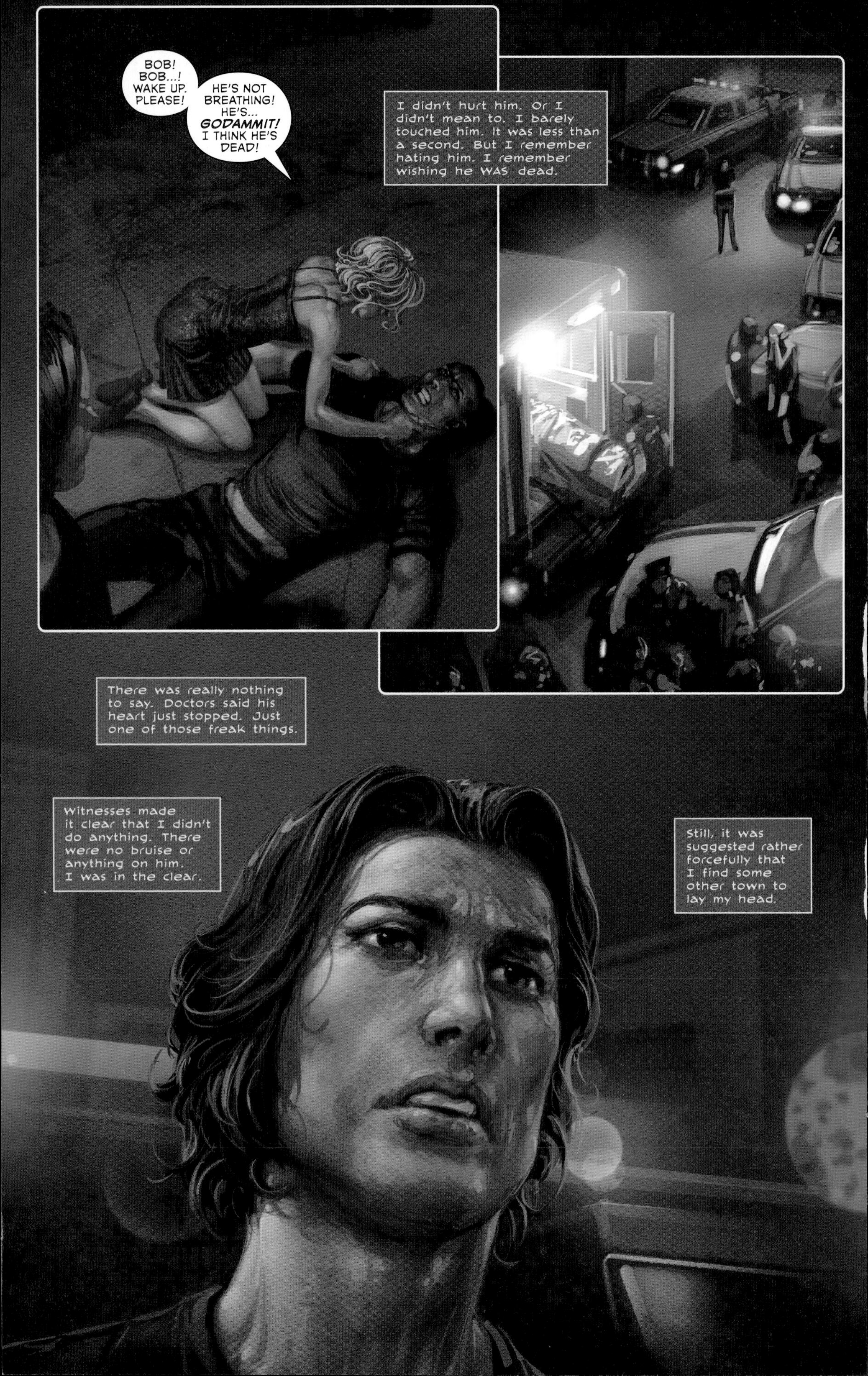
BOB! BOB...! WAKE UP. PLEASE!
HE'S NOT BREATHING! HE'S... GODAMMIT! I THINK HE'S DEAD!
I didn't hurt him. Or I didn't mean to. I barely touched him. It was less than a second. But I remember hating him. I remember wishing he WAS dead.
There was really nothing to say. Doctors said his heart just stopped. Just one of those freak things.
Witnesses made it clear that I didn't do anything. There were no bruise or anything on him. I was in the clear.
Still, it was suggested rather forcefully that I find some other town to lay my head.

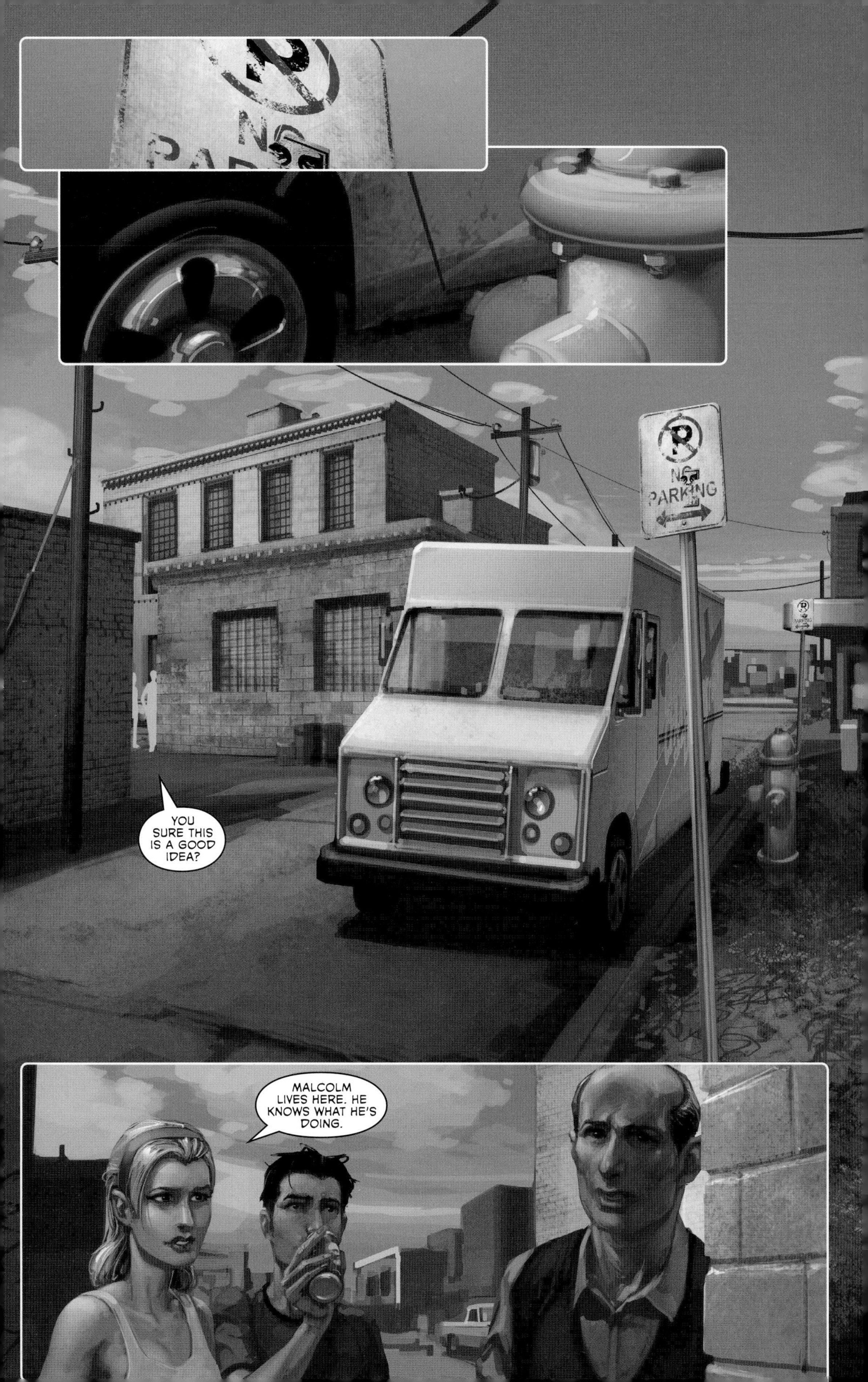
NO PAR
NO PARKING
YOU SURE THIS IS A GOOD IDEA?
MALCOLM LIVES HERE. HE KNOWS WHAT HE'S DOING.

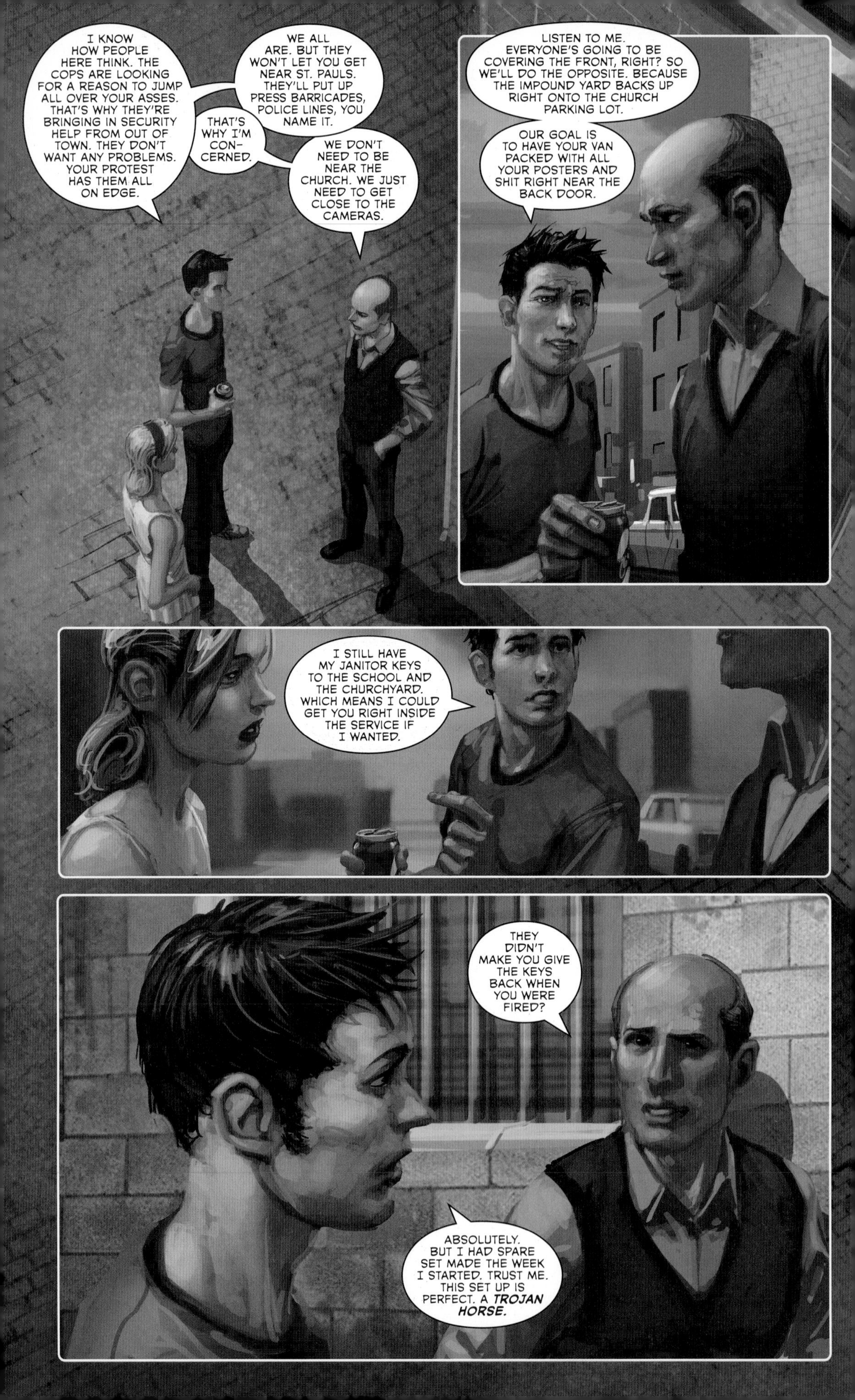
I KNOW HOW PEOPLE HERE THINK. THE COPS ARE LOOKING FOR A REASON TO JUMP ALL OVER YOUR ASSES. THAT'S WHY THEY'RE BRINGING IN SECURITY HELP FROM OUT OF TOWN. THEY DON'T WANT ANY PROBLEMS. YOUR PROTEST HAS THEM ALL ON EDGE.
WE ALL ARE. BUT THEY WON'T LET YOU GET NEAR ST. PAULS. THEY'LL PUT UP PRESS BARRICADES, POLICE LINES, YOU NAME IT.
THAT'S WHY I'M CON-CERNED.
WE DON'T NEED TO BE NEAR THE CHURCH. WE JUST NEED TO GET CLOSE TO THE CAMERAS.
LISTEN TO ME. EVERYONE'S GOING TO BE COVERING THE FRONT, RIGHT? SO WE'LL DO THE OPPOSITE. BECAUSE THE IMPOUND YARD BACKS UP RIGHT ONTO THE CHURCH PARKING LOT.
OUR GOAL IS TO HAVE YOUR VAN PACKED WITH ALL YOUR POSTERS AND SHIT RIGHT NEAR THE BACK DOOR.
I STILL HAVE MY JANITOR KEYS TO THE SCHOOL AND THE CHURCHYARD. WHICH MEANS I COULD GET YOU RIGHT INSIDE THE SERVICE IF I WANTED.
THEY DIDN'T MAKE YOU GIVE THE KEYS BACK WHEN YOU WERE FIRED?
ABSOLUTELY. BUT I HAD SPARE SET MADE THE WEEK I STARTED. TRUST ME. THIS SET UP IS PERFECT. A ***TROJAN HORSE.***

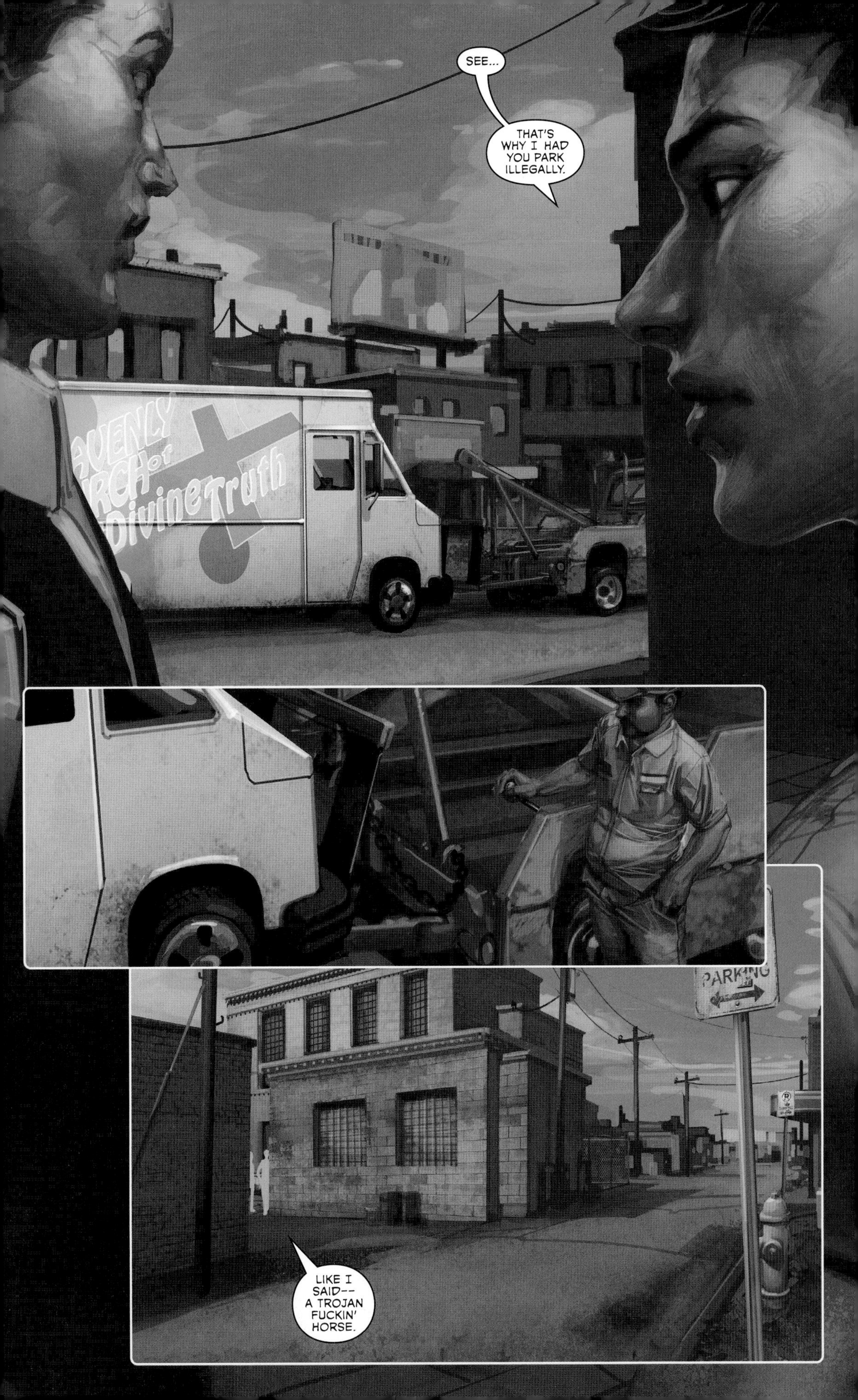
SEE...
THAT'S WHY I HAD YOU PARK ILLEGALLY.
HEAVENLY CHURCH of Divine Truth
PARKING
LIKE I SAID-- A TROJAN FUCKIN' HORSE.

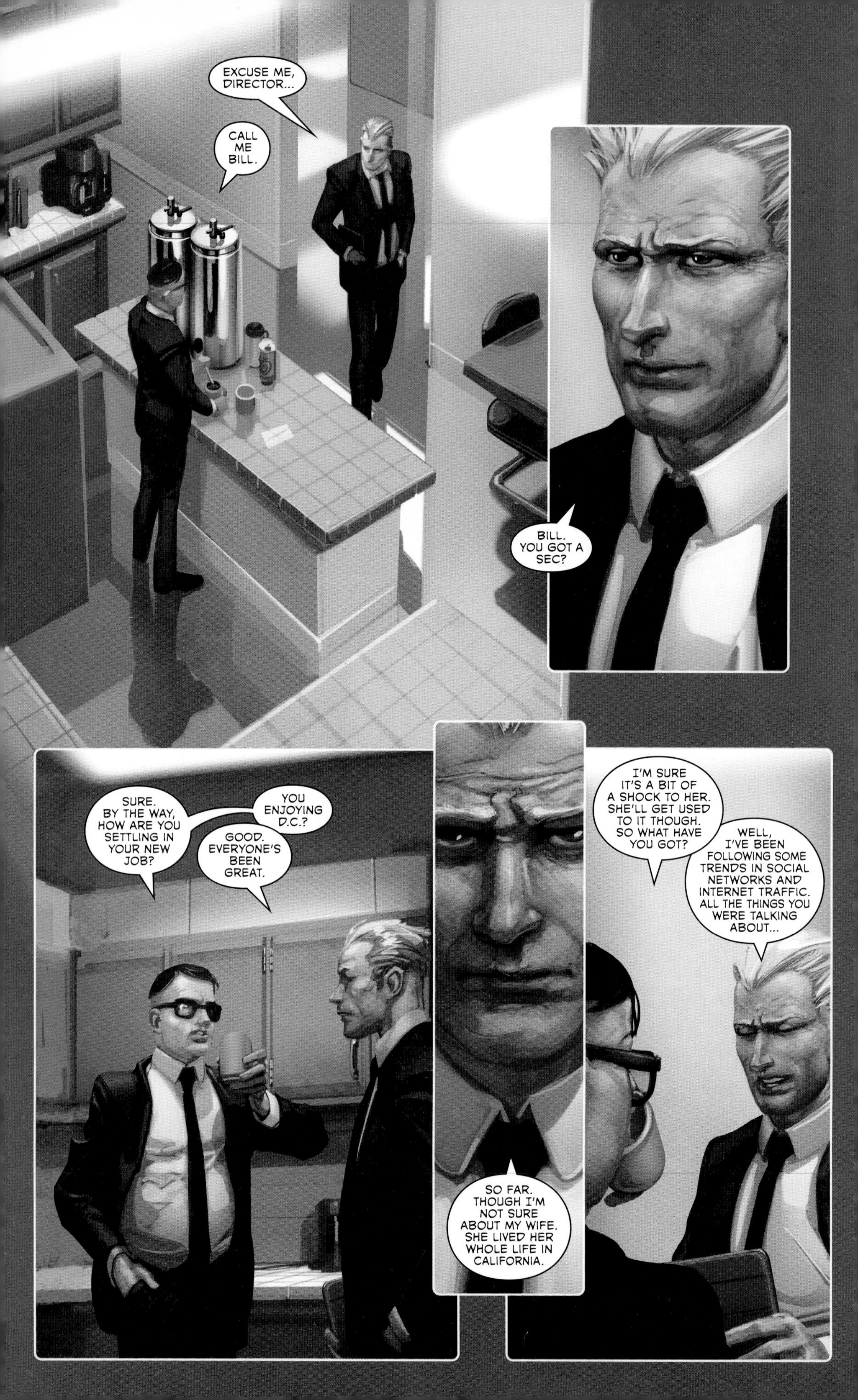
EXCUSE ME, DIRECTOR...
CALL ME BILL.
BILL. YOU GOT A SEC?
SURE. BY THE WAY, HOW ARE YOU SETTLING IN YOUR NEW JOB?
YOU ENJOYING D.C.?
GOOD. EVERYONE'S BEEN GREAT.
SO FAR. THOUGH I'M NOT SURE ABOUT MY WIFE. SHE LIVED HER WHOLE LIFE IN CALIFORNIA.
I'M SURE IT'S A BIT OF A SHOCK TO HER. SHE'LL GET USED TO IT THOUGH. SO WHAT HAVE YOU GOT?
WELL, I'VE BEEN FOLLOWING SOME TRENDS IN SOCIAL NETWORKS AND INTERNET TRAFFIC. ALL THE THINGS YOU WERE TALKING ABOUT...

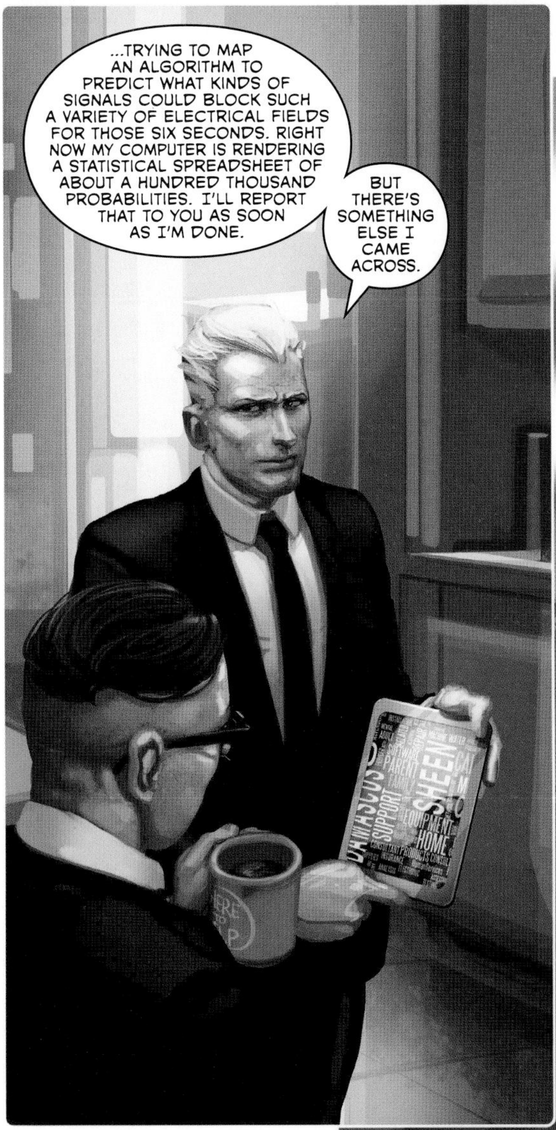

...TRYING TO MAP AN ALGORITHM TO PREDICT WHAT KINDS OF SIGNALS COULD BLOCK SUCH A VARIETY OF ELECTRICAL FIELDS FOR THOSE SIX SECONDS. RIGHT NOW MY COMPUTER IS RENDERING A STATISTICAL SPREADSHEET OF ABOUT A HUNDRED THOUSAND PROBABILITIES. I'LL REPORT THAT TO YOU AS SOON AS I'M DONE.
BUT THERE'S SOMETHING ELSE I CAME ACROSS.

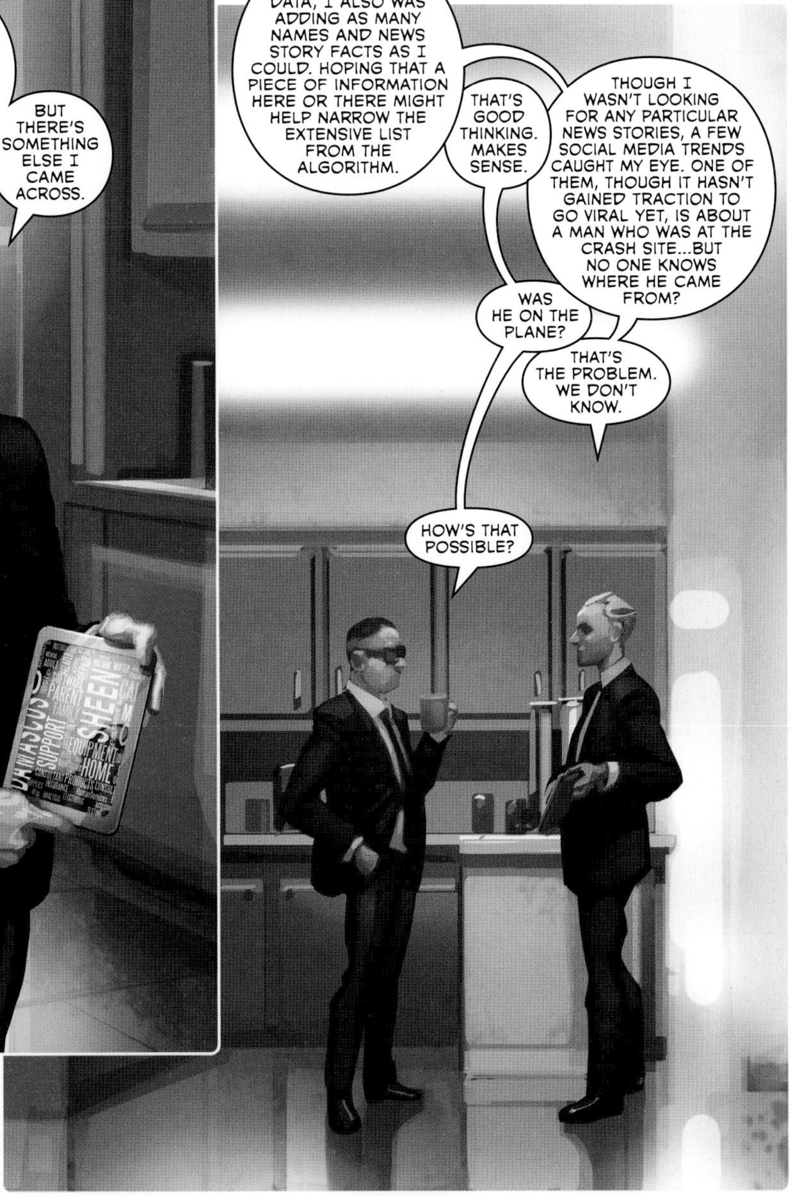

AS I WAS ENTERING MY DATA, I ALSO WAS ADDING AS MANY NAMES AND NEWS STORY FACTS AS I COULD. HOPING THAT A PIECE OF INFORMATION HERE OR THERE MIGHT HELP NARROW THE EXTENSIVE LIST FROM THE ALGORITHM.
THAT'S GOOD THINKING. MAKES SENSE.
THOUGH I WASN'T LOOKING FOR ANY PARTICULAR NEWS STORIES, A FEW SOCIAL MEDIA TRENDS CAUGHT MY EYE. ONE OF THEM, THOUGH IT HASN'T GAINED TRACTION TO GO VIRAL YET, IS ABOUT A MAN WHO WAS AT THE CRASH SITE...BUT NO ONE KNOWS WHERE HE CAME FROM?
WAS HE ON THE PLANE?
THAT'S THE PROBLEM. WE DON'T KNOW.
HOW'S THAT POSSIBLE?

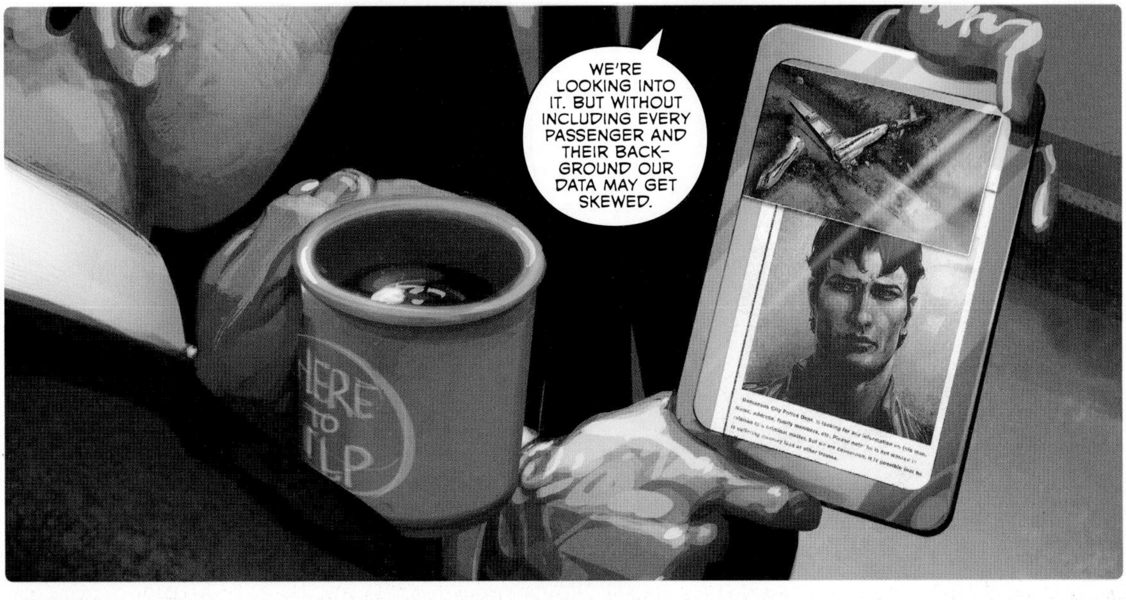

WE'RE LOOKING INTO IT. BUT WITHOUT INCLUDING EVERY PASSENGER AND THEIR BACK-GROUND OUR DATA MAY GET SKEWED.

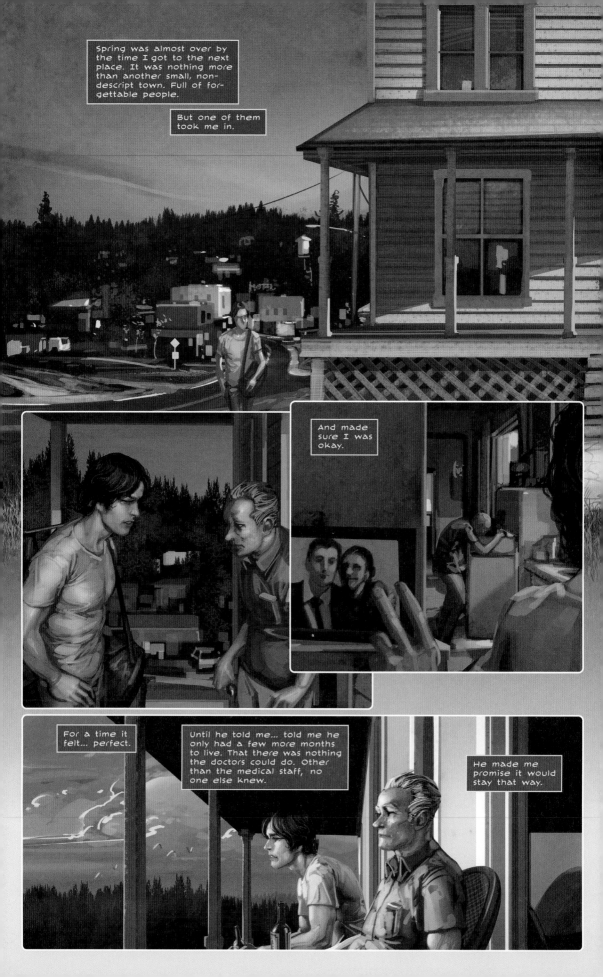

Spring was almost over by the time I got to the next place. It was nothing more than another small, nondescript town. Full of forgettable people.

But one of them took me in.

And made sure I was okay.

For a time it felt... perfect.

Until he told me... told me he only had a few more months to live. That there was nothing the doctors could do. Other than the medical staff, no one else knew.

He made me promise it would stay that way.

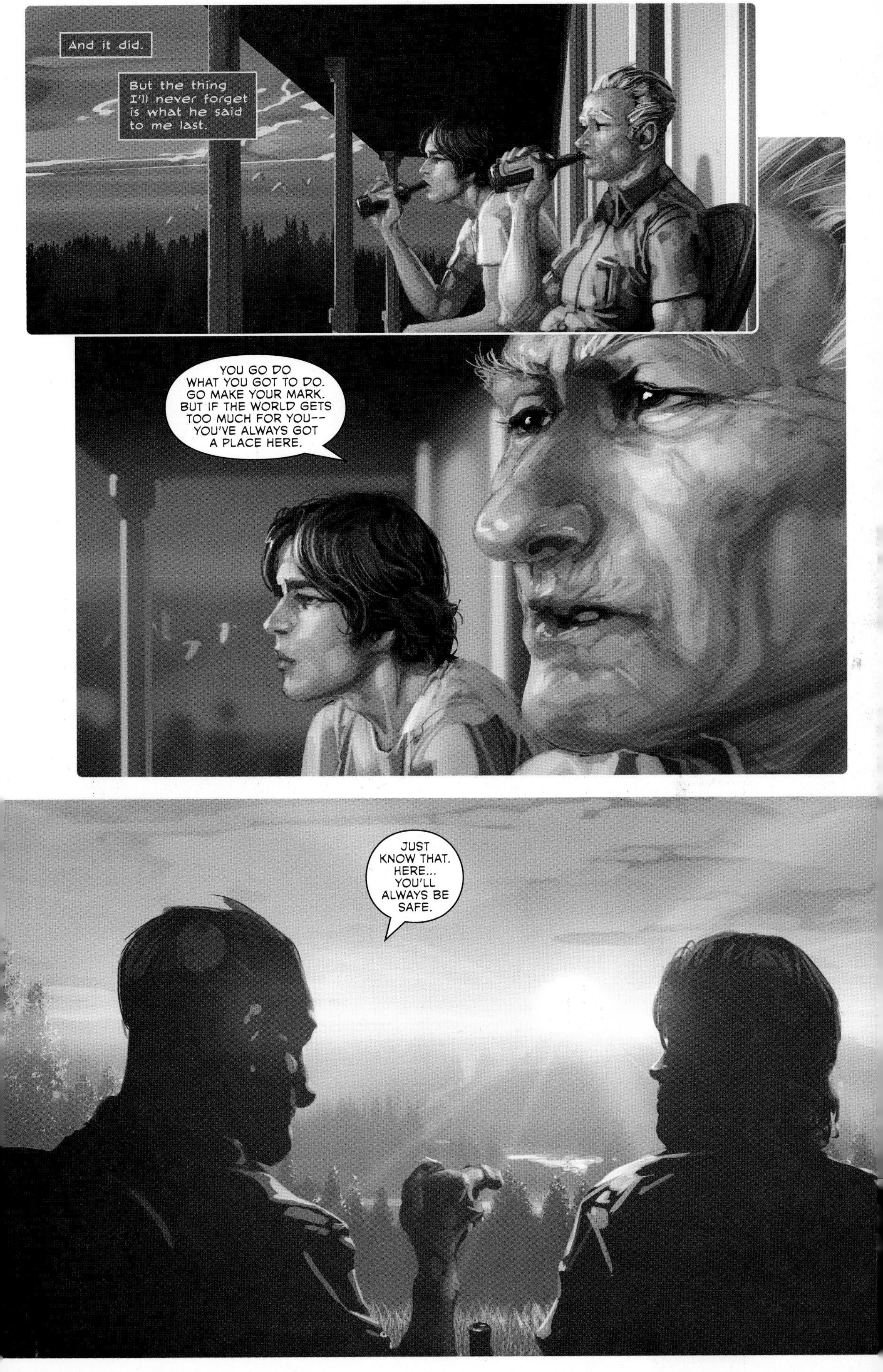
And it did.
But the thing I'll never forget is what he said to me last.
YOU GO DO WHAT YOU GOT TO DO. GO MAKE YOUR MARK. BUT IF THE WORLD GETS TOO MUCH FOR YOU-- YOU'VE ALWAYS GOT A PLACE HERE.
JUST KNOW THAT. HERE... YOU'LL ALWAYS BE SAFE.

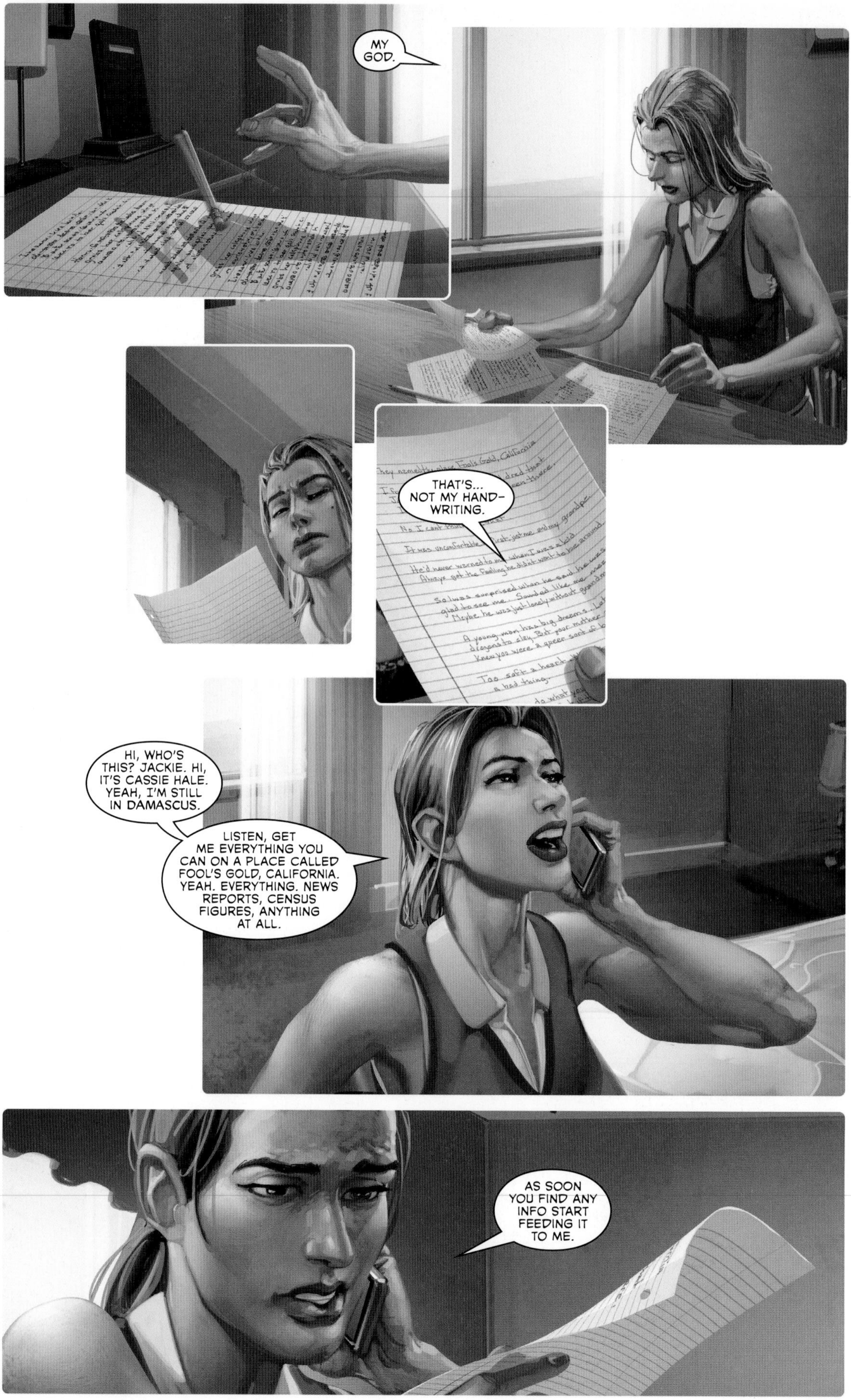
MY GOD.
THAT'S... NOT MY HAND-WRITING.
HI, WHO'S THIS? JACKIE. HI, IT'S CASSIE HALE. YEAH, I'M STILL IN DAMASCUS.
LISTEN, GET ME EVERYTHING YOU CAN ON A PLACE CALLED FOOL'S GOLD, CALIFORNIA. YEAH. EVERYTHING. NEWS REPORTS, CENSUS FIGURES, ANYTHING AT ALL.
AS SOON YOU FIND ANY INFO START FEEDING IT TO ME.

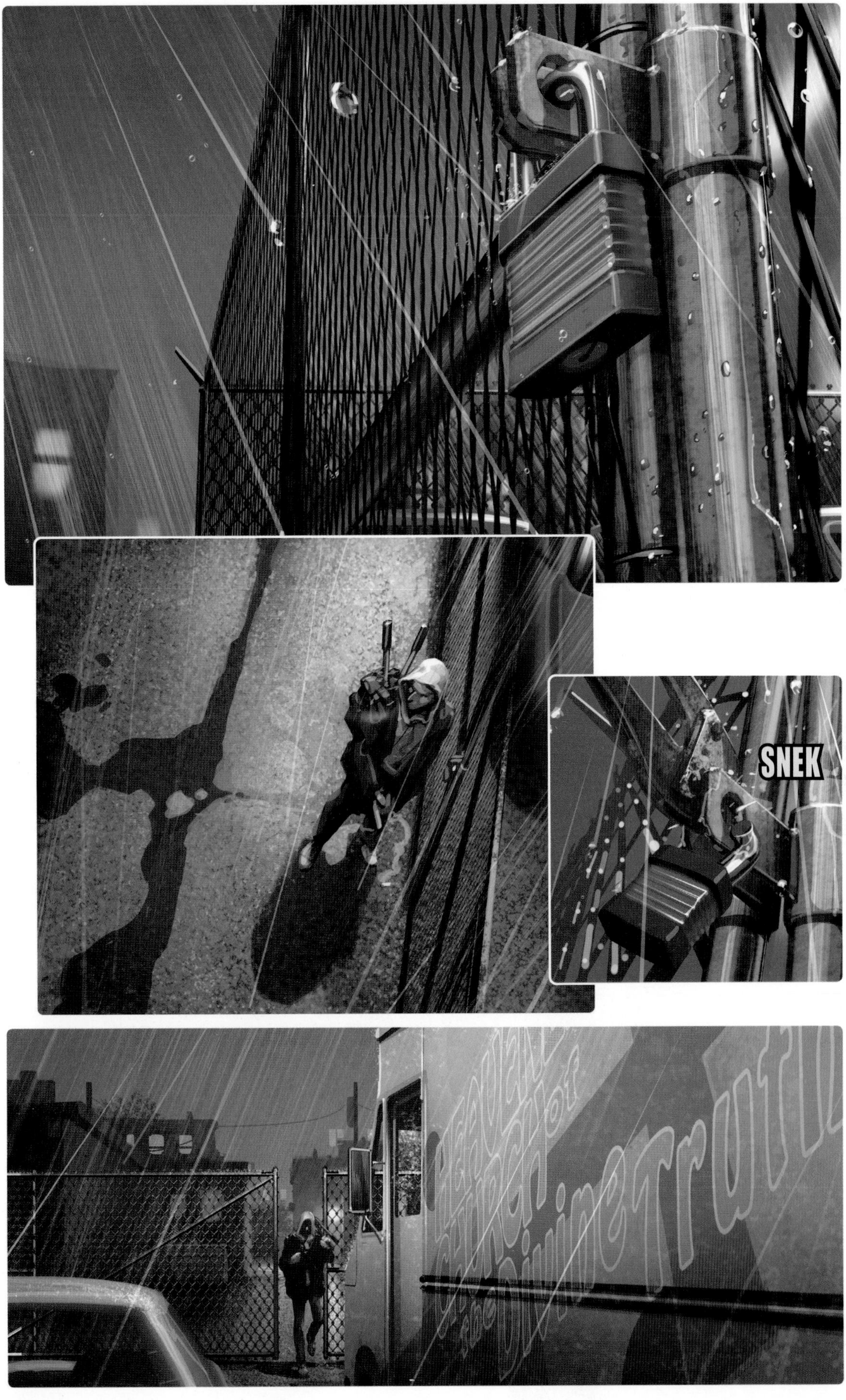
SNEK

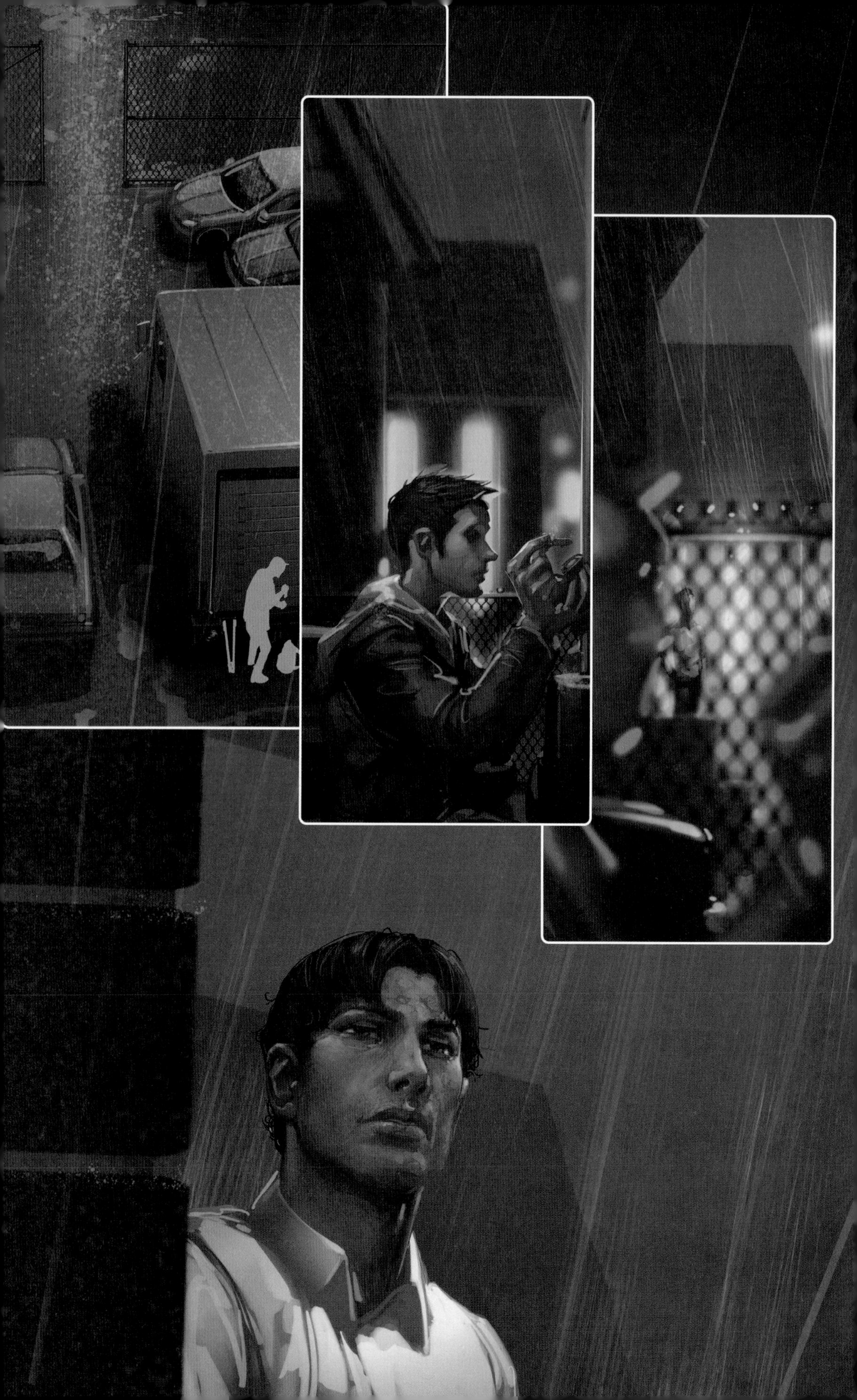

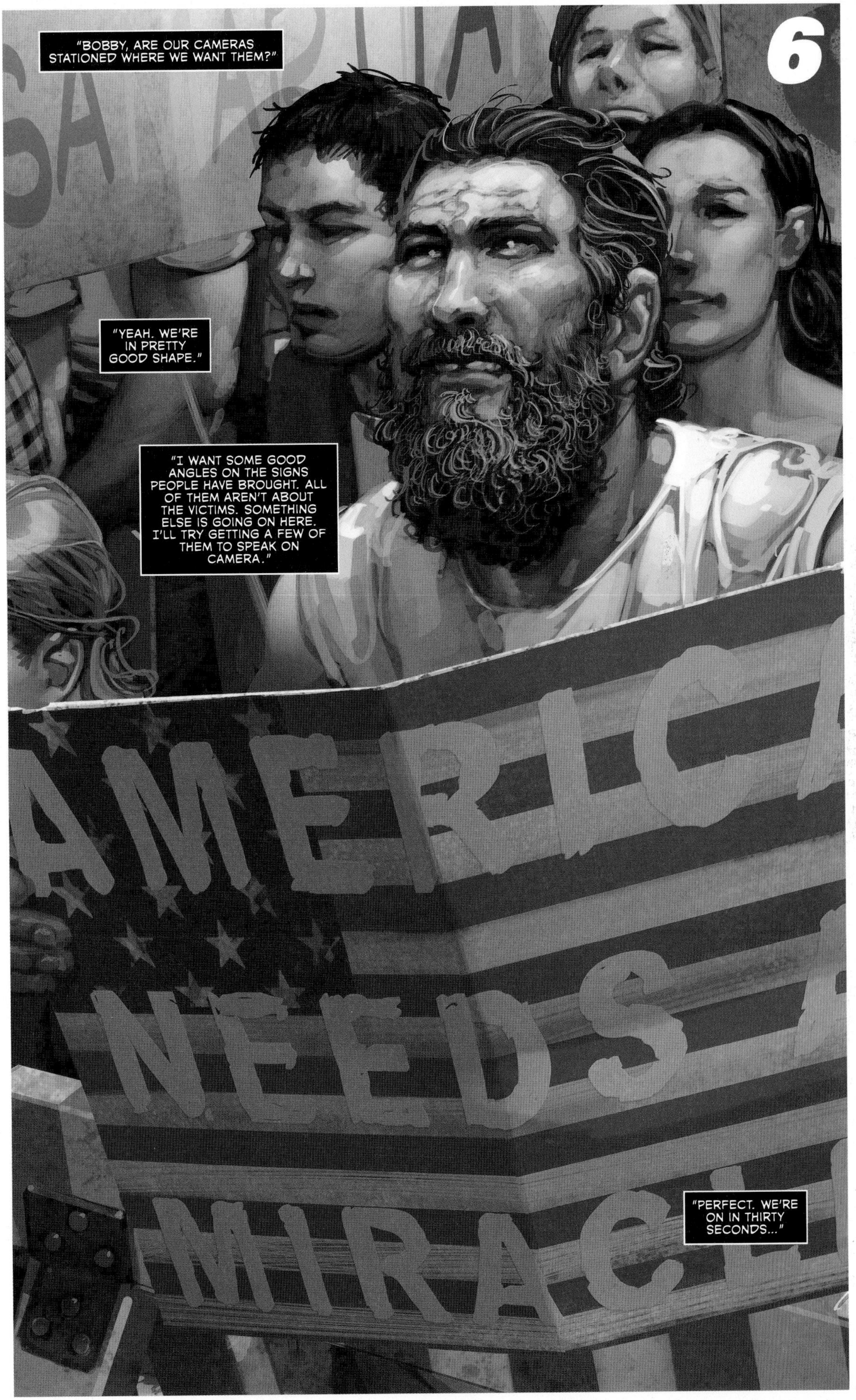
6
"BOBBY, ARE OUR CAMERAS STATIONED WHERE WE WANT THEM?"
"YEAH. WE'RE IN PRETTY GOOD SHAPE."
"I WANT SOME GOOD ANGLES ON THE SIGNS PEOPLE HAVE BROUGHT. ALL OF THEM AREN'T ABOUT THE VICTIMS. SOMETHING ELSE IS GOING ON HERE. I'LL TRY GETTING A FEW OF THEM TO SPEAK ON CAMERA."
NEEDS
"PERFECT. WE'RE ON IN THIRTY SECONDS..."

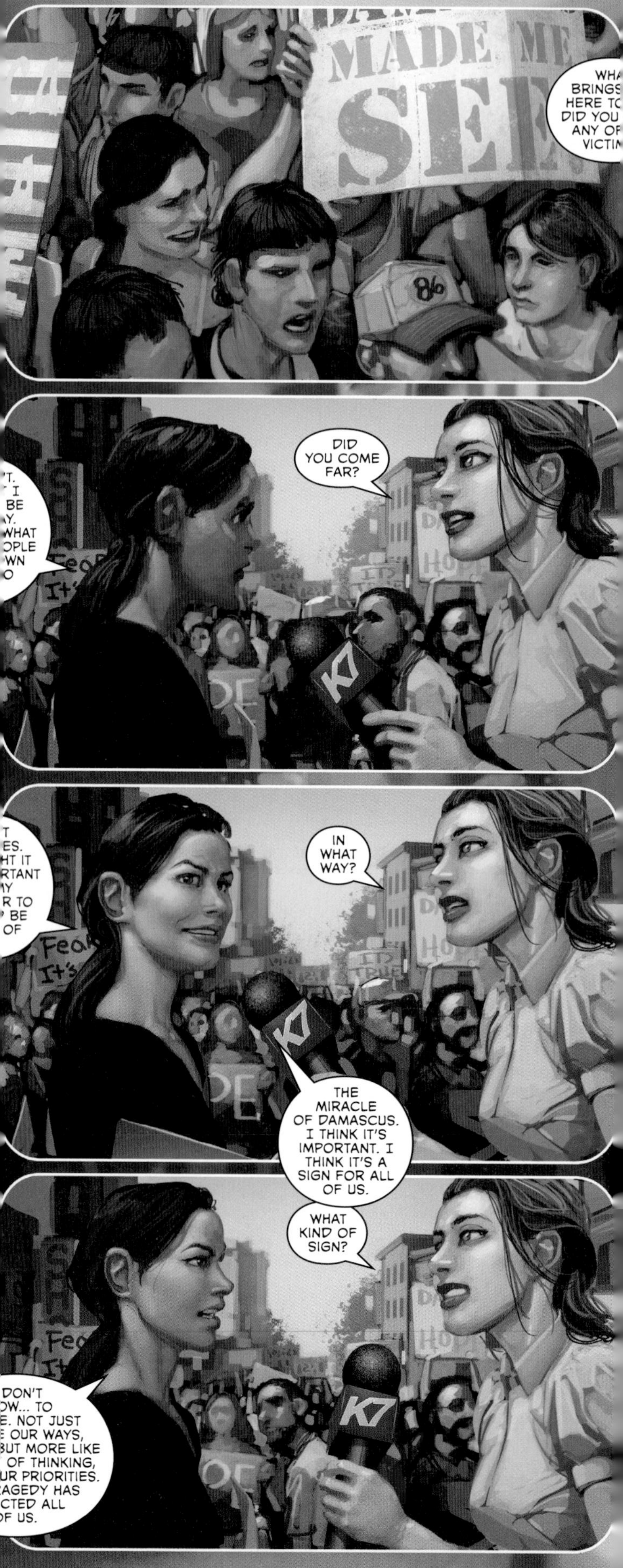
DID YOU COME FAR?
IN WHAT WAY?
THE MIRACLE OF DAMASCUS. I THINK IT'S IMPORTANT. I THINK IT'S A SIGN FOR ALL OF US.
WHAT KIND OF SIGN?

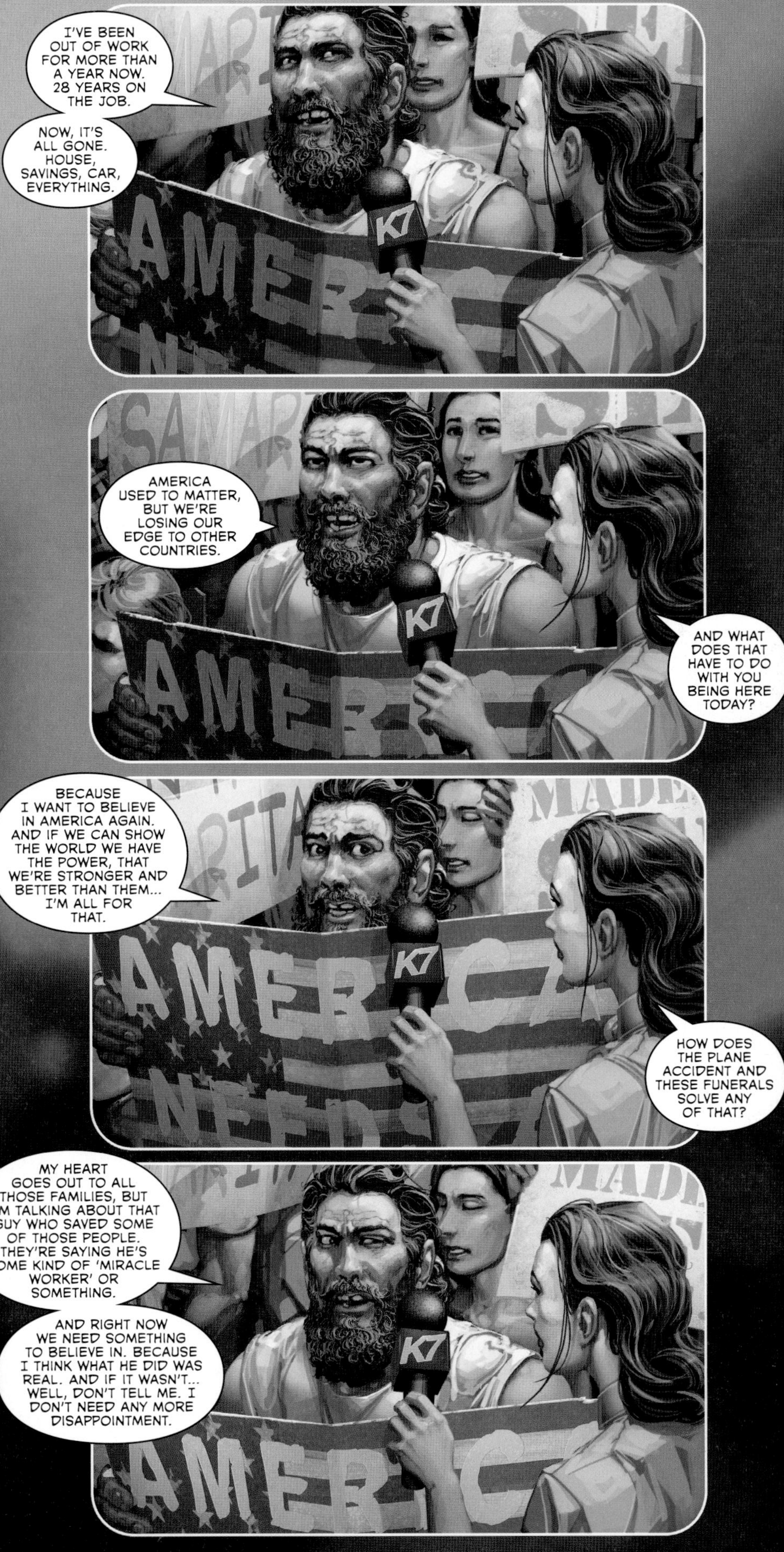
I'VE BEEN OUT OF WORK FOR MORE THAN A YEAR NOW. 28 YEARS ON THE JOB.
NOW, IT'S ALL GONE. HOUSE, SAVINGS, CAR, EVERYTHING.
AMERICA USED TO MATTER, BUT WE'RE LOSING OUR EDGE TO OTHER COUNTRIES.
AND WHAT DOES THAT HAVE TO DO WITH YOU BEING HERE TODAY?
BECAUSE I WANT TO BELIEVE IN AMERICA AGAIN. AND IF WE CAN SHOW THE WORLD WE HAVE THE POWER, THAT WE'RE STRONGER AND BETTER THAN THEM... I'M ALL FOR THAT.
HOW DOES THE PLANE ACCIDENT AND THESE FUNERALS SOLVE ANY OF THAT?
MY HEART GOES OUT TO ALL THOSE FAMILIES, BUT I'M TALKING ABOUT THAT GUY WHO SAVED SOME OF THOSE PEOPLE. THEY'RE SAYING HE'S SOME KIND OF 'MIRACLE WORKER' OR SOMETHING.
AND RIGHT NOW WE NEED SOMETHING TO BELIEVE IN. BECAUSE I THINK WHAT HE DID WAS REAL. AND IF IT WASN'T... WELL, DON'T TELL ME. I DON'T NEED ANY MORE DISAPPOINTMENT.

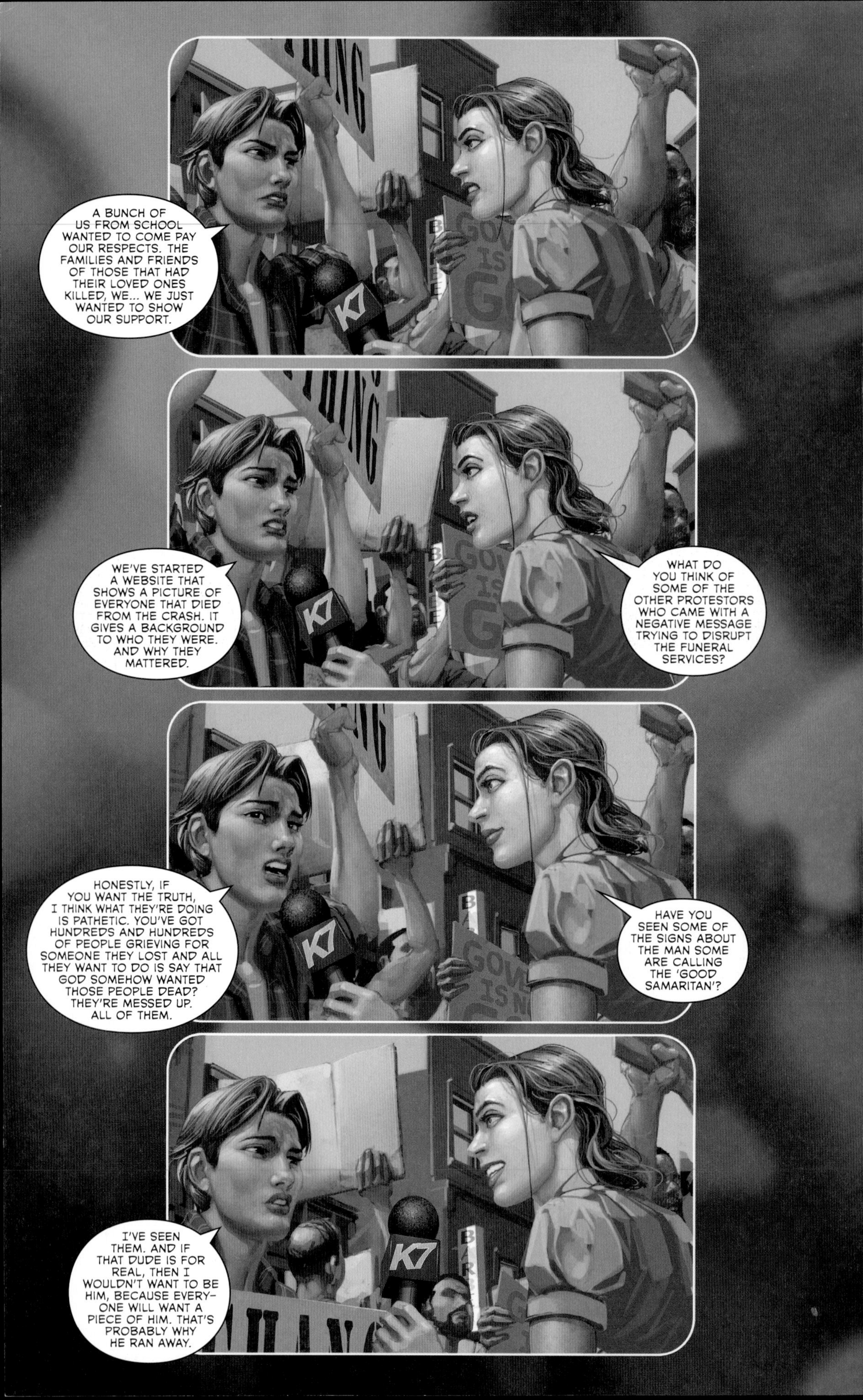

A BUNCH OF US FROM SCHOOL WANTED TO COME PAY OUR RESPECTS. THE FAMILIES AND FRIENDS OF THOSE THAT HAD THEIR LOVED ONES KILLED, WE... WE JUST WANTED TO SHOW OUR SUPPORT.
WE'VE STARTED A WEBSITE THAT SHOWS A PICTURE OF EVERYONE THAT DIED FROM THE CRASH. IT GIVES A BACKGROUND TO WHO THEY WERE. AND WHY THEY MATTERED.
WHAT DO YOU THINK OF SOME OF THE OTHER PROTESTORS WHO CAME WITH A NEGATIVE MESSAGE TRYING TO DISRUPT THE FUNERAL SERVICES?
HONESTLY, IF YOU WANT THE TRUTH, I THINK WHAT THEY'RE DOING IS PATHETIC. YOU'VE GOT HUNDREDS AND HUNDREDS OF PEOPLE GRIEVING FOR SOMEONE THEY LOST AND ALL THEY WANT TO DO IS SAY THAT GOD SOMEHOW WANTED THOSE PEOPLE DEAD? THEY'RE MESSED UP. ALL OF THEM.
HAVE YOU SEEN SOME OF THE SIGNS ABOUT THE MAN SOME ARE CALLING THE 'GOOD SAMARITAN'?
I'VE SEEN THEM. AND IF THAT DUDE IS FOR REAL, THEN I WOULDN'T WANT TO BE HIM, BECAUSE EVERY-ONE WILL WANT A PIECE OF HIM. THAT'S PROBABLY WHY HE RAN AWAY.

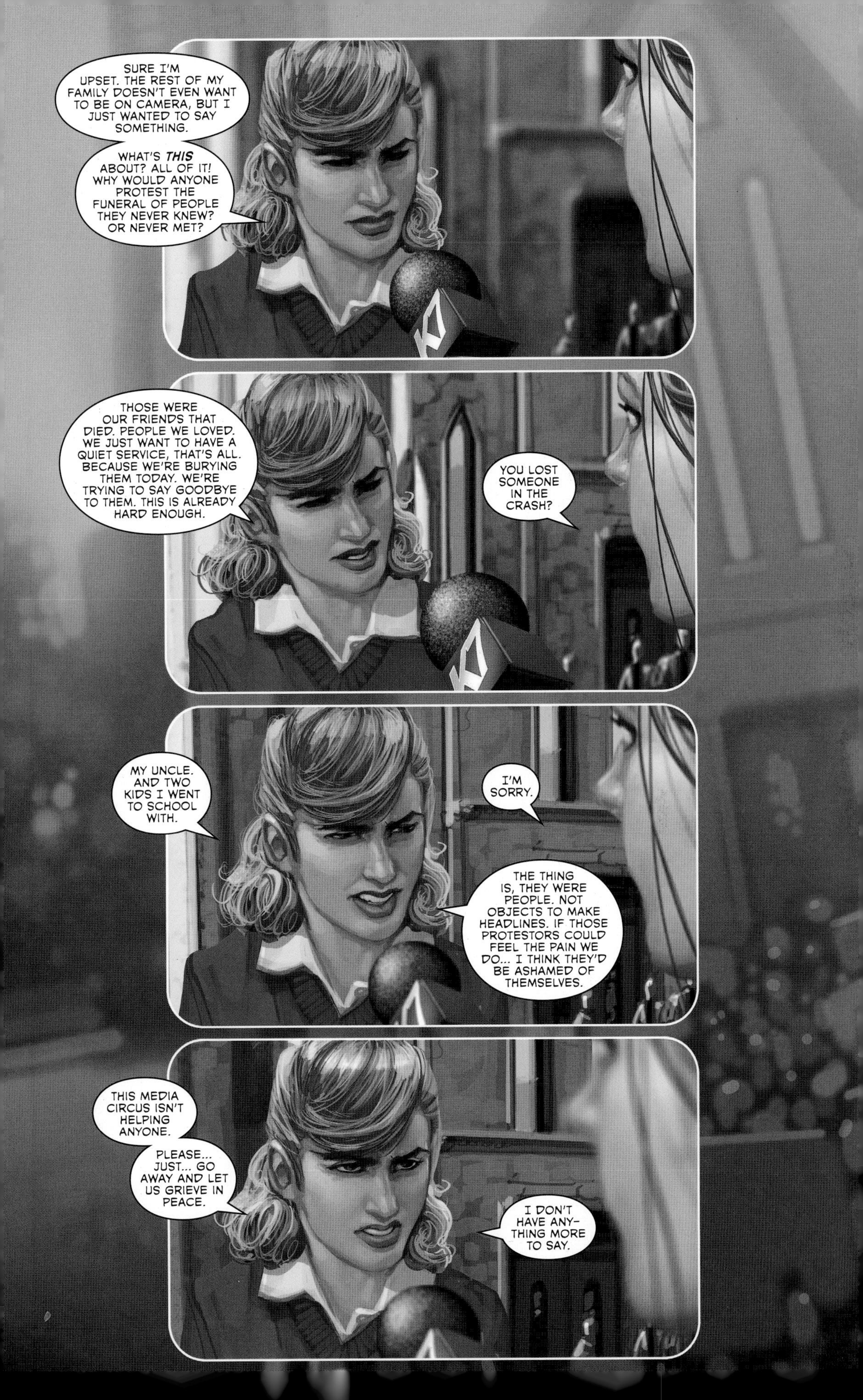
SURE I'M UPSET. THE REST OF MY FAMILY DOESN'T EVEN WANT TO BE ON CAMERA, BUT I JUST WANTED TO SAY SOMETHING.
WHAT'S *THIS* ABOUT? ALL OF IT! WHY WOULD ANYONE PROTEST THE FUNERAL OF PEOPLE THEY NEVER KNEW? OR NEVER MET?
THOSE WERE OUR FRIENDS THAT DIED. PEOPLE WE LOVED. WE JUST WANT TO HAVE A QUIET SERVICE, THAT'S ALL. BECAUSE WE'RE BURYING THEM TODAY. WE'RE TRYING TO SAY GOODBYE TO THEM. THIS IS ALREADY HARD ENOUGH.
YOU LOST SOMEONE IN THE CRASH?
MY UNCLE. AND TWO KIDS I WENT TO SCHOOL WITH.
I'M SORRY.
THE THING IS, THEY WERE PEOPLE. NOT OBJECTS TO MAKE HEADLINES. IF THOSE PROTESTORS COULD FEEL THE PAIN WE DO... I THINK THEY'D BE ASHAMED OF THEMSELVES.
THIS MEDIA CIRCUS ISN'T HELPING ANYONE.
PLEASE... JUST... GO AWAY AND LET US GRIEVE IN PEACE.
I DON'T HAVE ANY-THING MORE TO SAY.

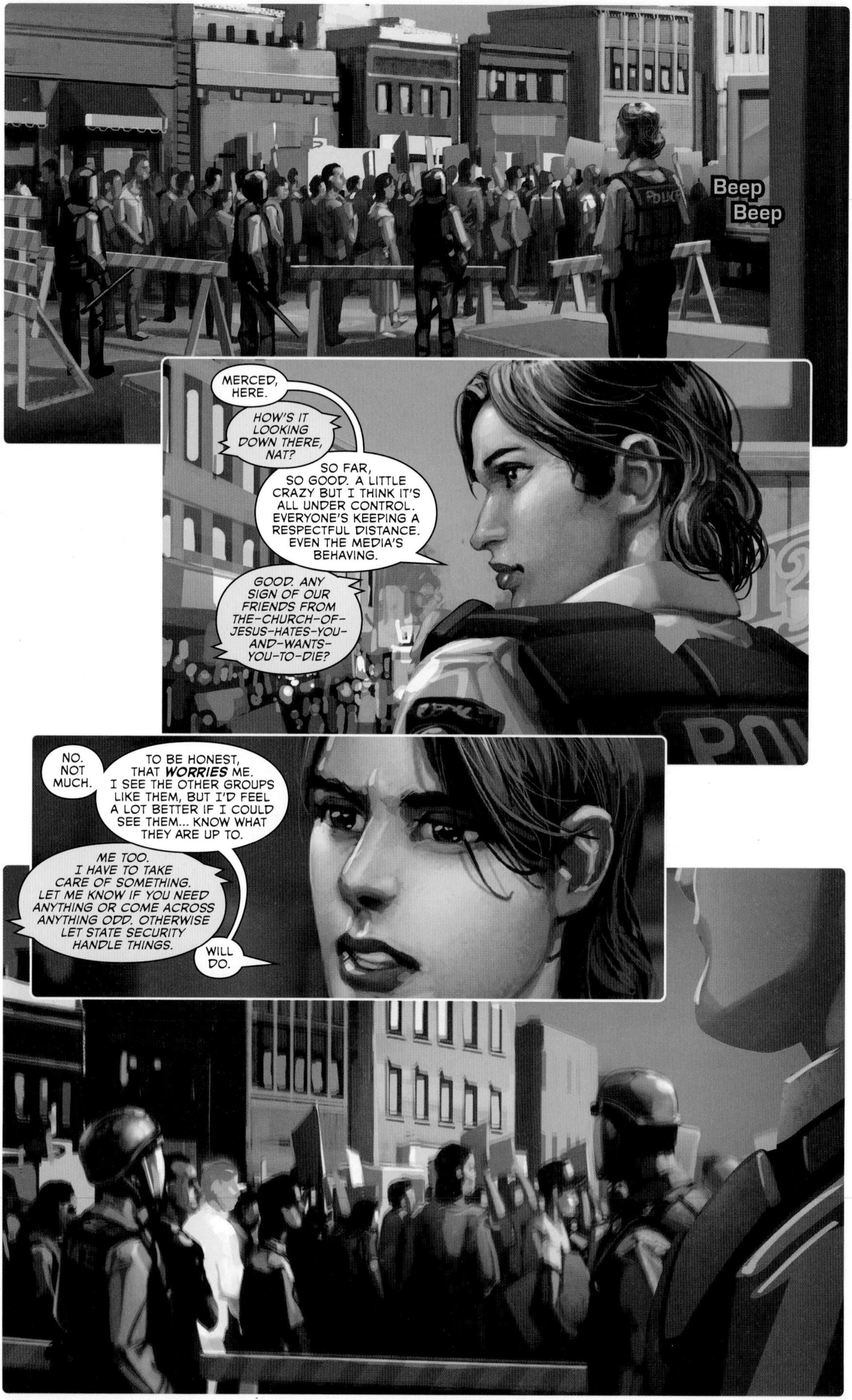
Beep
Beep
MERCED, HERE.
HOW'S IT LOOKING DOWN THERE, NAT?
SO FAR, SO GOOD. A LITTLE CRAZY BUT I THINK IT'S ALL UNDER CONTROL. EVERYONE'S KEEPING A RESPECTFUL DISTANCE. EVEN THE MEDIA'S BEHAVING.
GOOD. ANY SIGN OF OUR FRIENDS FROM THE-CHURCH-OF-JESUS-HATES-YOU-AND-WANTS-YOU-TO-DIE?
NO. NOT MUCH.
TO BE HONEST, THAT WORRIES ME. I SEE THE OTHER GROUPS LIKE THEM, BUT I'D FEEL A LOT BETTER IF I COULD SEE THEM... KNOW WHAT THEY ARE UP TO.
ME TOO. I HAVE TO TAKE CARE OF SOMETHING. LET ME KNOW IF YOU NEED ANYTHING OR COME ACROSS ANYTHING ODD. OTHERWISE LET STATE SECURITY HANDLE THINGS.
WILL DO.

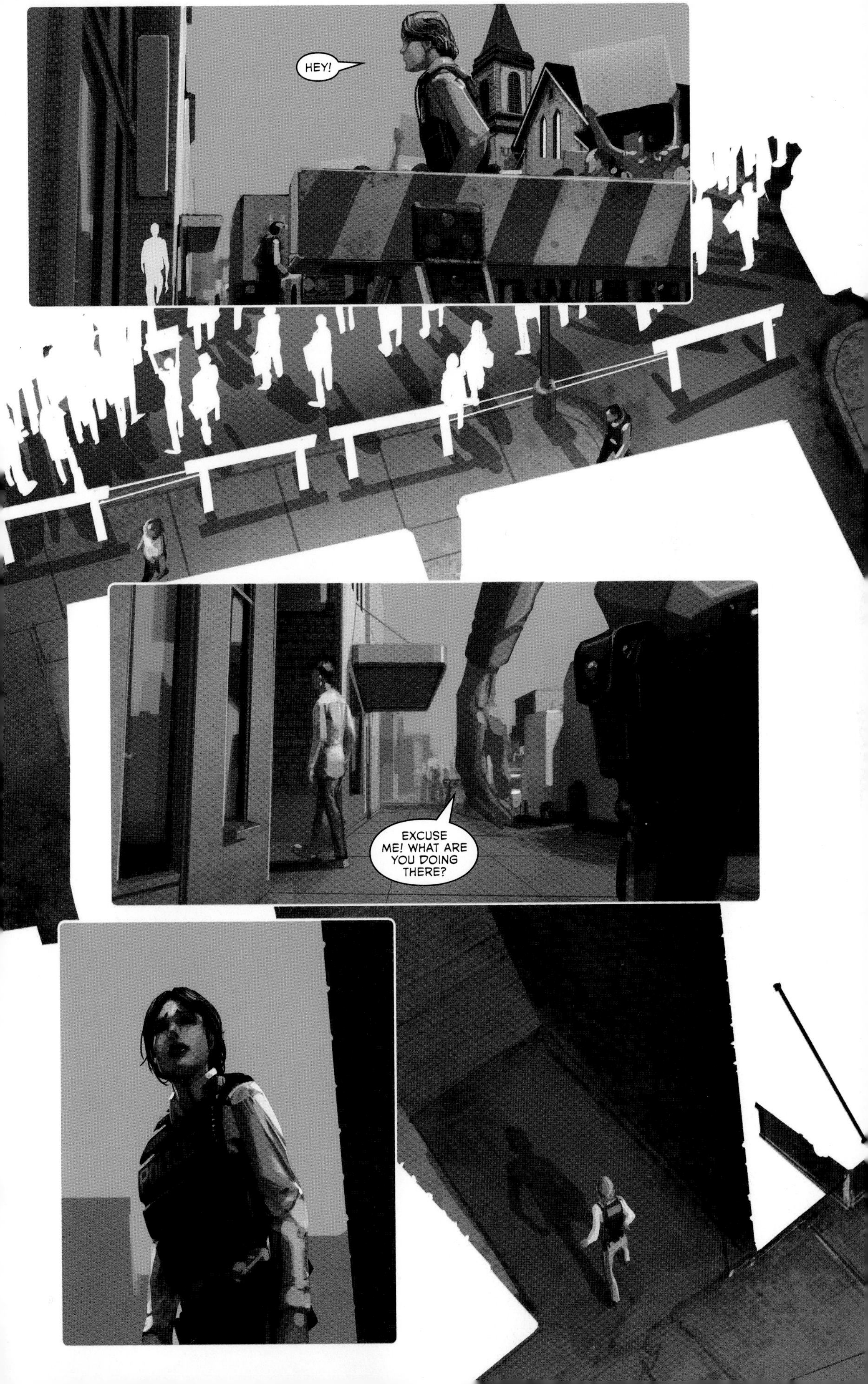
HEY!
EXCUSE ME! WHAT ARE YOU DOING THERE?

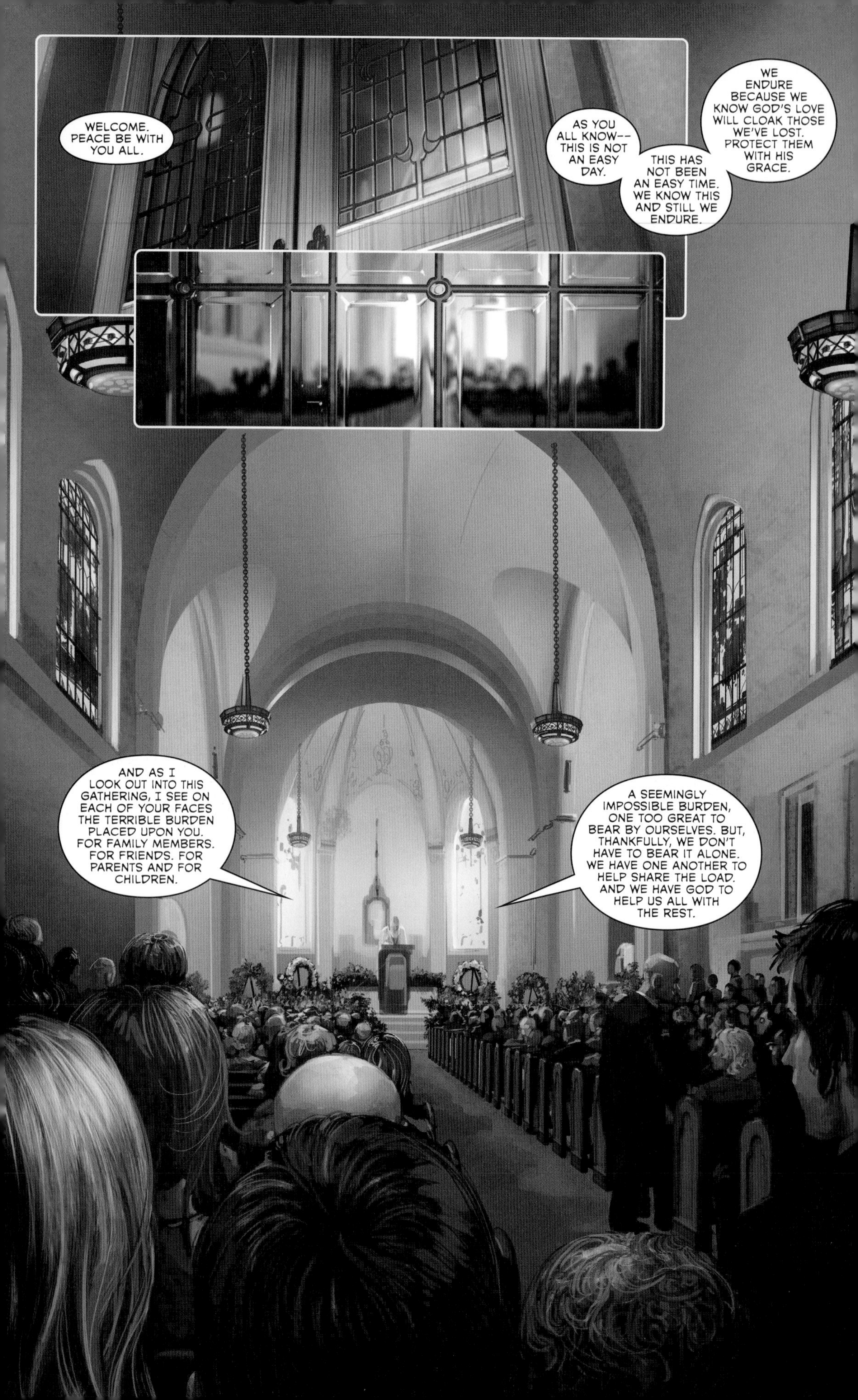
WELCOME. PEACE BE WITH YOU ALL.
AS YOU ALL KNOW-- THIS IS NOT AN EASY DAY.
THIS HAS NOT BEEN AN EASY TIME. WE KNOW THIS AND STILL WE ENDURE.
WE ENDURE BECAUSE WE KNOW GOD'S LOVE WILL CLOAK THOSE WE'VE LOST. PROTECT THEM WITH HIS GRACE.
AND AS I LOOK OUT INTO THIS GATHERING, I SEE ON EACH OF YOUR FACES THE TERRIBLE BURDEN PLACED UPON YOU. FOR FAMILY MEMBERS. FOR FRIENDS. FOR PARENTS AND FOR CHILDREN.
A SEEMINGLY IMPOSSIBLE BURDEN, ONE TOO GREAT TO BEAR BY OURSELVES. BUT, THANKFULLY, WE DON'T HAVE TO BEAR IT ALONE. WE HAVE ONE ANOTHER TO HELP SHARE THE LOAD. AND WE HAVE GOD TO HELP US ALL WITH THE REST.

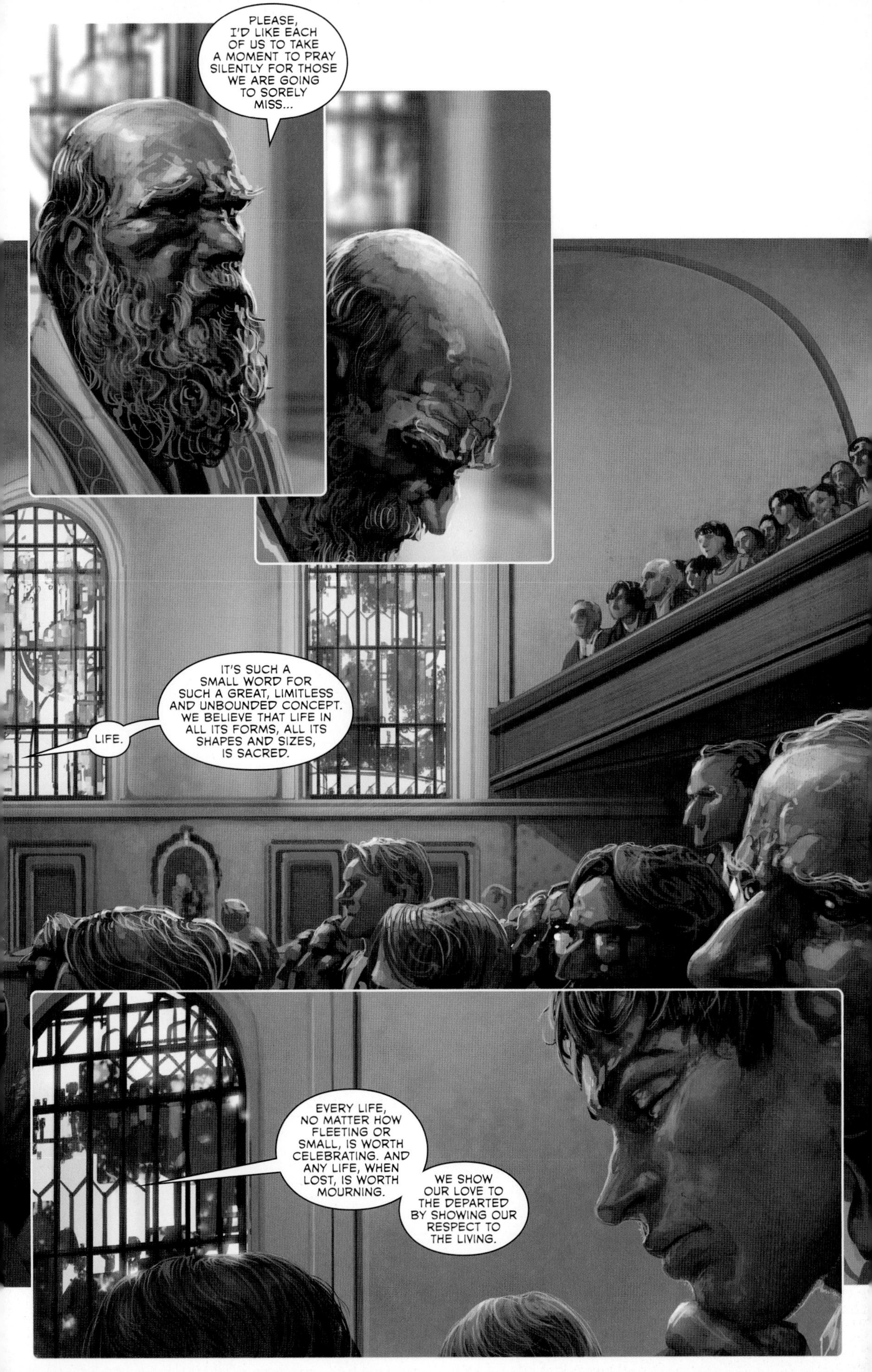
PLEASE, I'D LIKE EACH OF US TO TAKE A MOMENT TO PRAY SILENTLY FOR THOSE WE ARE GOING TO SORELY MISS...
LIFE.
IT'S SUCH A SMALL WORD FOR SUCH A GREAT, LIMITLESS AND UNBOUNDED CONCEPT. WE BELIEVE THAT LIFE IN ALL ITS FORMS, ALL ITS SHAPES AND SIZES, IS SACRED.
EVERY LIFE, NO MATTER HOW FLEETING OR SMALL, IS WORTH CELEBRATING. AND ANY LIFE, WHEN LOST, IS WORTH MOURNING.
WE SHOW OUR LOVE TO THE DEPARTED BY SHOWING OUR RESPECT TO THE LIVING.

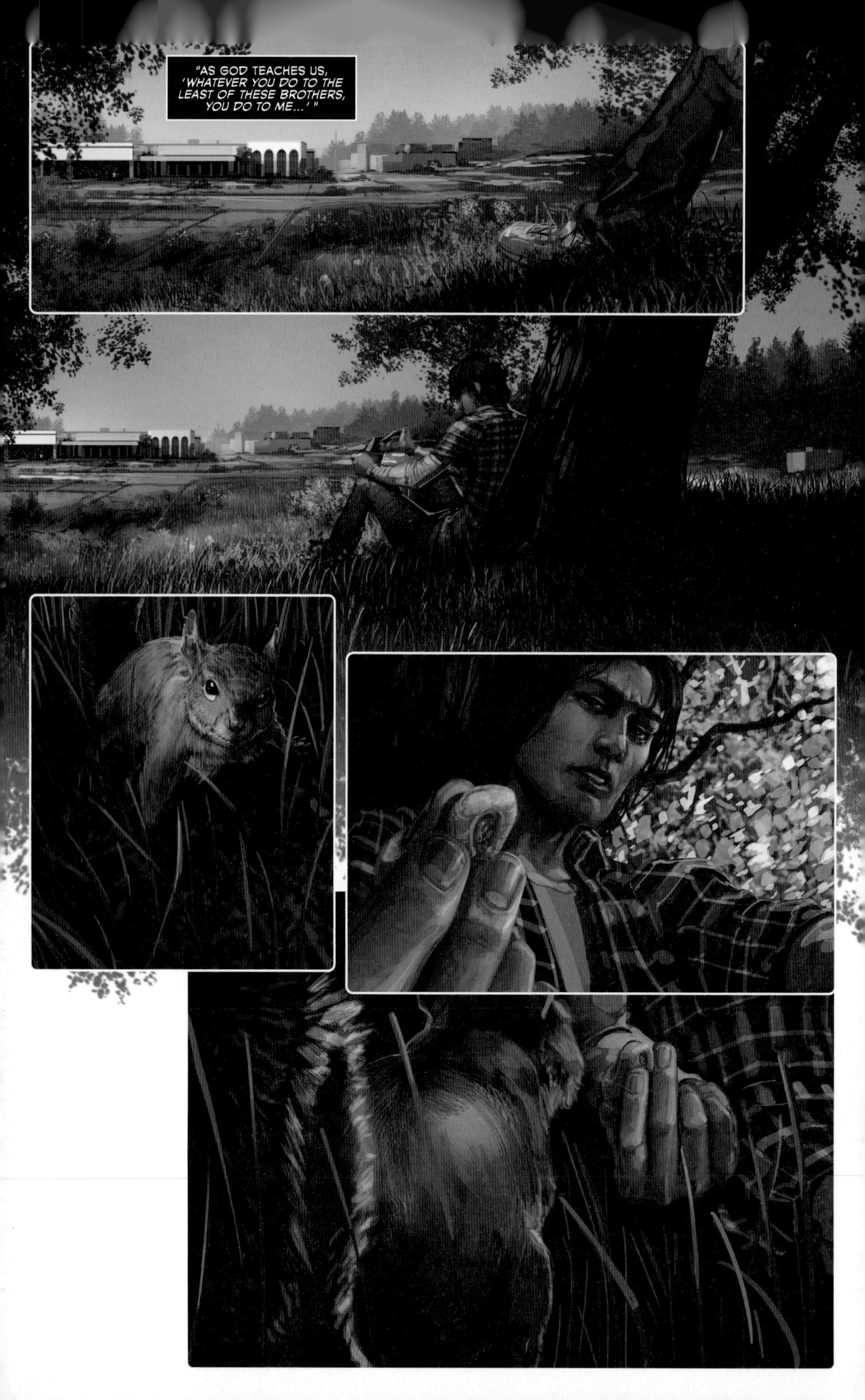
"AS GOD TEACHES US, 'WHATEVER YOU DO TO THE LEAST OF THESE BROTHERS, YOU DO TO ME...' "

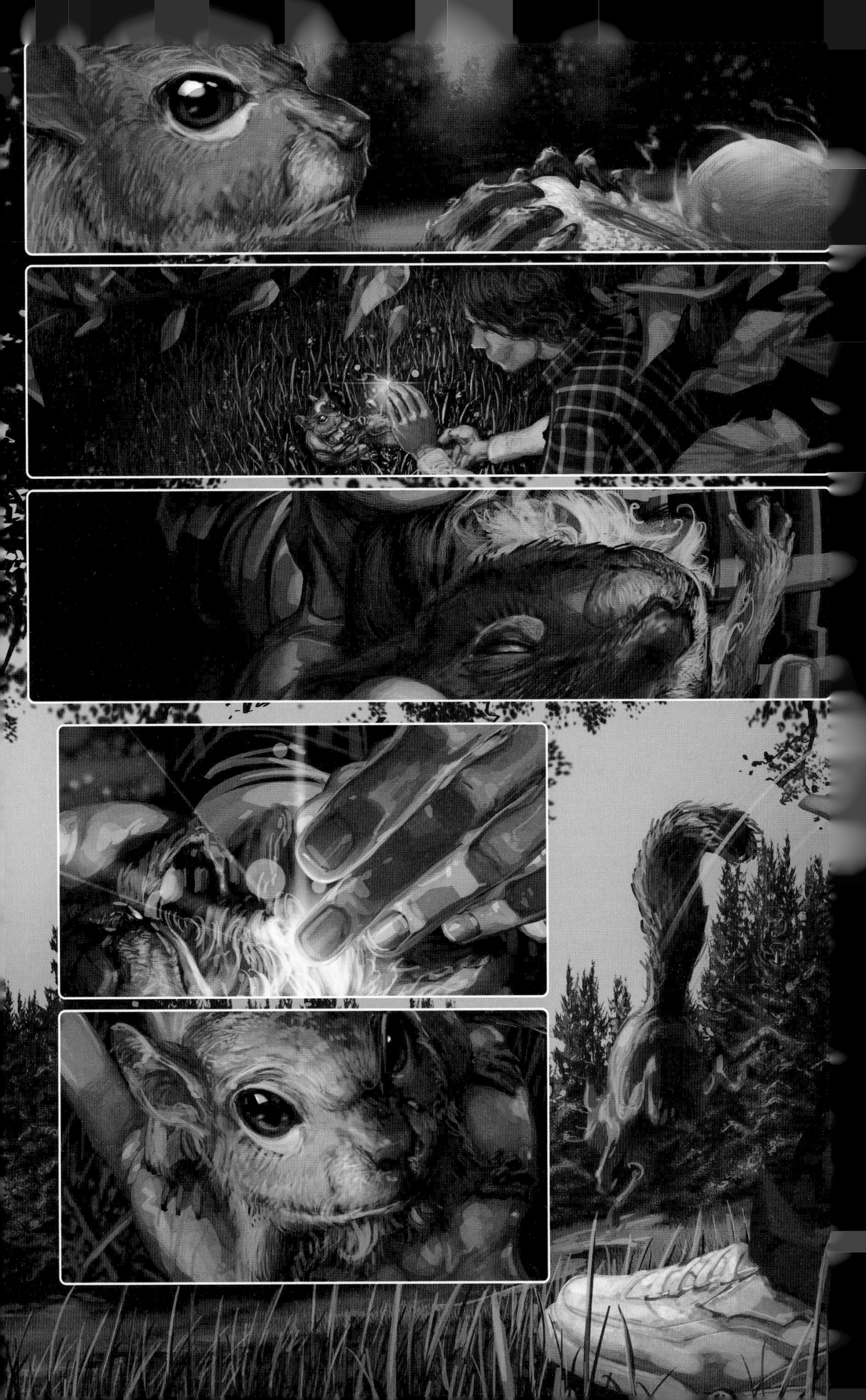

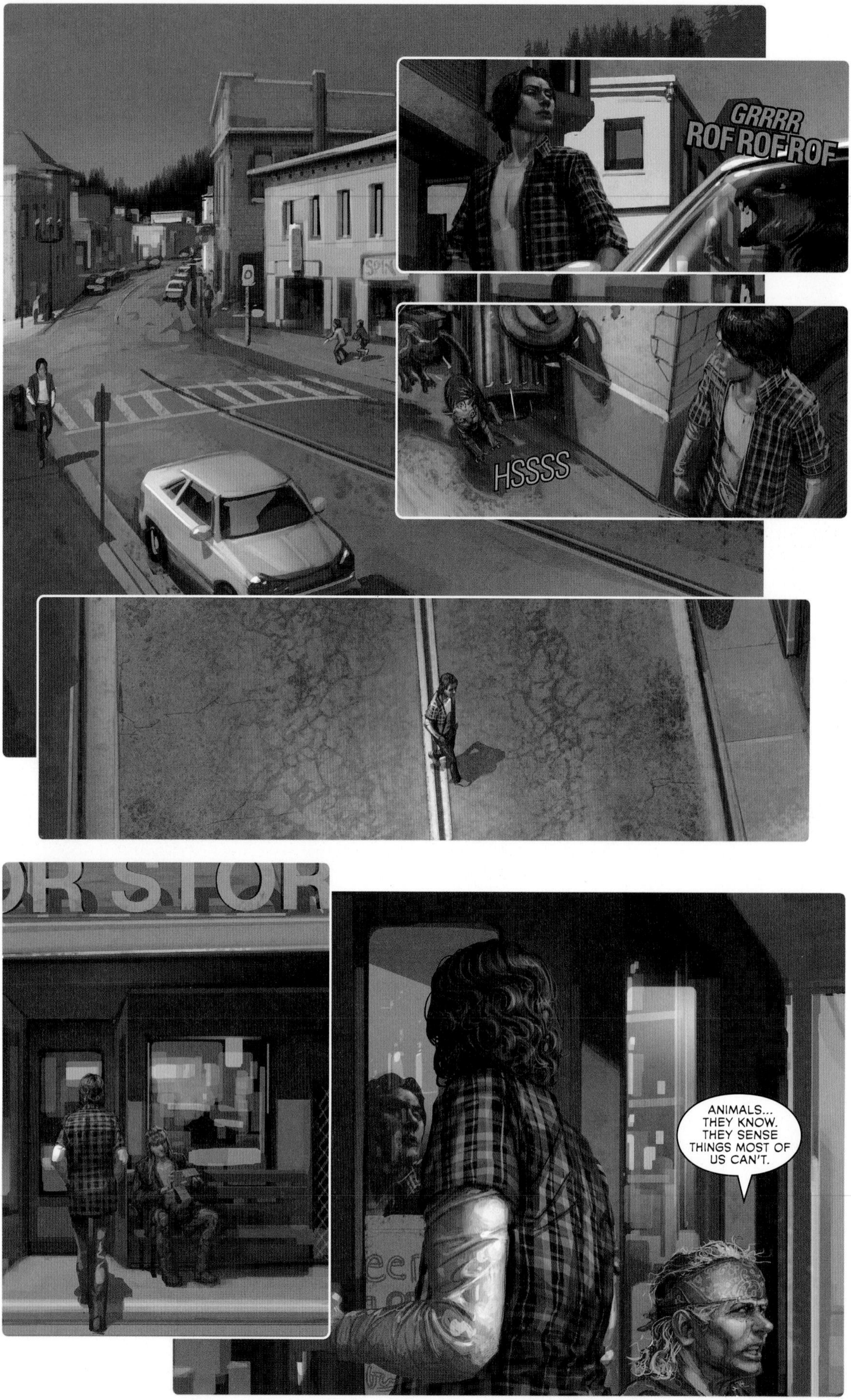
GRRRR
ROF ROF ROF
HSSSS
OR STOR
ANIMALS... THEY KNOW. THEY SENSE THINGS MOST OF US CAN'T.

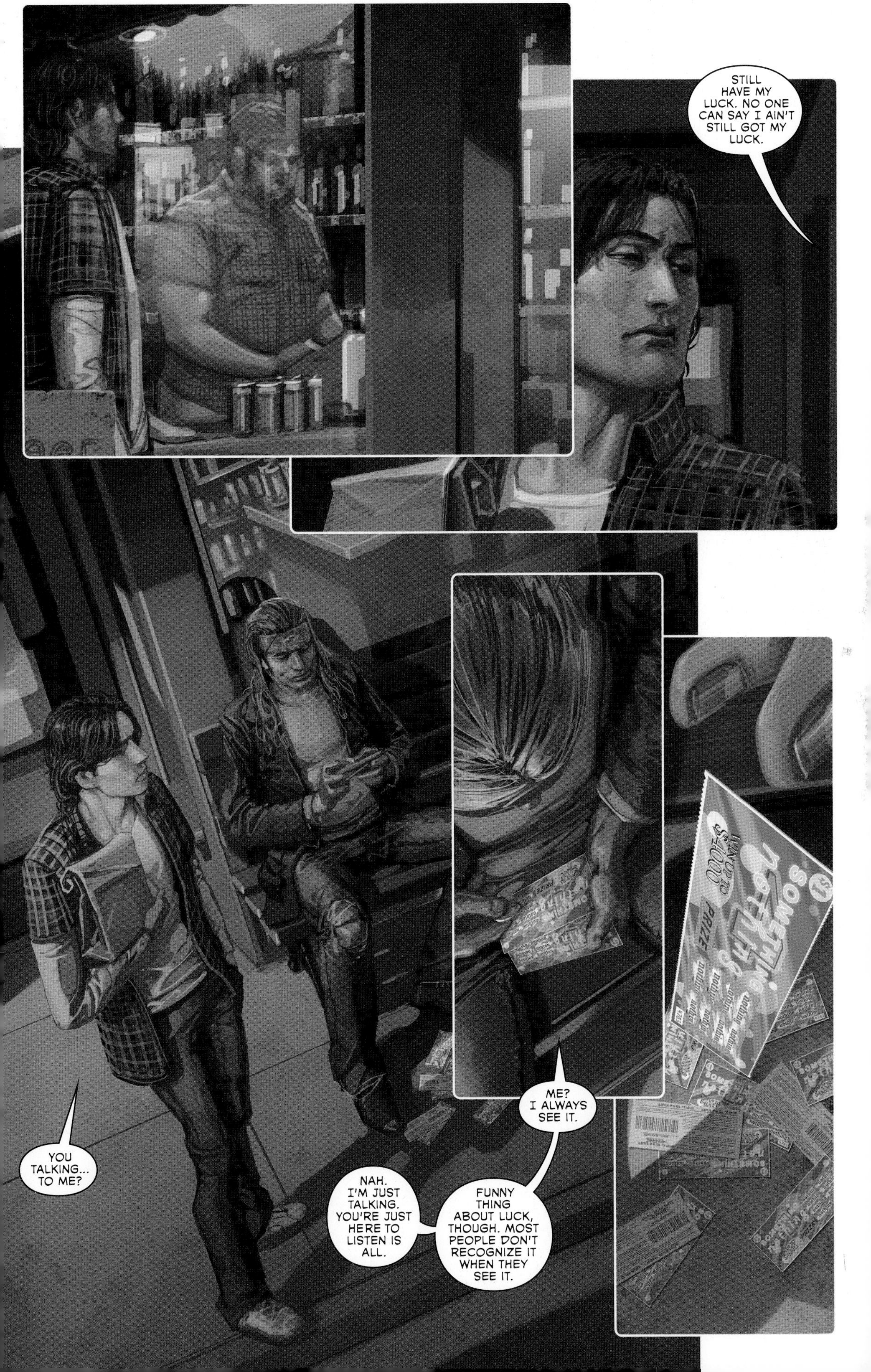
STILL HAVE MY LUCK. NO ONE CAN SAY I AIN'T STILL GOT MY LUCK.
YOU TALKING... TO ME?
NAH. I'M JUST TALKING. YOU'RE JUST HERE TO LISTEN IS ALL.
FUNNY THING ABOUT LUCK, THOUGH. MOST PEOPLE DON'T RECOGNIZE IT WHEN THEY SEE IT.
ME? I ALWAYS SEE IT.

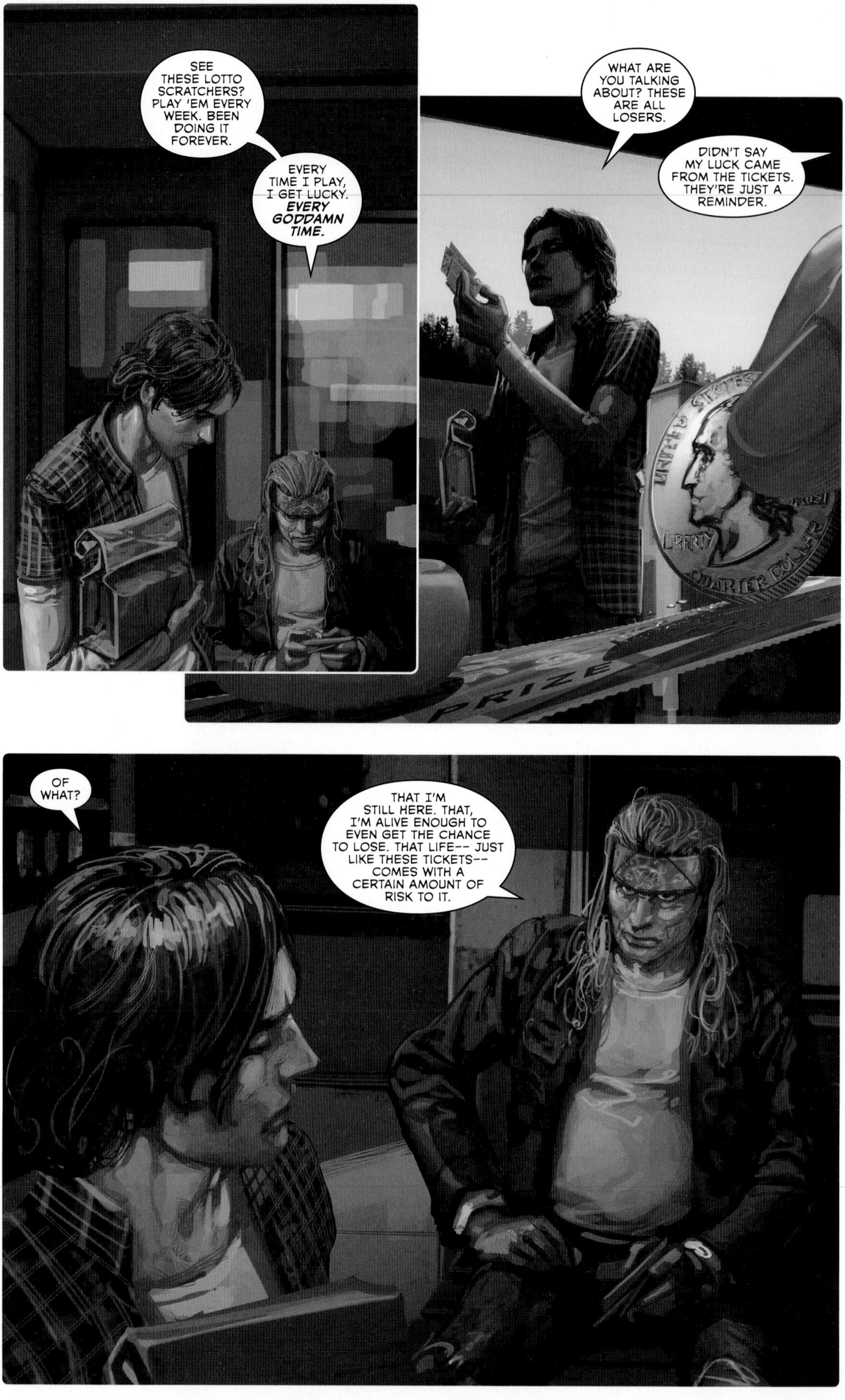

SEE THESE LOTTO SCRATCHERS? PLAY 'EM EVERY WEEK. BEEN DOING IT FOREVER.
EVERY TIME I PLAY, I GET LUCKY. *EVERY GODDAMN TIME.*
WHAT ARE YOU TALKING ABOUT? THESE ARE ALL LOSERS.
DIDN'T SAY MY LUCK CAME FROM THE TICKETS. THEY'RE JUST A REMINDER.
PRIZE
OF WHAT?
THAT I'M STILL HERE. THAT, I'M ALIVE ENOUGH TO EVEN GET THE CHANCE TO LOSE. THAT LIFE-- JUST LIKE THESE TICKETS-- COMES WITH A CERTAIN AMOUNT OF RISK TO IT.

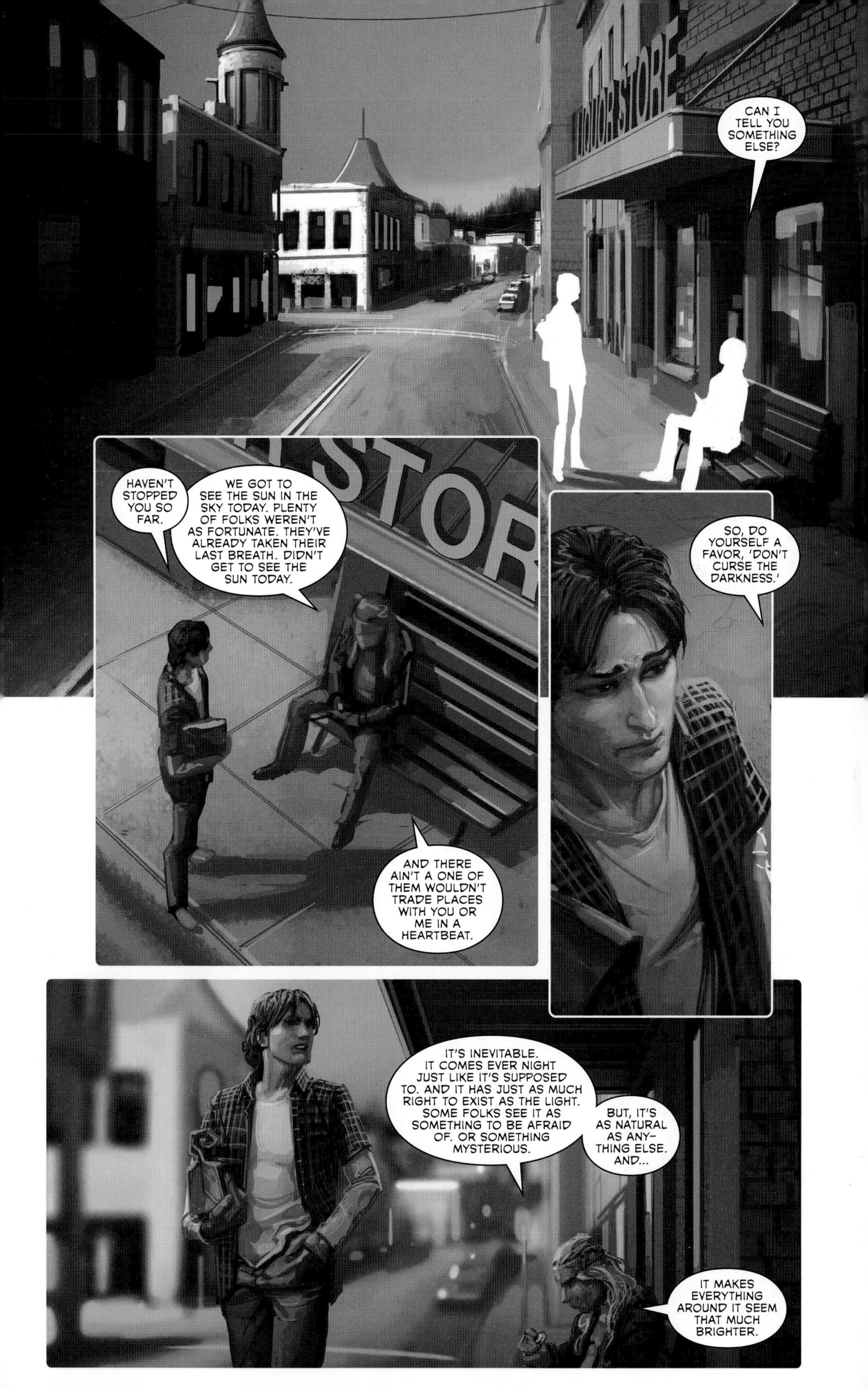
LIQUOR STORE
CAN I TELL YOU SOMETHING ELSE?
STOR
HAVEN'T STOPPED YOU SO FAR.
WE GOT TO SEE THE SUN IN THE SKY TODAY. PLENTY OF FOLKS WEREN'T AS FORTUNATE. THEY'VE ALREADY TAKEN THEIR LAST BREATH. DIDN'T GET TO SEE THE SUN TODAY.
AND THERE AIN'T A ONE OF THEM WOULDN'T TRADE PLACES WITH YOU OR ME IN A HEARTBEAT.
SO, DO YOURSELF A FAVOR, 'DON'T CURSE THE DARKNESS.'
IT'S INEVITABLE. IT COMES EVER NIGHT JUST LIKE IT'S SUPPOSED TO. AND IT HAS JUST AS MUCH RIGHT TO EXIST AS THE LIGHT. SOME FOLKS SEE IT AS SOMETHING TO BE AFRAID OF. OR SOMETHING MYSTERIOUS.
BUT, IT'S AS NATURAL AS ANY-THING ELSE. AND...
IT MAKES EVERYTHING AROUND IT SEEM THAT MUCH BRIGHTER.

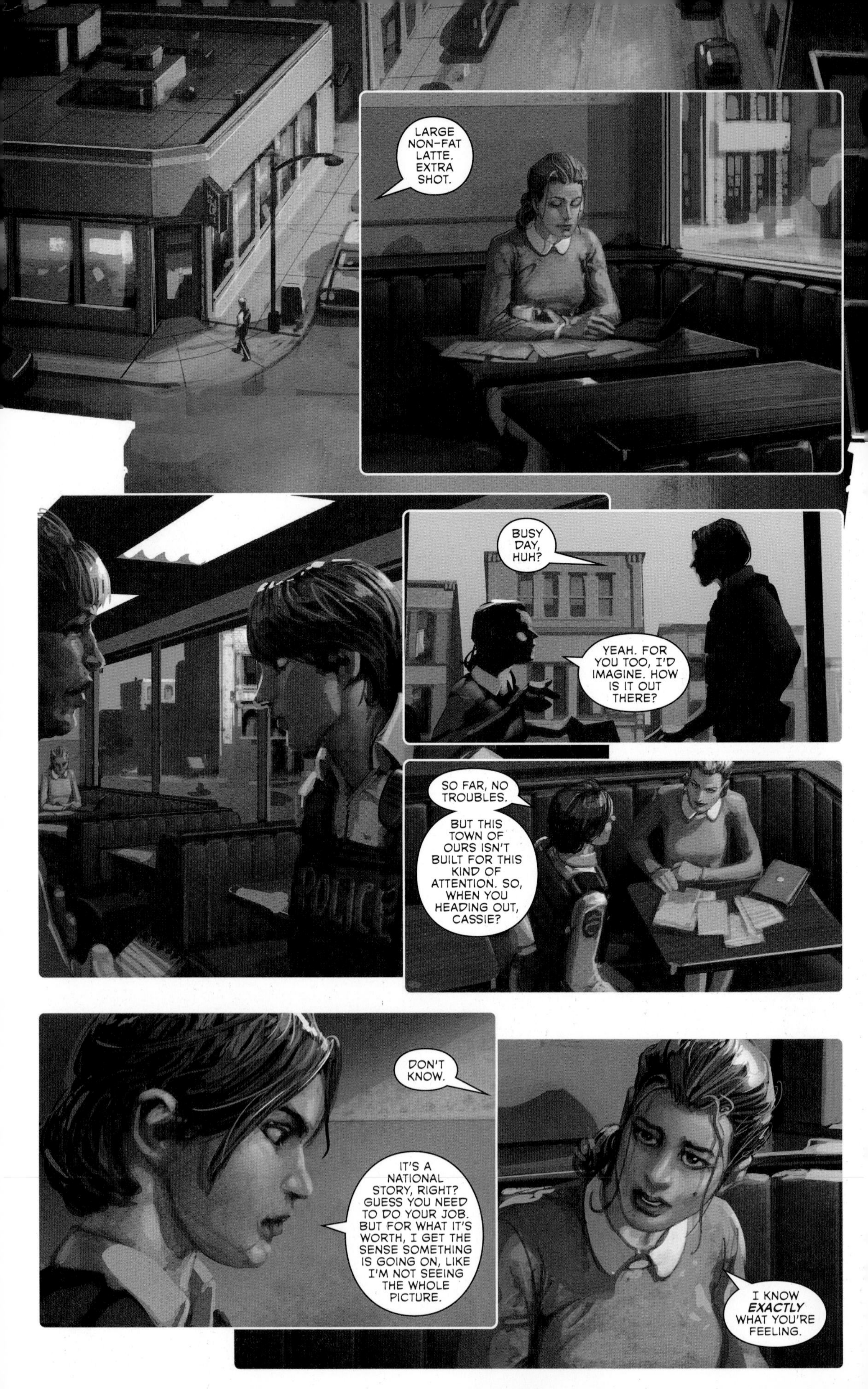
LARGE NON-FAT LATTE. EXTRA SHOT.
BUSY DAY, HUH?
YEAH. FOR YOU TOO, I'D IMAGINE. HOW IS IT OUT THERE?
SO FAR, NO TROUBLES.
BUT THIS TOWN OF OURS ISN'T BUILT FOR THIS KIND OF ATTENTION. SO, WHEN YOU HEADING OUT, CASSIE?
DON'T KNOW.
IT'S A NATIONAL STORY, RIGHT? GUESS YOU NEED TO DO YOUR JOB. BUT FOR WHAT IT'S WORTH, I GET THE SENSE SOMETHING IS GOING ON, LIKE I'M NOT SEEING THE WHOLE PICTURE.
I KNOW *EXACTLY* WHAT YOU'RE FEELING.
POLICE

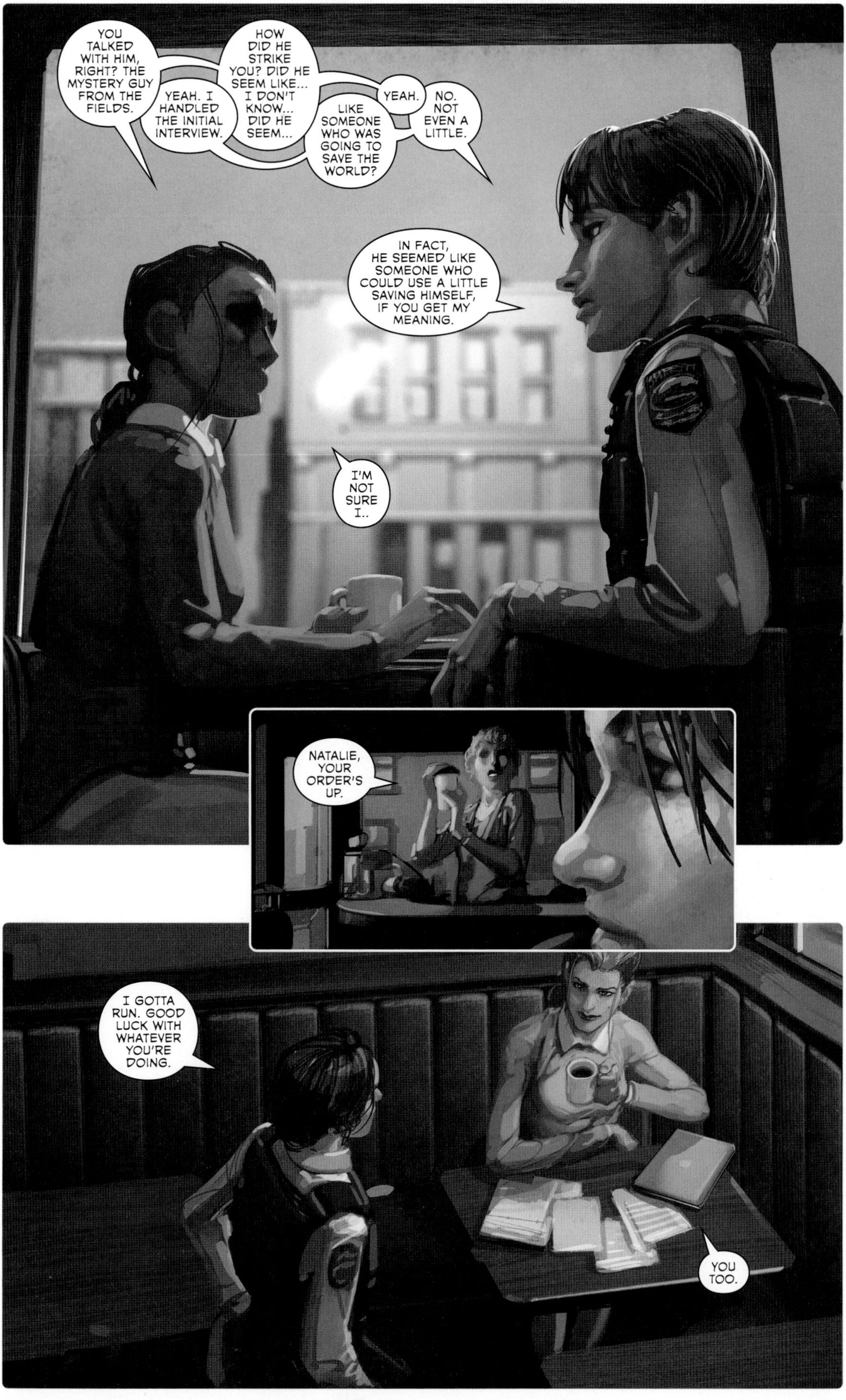
YOU TALKED WITH HIM, RIGHT? THE MYSTERY GUY FROM THE FIELDS.
YEAH. I HANDLED THE INITIAL INTERVIEW.
HOW DID HE STRIKE YOU? DID HE SEEM LIKE... I DON'T KNOW... DID HE SEEM...
LIKE SOMEONE WHO WAS GOING TO SAVE THE WORLD?
YEAH.
NO. NOT EVEN A LITTLE.
IN FACT, HE SEEMED LIKE SOMEONE WHO COULD USE A LITTLE SAVING HIMSELF, IF YOU GET MY MEANING.
I'M NOT SURE I..
NATALIE, YOUR ORDER'S UP.
I GOTTA RUN. GOOD LUCK WITH WHATEVER YOU'RE DOING.
YOU TOO.

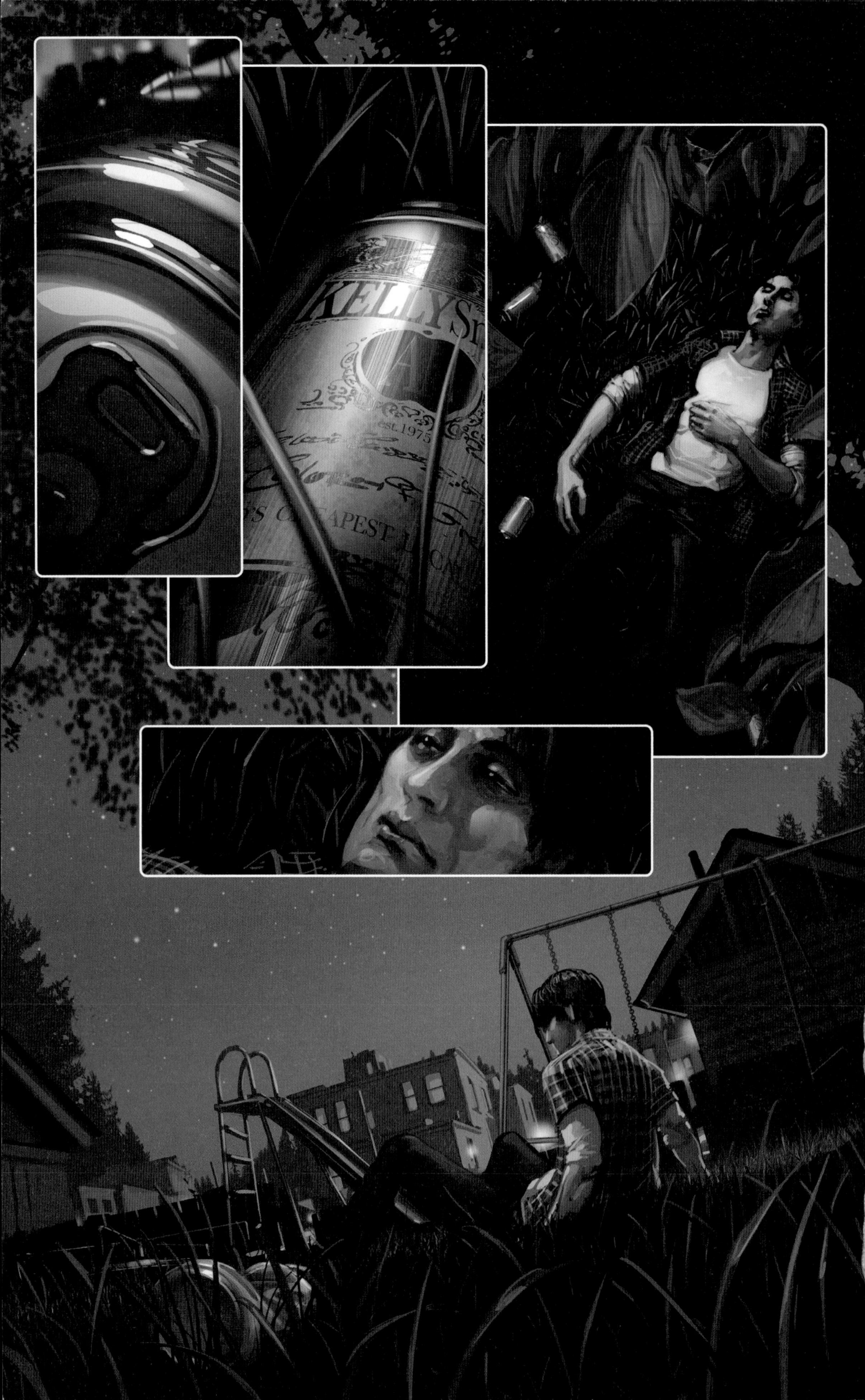
est.1975

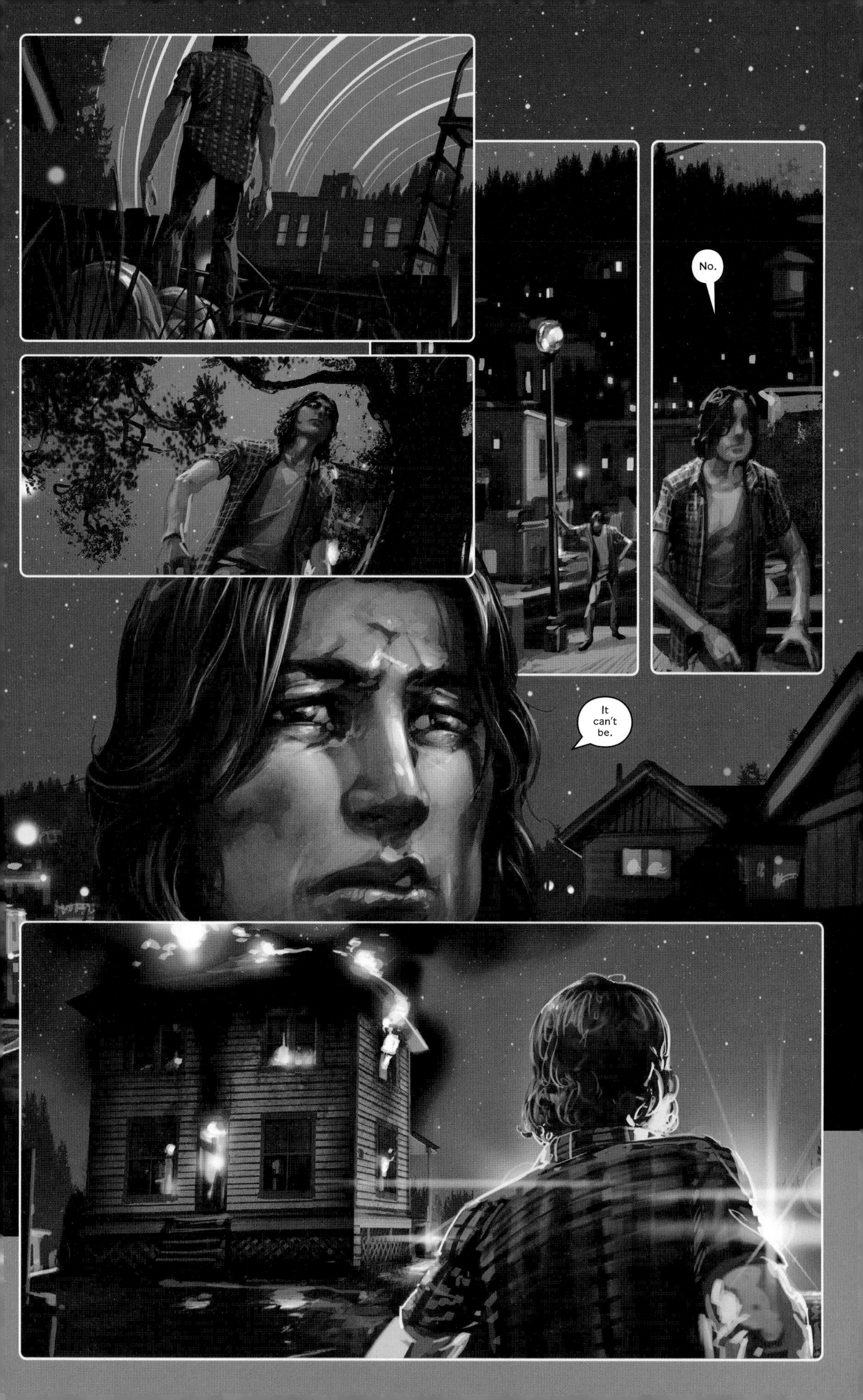
No.
It can't be.

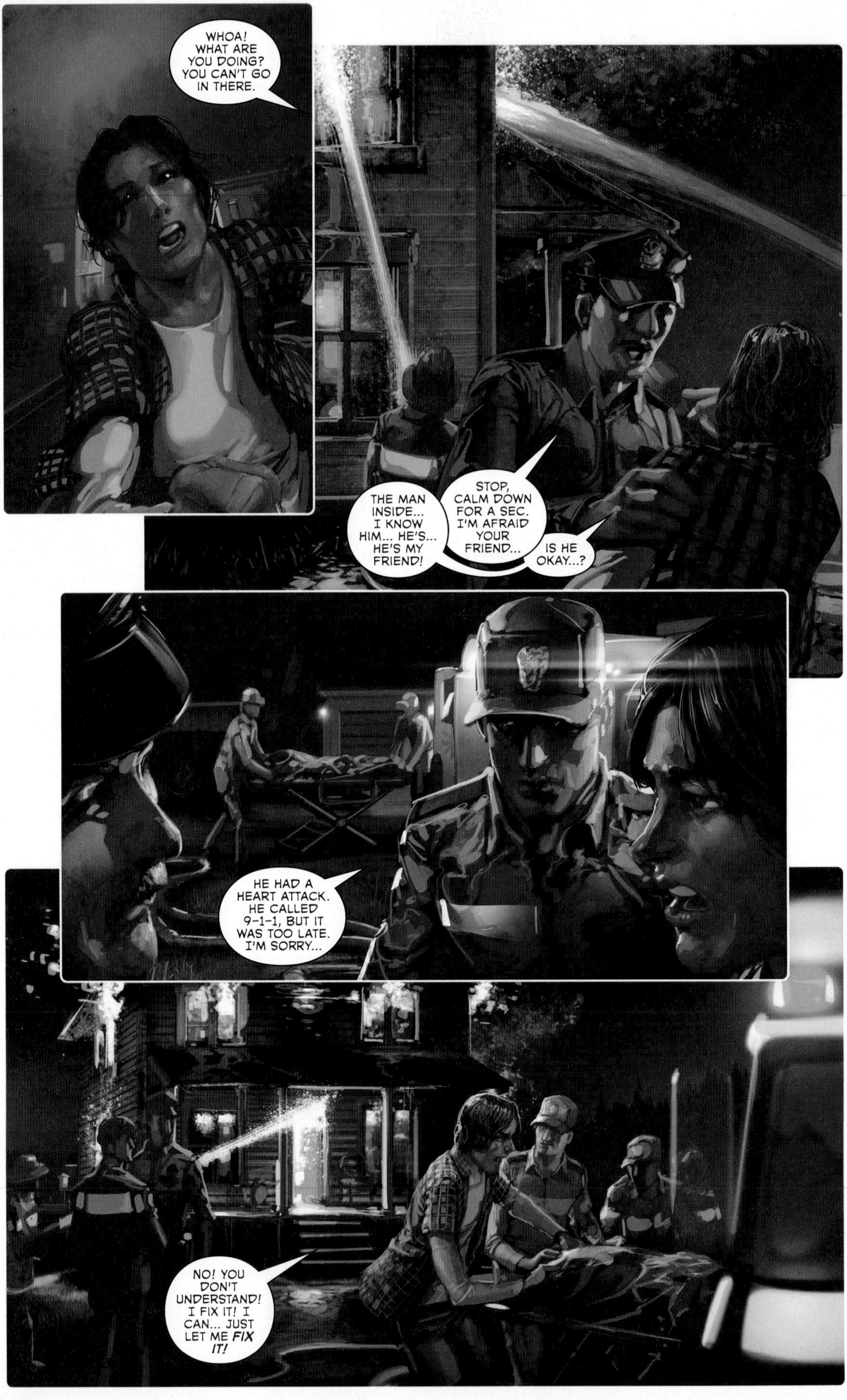
WHOA! WHAT ARE YOU DOING? YOU CAN'T GO IN THERE.
THE MAN INSIDE... I KNOW HIM... HE'S... HE'S MY FRIEND!
STOP, CALM DOWN FOR A SEC. I'M AFRAID YOUR FRIEND...
IS HE OKAY...?
HE HAD A HEART ATTACK. HE CALLED 9-1-1, BUT IT WAS TOO LATE. I'M SORRY...
NO! YOU DON'T UNDERSTAND! I FIX IT! I CAN... JUST LET ME *FIX IT!*

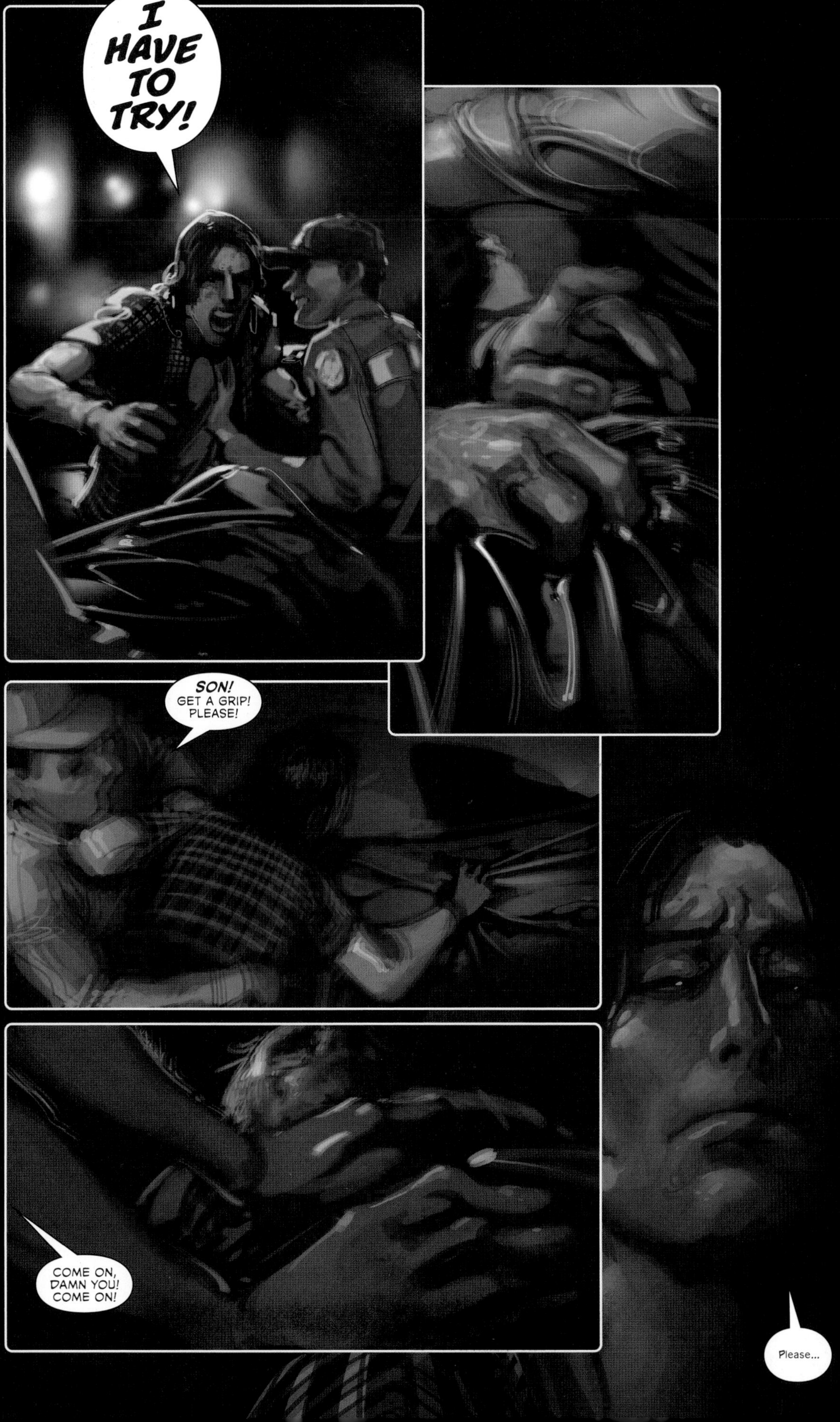
I HAVE TO TRY!
SON! GET A GRIP! PLEASE!
COME ON, DAMN YOU! COME ON!
Please...

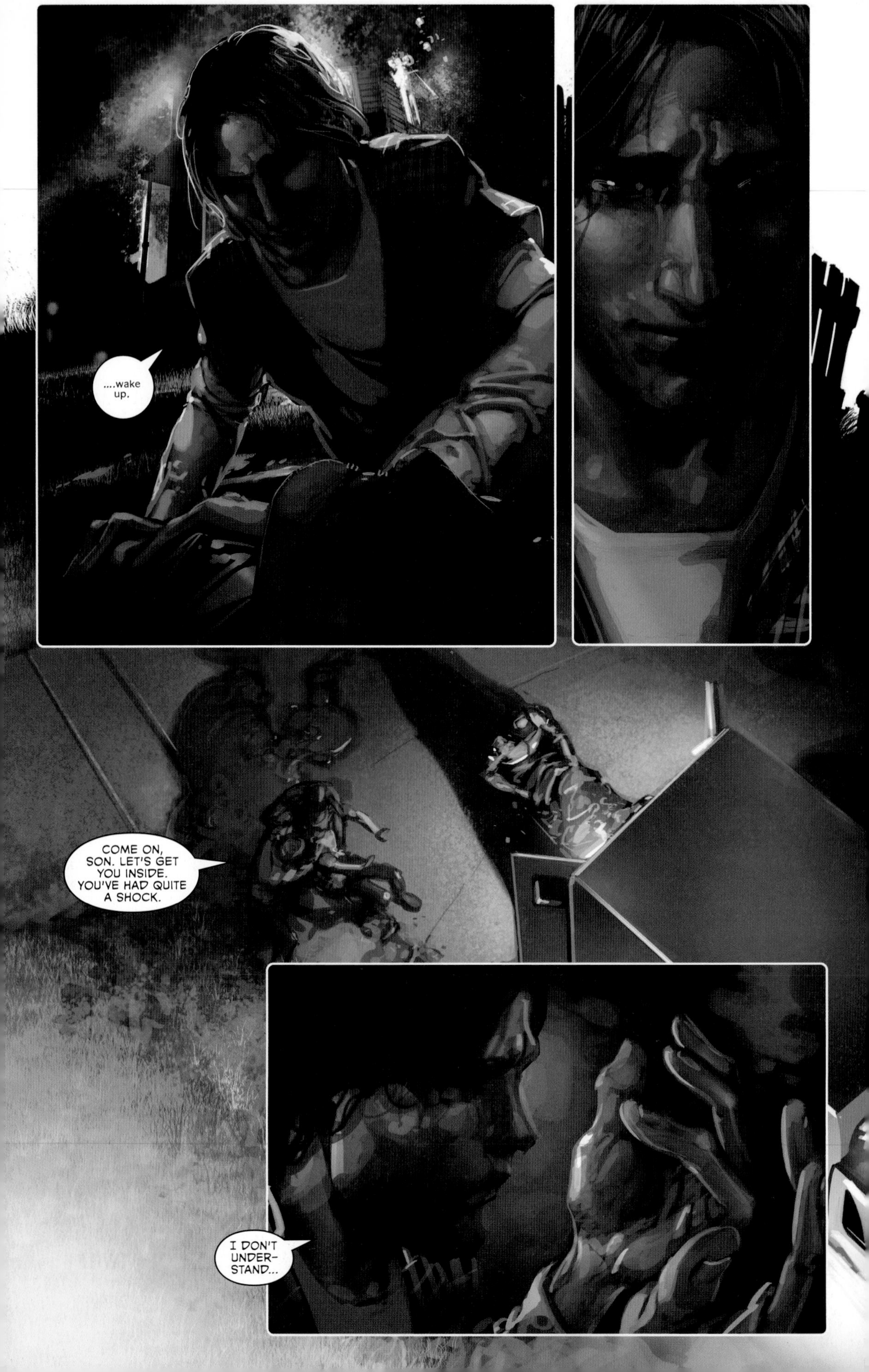
....wake up.
COME ON, SON. LET'S GET YOU INSIDE. YOU'VE HAD QUITE A SHOCK.
I DON'T UNDER-STAND...

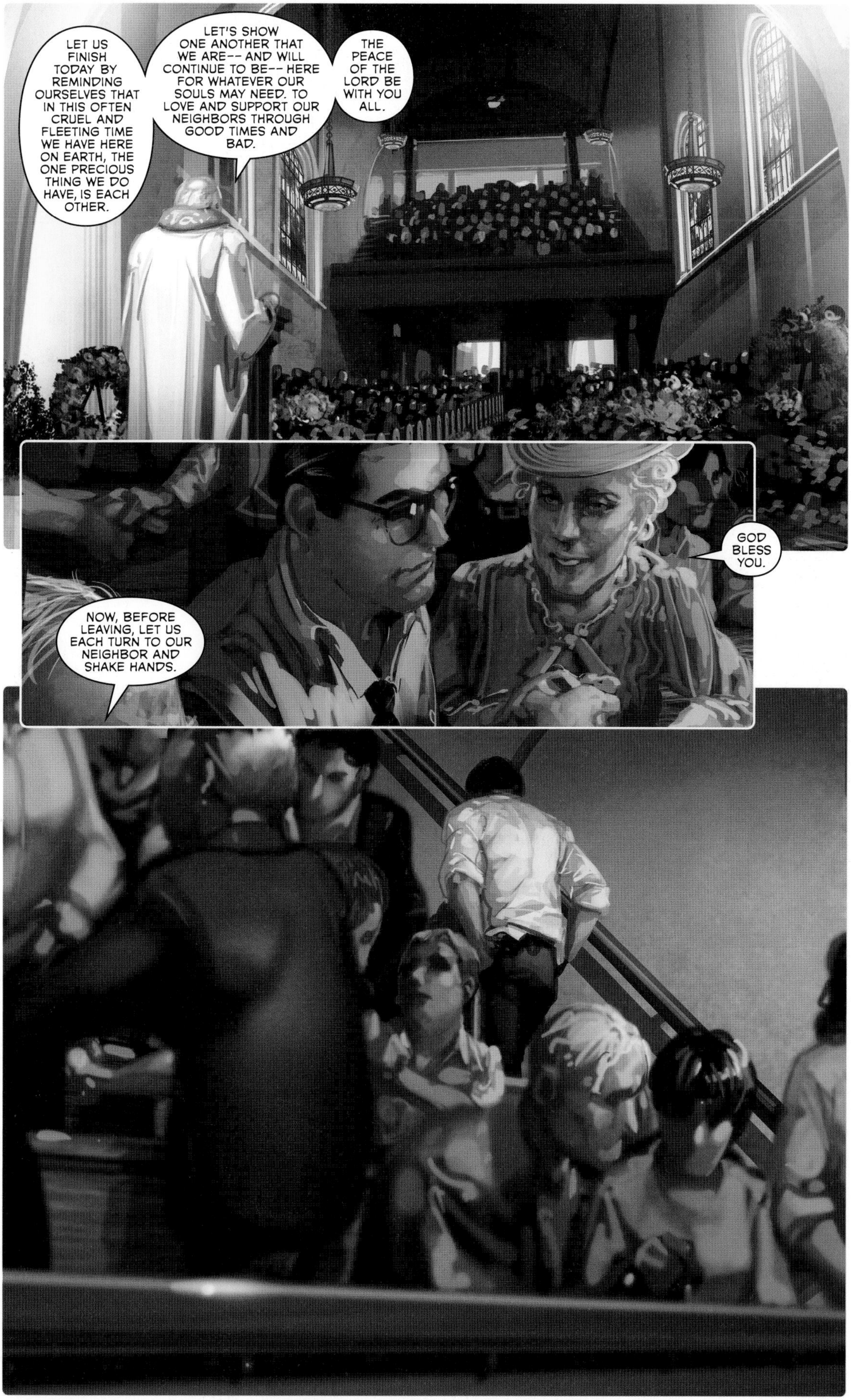
LET US FINISH TODAY BY REMINDING OURSELVES THAT IN THIS OFTEN CRUEL AND FLEETING TIME WE HAVE HERE ON EARTH, THE ONE PRECIOUS THING WE DO HAVE, IS EACH OTHER.
LET'S SHOW ONE ANOTHER THAT WE ARE-- AND WILL CONTINUE TO BE-- HERE FOR WHATEVER OUR SOULS MAY NEED. TO LOVE AND SUPPORT OUR NEIGHBORS THROUGH GOOD TIMES AND BAD.
THE PEACE OF THE LORD BE WITH YOU ALL.
NOW, BEFORE LEAVING, LET US EACH TURN TO OUR NEIGHBOR AND SHAKE HANDS.
GOD BLESS YOU.

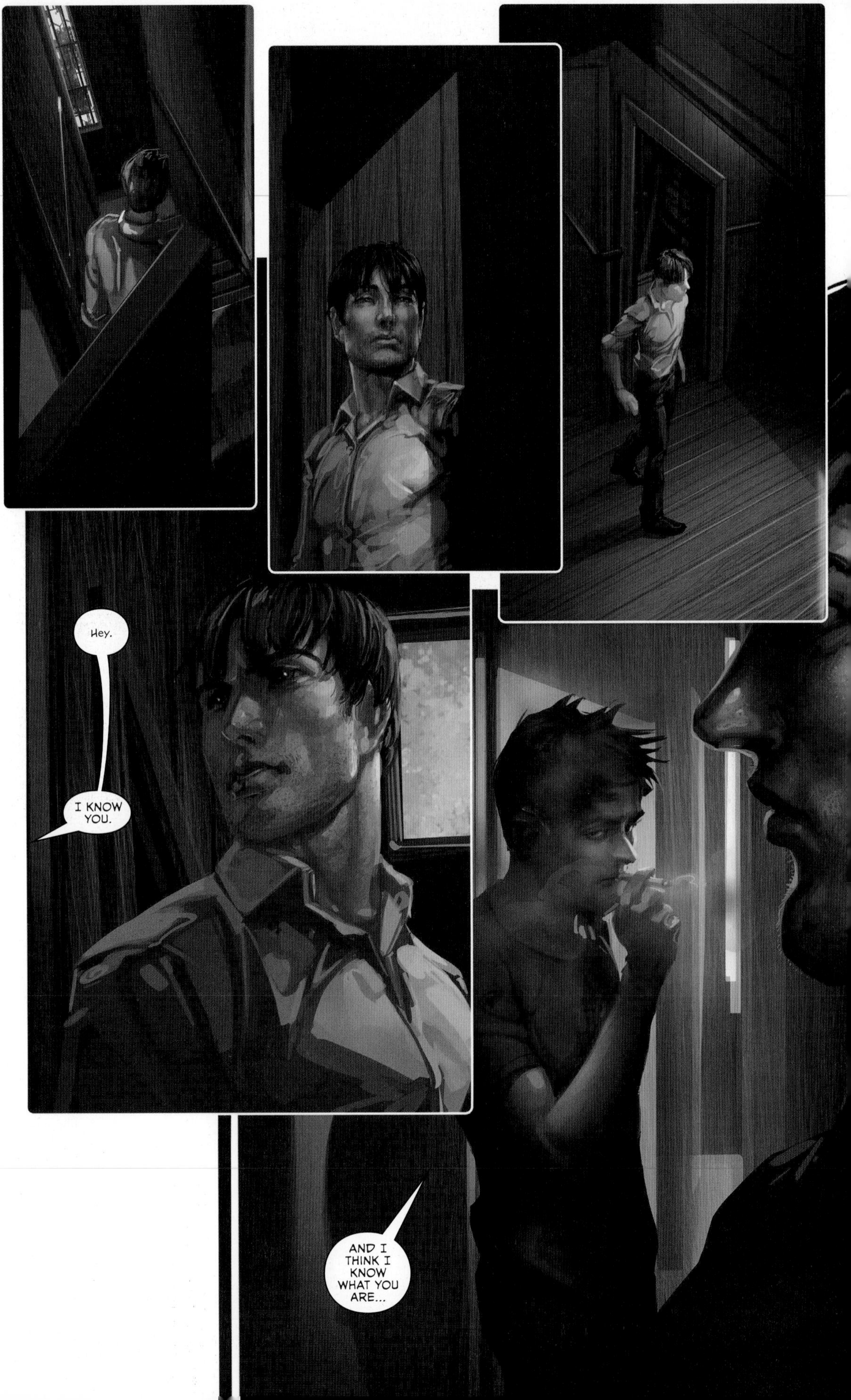
Hey.
I KNOW YOU.
AND I THINK I KNOW WHAT YOU ARE...

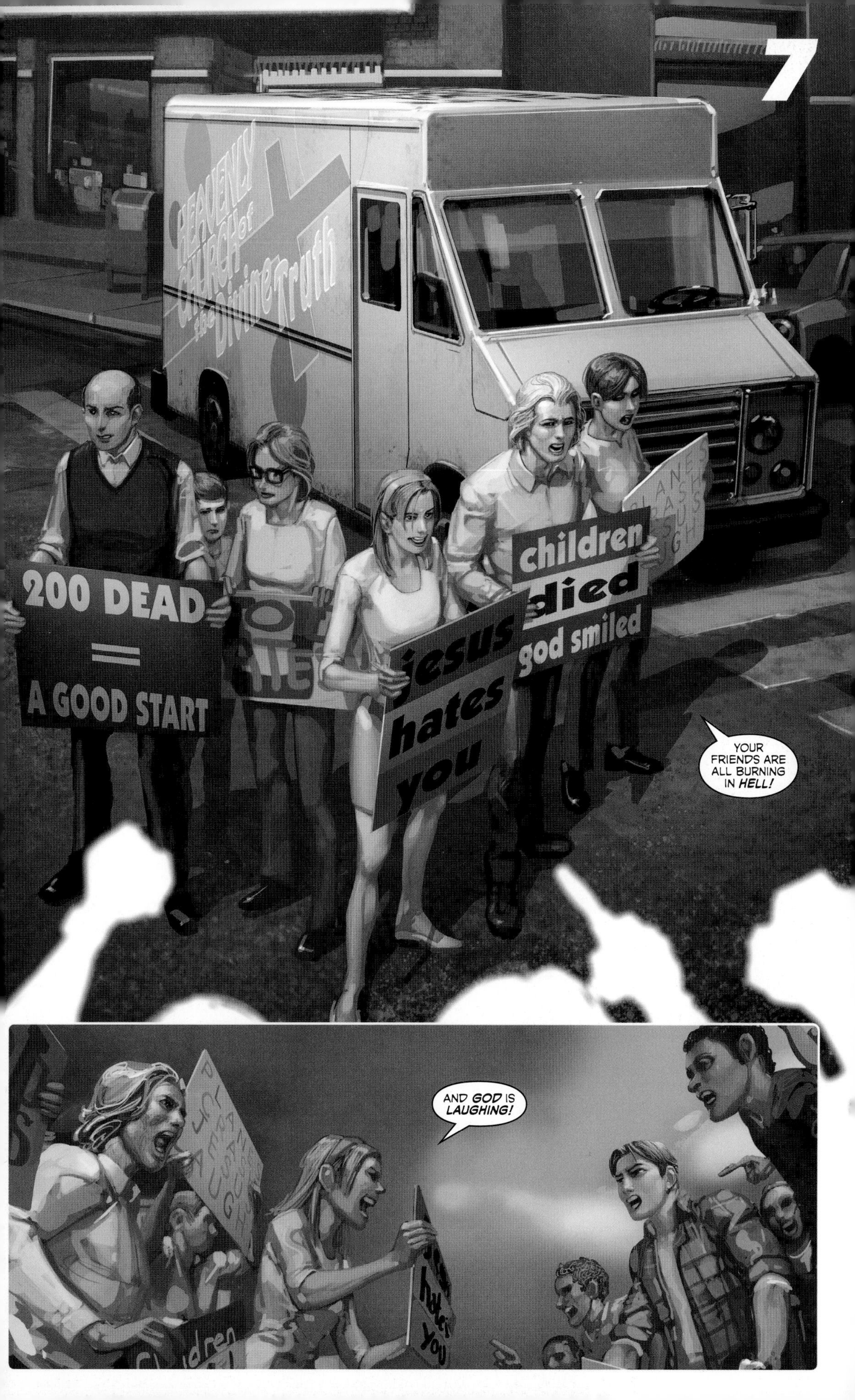
7
HEAVENLY CHURCH of the Divine Truth
200 DEAD = A GOOD START
jesus hates you
children died god smiled
YOUR FRIENDS ARE ALL BURNING IN *HELL!*
AND *GOD* IS *LAUGHING!*

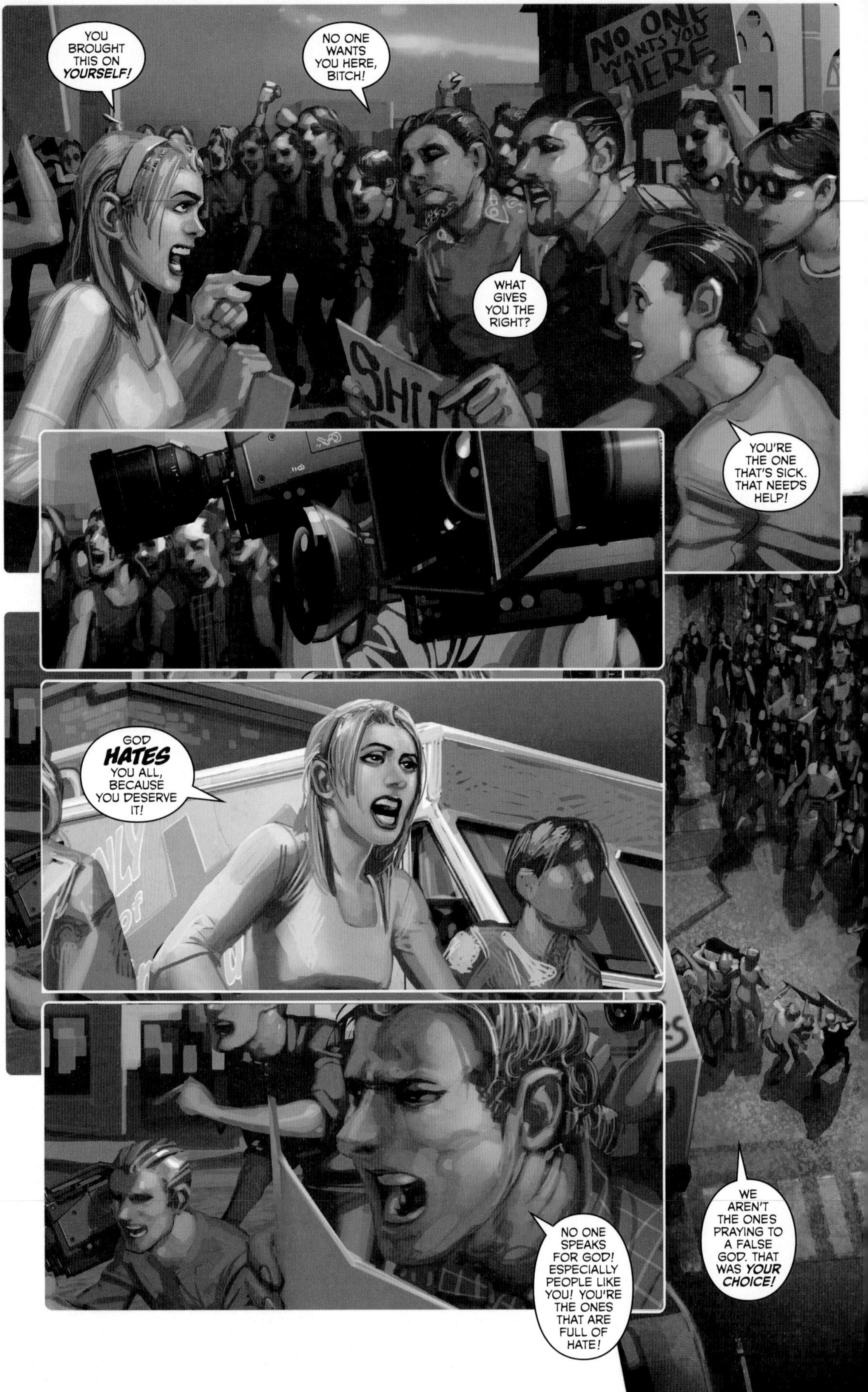
NO ONE WANTS YOU HERE
YOU BROUGHT THIS ON *YOURSELF!*
NO ONE WANTS YOU HERE, BITCH!
WHAT GIVES YOU THE RIGHT?
YOU'RE THE ONE THAT'S SICK. THAT NEEDS HELP!
GOD **HATES** YOU ALL, BECAUSE YOU DESERVE IT!
NO ONE SPEAKS FOR GOD! ESPECIALLY PEOPLE LIKE YOU! YOU'RE THE ONES THAT ARE FULL OF HATE!
WE AREN'T THE ONES PRAYING TO A FALSE GOD. THAT WAS ***YOUR CHOICE!***

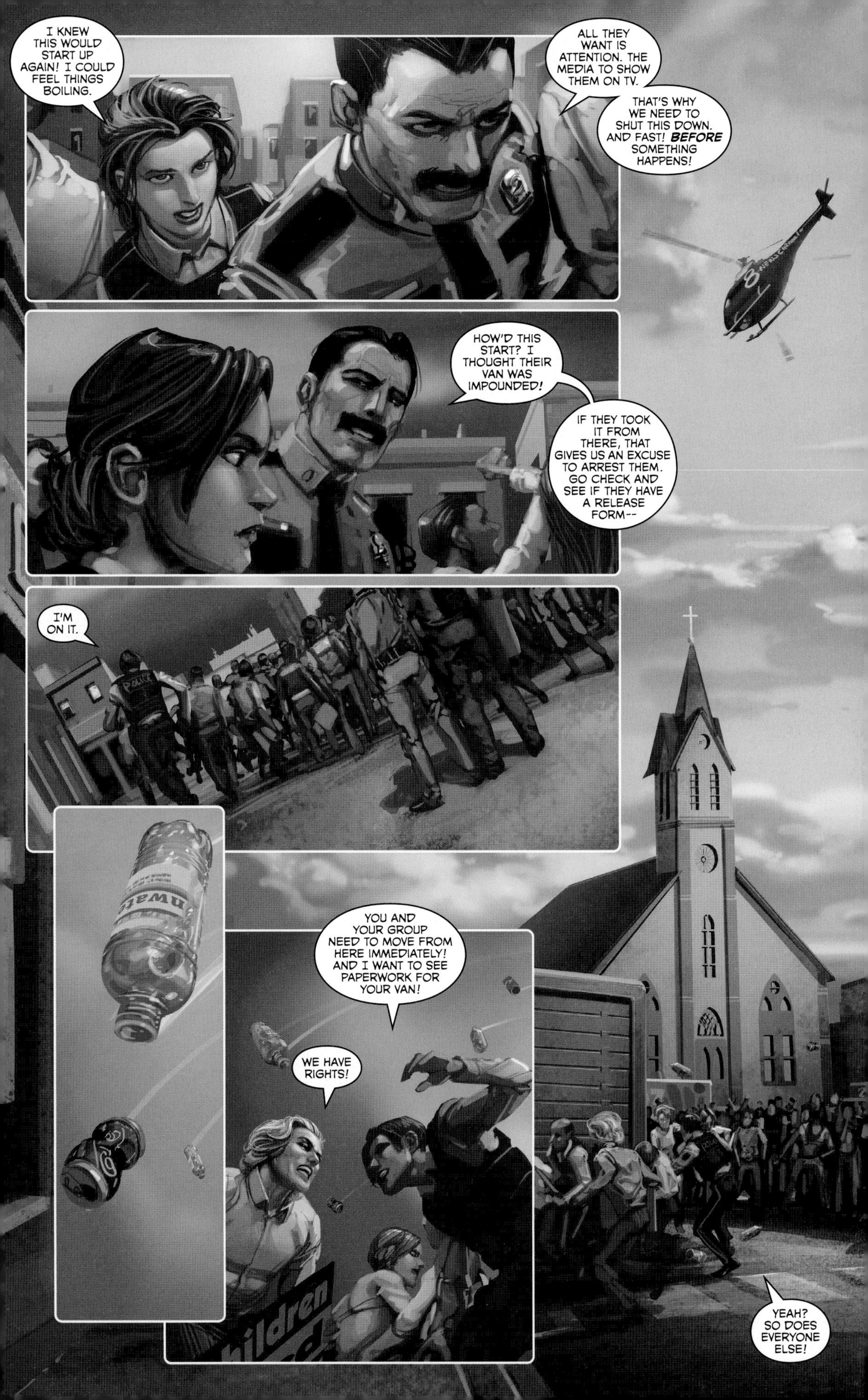
I KNEW THIS WOULD START UP AGAIN! I COULD FEEL THINGS BOILING.
ALL THEY WANT IS ATTENTION. THE MEDIA TO SHOW THEM ON TV.
THAT'S WHY WE NEED TO SHUT THIS DOWN. AND FAST! ***BEFORE*** SOMETHING HAPPENS!
HOW'D THIS START? I THOUGHT THEIR VAN WAS IMPOUNDED!
IF THEY TOOK IT FROM THERE, THAT GIVES US AN EXCUSE TO ARREST THEM. GO CHECK AND SEE IF THEY HAVE A RELEASE FORM--
I'M ON IT.
POLICE
YOU AND YOUR GROUP NEED TO MOVE FROM HERE IMMEDIATELY! AND I WANT TO SEE PAPERWORK FOR YOUR VAN!
WE HAVE RIGHTS!
YEAH? SO DOES EVERYONE ELSE!

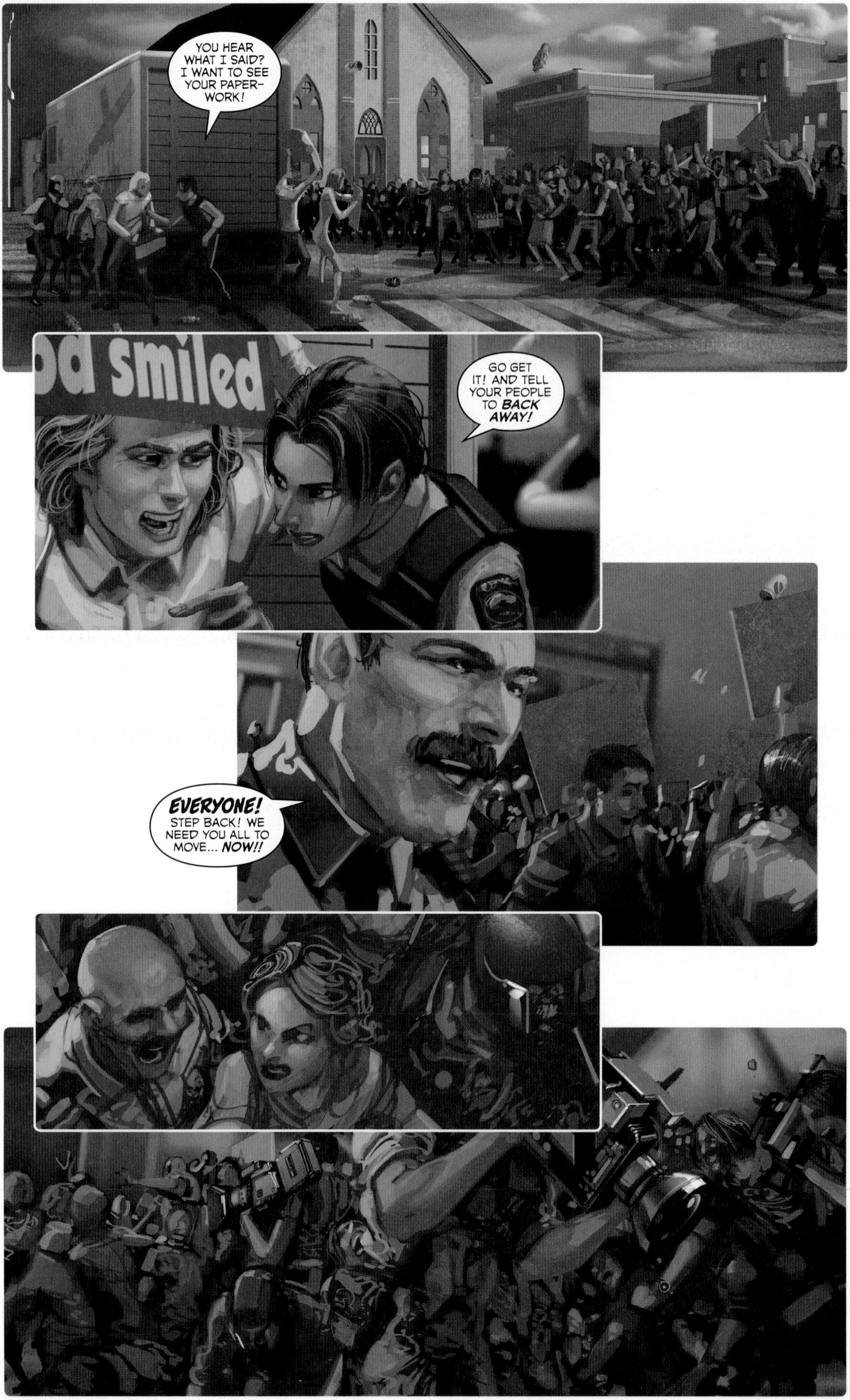
YOU HEAR WHAT I SAID? I WANT TO SEE YOUR PAPER-WORK!
od smiled
GO GET IT! AND TELL YOUR PEOPLE TO BACK AWAY!
EVERYONE! STEP BACK! WE NEED YOU ALL TO MOVE... NOW!!

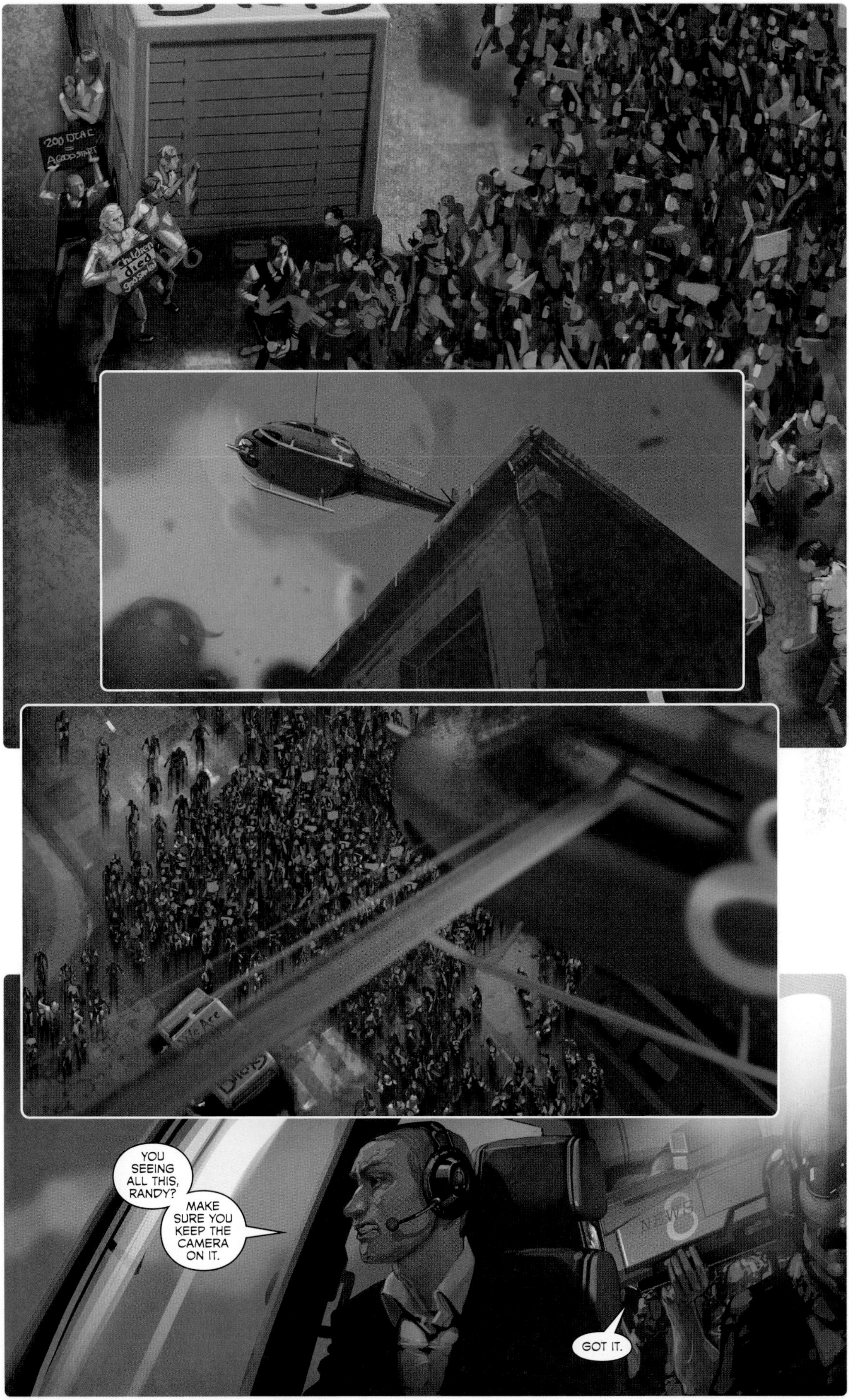
YOU SEEING ALL THIS, RANDY?
MAKE SURE YOU KEEP THE CAMERA ON IT.
GOT IT.

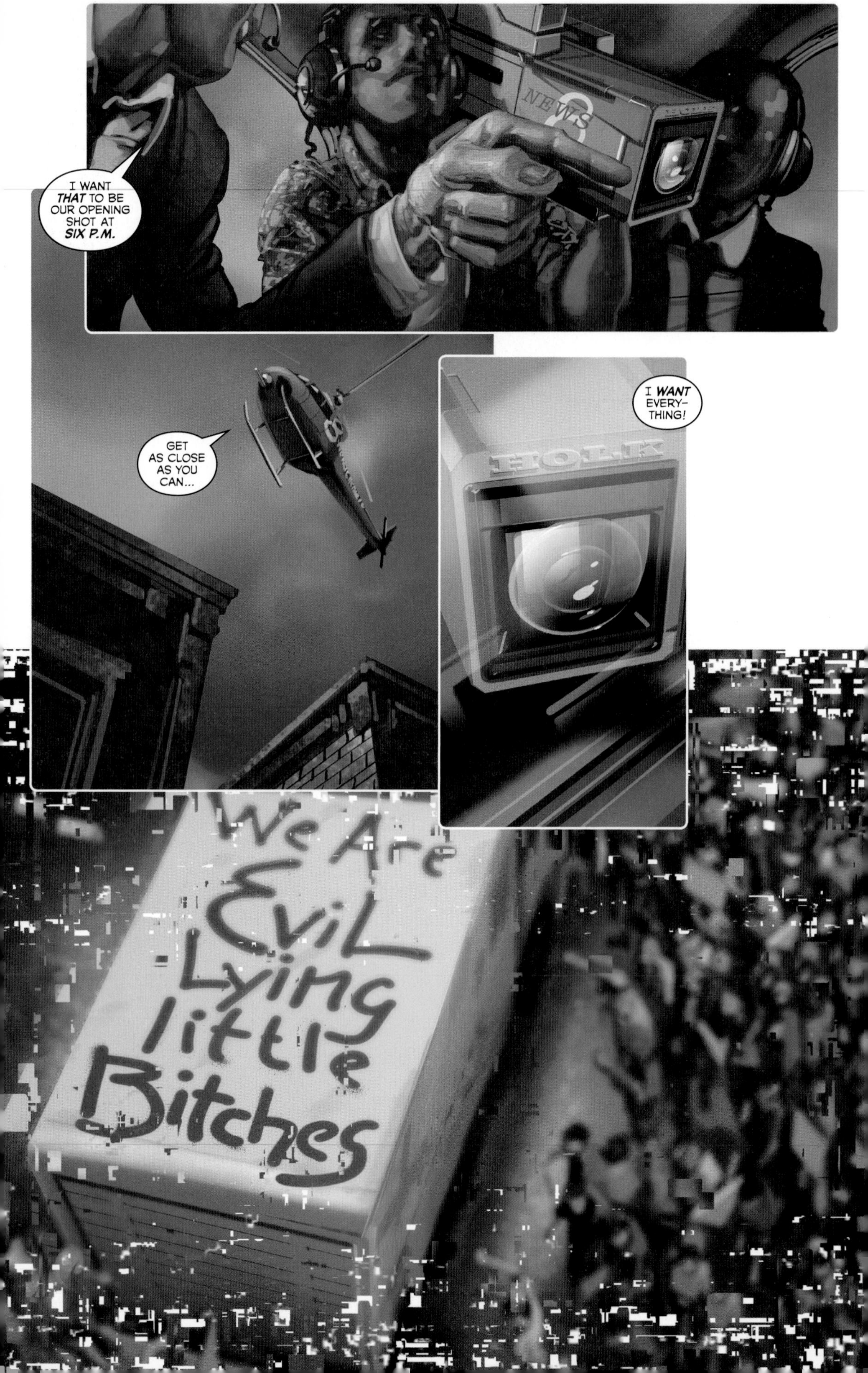
I WANT THAT TO BE OUR OPENING SHOT AT SIX P.M.
NEWS 8
HOLK
GET AS CLOSE AS YOU CAN...
I WANT EVERY-THING!
HOLK
We Are Evil Lying little Bitches

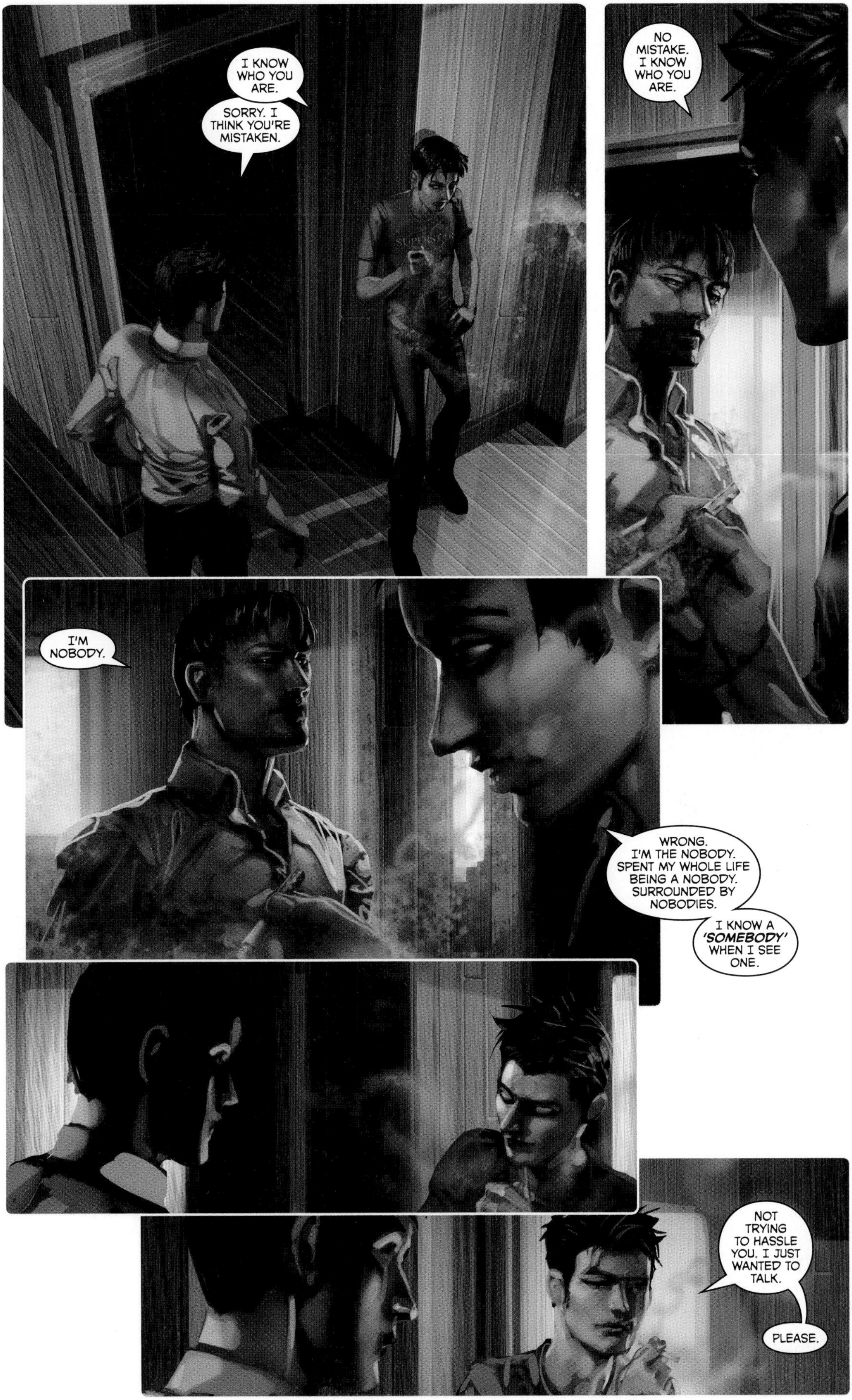
I KNOW WHO YOU ARE.
SORRY. I THINK YOU'RE MISTAKEN.
NO MISTAKE. I KNOW WHO YOU ARE.
I'M NOBODY.
WRONG. I'M THE NOBODY. SPENT MY WHOLE LIFE BEING A NOBODY. SURROUNDED BY NOBODIES.
I KNOW A *'SOMEBODY'* WHEN I SEE ONE.
NOT TRYING TO HASSLE YOU. I JUST WANTED TO TALK.
PLEASE.

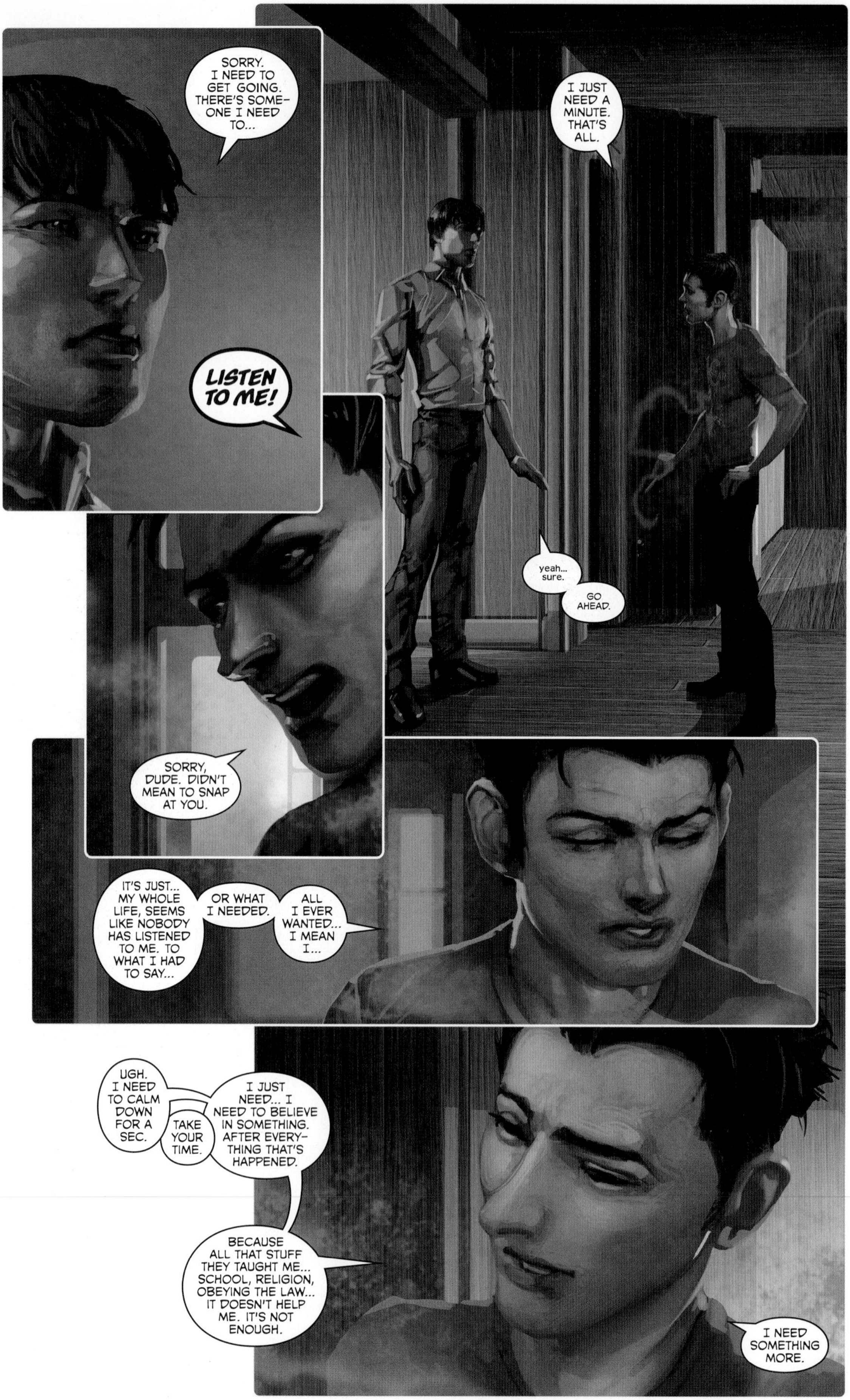
SORRY. I NEED TO GET GOING. THERE'S SOME-ONE I NEED TO...
I JUST NEED A MINUTE. THAT'S ALL.
LISTEN TO ME!
yeah... sure.
GO AHEAD.
SORRY, DUDE. DIDN'T MEAN TO SNAP AT YOU.
IT'S JUST... MY WHOLE LIFE, SEEMS LIKE NOBODY HAS LISTENED TO ME. TO WHAT I HAD TO SAY...
OR WHAT I NEEDED.
ALL I EVER WANTED... I MEAN I...
UGH. I NEED TO CALM DOWN FOR A SEC.
TAKE YOUR TIME.
I JUST NEED... I NEED TO BELIEVE IN SOMETHING. AFTER EVERY-THING THAT'S HAPPENED.
BECAUSE ALL THAT STUFF THEY TAUGHT ME... SCHOOL, RELIGION, OBEYING THE LAW... IT DOESN'T HELP ME. IT'S NOT ENOUGH.
I NEED SOMETHING MORE.

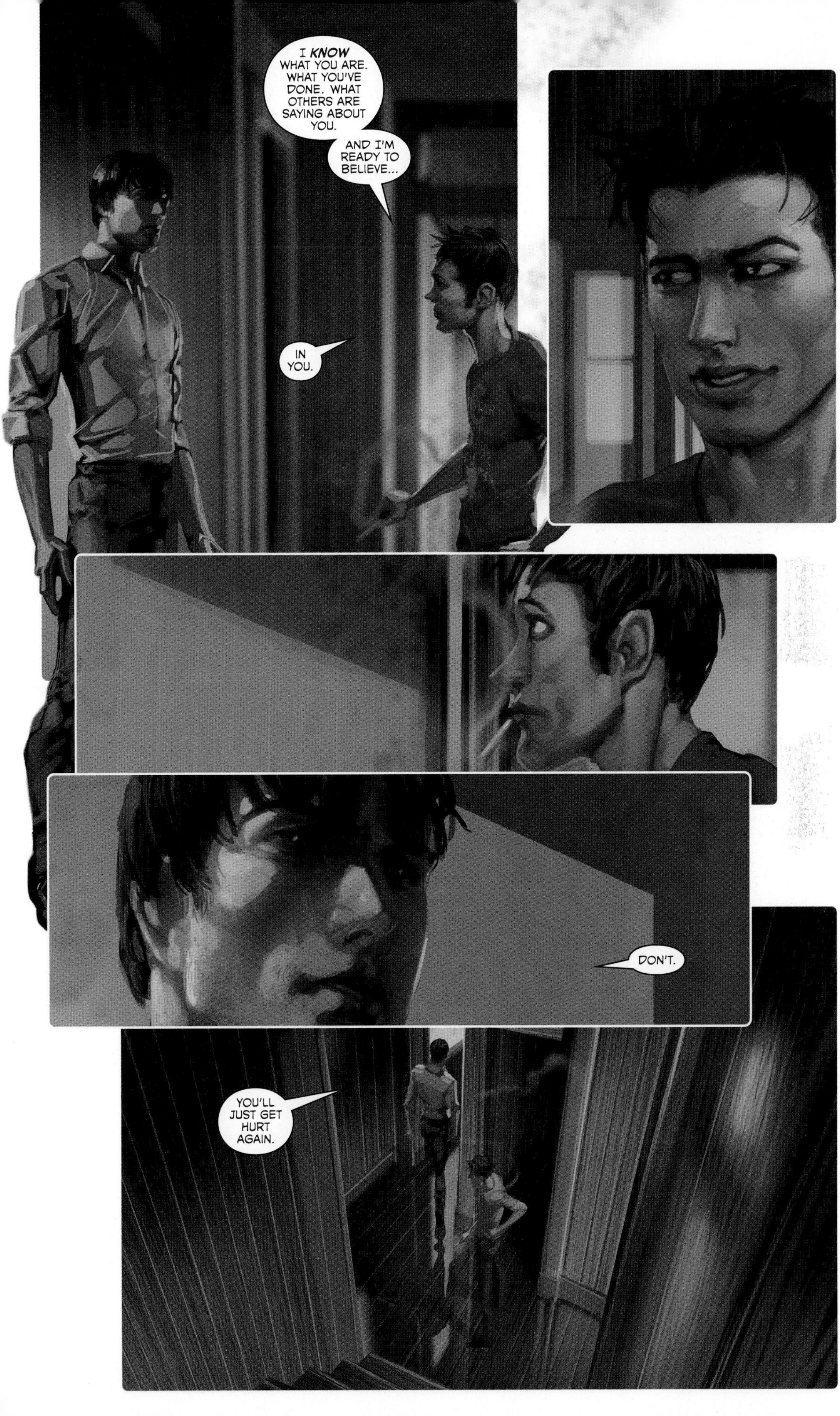
I KNOW WHAT YOU ARE. WHAT YOU'VE DONE. WHAT OTHERS ARE SAYING ABOUT YOU.
AND I'M READY TO BELIEVE...
IN YOU.
DON'T.
YOU'LL JUST GET HURT AGAIN.

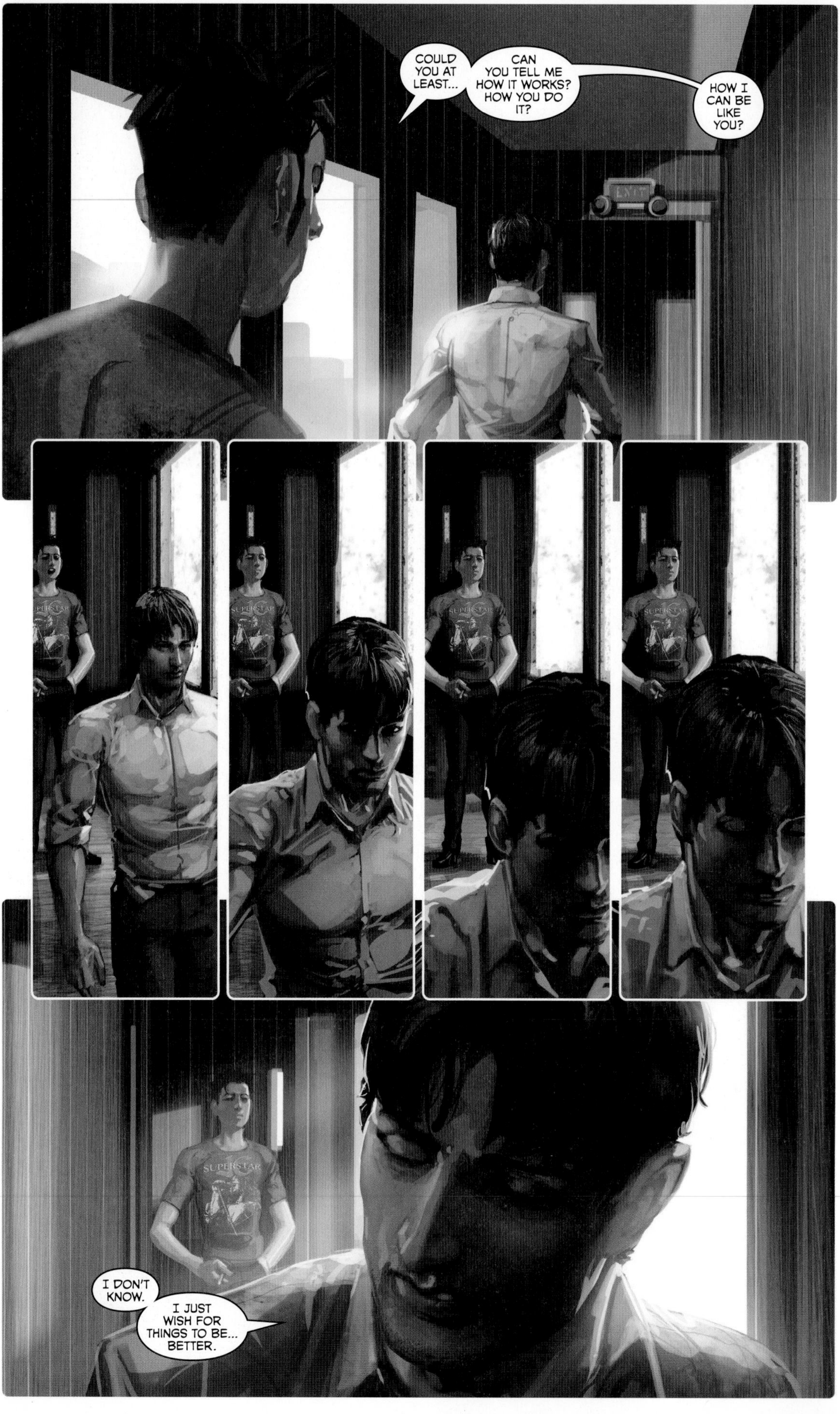
COULD YOU AT LEAST...
CAN YOU TELL ME HOW IT WORKS? HOW YOU DO IT?
HOW I CAN BE LIKE YOU?
EXIT
SUPERSTAR
I DON'T KNOW.
I JUST WISH FOR THINGS TO BE... BETTER.

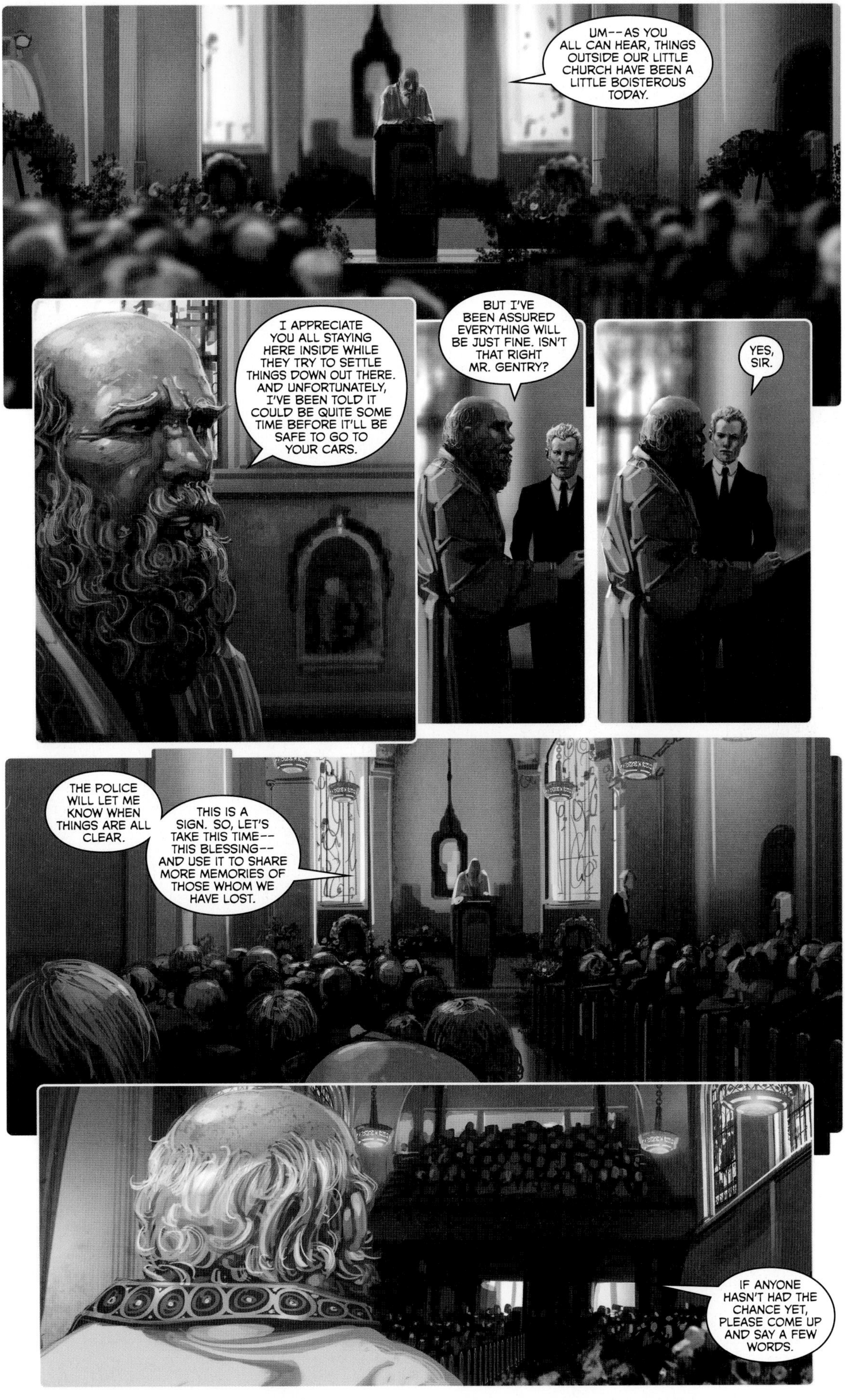
UM--AS YOU ALL CAN HEAR, THINGS OUTSIDE OUR LITTLE CHURCH HAVE BEEN A LITTLE BOISTEROUS TODAY.
I APPRECIATE YOU ALL STAYING HERE INSIDE WHILE THEY TRY TO SETTLE THINGS DOWN OUT THERE. AND UNFORTUNATELY, I'VE BEEN TOLD IT COULD BE QUITE SOME TIME BEFORE IT'LL BE SAFE TO GO TO YOUR CARS.
BUT I'VE BEEN ASSURED EVERYTHING WILL BE JUST FINE. ISN'T THAT RIGHT MR. GENTRY?
YES, SIR.
THE POLICE WILL LET ME KNOW WHEN THINGS ARE ALL CLEAR.
THIS IS A SIGN. SO, LET'S TAKE THIS TIME-- THIS BLESSING-- AND USE IT TO SHARE MORE MEMORIES OF THOSE WHOM WE HAVE LOST.
IF ANYONE HASN'T HAD THE CHANCE YET, PLEASE COME UP AND SAY A FEW WORDS.

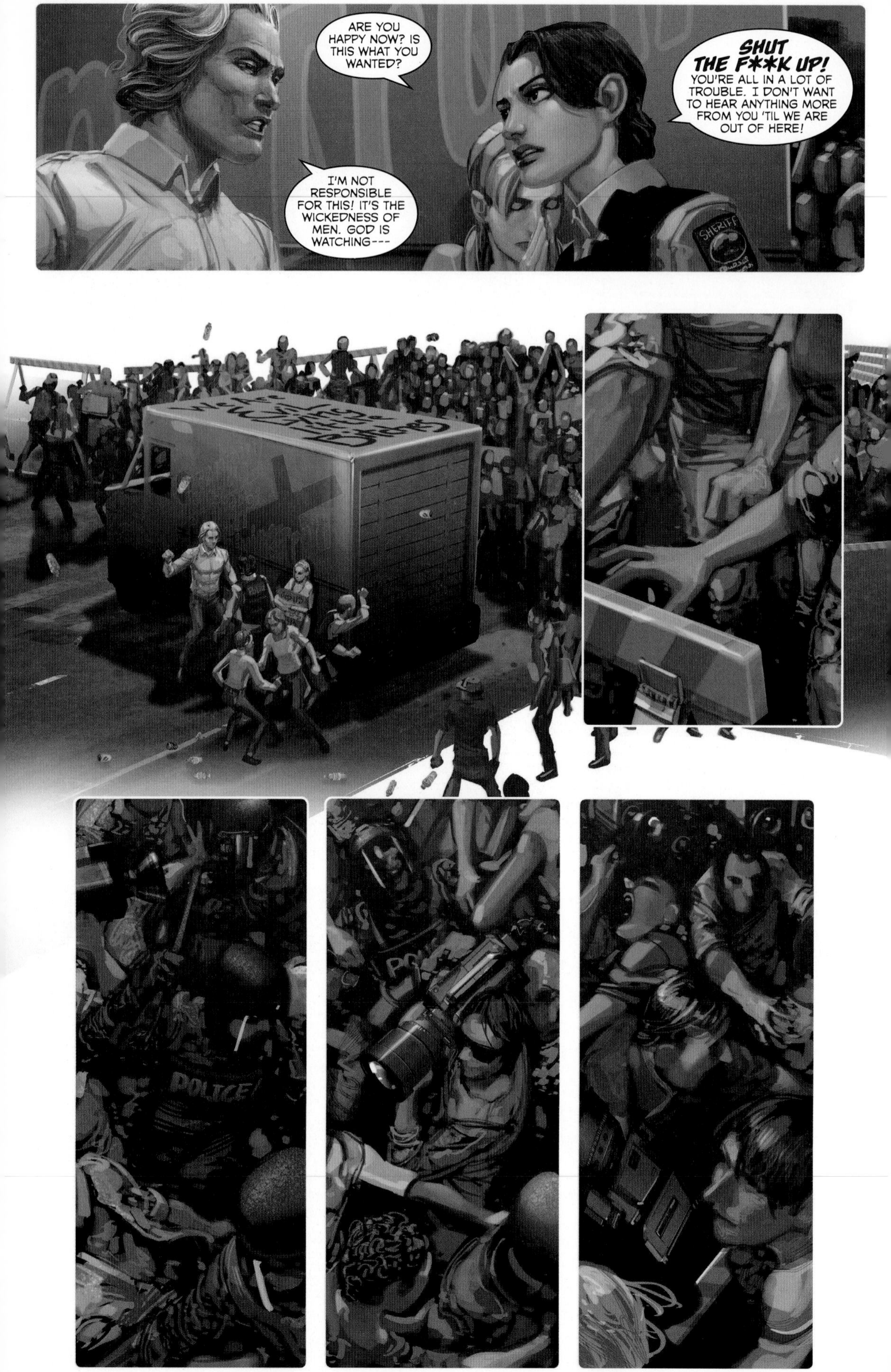
ARE YOU HAPPY NOW? IS THIS WHAT YOU WANTED?
I'M NOT RESPONSIBLE FOR THIS! IT'S THE WICKEDNESS OF MEN. GOD IS WATCHING---
SHUT THE F**K UP! YOU'RE ALL IN A LOT OF TROUBLE. I DON'T WANT TO HEAR ANYTHING MORE FROM YOU 'TIL WE ARE OUT OF HERE!
SHERIFF
POLICE

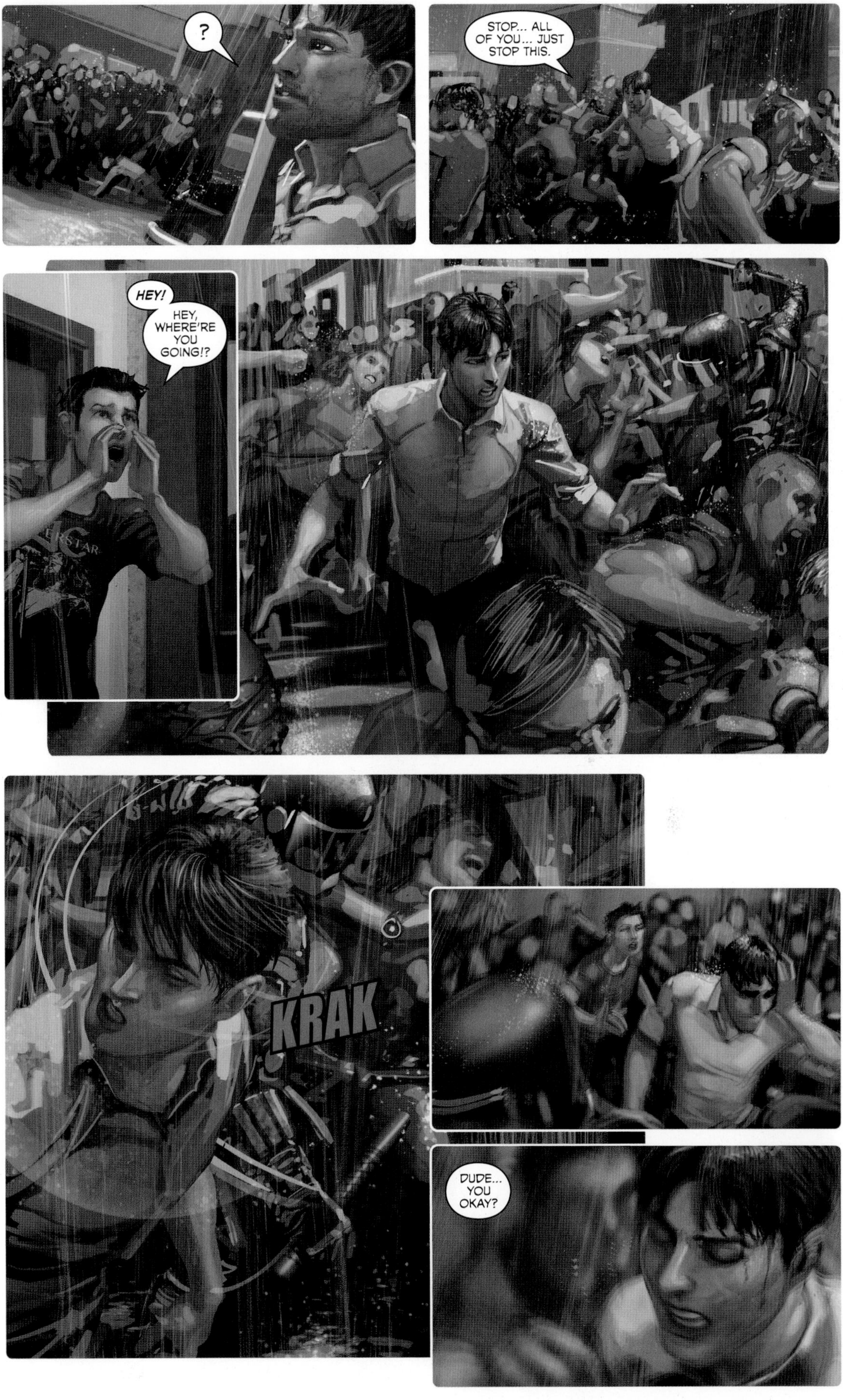
?
STOP... ALL OF YOU... JUST STOP THIS.
HEY!
HEY, WHERE'RE YOU GOING!?
KRAK
DUDE... YOU OKAY?

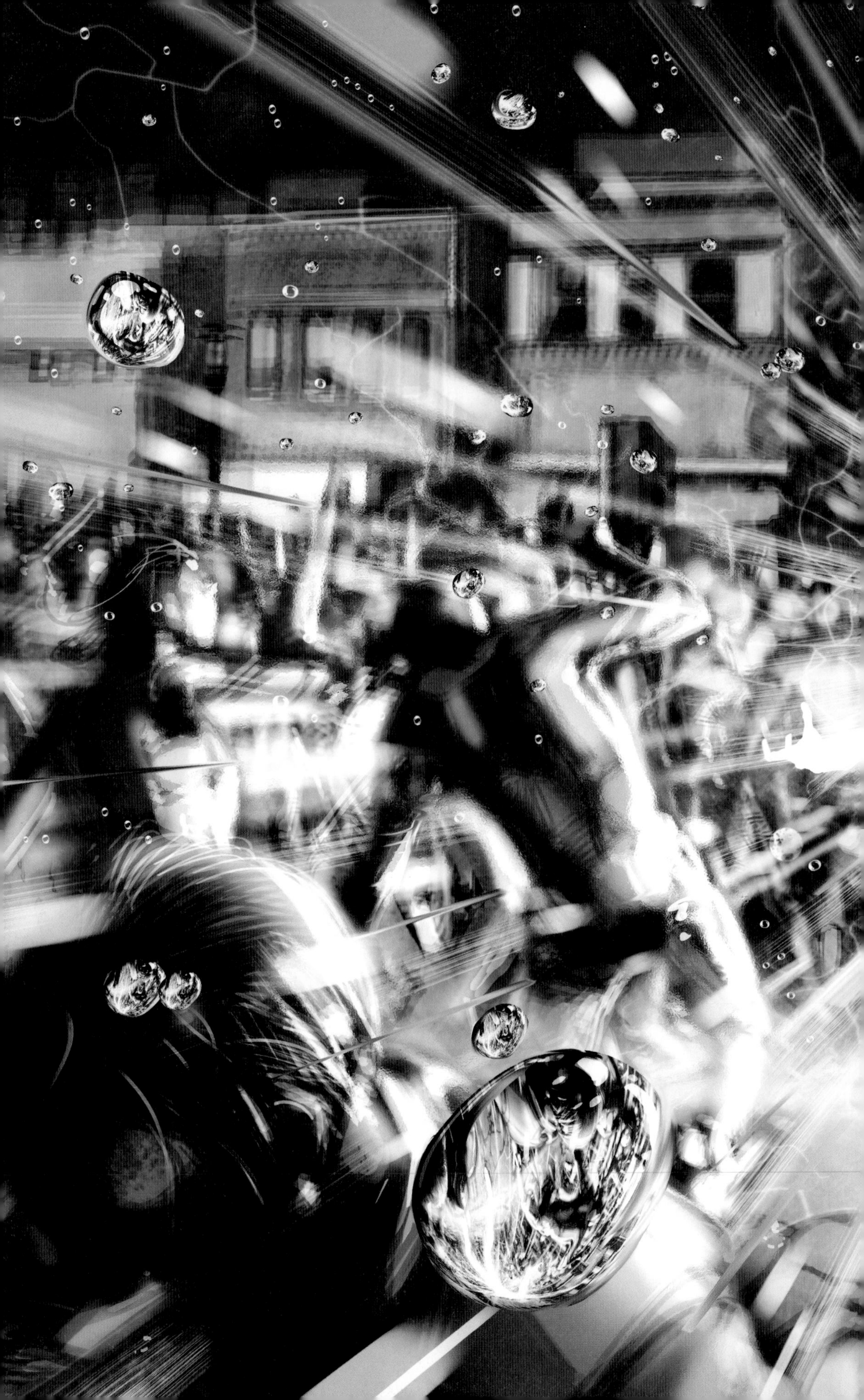

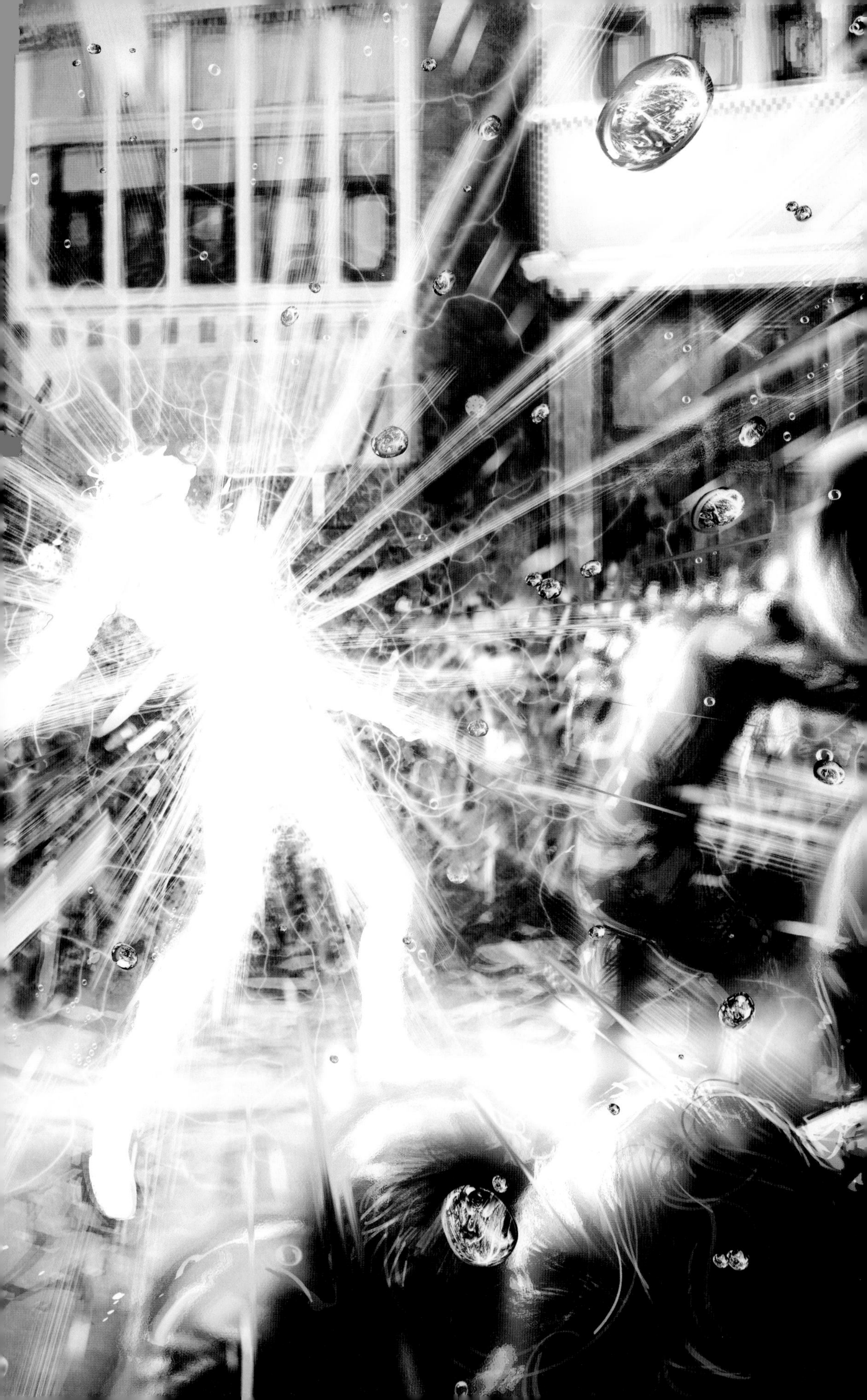

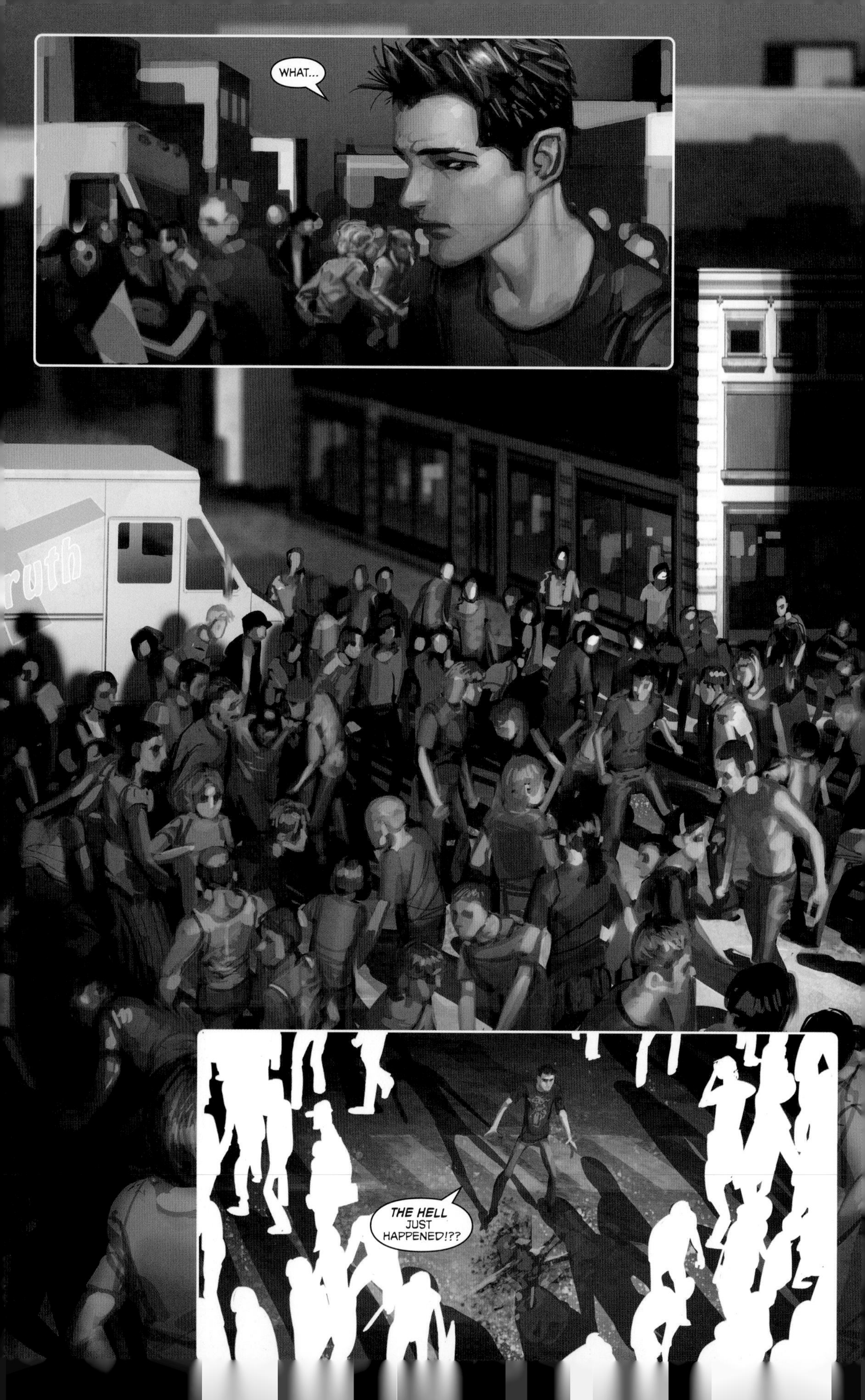
WHAT...
THE HELL JUST HAPPENED!??

Later.

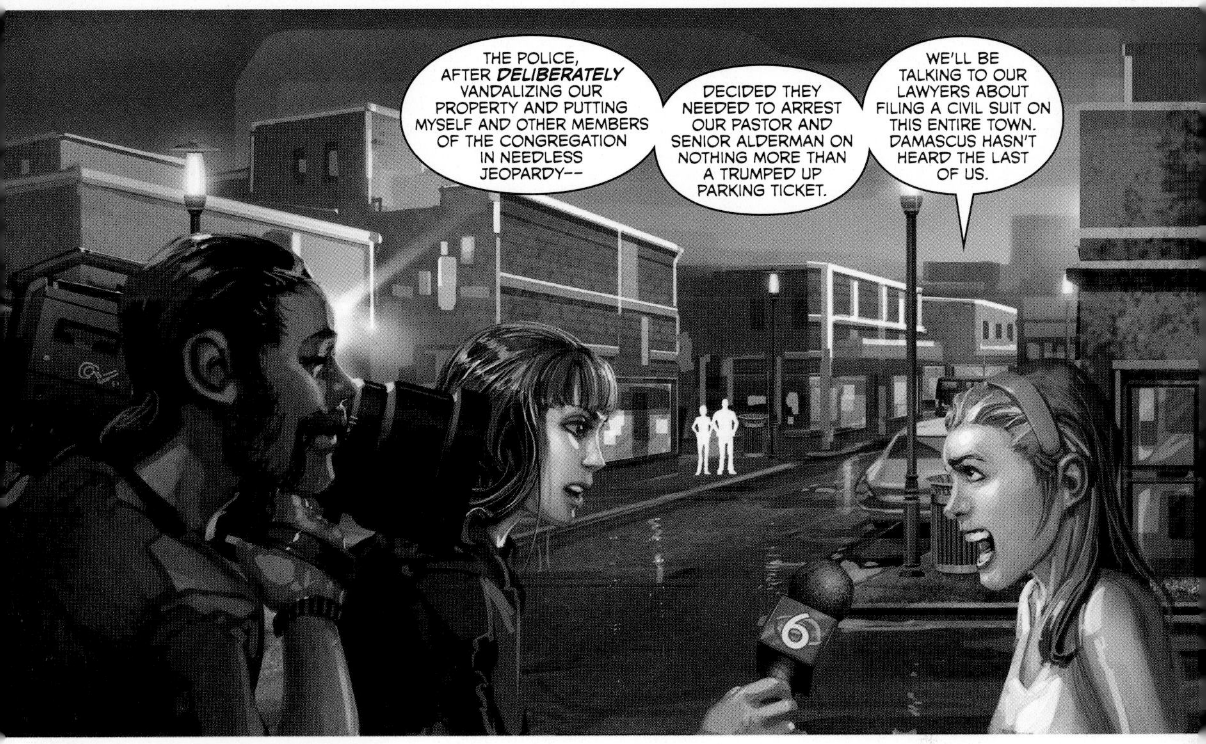

THE POLICE, AFTER ***DELIBERATELY*** VANDALIZING OUR PROPERTY AND PUTTING MYSELF AND OTHER MEMBERS OF THE CONGREGATION IN NEEDLESS JEOPARDY--
DECIDED THEY NEEDED TO ARREST OUR PASTOR AND SENIOR ALDERMAN ON NOTHING MORE THAN A TRUMPED UP PARKING TICKET.
WE'LL BE TALKING TO OUR LAWYERS ABOUT FILING A CIVIL SUIT ON THIS ENTIRE TOWN. DAMASCUS HASN'T HEARD THE LAST OF US.
6

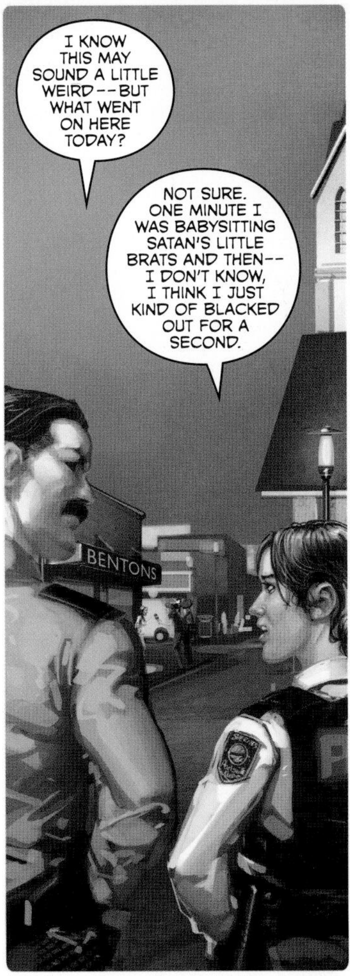

I KNOW THIS MAY SOUND A LITTLE WEIRD--BUT WHAT WENT ON HERE TODAY?
NOT SURE. ONE MINUTE I WAS BABYSITTING SATAN'S LITTLE BRATS AND THEN--I DON'T KNOW, I THINK I JUST KIND OF BLACKED OUT FOR A SECOND.
BENTONS

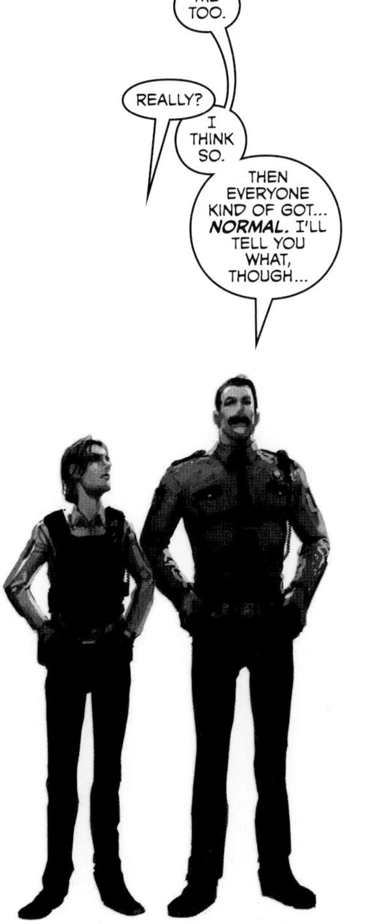

ME TOO.
REALLY?
I THINK SO.
THEN EVERYONE KIND OF GOT... ***NORMAL.*** I'LL TELL YOU WHAT, THOUGH...

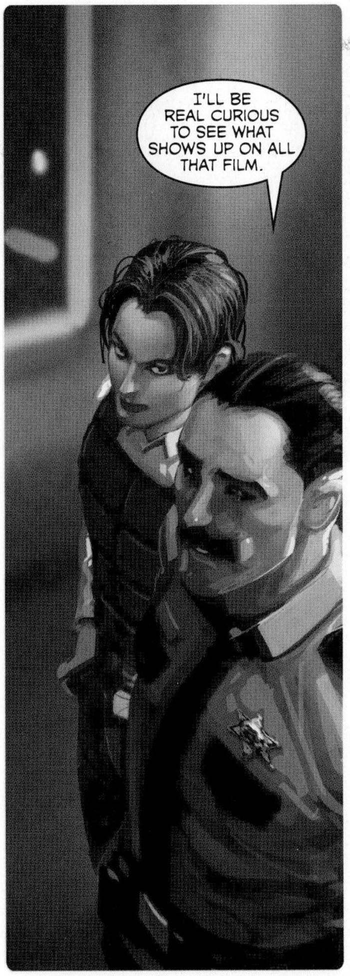

I'LL BE REAL CURIOUS TO SEE WHAT SHOWS UP ON ALL THAT FILM.

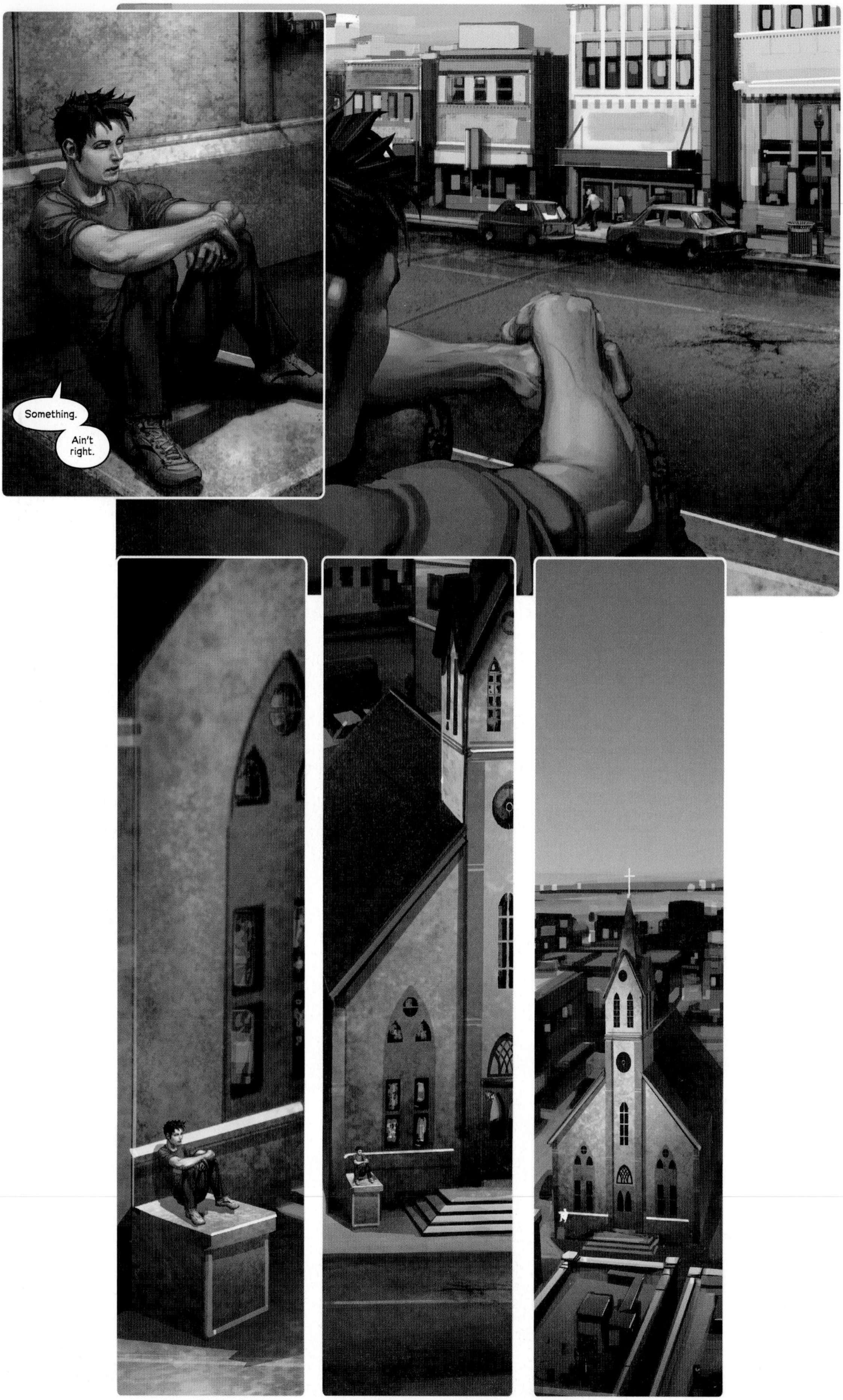
Something.
Ain't right.

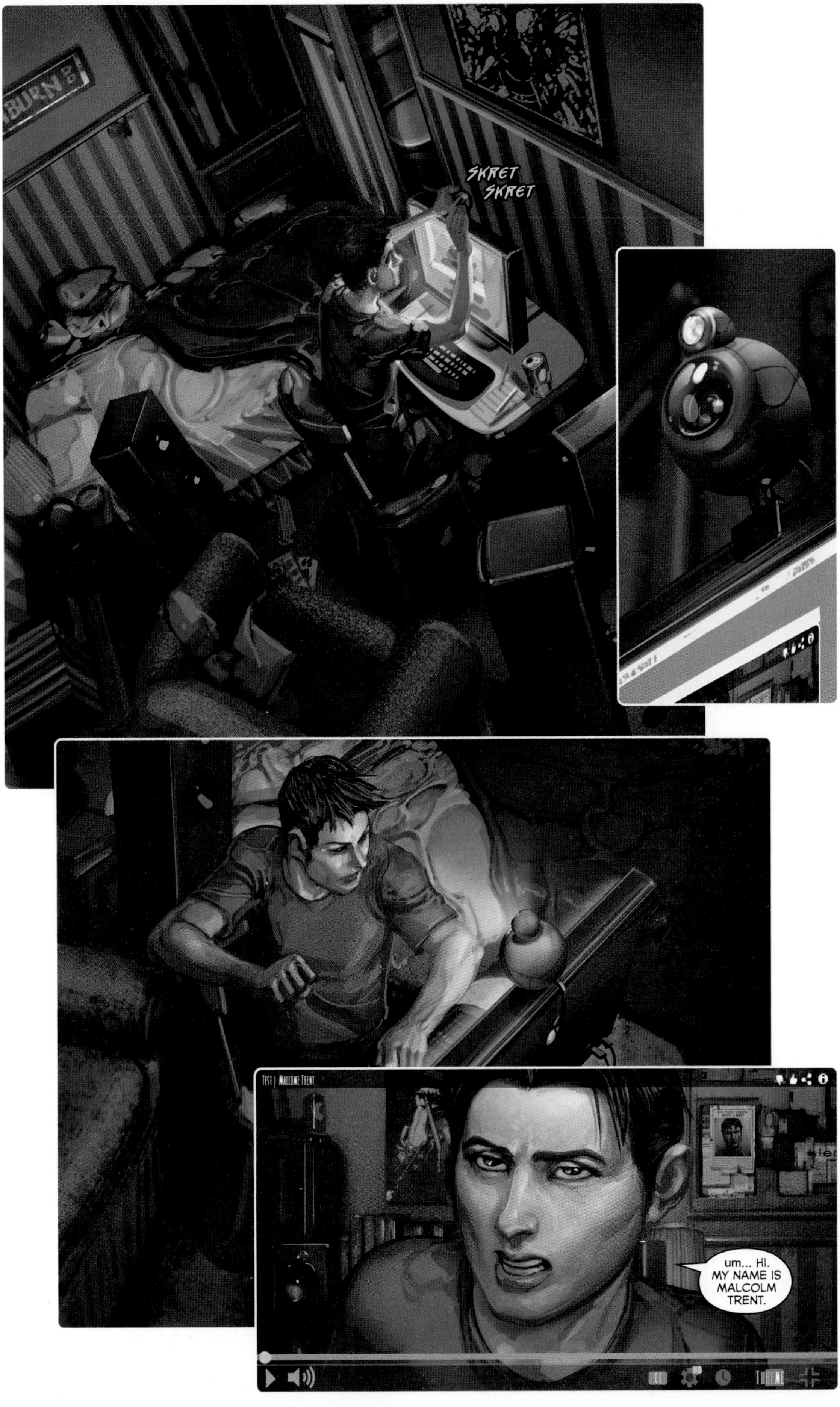
SKRET
SKRET
um... HI.
MY NAME IS
MALCOLM
TRENT.

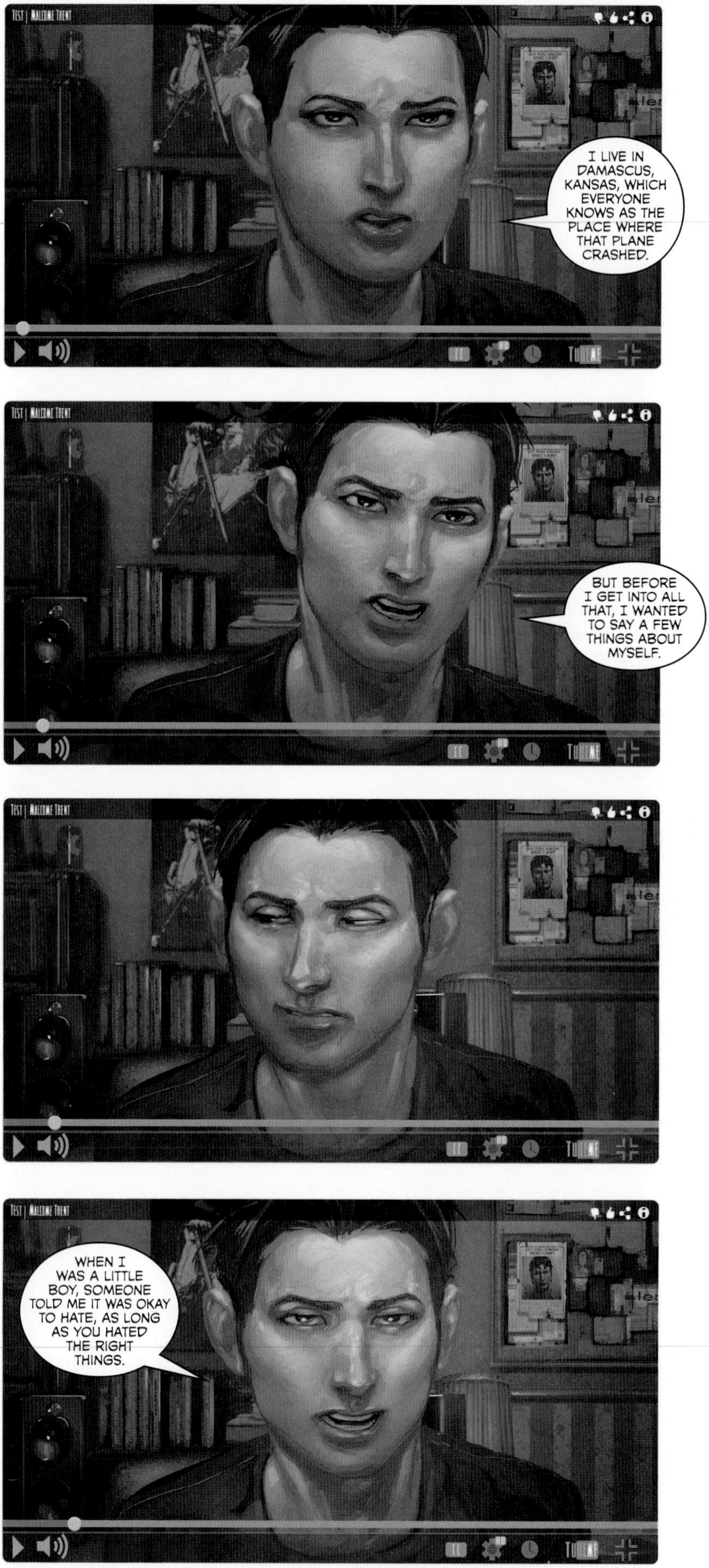
I LIVE IN DAMASCUS, KANSAS, WHICH EVERYONE KNOWS AS THE PLACE WHERE THAT PLANE CRASHED.
BUT BEFORE I GET INTO ALL THAT, I WANTED TO SAY A FEW THINGS ABOUT MYSELF.
WHEN I WAS A LITTLE BOY, SOMEONE TOLD ME IT WAS OKAY TO HATE, AS LONG AS YOU HATED THE RIGHT THINGS.

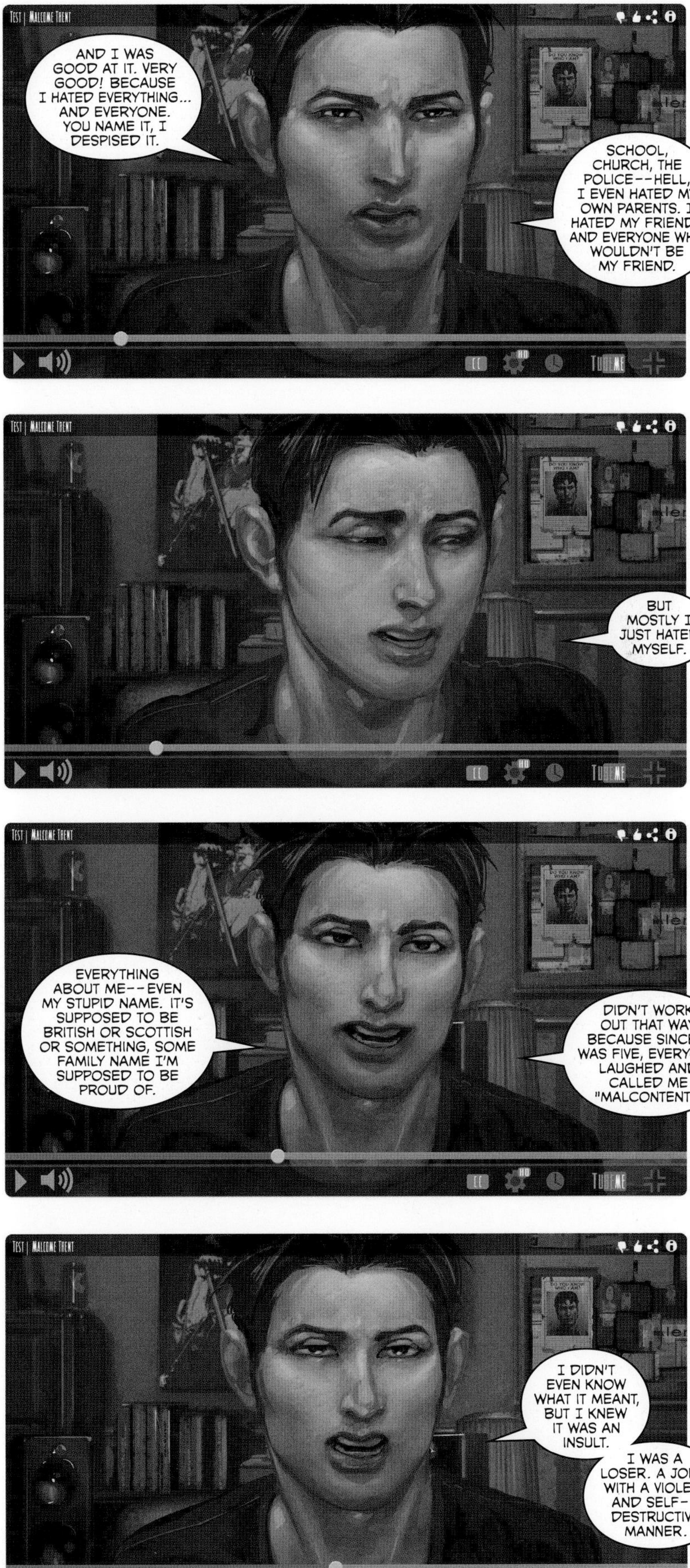
TEST | MALCOME TRENT
AND I WAS GOOD AT IT. VERY GOOD! BECAUSE I HATED EVERYTHING... AND EVERYONE. YOU NAME IT, I DESPISED IT.
SCHOOL, CHURCH, THE POLICE--HELL, I EVEN HATED MY OWN PARENTS. I HATED MY FRIENDS AND EVERYONE WHO WOULDN'T BE MY FRIEND.
BUT MOSTLY I JUST HATED MYSELF.
EVERYTHING ABOUT ME--EVEN MY STUPID NAME. IT'S SUPPOSED TO BE BRITISH OR SCOTTISH OR SOMETHING, SOME FAMILY NAME I'M SUPPOSED TO BE PROUD OF.
DIDN'T WORK OUT THAT WAY BECAUSE SINCE I WAS FIVE, EVERYONE LAUGHED AND CALLED ME "MALCONTENT."
I DIDN'T EVEN KNOW WHAT IT MEANT, BUT I KNEW IT WAS AN INSULT.
I WAS A LOSER. A JOKE. WITH A VIOLENT AND SELF-DESTRUCTIVE MANNER.

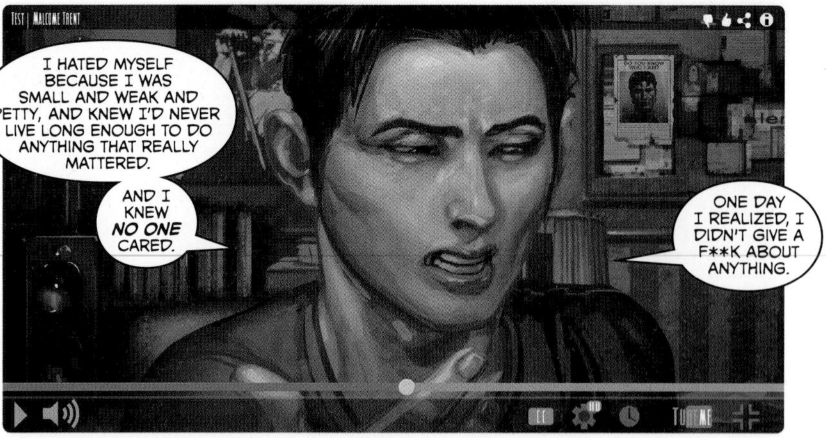
I HATED MYSELF BECAUSE I WAS SMALL AND WEAK AND PETTY, AND KNEW I'D NEVER LIVE LONG ENOUGH TO DO ANYTHING THAT REALLY MATTERED.
AND I KNEW ***NO ONE*** CARED.
ONE DAY I REALIZED, I DIDN'T GIVE A F**K ABOUT ANYTHING.

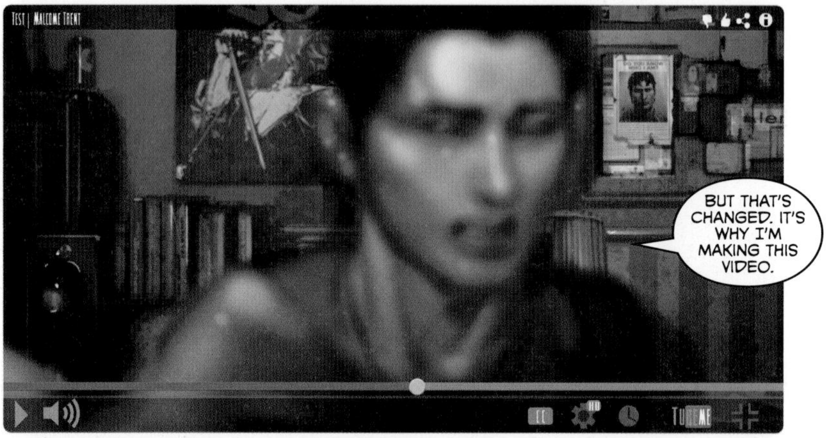
BUT THAT'S CHANGED. IT'S WHY I'M MAKING THIS VIDEO.

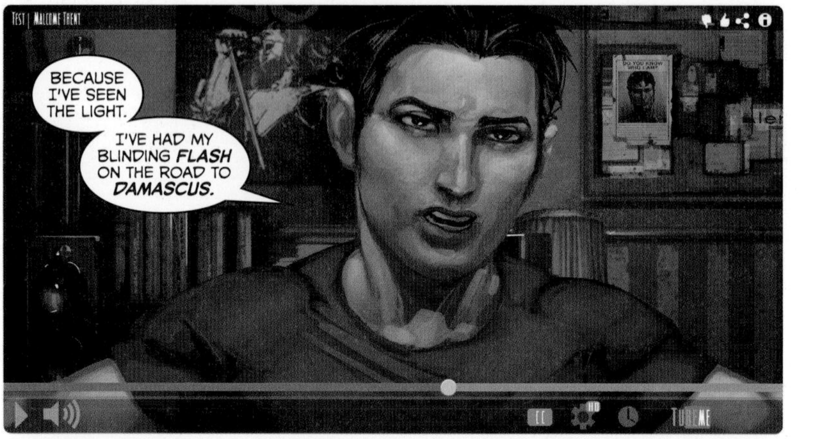
BECAUSE I'VE SEEN THE LIGHT.
I'VE HAD MY BLINDING ***FLASH*** ON THE ROAD TO ***DAMASCUS.***

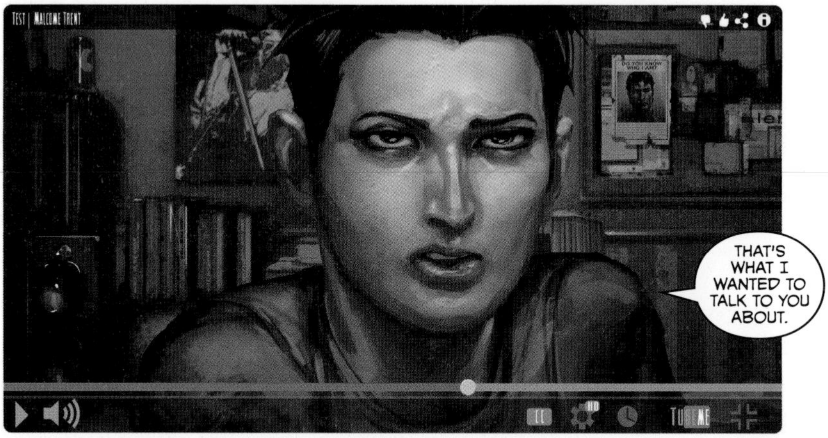
THAT'S WHAT I WANTED TO TALK TO YOU ABOUT.

Defense Advanced Research Projects Agency. Arlington, Virginia.

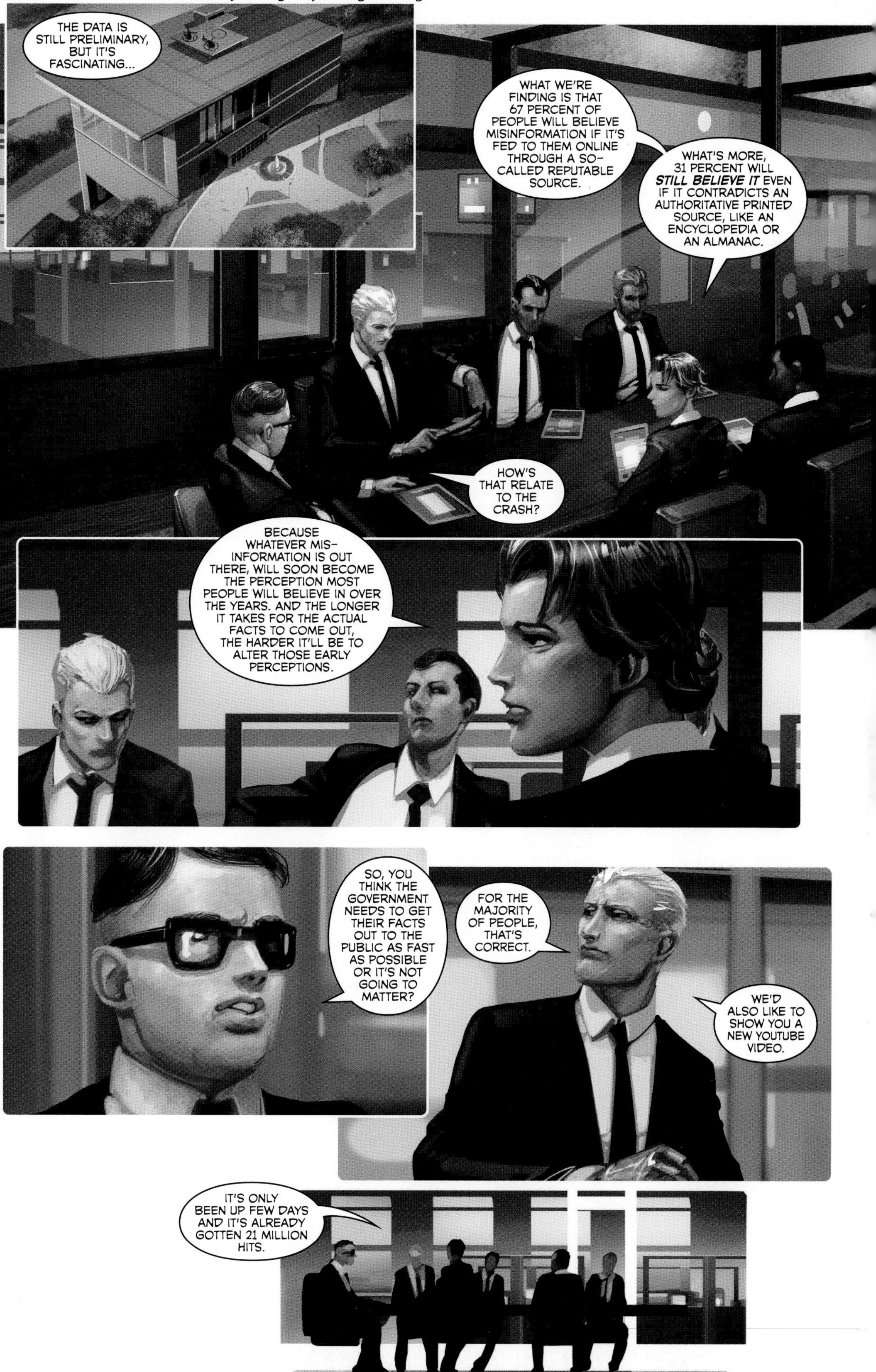
THE DATA IS STILL PRELIMINARY, BUT IT'S FASCINATING...
WHAT WE'RE FINDING IS THAT 67 PERCENT OF PEOPLE WILL BELIEVE MISINFORMATION IF IT'S FED TO THEM ONLINE THROUGH A SO-CALLED REPUTABLE SOURCE.
WHAT'S MORE, 31 PERCENT WILL STILL BELIEVE IT EVEN IF IT CONTRADICTS AN AUTHORITATIVE PRINTED SOURCE, LIKE AN ENCYCLOPEDIA OR AN ALMANAC.
HOW'S THAT RELATE TO THE CRASH?
BECAUSE WHATEVER MIS-INFORMATION IS OUT THERE, WILL SOON BECOME THE PERCEPTION MOST PEOPLE WILL BELIEVE IN OVER THE YEARS. AND THE LONGER IT TAKES FOR THE ACTUAL FACTS TO COME OUT, THE HARDER IT'LL BE TO ALTER THOSE EARLY PERCEPTIONS.
SO, YOU THINK THE GOVERNMENT NEEDS TO GET THEIR FACTS OUT TO THE PUBLIC AS FAST AS POSSIBLE OR IT'S NOT GOING TO MATTER?
FOR THE MAJORITY OF PEOPLE, THAT'S CORRECT.
WE'D ALSO LIKE TO SHOW YOU A NEW YOUTUBE VIDEO.
IT'S ONLY BEEN UP FEW DAYS AND IT'S ALREADY GOTTEN 21 MILLION HITS.

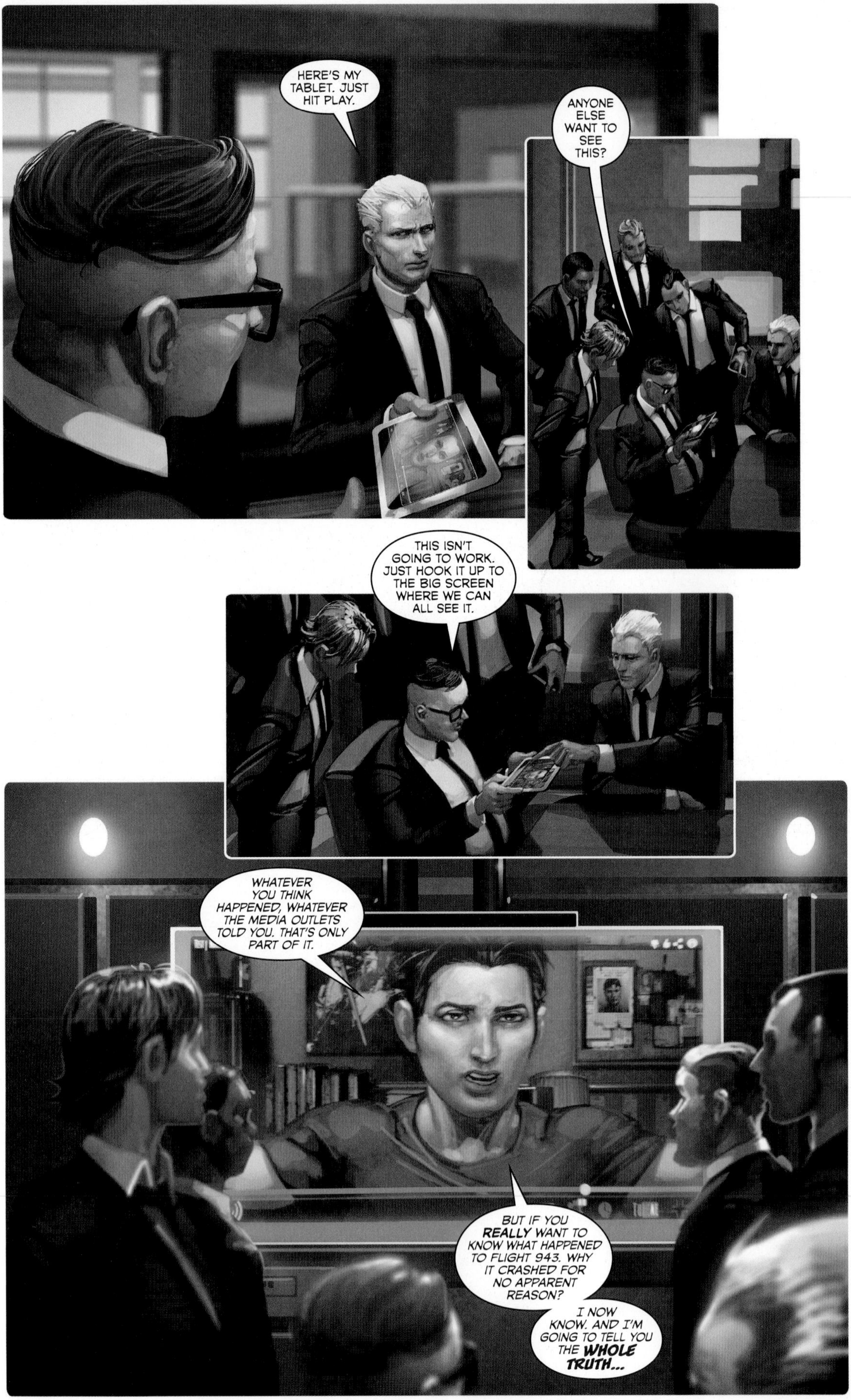
HERE'S MY TABLET. JUST HIT PLAY.
ANYONE ELSE WANT TO SEE THIS?
THIS ISN'T GOING TO WORK. JUST HOOK IT UP TO THE BIG SCREEN WHERE WE CAN ALL SEE IT.
WHATEVER YOU THINK HAPPENED, WHATEVER THE MEDIA OUTLETS TOLD YOU. THAT'S ONLY PART OF IT.
BUT IF YOU REALLY WANT TO KNOW WHAT HAPPENED TO FLIGHT 943. WHY IT CRASHED FOR NO APPARENT REASON?
I NOW KNOW. AND I'M GOING TO TELL YOU THE WHOLE TRUTH...

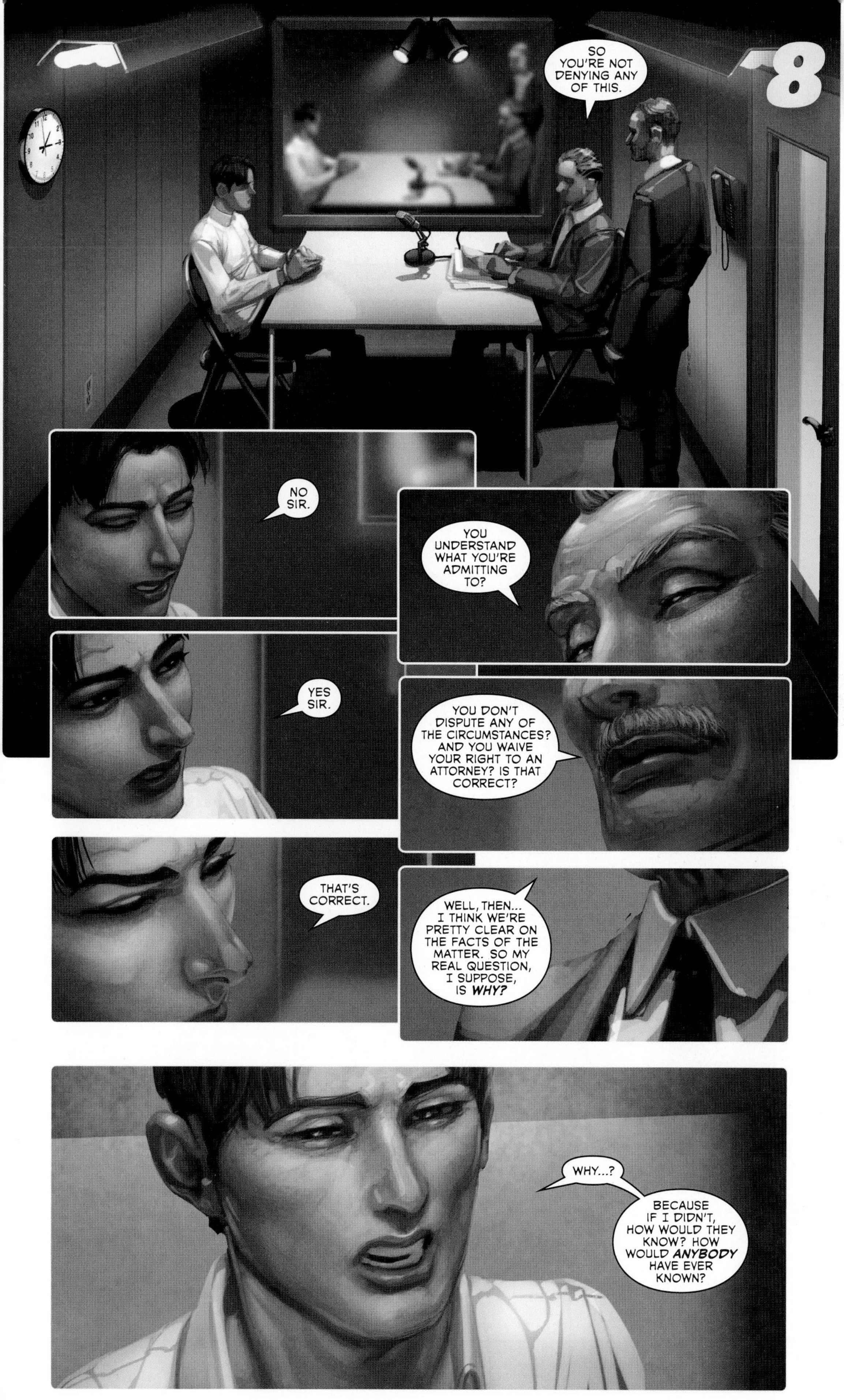
8
SO YOU'RE NOT DENYING ANY OF THIS.
NO SIR.
YOU UNDERSTAND WHAT YOU'RE ADMITTING TO?
YES SIR.
YOU DON'T DISPUTE ANY OF THE CIRCUMSTANCES? AND YOU WAIVE YOUR RIGHT TO AN ATTORNEY? IS THAT CORRECT?
THAT'S CORRECT.
WELL, THEN... I THINK WE'RE PRETTY CLEAR ON THE FACTS OF THE MATTER. SO MY REAL QUESTION, I SUPPOSE, IS *WHY?*
WHY...?
BECAUSE IF I DIDN'T, HOW WOULD THEY KNOW? HOW WOULD *ANYBODY* HAVE EVER KNOWN?

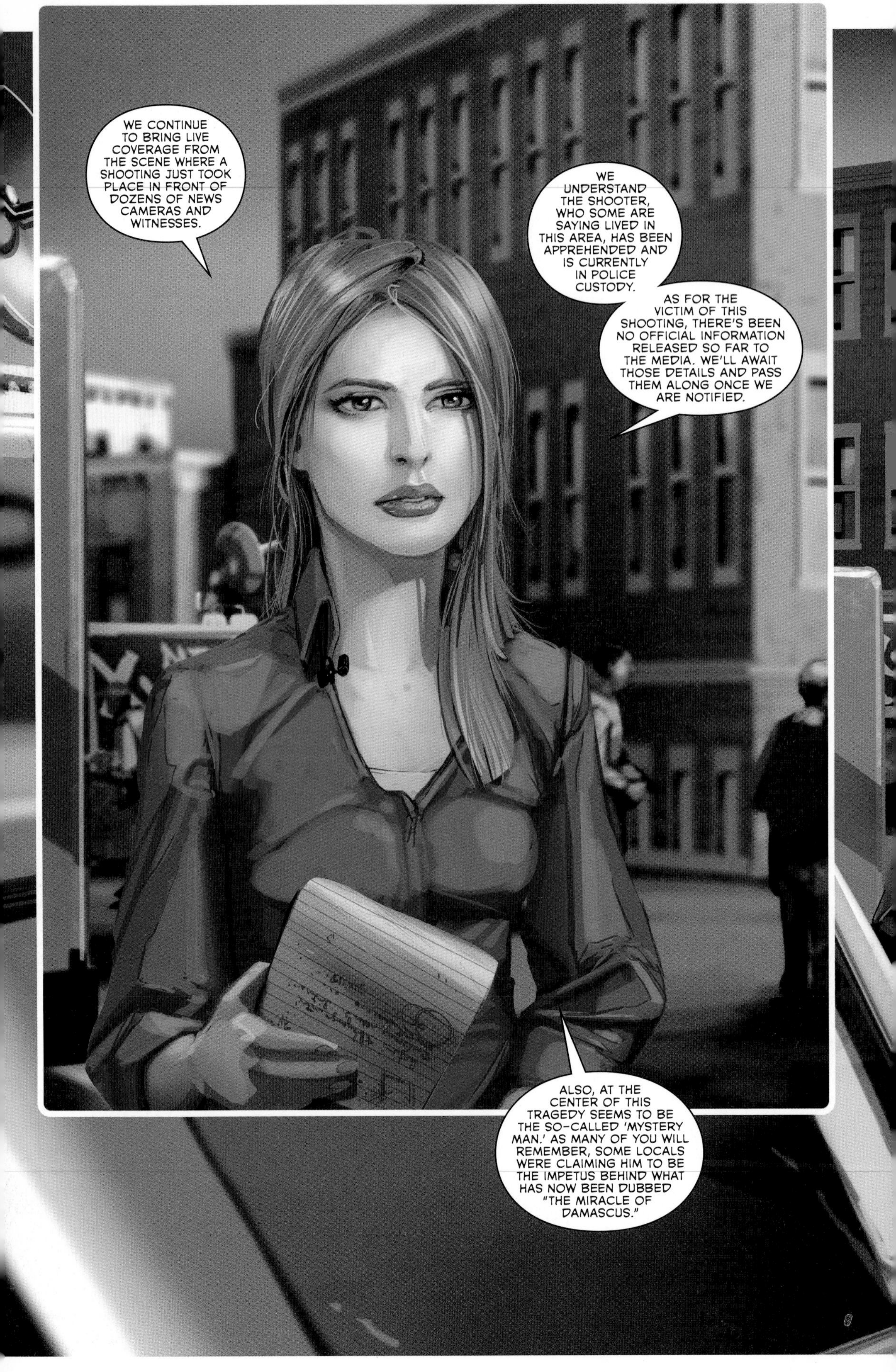
WE CONTINUE TO BRING LIVE COVERAGE FROM THE SCENE WHERE A SHOOTING JUST TOOK PLACE IN FRONT OF DOZENS OF NEWS CAMERAS AND WITNESSES.
WE UNDERSTAND THE SHOOTER, WHO SOME ARE SAYING LIVED IN THIS AREA, HAS BEEN APPREHENDED AND IS CURRENTLY IN POLICE CUSTODY.
AS FOR THE VICTIM OF THIS SHOOTING, THERE'S BEEN NO OFFICIAL INFORMATION RELEASED SO FAR TO THE MEDIA. WE'LL AWAIT THOSE DETAILS AND PASS THEM ALONG ONCE WE ARE NOTIFIED.
ALSO, AT THE CENTER OF THIS TRAGEDY SEEMS TO BE THE SO-CALLED 'MYSTERY MAN.' AS MANY OF YOU WILL REMEMBER, SOME LOCALS WERE CLAIMING HIM TO BE THE IMPETUS BEHIND WHAT HAS NOW BEEN DUBBED "THE MIRACLE OF DAMASCUS."

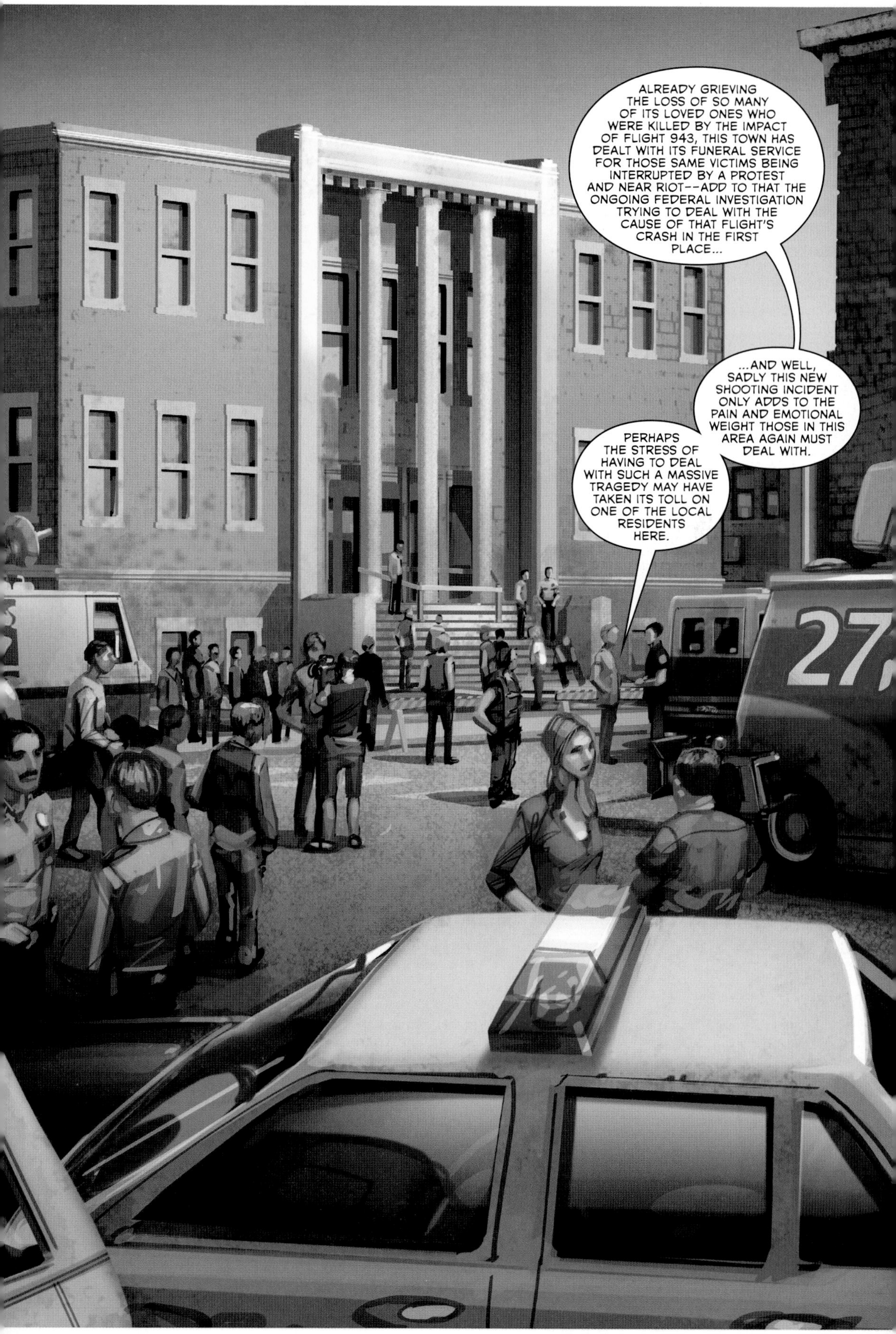
ALREADY GRIEVING THE LOSS OF SO MANY OF ITS LOVED ONES WHO WERE KILLED BY THE IMPACT OF FLIGHT 943, THIS TOWN HAS DEALT WITH ITS FUNERAL SERVICE FOR THOSE SAME VICTIMS BEING INTERRUPTED BY A PROTEST AND NEAR RIOT--ADD TO THAT THE ONGOING FEDERAL INVESTIGATION TRYING TO DEAL WITH THE CAUSE OF THAT FLIGHT'S CRASH IN THE FIRST PLACE...
...AND WELL, SADLY THIS NEW SHOOTING INCIDENT ONLY ADDS TO THE PAIN AND EMOTIONAL WEIGHT THOSE IN THIS AREA AGAIN MUST DEAL WITH.
PERHAPS THE STRESS OF HAVING TO DEAL WITH SUCH A MASSIVE TRAGEDY MAY HAVE TAKEN ITS TOLL ON ONE OF THE LOCAL RESIDENTS HERE.
27

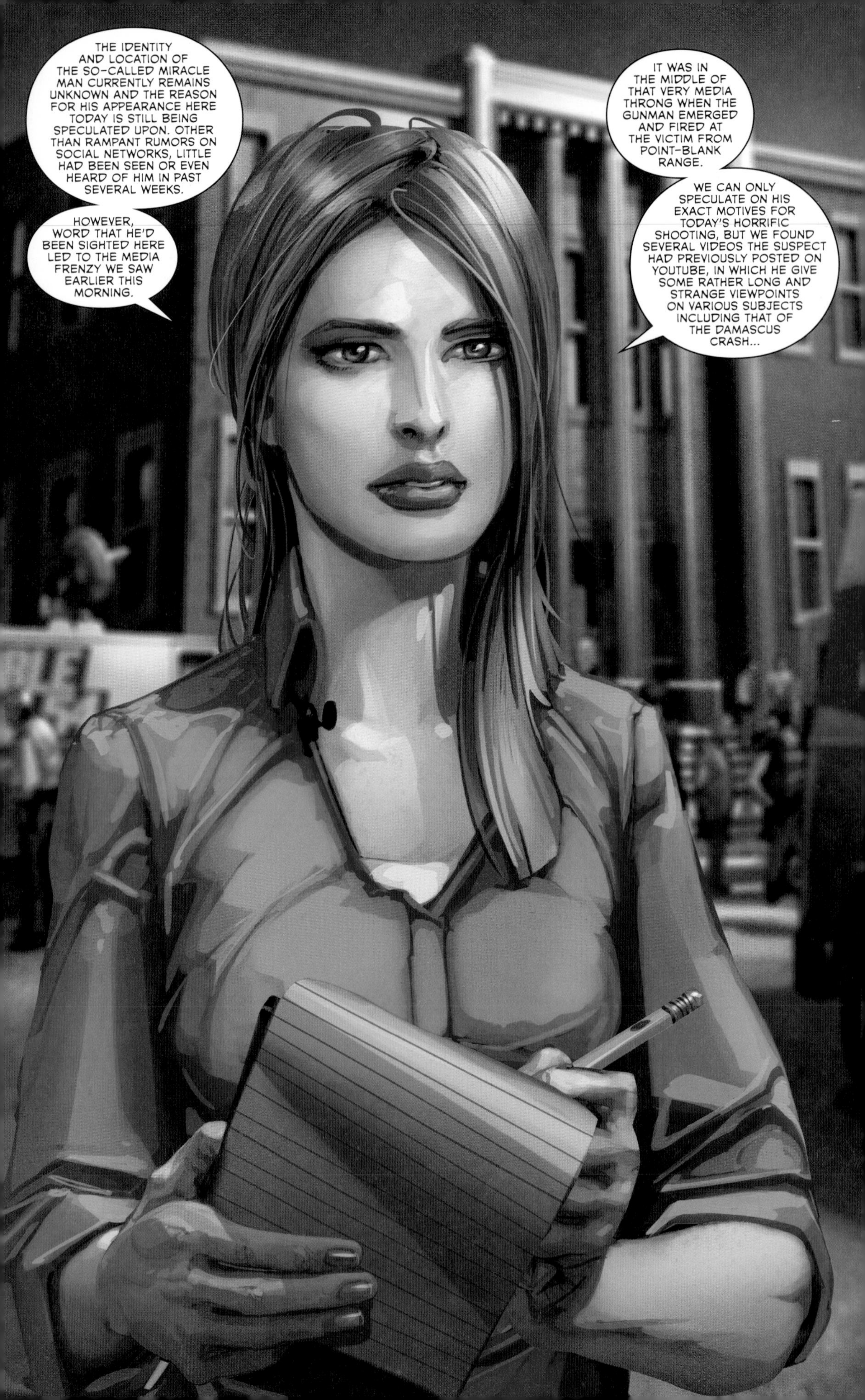
THE IDENTITY AND LOCATION OF THE SO-CALLED MIRACLE MAN CURRENTLY REMAINS UNKNOWN AND THE REASON FOR HIS APPEARANCE HERE TODAY IS STILL BEING SPECULATED UPON. OTHER THAN RAMPANT RUMORS ON SOCIAL NETWORKS, LITTLE HAD BEEN SEEN OR EVEN HEARD OF HIM IN PAST SEVERAL WEEKS.
HOWEVER, WORD THAT HE'D BEEN SIGHTED HERE LED TO THE MEDIA FRENZY WE SAW EARLIER THIS MORNING.
IT WAS IN THE MIDDLE OF THAT VERY MEDIA THRONG WHEN THE GUNMAN EMERGED AND FIRED AT THE VICTIM FROM POINT-BLANK RANGE.
WE CAN ONLY SPECULATE ON HIS EXACT MOTIVES FOR TODAY'S HORRIFIC SHOOTING, BUT WE FOUND SEVERAL VIDEOS THE SUSPECT HAD PREVIOUSLY POSTED ON YOUTUBE, IN WHICH HE GIVE SOME RATHER LONG AND STRANGE VIEWPOINTS ON VARIOUS SUBJECTS INCLUDING THAT OF THE DAMASCUS CRASH...

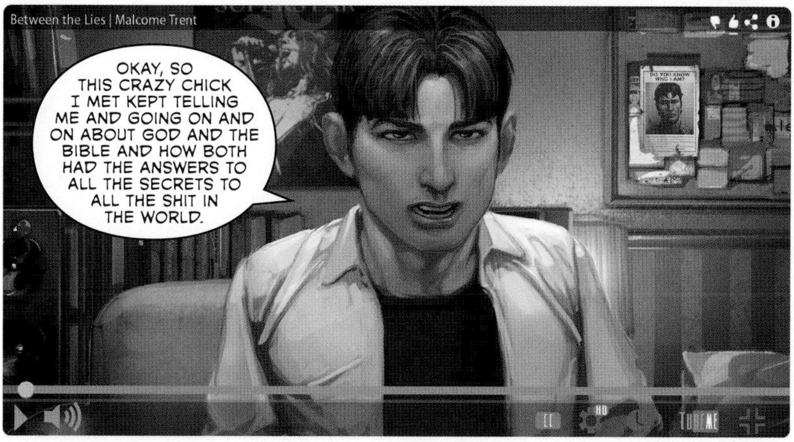
Between the Lies | Malcome Trent
OKAY, SO THIS CRAZY CHICK I MET KEPT TELLING ME AND GOING ON AND ON ABOUT GOD AND THE BIBLE AND HOW BOTH HAD THE ANSWERS TO ALL THE SECRETS TO ALL THE SHIT IN THE WORLD.
DO YOU KNOW WHO I AM?

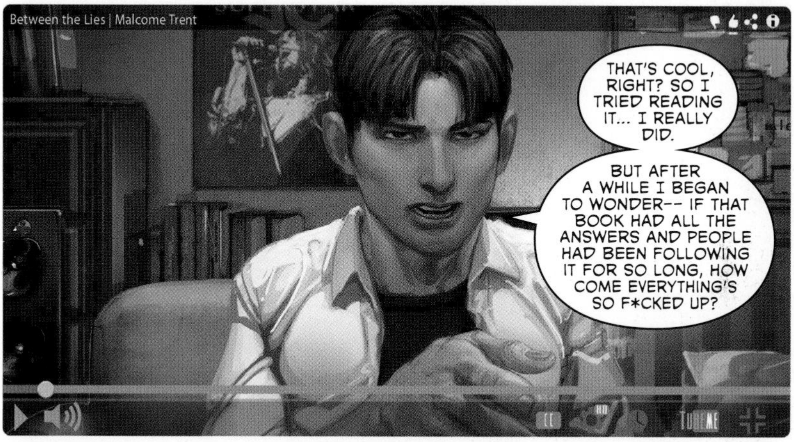
Between the Lies | Malcome Trent
THAT'S COOL, RIGHT? SO I TRIED READING IT... I REALLY DID.
BUT AFTER A WHILE I BEGAN TO WONDER-- IF THAT BOOK HAD ALL THE ANSWERS AND PEOPLE HAD BEEN FOLLOWING IT FOR SO LONG, HOW COME EVERYTHING'S SO F*CKED UP?

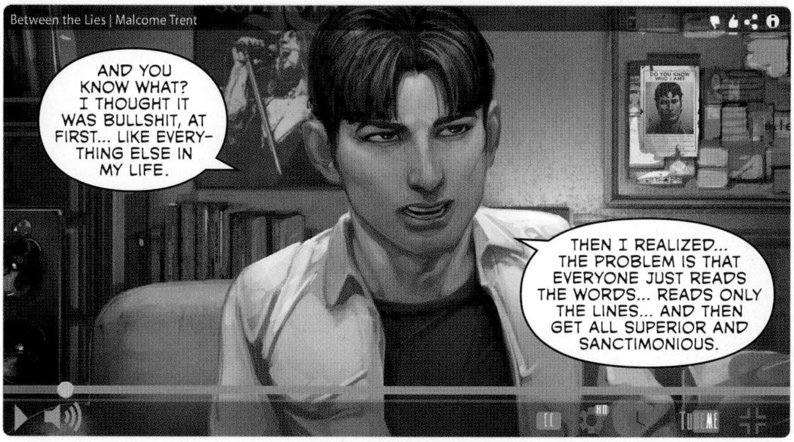
Between the Lies | Malcome Trent
AND YOU KNOW WHAT? I THOUGHT IT WAS BULLSHIT, AT FIRST... LIKE EVERYTHING ELSE IN MY LIFE.
THEN I REALIZED... THE PROBLEM IS THAT EVERYONE JUST READS THE WORDS... READS ONLY THE LINES... AND THEN GET ALL SUPERIOR AND SANCTIMONIOUS.
DO YOU KNOW WHO I AM?

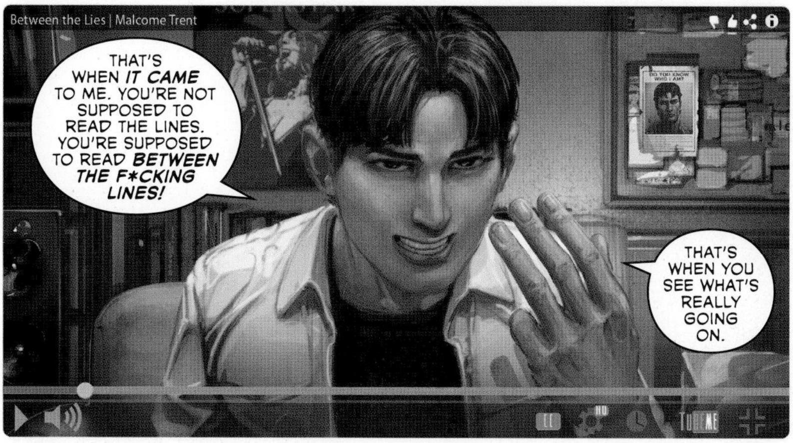
Between the Lies | Malcome Trent
THAT'S WHEN *IT CAME* TO ME. YOU'RE NOT SUPPOSED TO READ THE LINES. YOU'RE SUPPOSED TO READ ***BETWEEN THE F*CKING LINES!***
THAT'S WHEN YOU SEE WHAT'S REALLY GOING ON.
DO YOU KNOW WHO I AM?

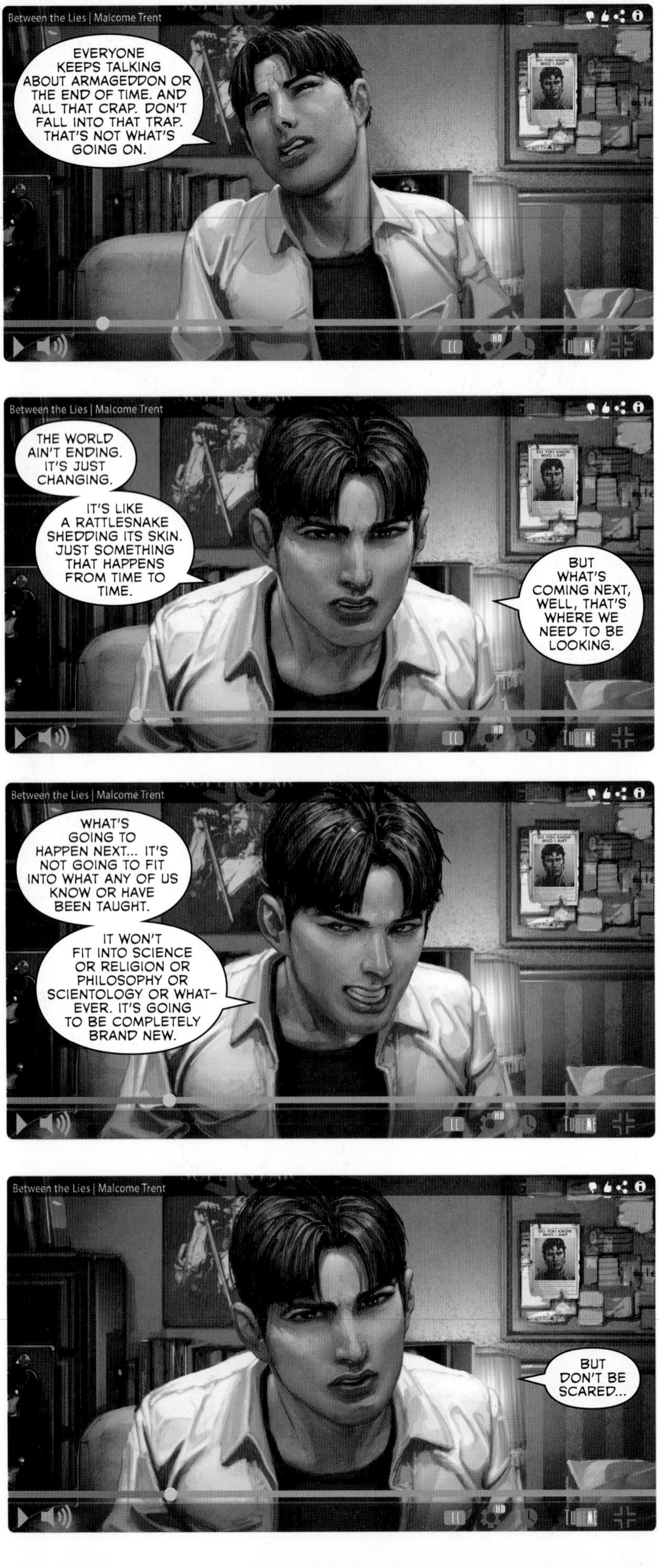
Between the Lies | Malcome Trent
EVERYONE KEEPS TALKING ABOUT ARMAGEDDON OR THE END OF TIME. AND ALL THAT CRAP. DON'T FALL INTO THAT TRAP. THAT'S NOT WHAT'S GOING ON.
Between the Lies | Malcome Trent
THE WORLD AIN'T ENDING. IT'S JUST CHANGING.
IT'S LIKE A RATTLESNAKE SHEDDING ITS SKIN. JUST SOMETHING THAT HAPPENS FROM TIME TO TIME.
BUT WHAT'S COMING NEXT, WELL, THAT'S WHERE WE NEED TO BE LOOKING.
Between the Lies | Malcome Trent
WHAT'S GOING TO HAPPEN NEXT... IT'S NOT GOING TO FIT INTO WHAT ANY OF US KNOW OR HAVE BEEN TAUGHT.
IT WON'T FIT INTO SCIENCE OR RELIGION OR PHILOSOPHY OR SCIENTOLOGY OR WHAT-EVER. IT'S GOING TO BE COMPLETELY BRAND NEW.
Between the Lies | Malcome Trent
BUT DON'T BE SCARED...

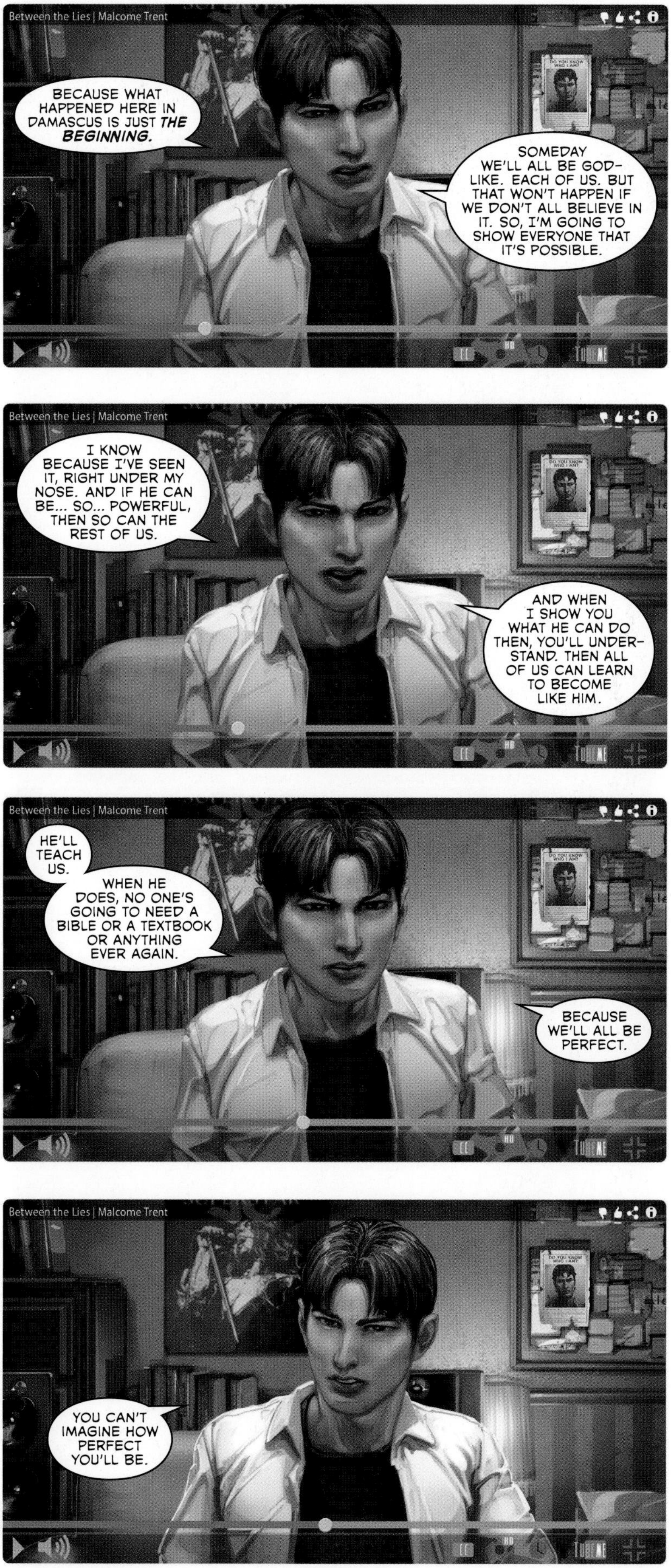
Between the Lies | Malcome Trent
BECAUSE WHAT HAPPENED HERE IN DAMASCUS IS JUST ***THE BEGINNING.***
SOMEDAY WE'LL ALL BE GOD-LIKE. EACH OF US. BUT THAT WON'T HAPPEN IF WE DON'T ALL BELIEVE IN IT. SO, I'M GOING TO SHOW EVERYONE THAT IT'S POSSIBLE.
Between the Lies | Malcome Trent
I KNOW BECAUSE I'VE SEEN IT, RIGHT UNDER MY NOSE. AND IF HE CAN BE... SO... POWERFUL, THEN SO CAN THE REST OF US.
AND WHEN I SHOW YOU WHAT HE CAN DO THEN, YOU'LL UNDER-STAND. THEN ALL OF US CAN LEARN TO BECOME LIKE HIM.
Between the Lies | Malcome Trent
HE'LL TEACH US.
WHEN HE DOES, NO ONE'S GOING TO NEED A BIBLE OR A TEXTBOOK OR ANYTHING EVER AGAIN.
BECAUSE WE'LL ALL BE PERFECT.
Between the Lies | Malcome Trent
YOU CAN'T IMAGINE HOW PERFECT YOU'LL BE.

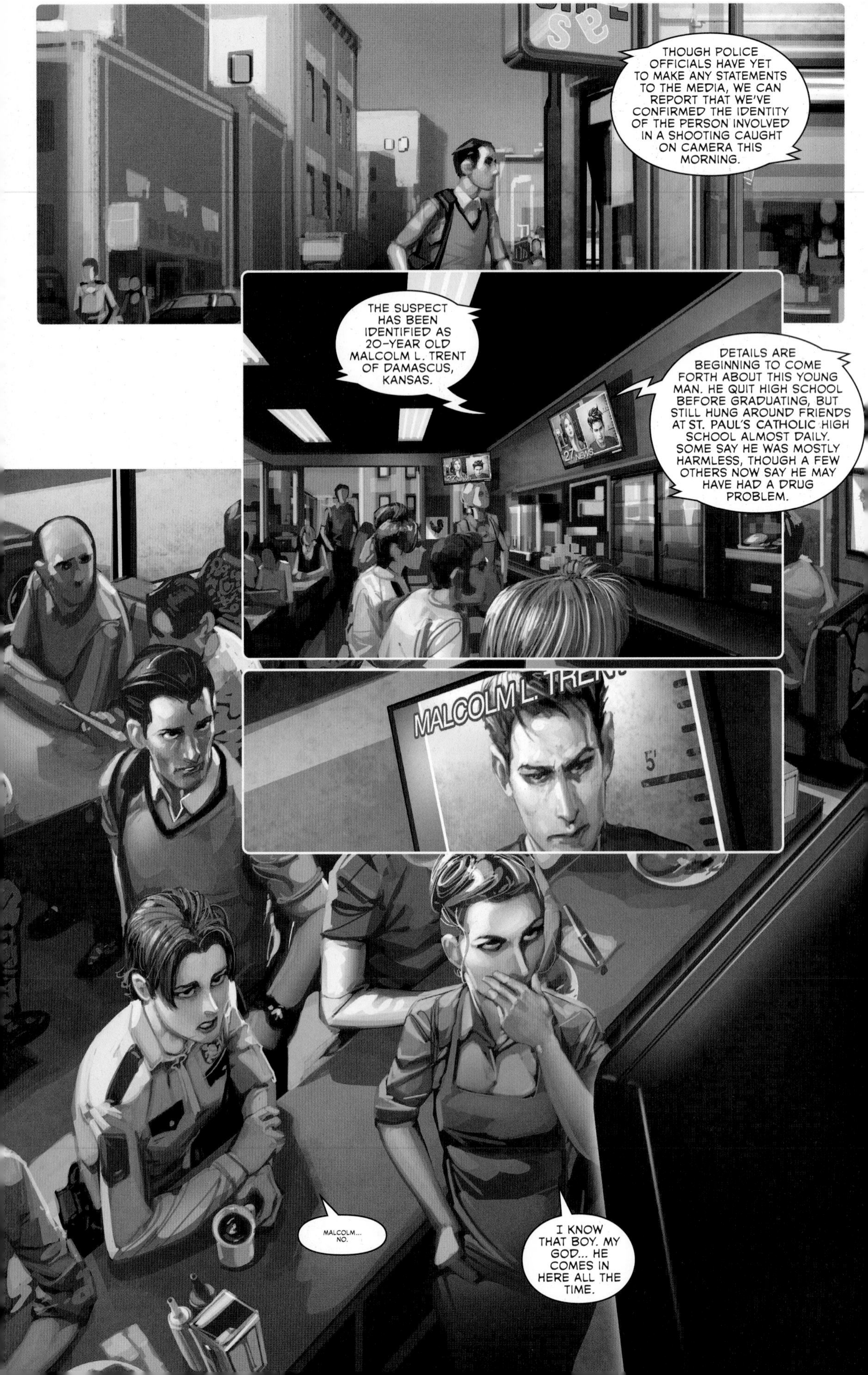
THOUGH POLICE OFFICIALS HAVE YET TO MAKE ANY STATEMENTS TO THE MEDIA, WE CAN REPORT THAT WE'VE CONFIRMED THE IDENTITY OF THE PERSON INVOLVED IN A SHOOTING CAUGHT ON CAMERA THIS MORNING.
THE SUSPECT HAS BEEN IDENTIFIED AS 20-YEAR OLD MALCOLM L. TRENT OF DAMASCUS, KANSAS.
DETAILS ARE BEGINNING TO COME FORTH ABOUT THIS YOUNG MAN. HE QUIT HIGH SCHOOL BEFORE GRADUATING, BUT STILL HUNG AROUND FRIENDS AT ST. PAUL'S CATHOLIC HIGH SCHOOL ALMOST DAILY. SOME SAY HE WAS MOSTLY HARMLESS, THOUGH A FEW OTHERS NOW SAY HE MAY HAVE HAD A DRUG PROBLEM.
27 NEWS
MALCOLM L. TREN
5'
MALCOLM... NO.
I KNOW THAT BOY. MY GOD... HE COMES IN HERE ALL THE TIME.

D.A.R.P.A. Headquarters.

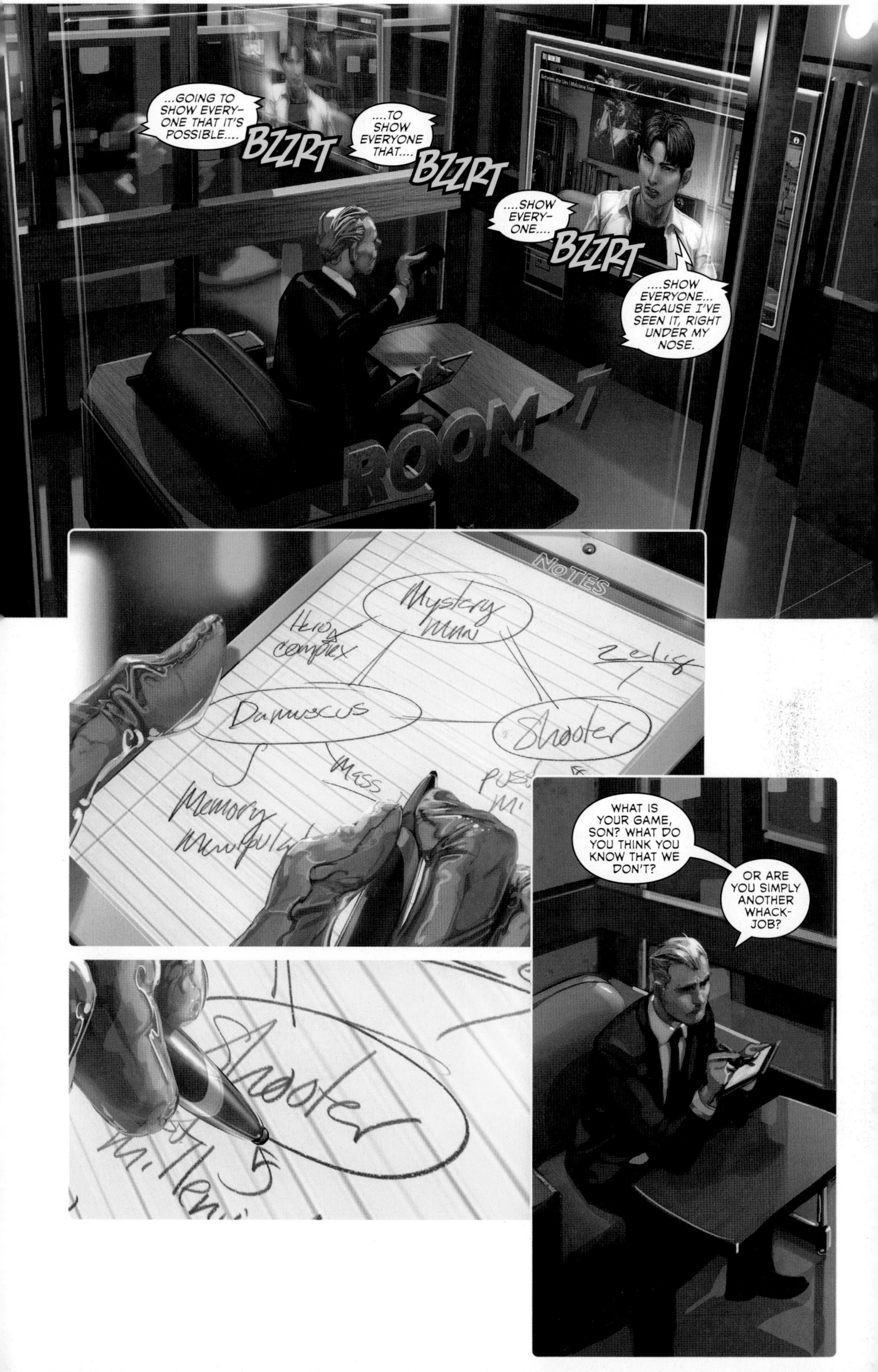

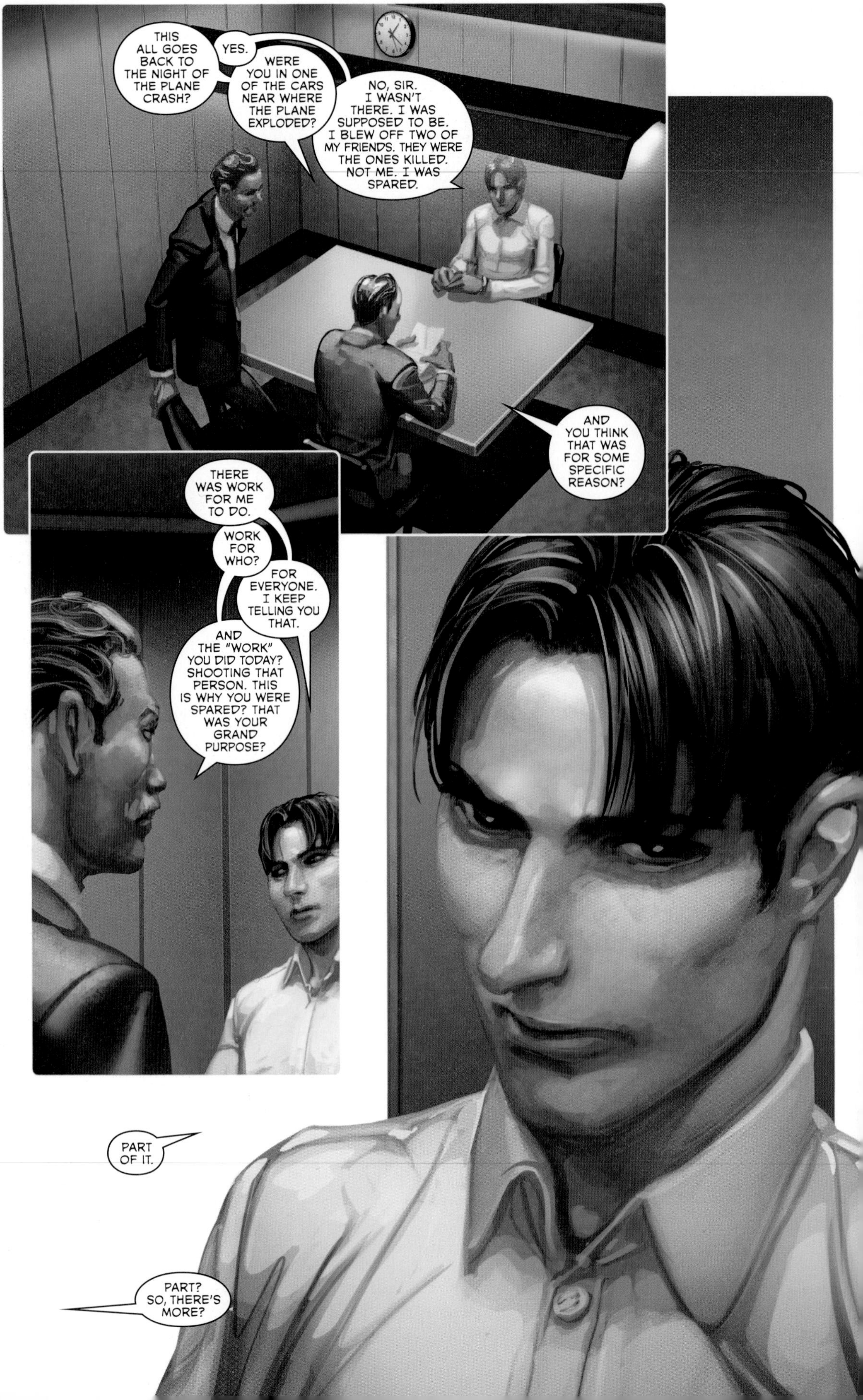
THIS ALL GOES BACK TO THE NIGHT OF THE PLANE CRASH?
YES.
WERE YOU IN ONE OF THE CARS NEAR WHERE THE PLANE EXPLODED?
NO, SIR. I WASN'T THERE. I WAS SUPPOSED TO BE. I BLEW OFF TWO OF MY FRIENDS. THEY WERE THE ONES KILLED. NOT ME. I WAS SPARED.
AND YOU THINK THAT WAS FOR SOME SPECIFIC REASON?
THERE WAS WORK FOR ME TO DO.
WORK FOR WHO?
FOR EVERYONE. I KEEP TELLING YOU THAT.
AND THE "WORK" YOU DID TODAY? SHOOTING THAT PERSON. THIS IS WHY YOU WERE SPARED? THAT WAS YOUR GRAND PURPOSE?
PART OF IT.
PART? SO, THERE'S MORE?

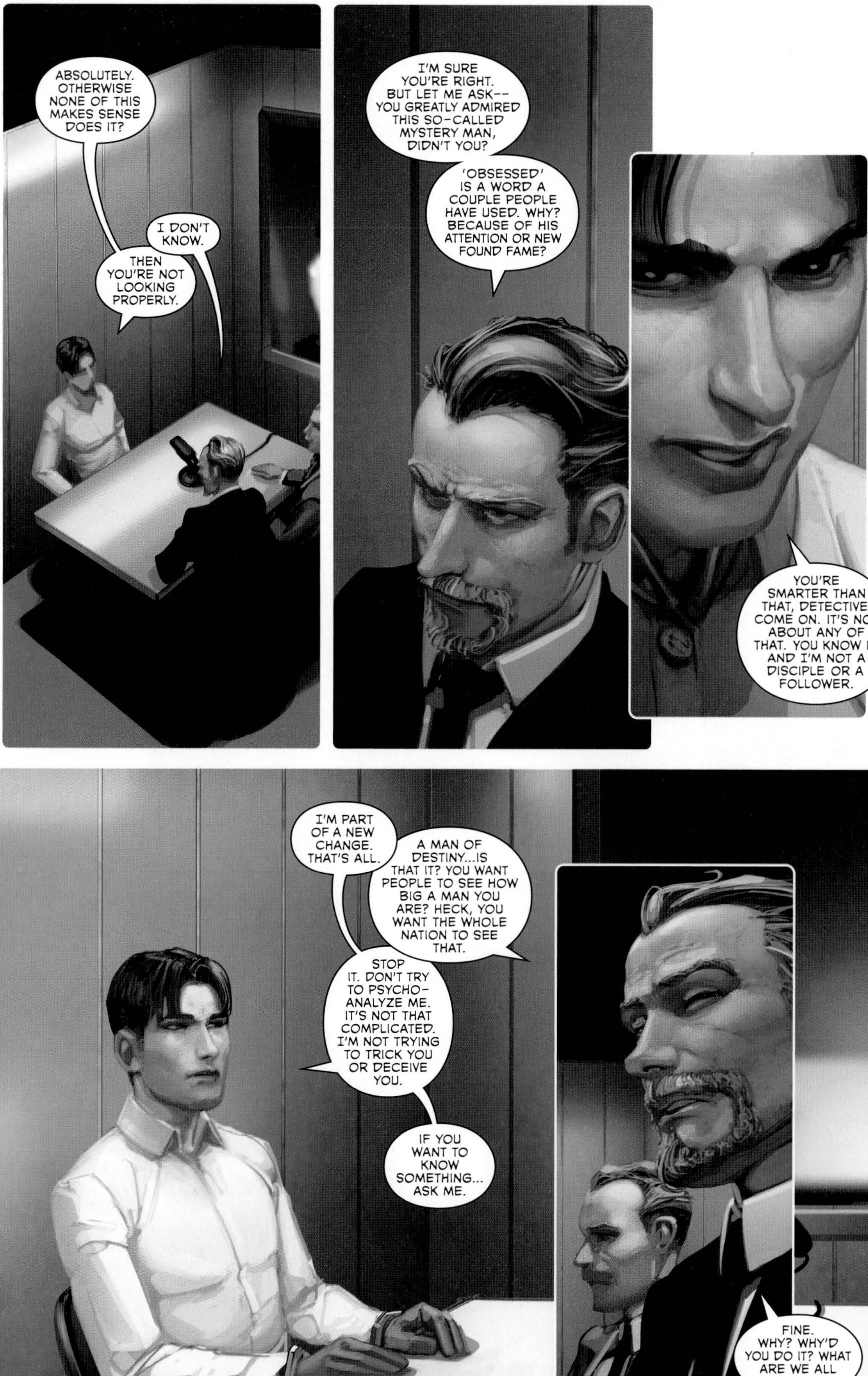
ABSOLUTELY. OTHERWISE NONE OF THIS MAKES SENSE DOES IT?
I DON'T KNOW.
THEN YOU'RE NOT LOOKING PROPERLY.
I'M SURE YOU'RE RIGHT. BUT LET ME ASK-- YOU GREATLY ADMIRED THIS SO-CALLED MYSTERY MAN, DIDN'T YOU?
'OBSESSED' IS A WORD A COUPLE PEOPLE HAVE USED. WHY? BECAUSE OF HIS ATTENTION OR NEW FOUND FAME?
YOU'RE SMARTER THAN THAT, DETECTIVE. COME ON. IT'S NOT ABOUT ANY OF THAT. YOU KNOW IT. AND I'M NOT A DISCIPLE OR A FOLLOWER.
I'M PART OF A NEW CHANGE. THAT'S ALL.
A MAN OF DESTINY...IS THAT IT? YOU WANT PEOPLE TO SEE HOW BIG A MAN YOU ARE? HECK, YOU WANT THE WHOLE NATION TO SEE THAT.
STOP IT. DON'T TRY TO PSYCHO-ANALYZE ME. IT'S NOT THAT COMPLICATED. I'M NOT TRYING TO TRICK YOU OR DECEIVE YOU.
IF YOU WANT TO KNOW SOMETHING... ASK ME.
FINE. WHY? WHY'D YOU DO IT? WHAT ARE WE ALL MISSING?

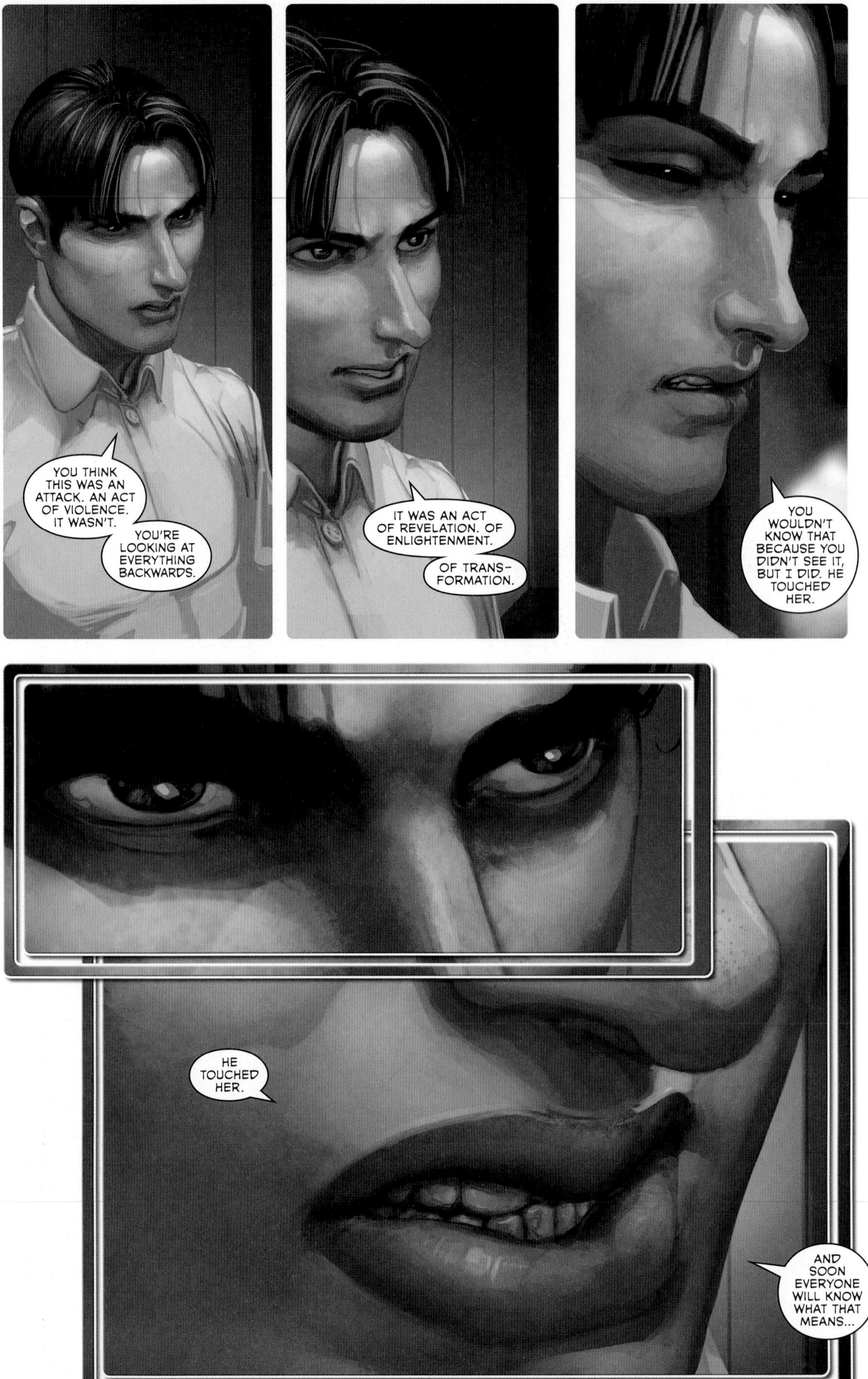
YOU THINK THIS WAS AN ATTACK. AN ACT OF VIOLENCE. IT WASN'T.
YOU'RE LOOKING AT EVERYTHING BACKWARDS.
IT WAS AN ACT OF REVELATION. OF ENLIGHTENMENT.
OF TRANS-FORMATION.
YOU WOULDN'T KNOW THAT BECAUSE YOU DIDN'T SEE IT, BUT I DID. HE TOUCHED HER.
HE TOUCHED HER.
AND SOON EVERYONE WILL KNOW WHAT THAT MEANS...

Earlier.

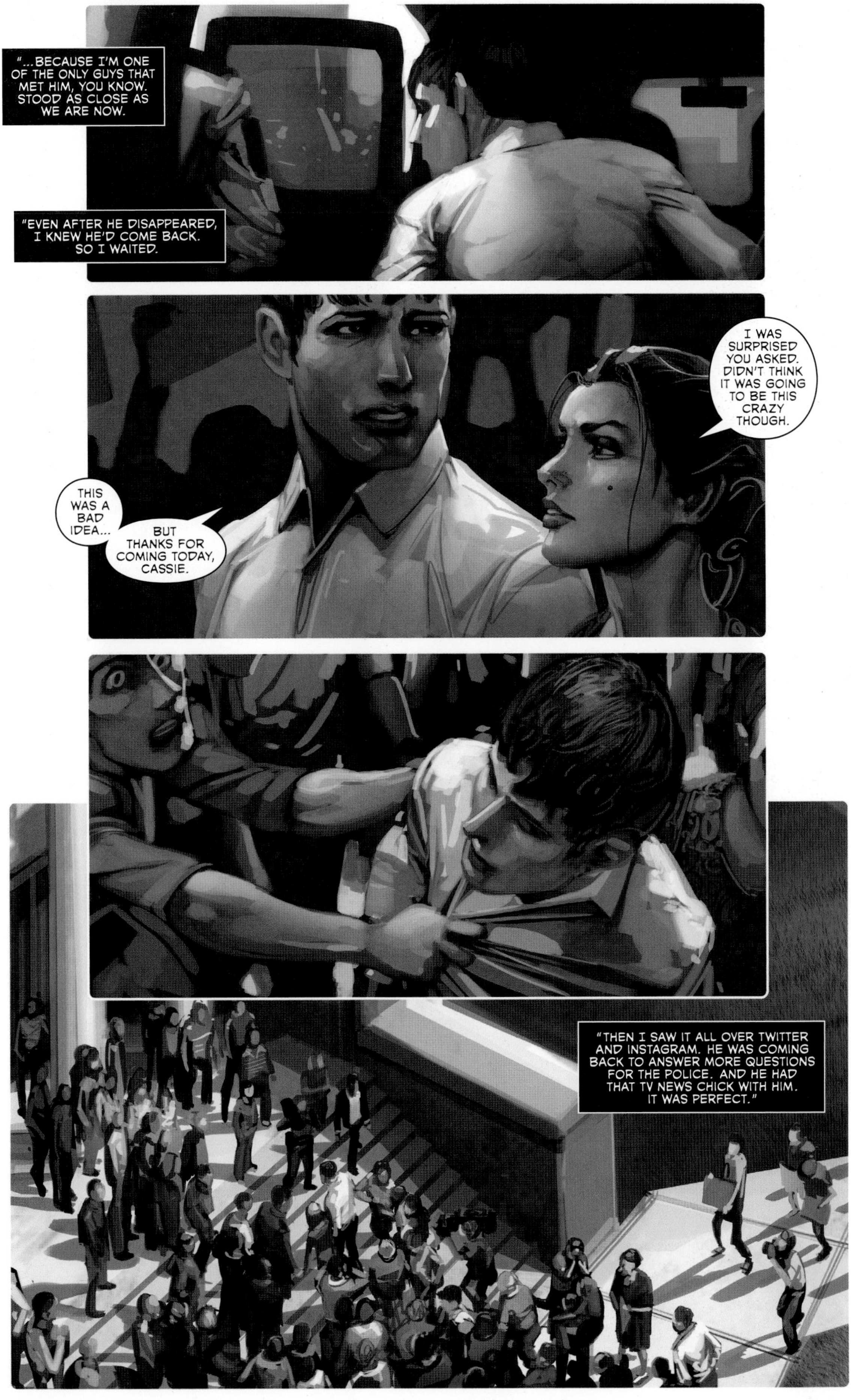

"...BECAUSE I'M ONE OF THE ONLY GUYS THAT MET HIM, YOU KNOW. STOOD AS CLOSE AS WE ARE NOW.
"EVEN AFTER HE DISAPPEARED, I KNEW HE'D COME BACK. SO I WAITED.
I WAS SURPRISED YOU ASKED. DIDN'T THINK IT WAS GOING TO BE THIS CRAZY THOUGH.
THIS WAS A BAD IDEA...
BUT THANKS FOR COMING TODAY, CASSIE.
"THEN I SAW IT ALL OVER TWITTER AND INSTAGRAM. HE WAS COMING BACK TO ANSWER MORE QUESTIONS FOR THE POLICE. AND HE HAD THAT TV NEWS CHICK WITH HIM. IT WAS PERFECT."

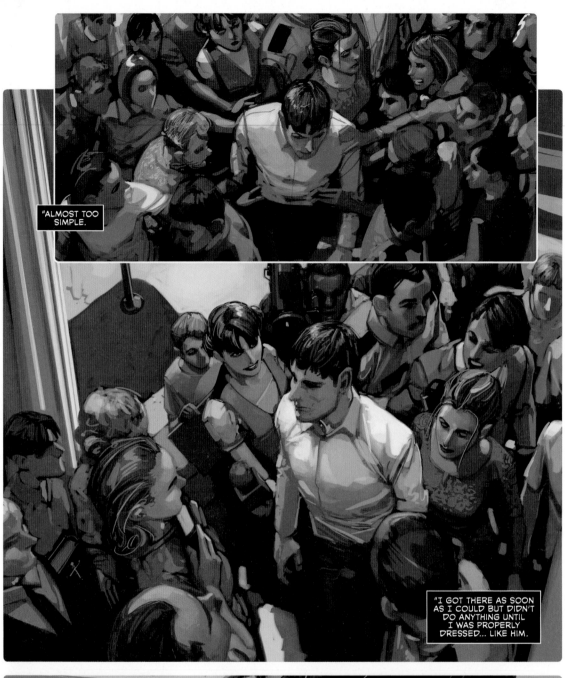

"ALMOST TOO SIMPLE.

"I GOT THERE AS SOON AS I COULD BUT DIDN'T DO ANYTHING UNTIL I WAS PROPERLY DRESSED... LIKE HIM.

"SO I BOUGHT THIS SHIRT, COMBED MY HAIR...

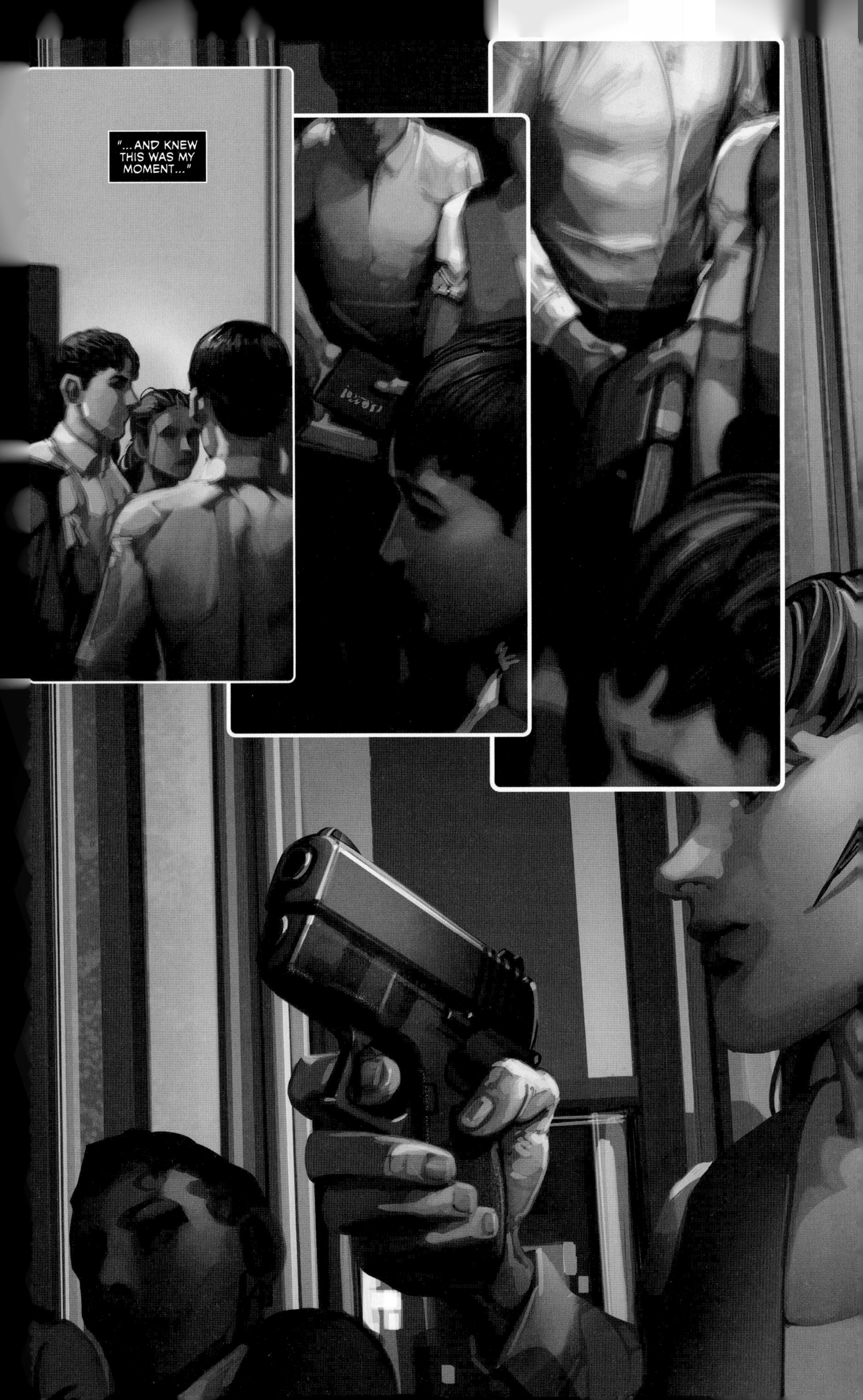
"...AND KNEW THIS WAS MY MOMENT..."

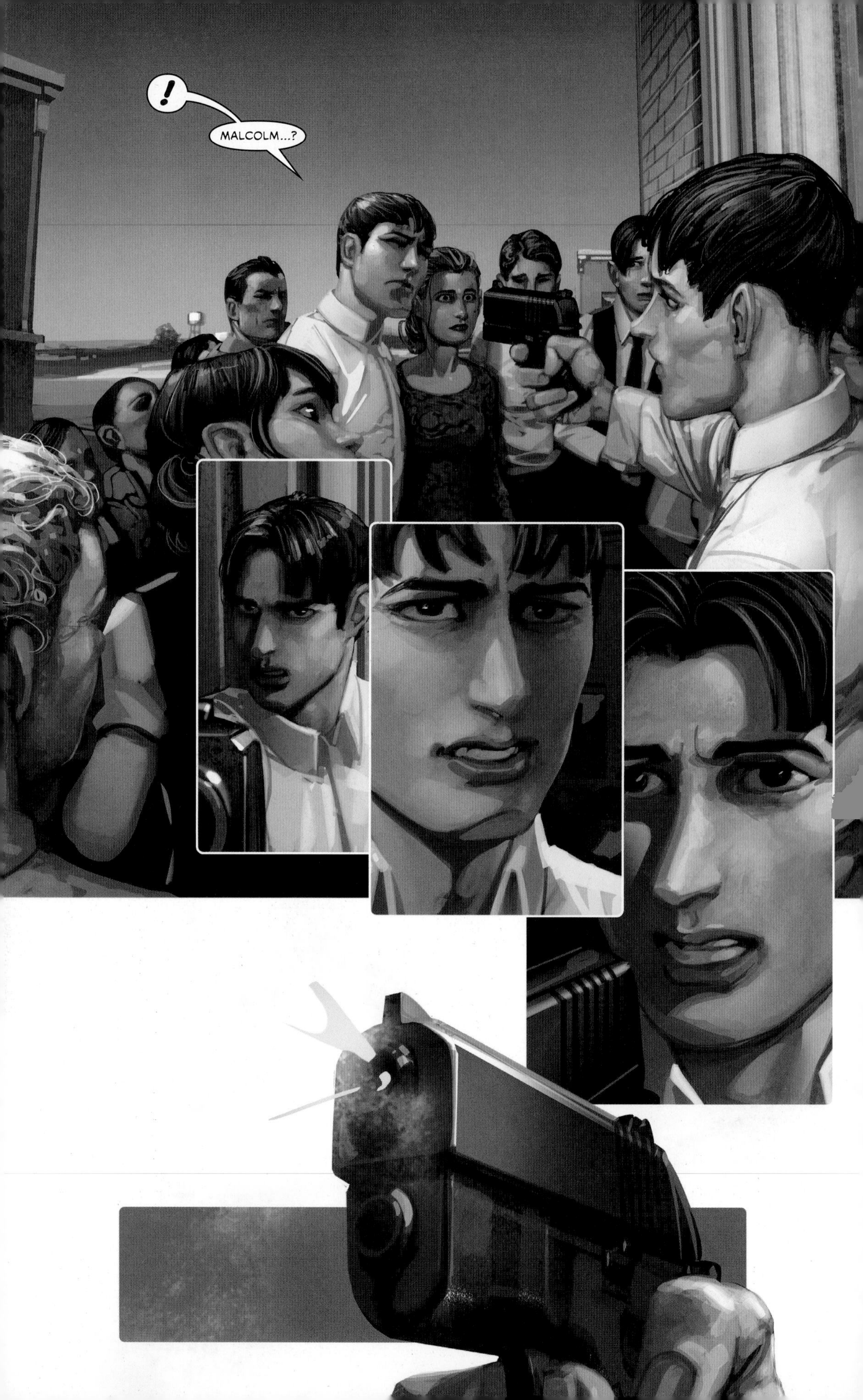
!
MALCOLM...?

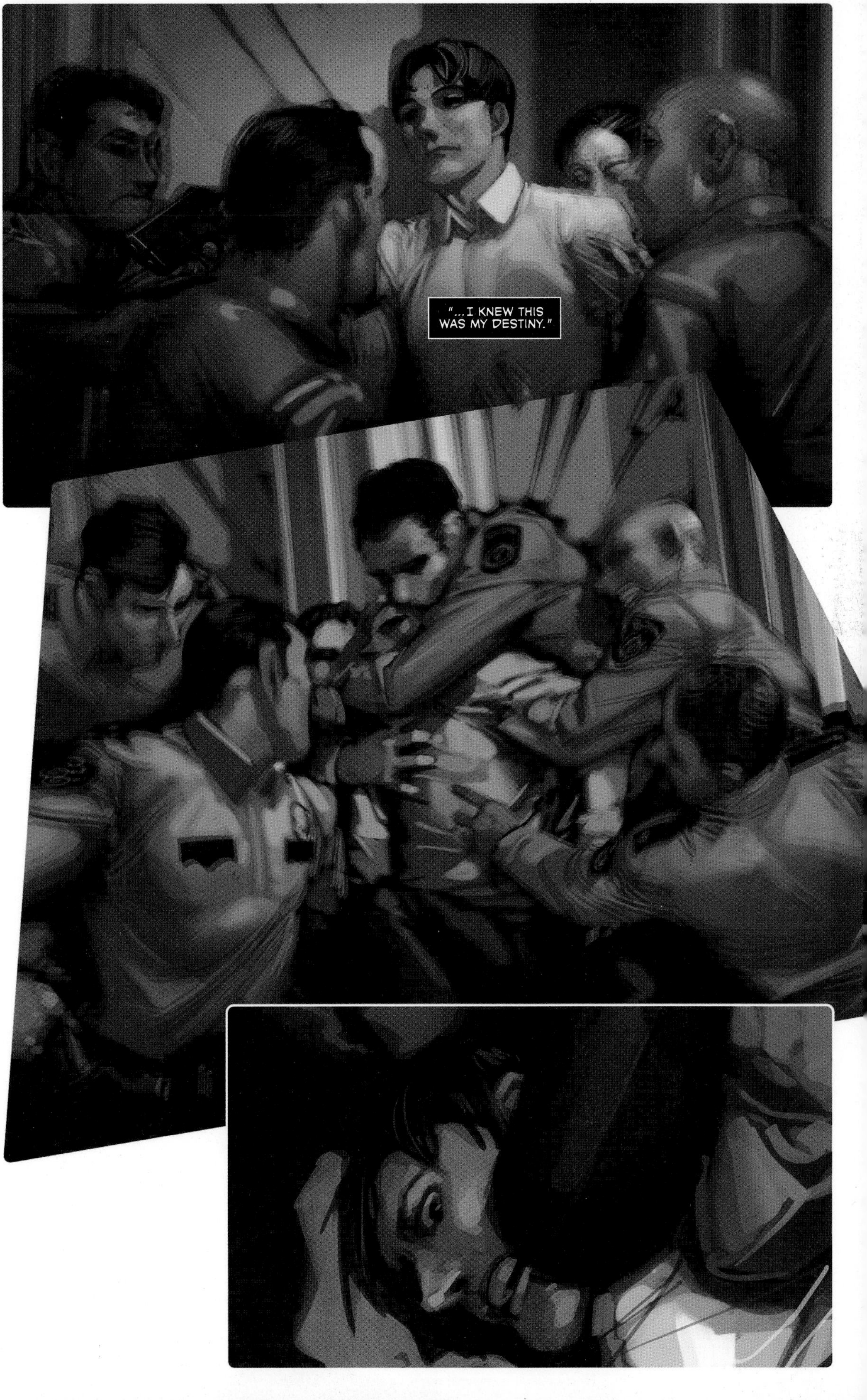
"...I KNEW THIS WAS MY DESTINY."

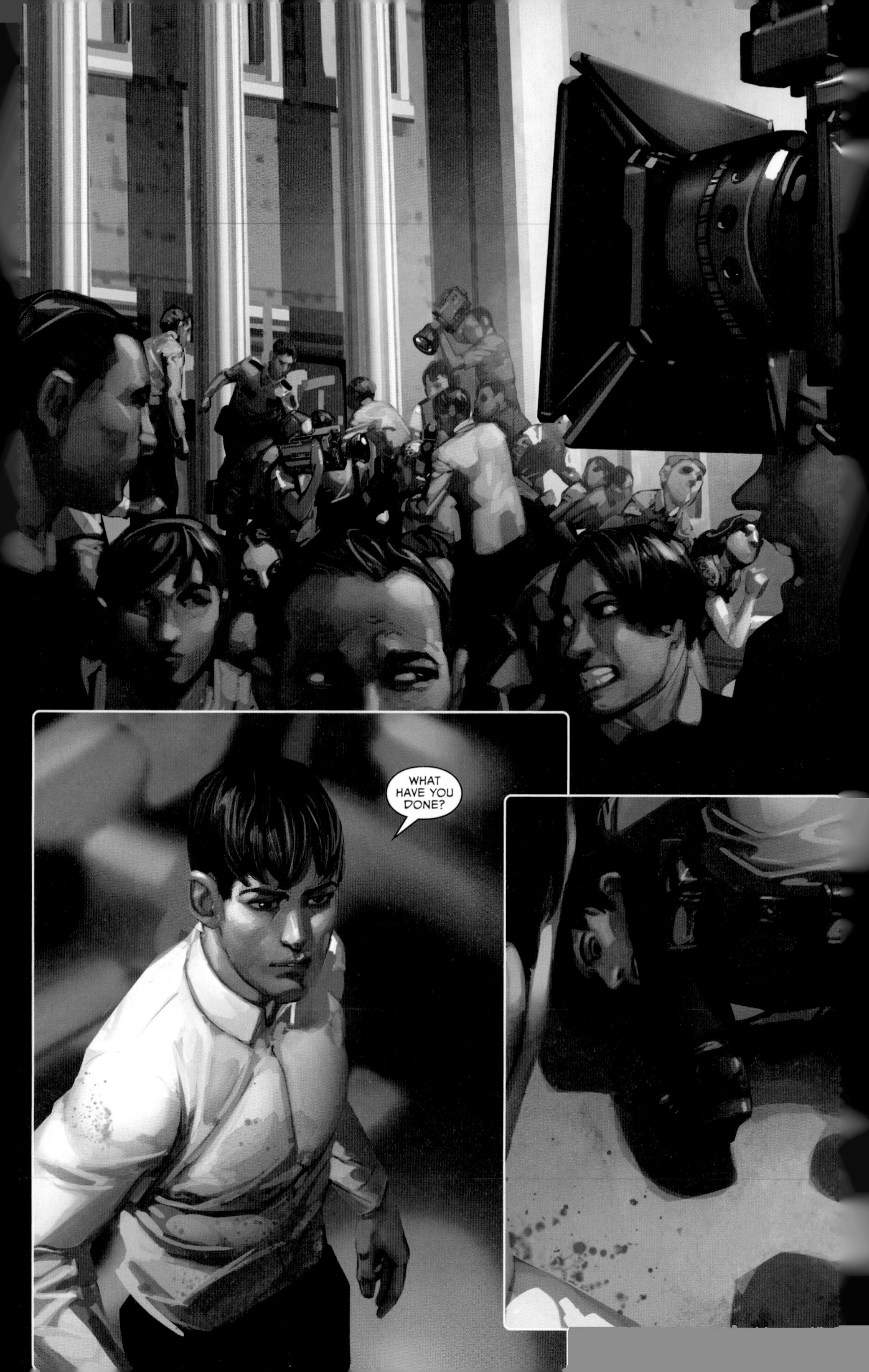
WHAT HAVE YOU DONE?

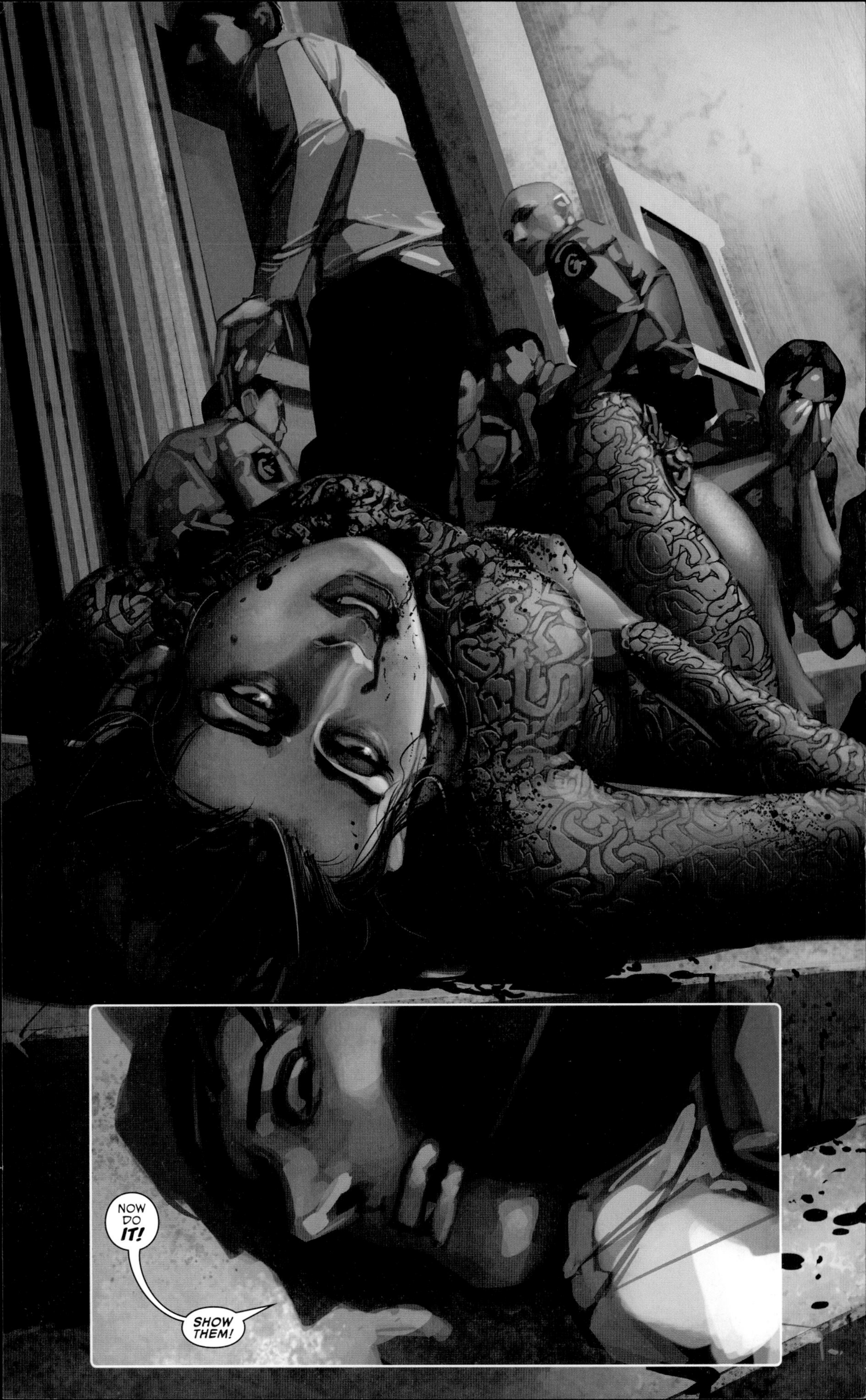
NOW DO IT!
SHOW THEM!

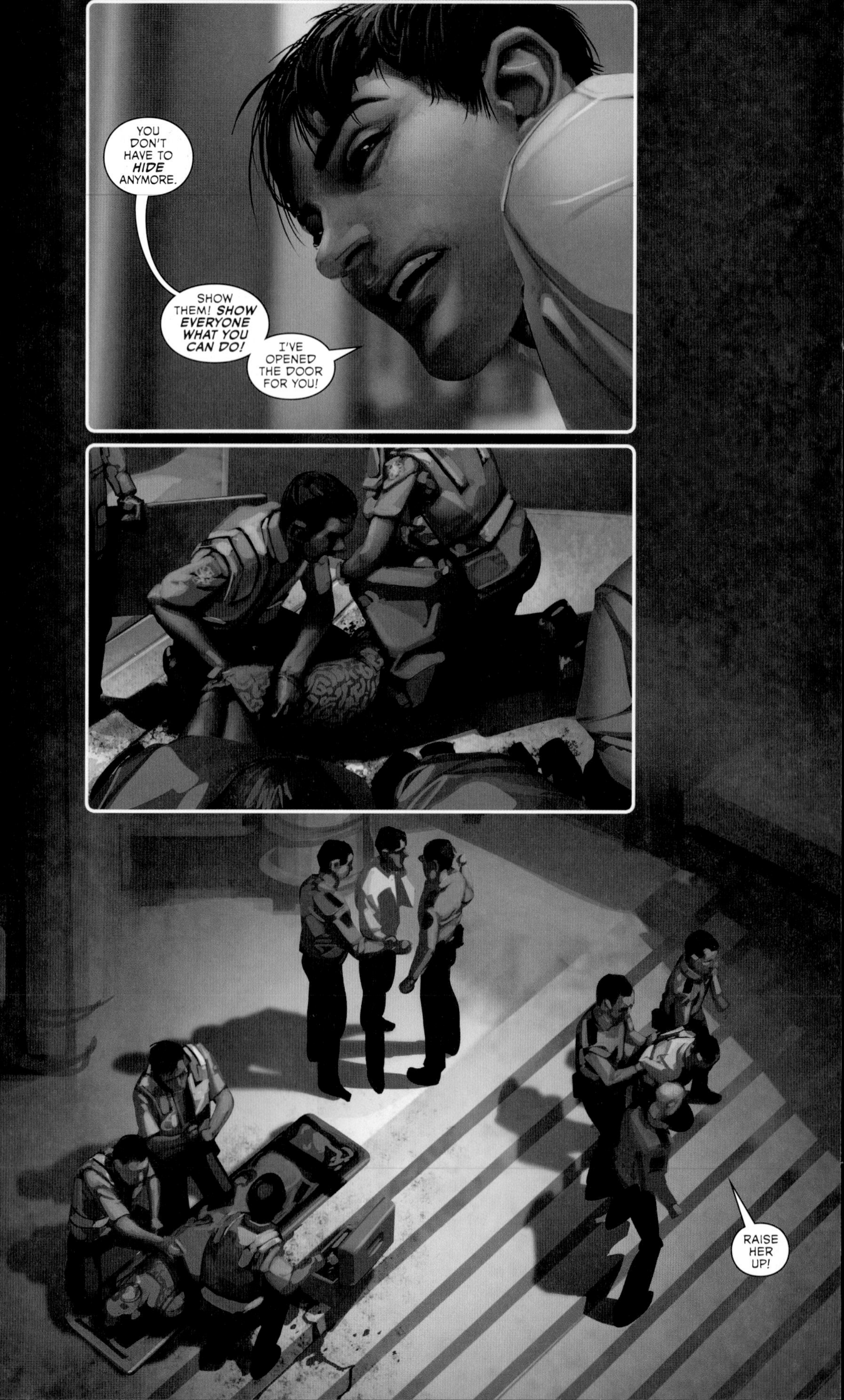
YOU DON'T HAVE TO *HIDE* ANYMORE.
SHOW THEM! ***SHOW EVERYONE WHAT YOU CAN DO!***
I'VE OPENED THE DOOR FOR YOU!
RAISE HER UP!

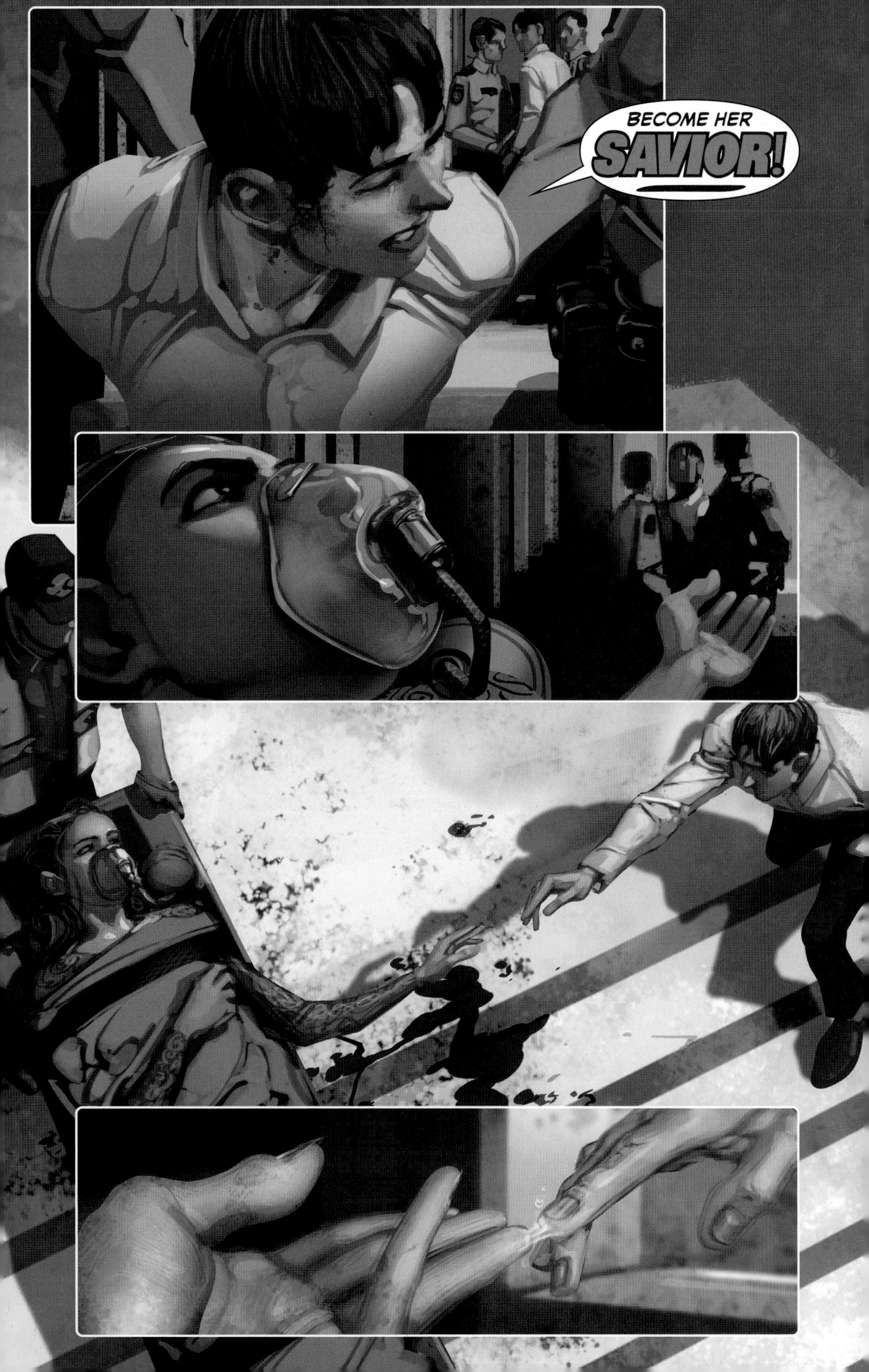
BECOME HER SAVIOR!

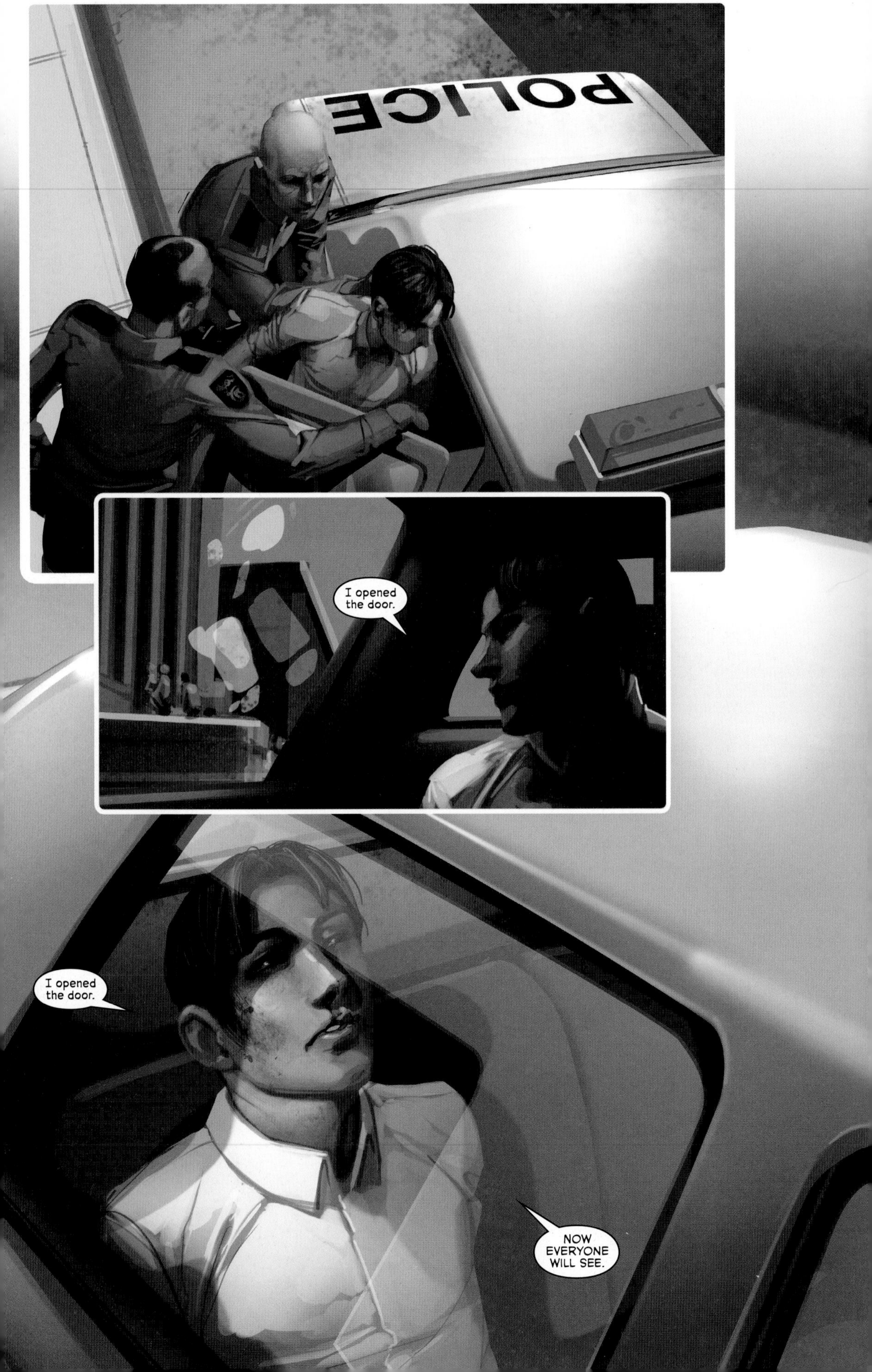
POLICE
I opened the door.
I opened the door.
NOW EVERYONE WILL SEE.

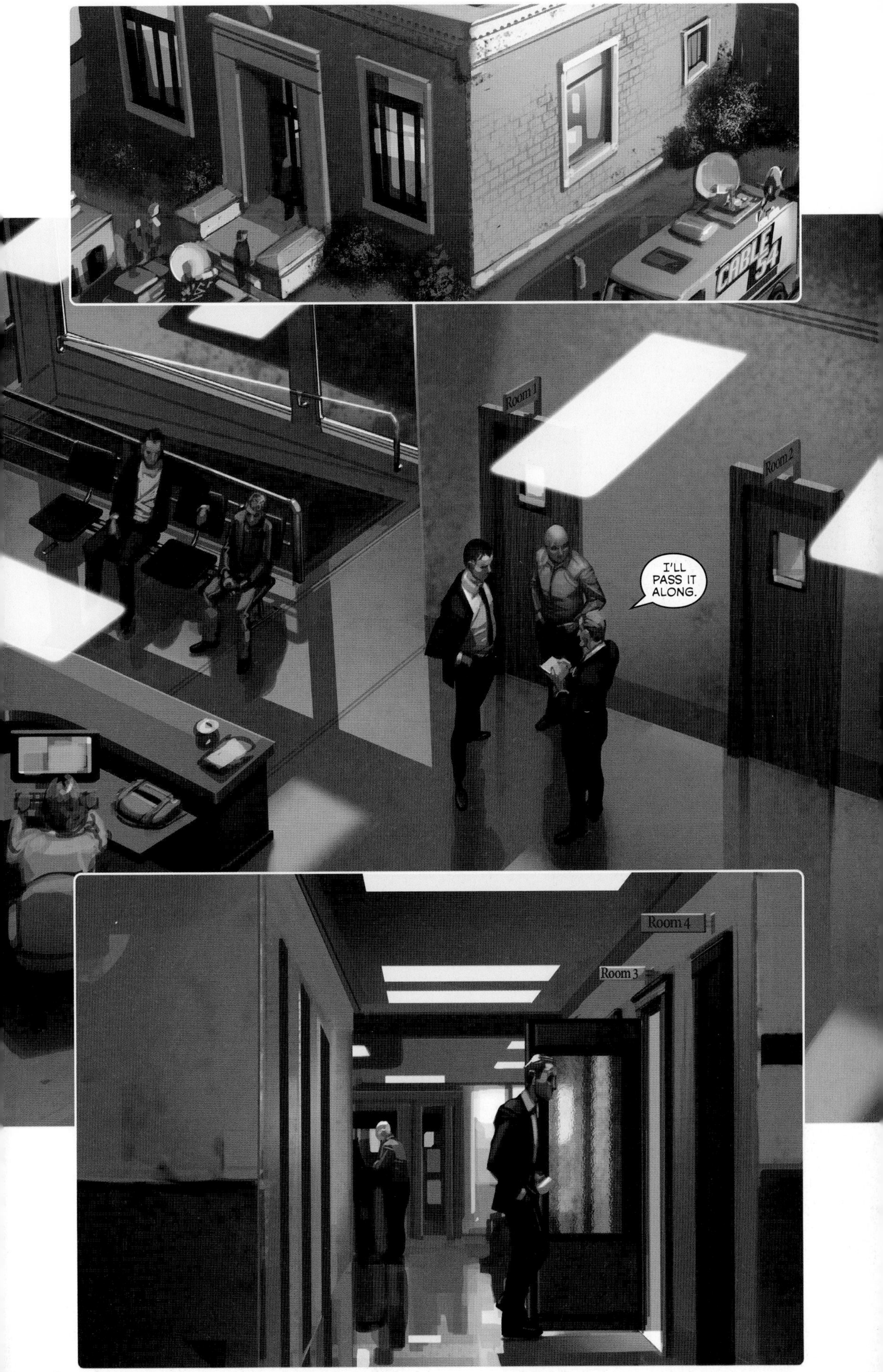
CABLE 54
Room 1
Room 2
I'LL PASS IT ALONG.
Room 4
Room 3

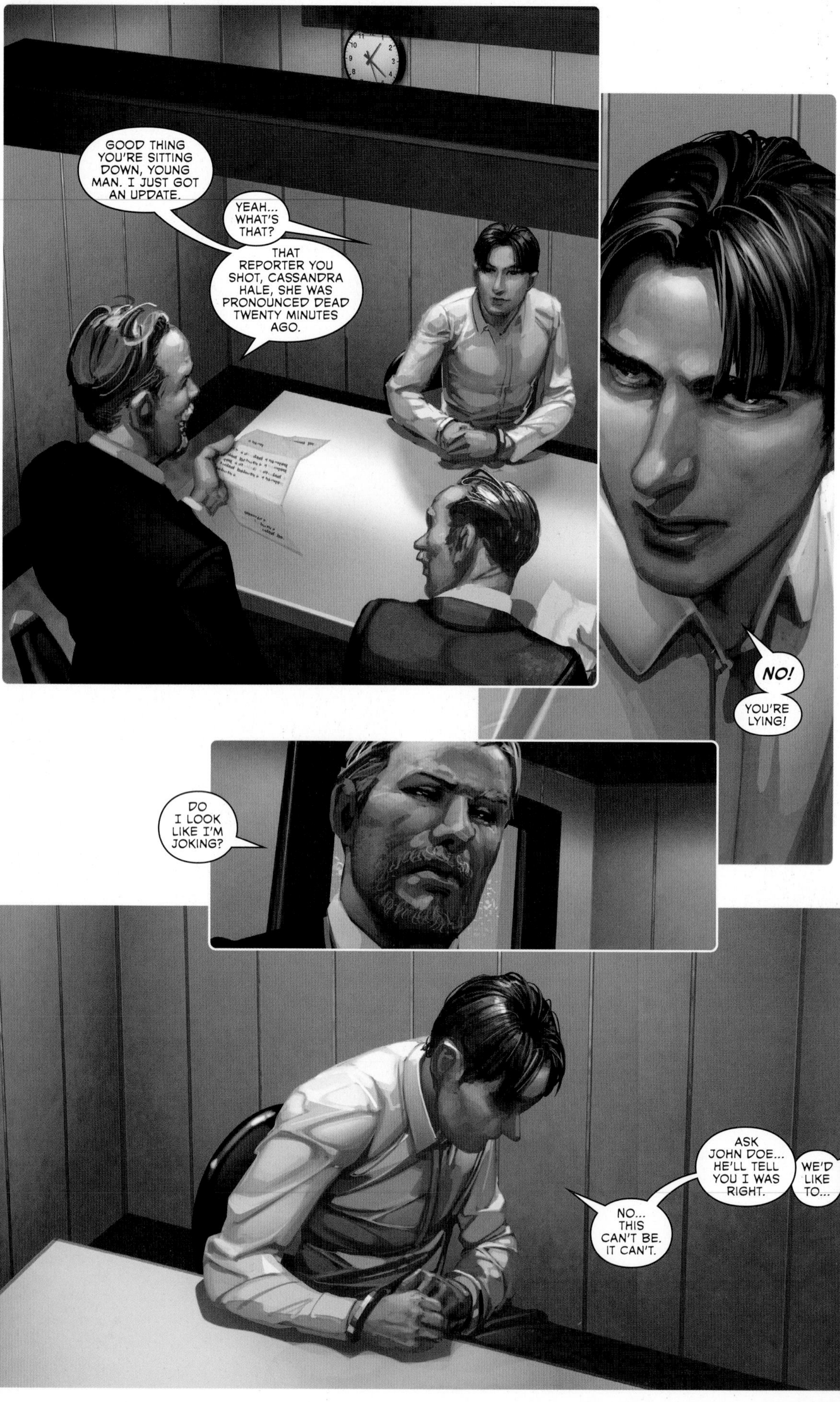
GOOD THING YOU'RE SITTING DOWN, YOUNG MAN. I JUST GOT AN UPDATE.
YEAH... WHAT'S THAT?
THAT REPORTER YOU SHOT, CASSANDRA HALE, SHE WAS PRONOUNCED DEAD TWENTY MINUTES AGO.
NO!
YOU'RE LYING!
DO I LOOK LIKE I'M JOKING?
NO... THIS CAN'T BE. IT CAN'T.
ASK JOHN DOE... HE'LL TELL YOU I WAS RIGHT.
WE'D LIKE TO...

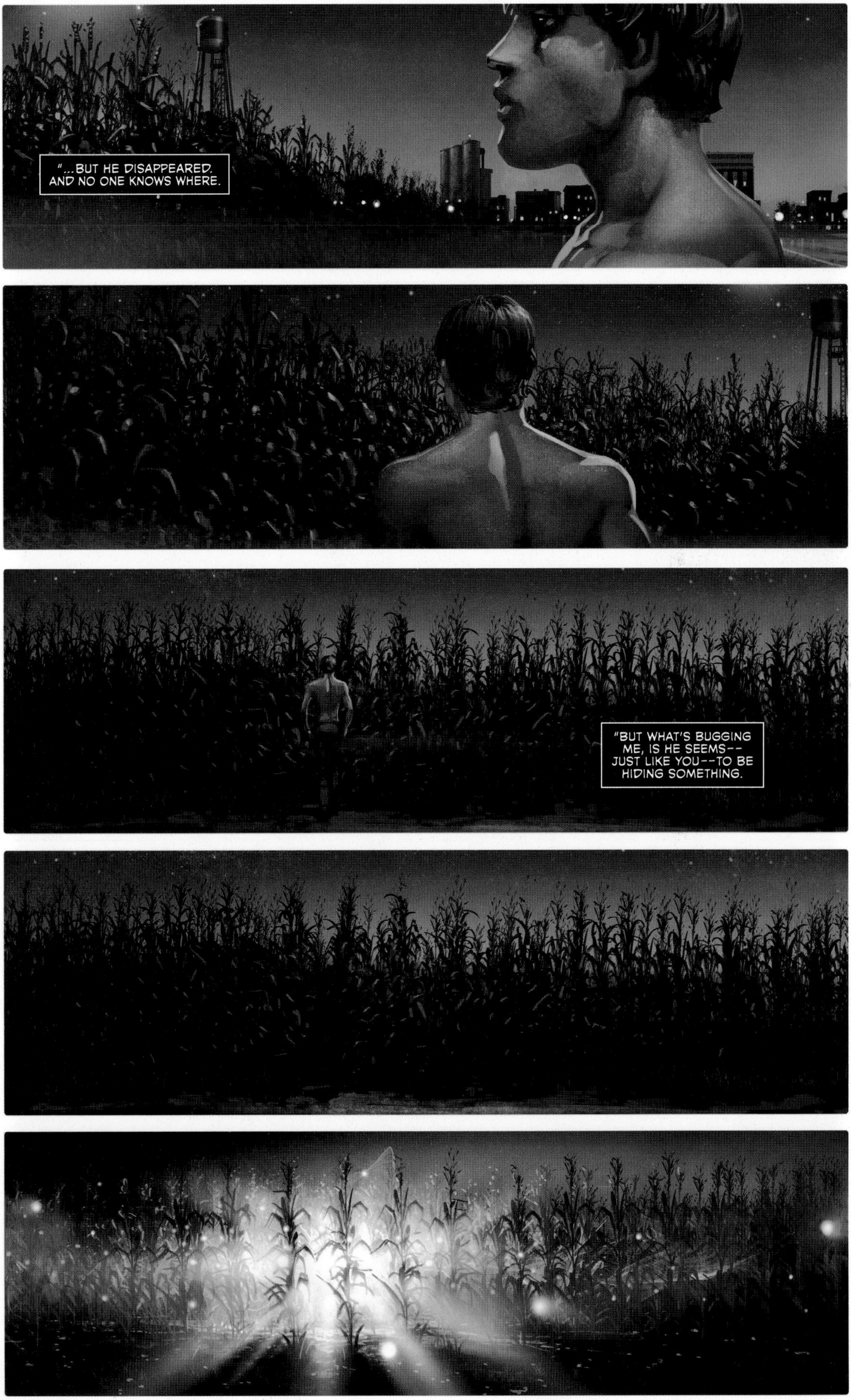
"...BUT HE DISAPPEARED. AND NO ONE KNOWS WHERE.
"BUT WHAT'S BUGGING ME, IS HE SEEMS-- JUST LIKE YOU--TO BE HIDING SOMETHING.

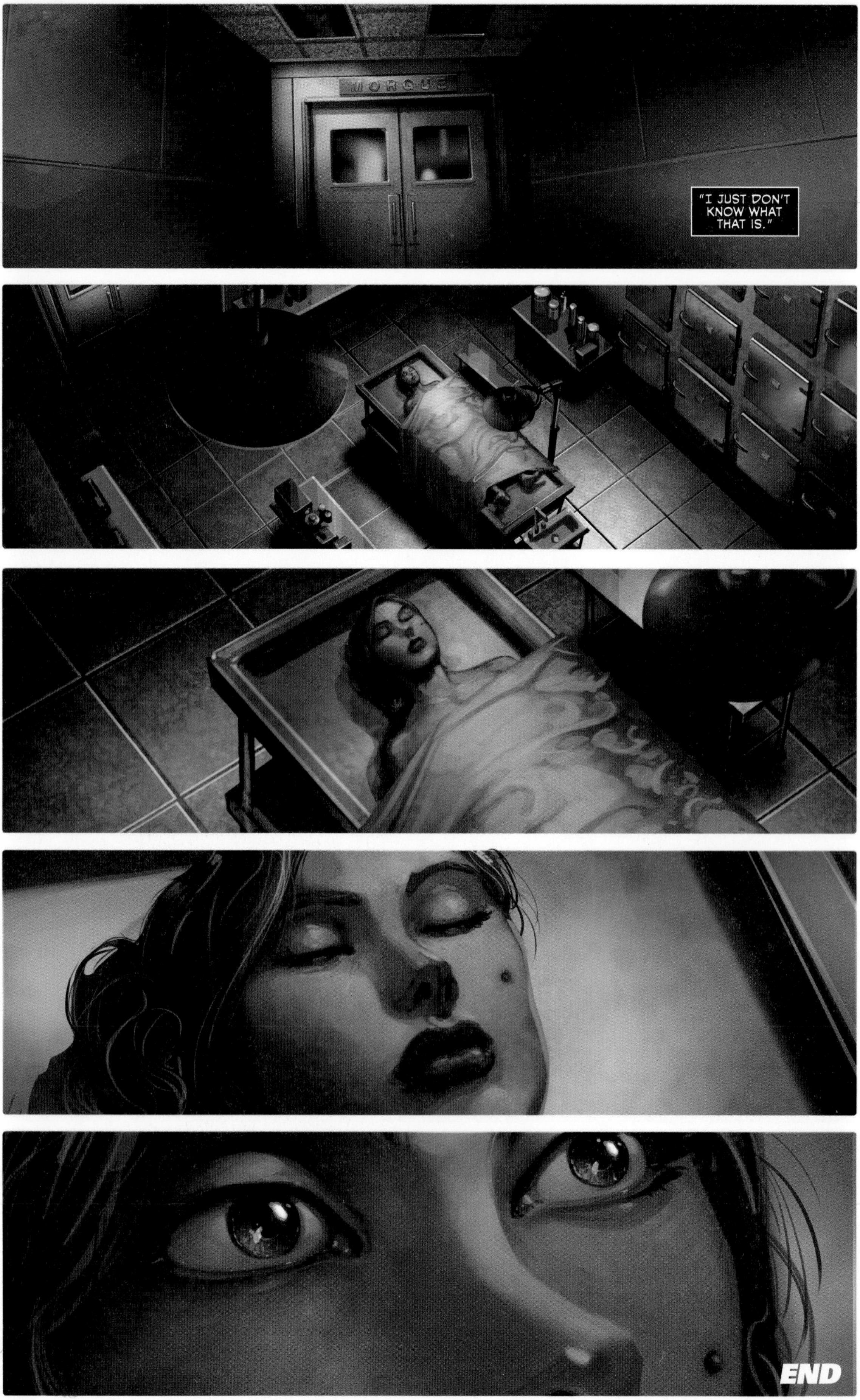
MORGUE
"I JUST DON'T KNOW WHAT THAT IS."
END

COVER ART GALLERY

COVER, ISSUE 1

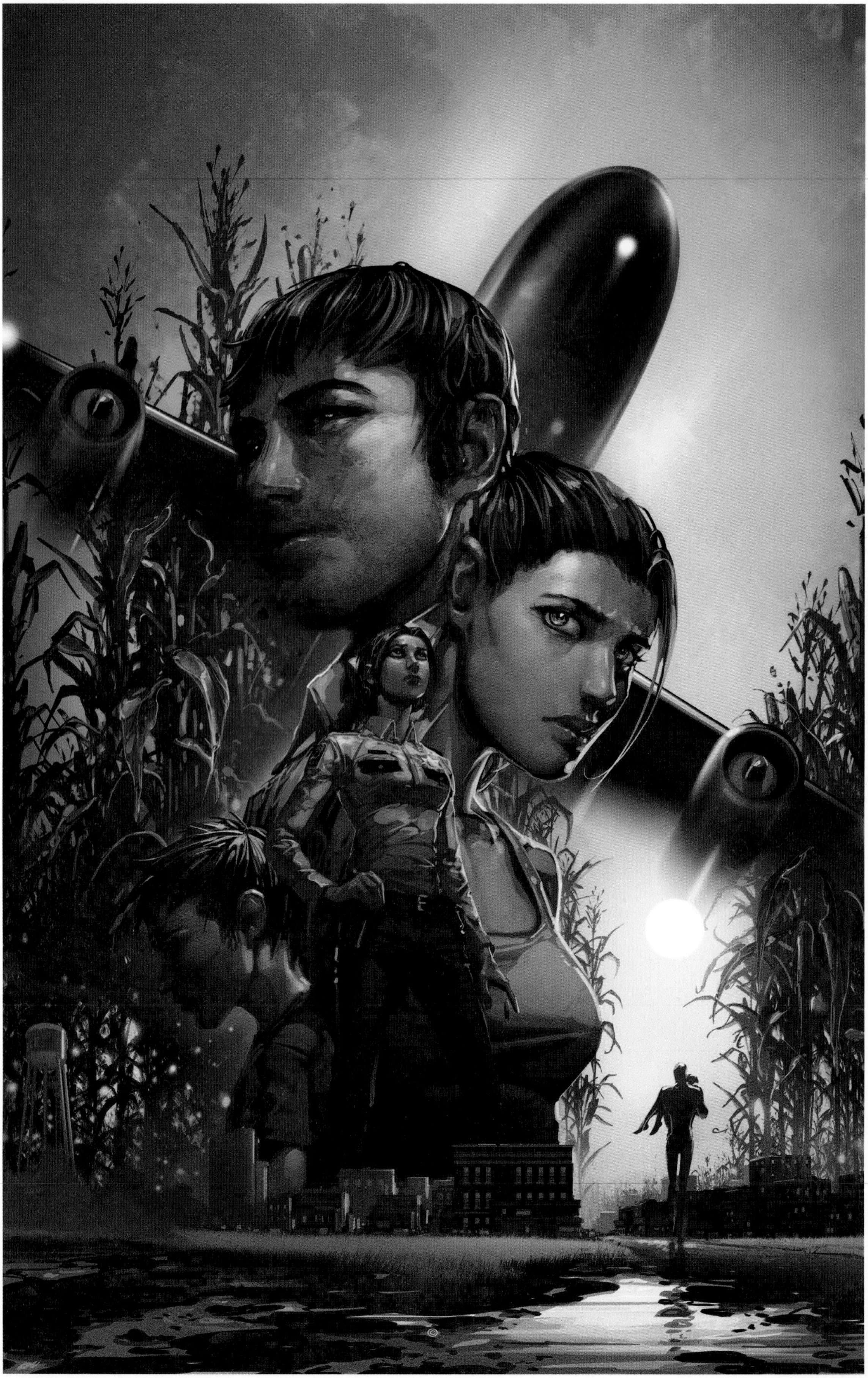

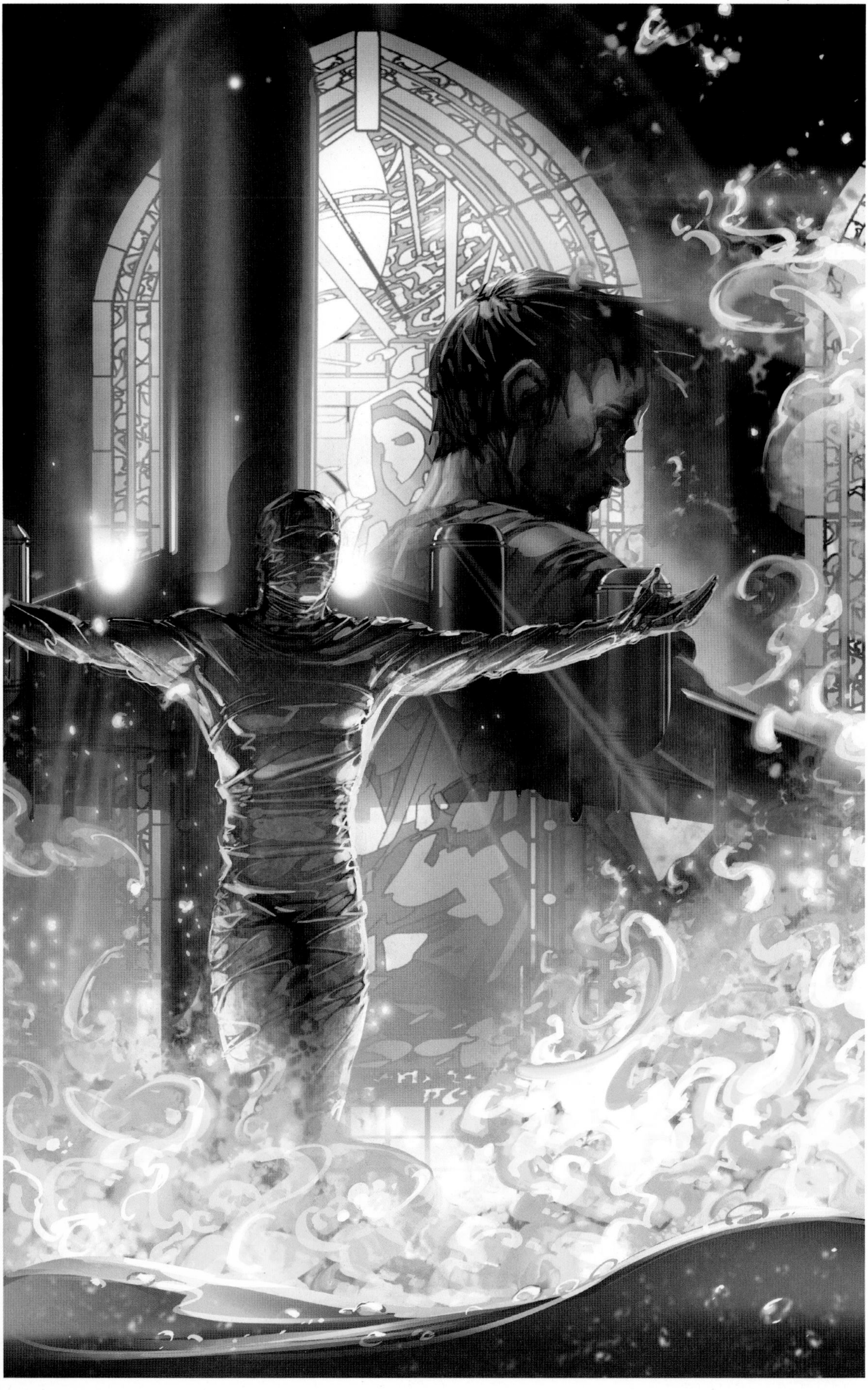

COVER CONCEPT ART, ISSUE 3

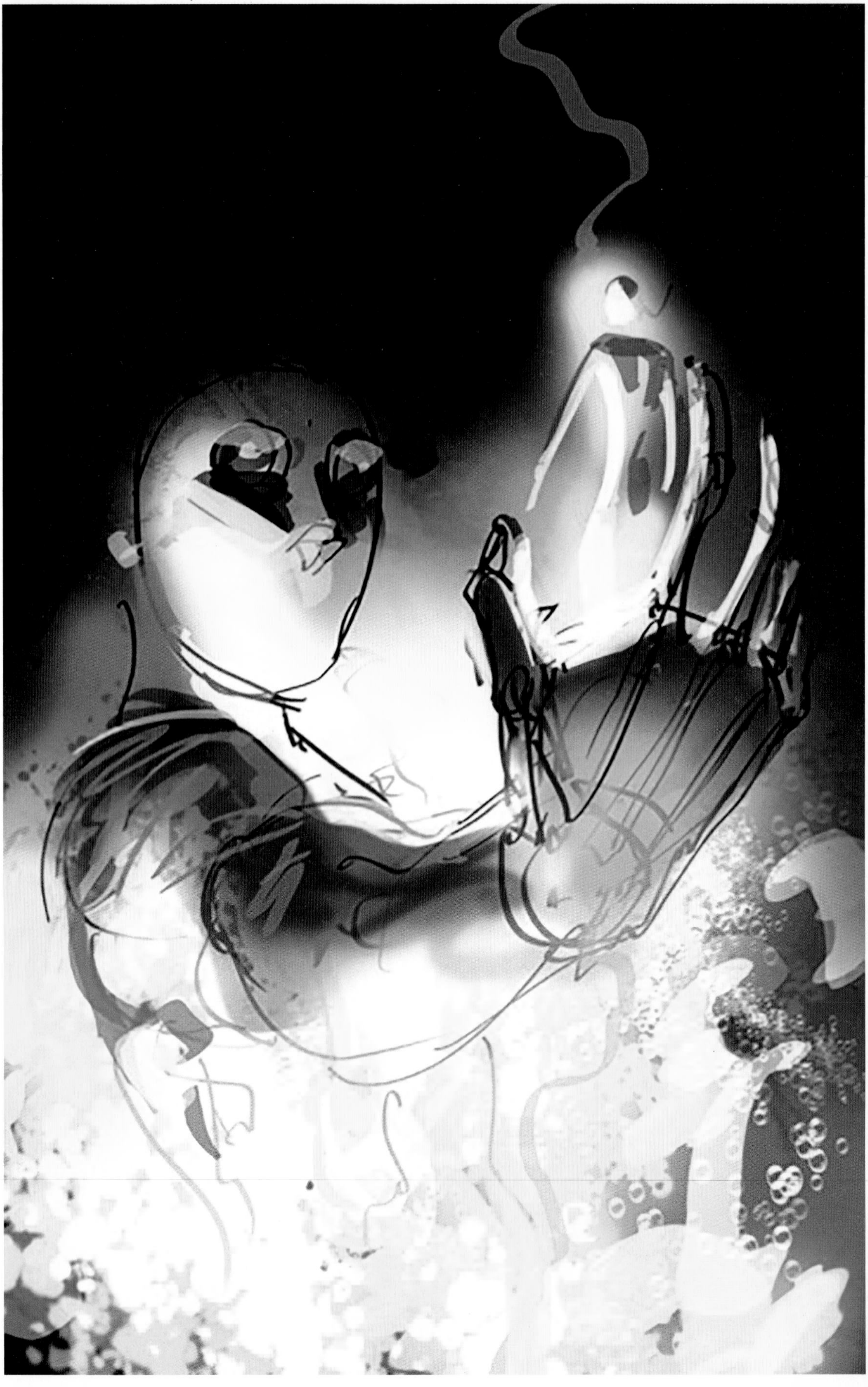

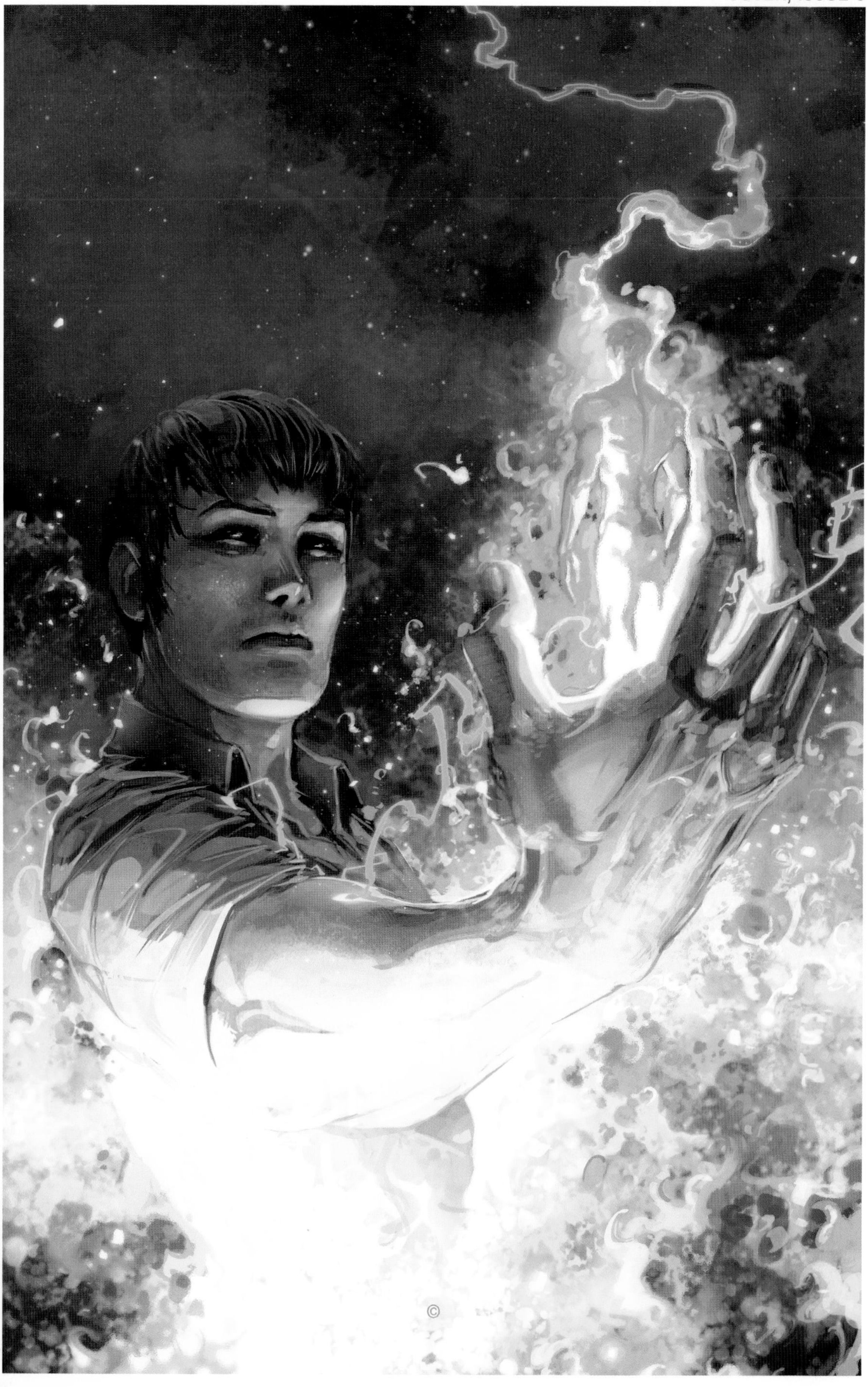

COVER CONCEPT ART (UNUSED)

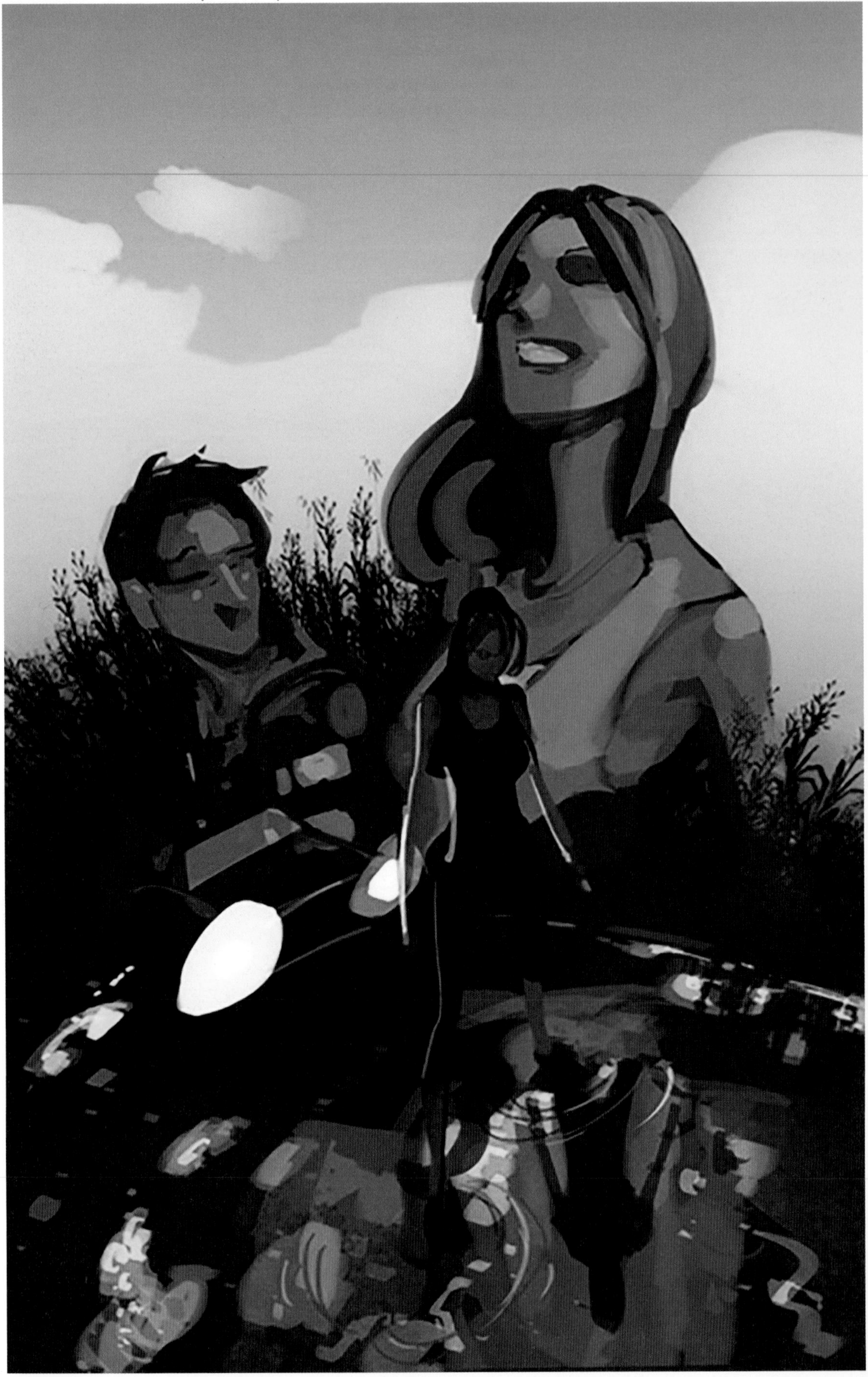

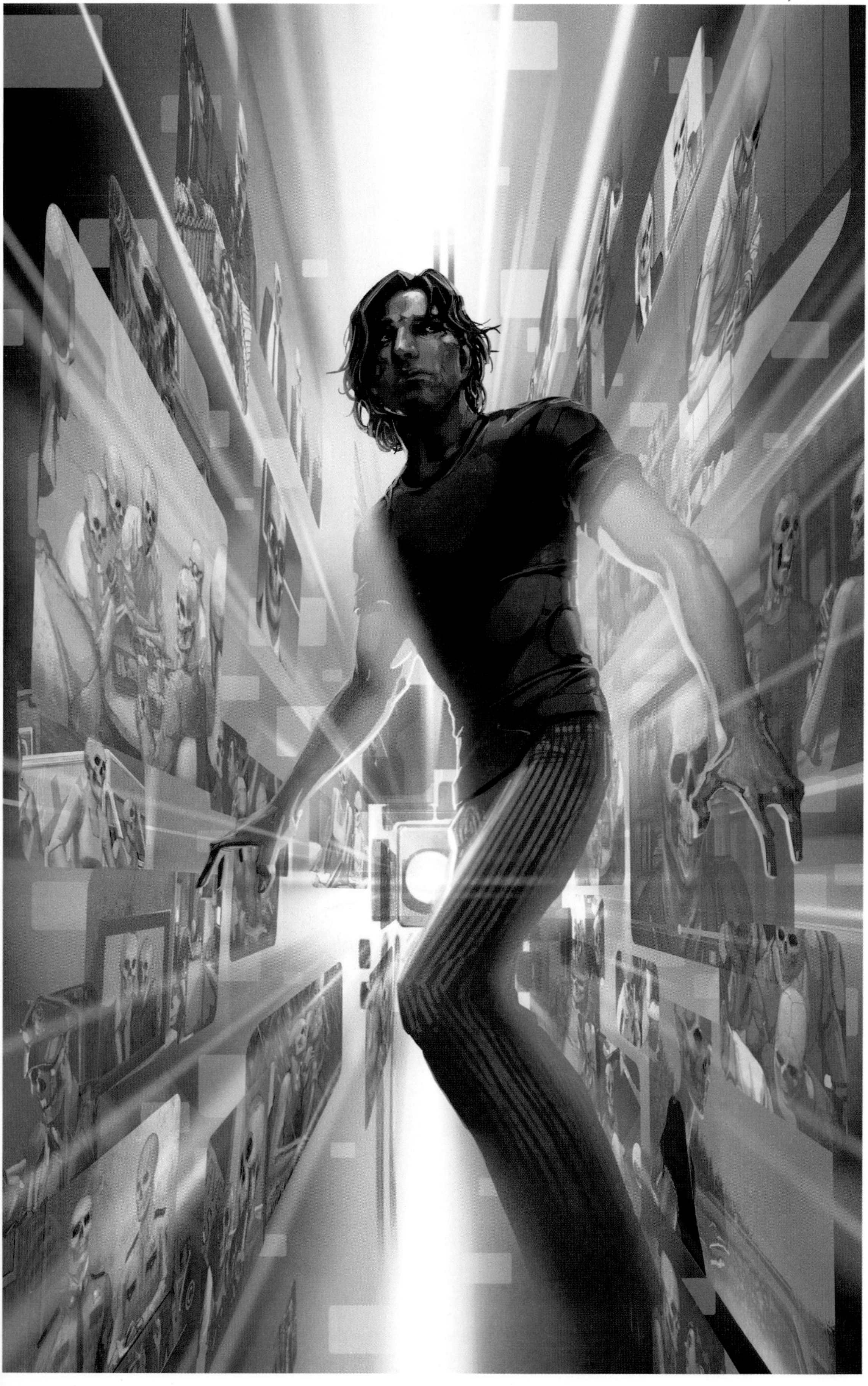

COVER, ISSUE 4

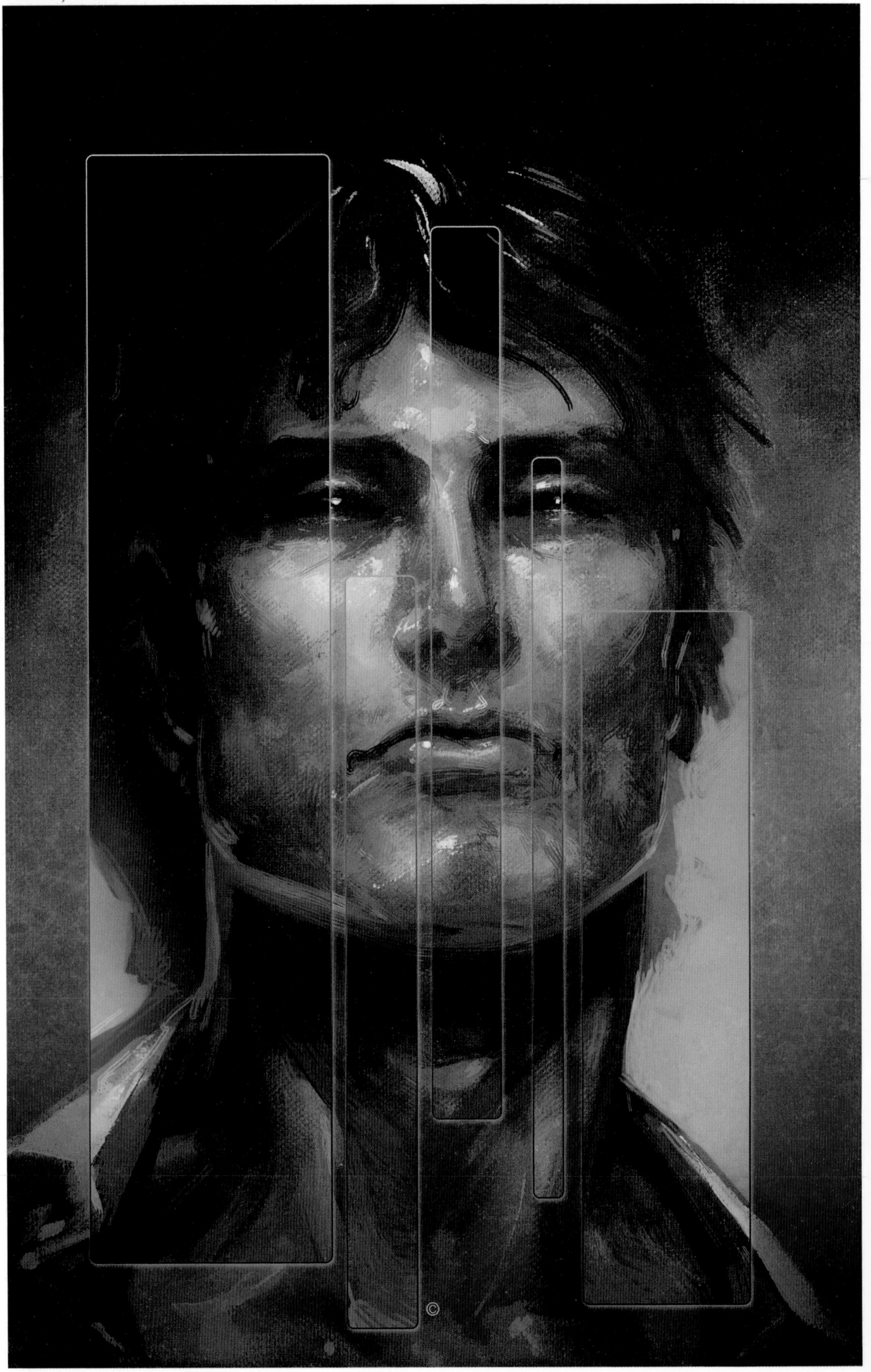

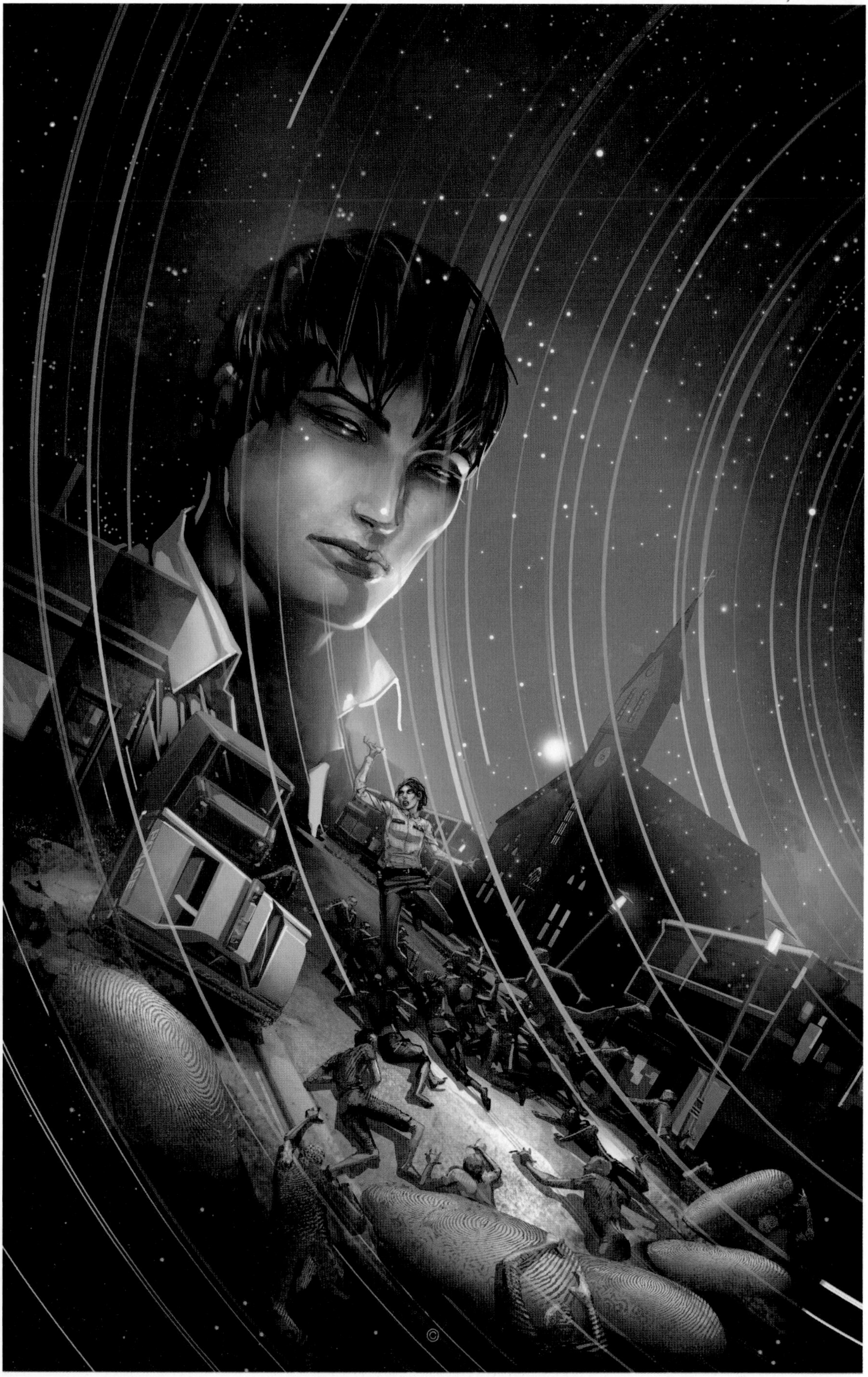

COVER CONCEPT ART (UNUSED)

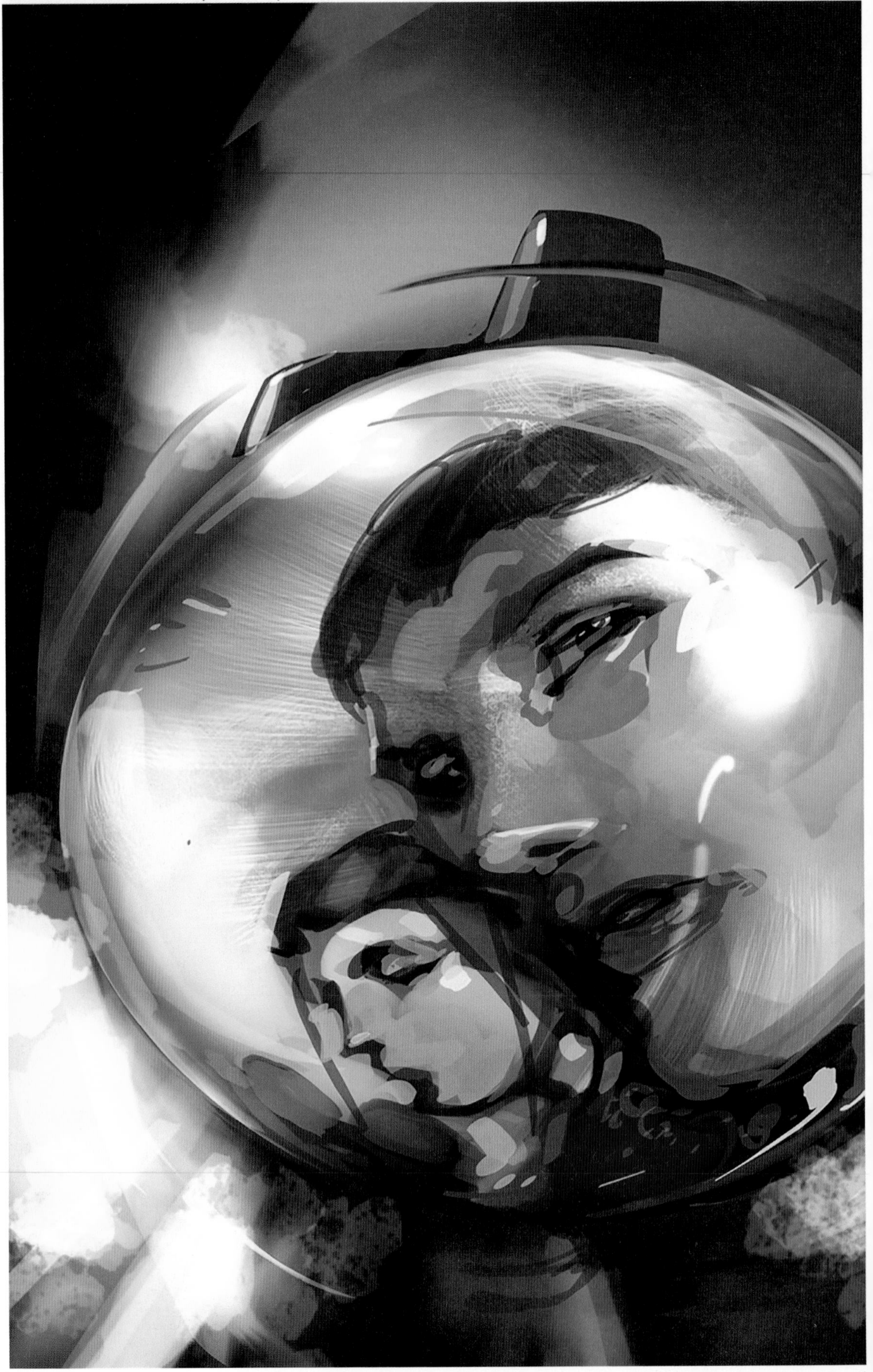

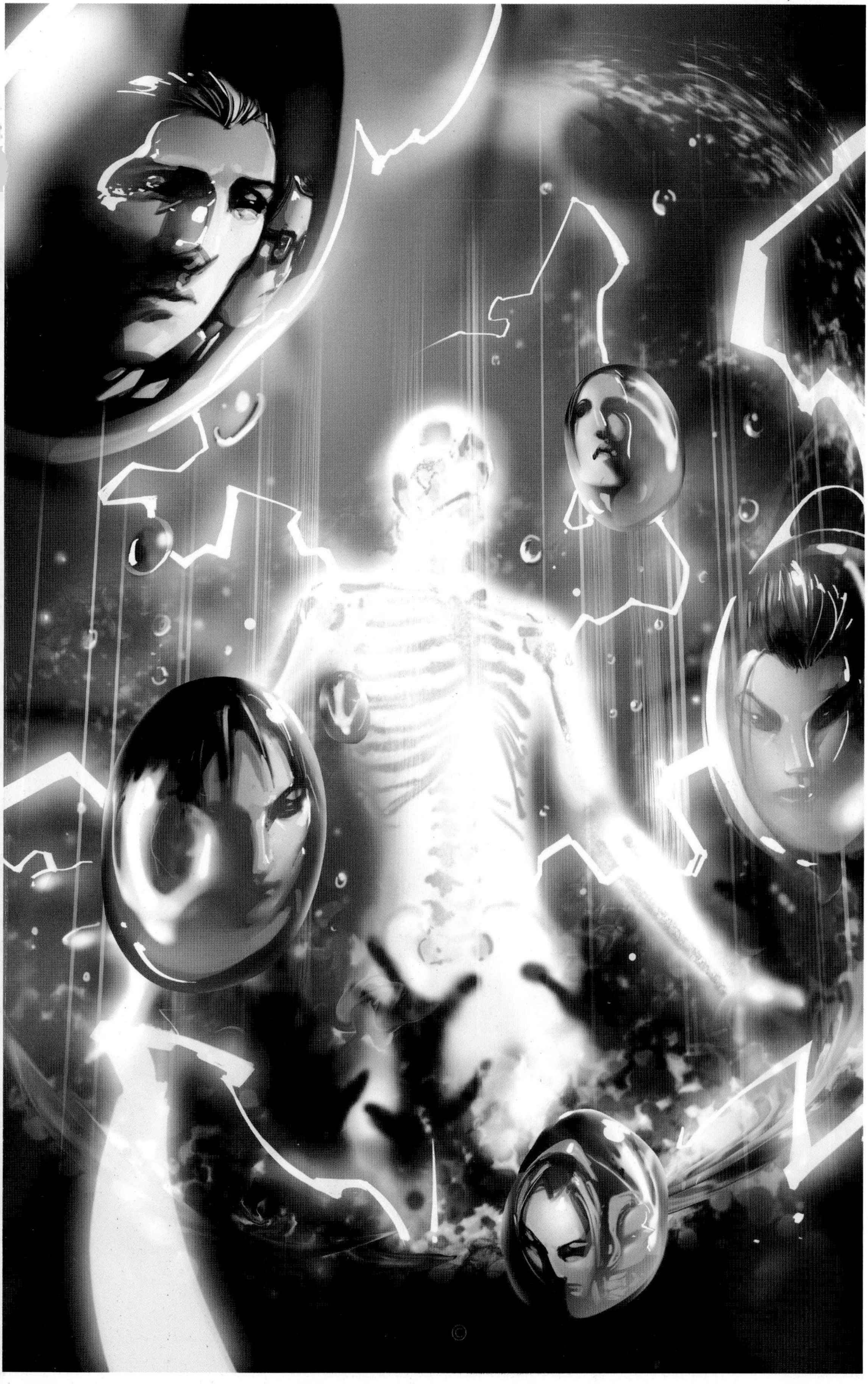

COVER, ISSUE 8

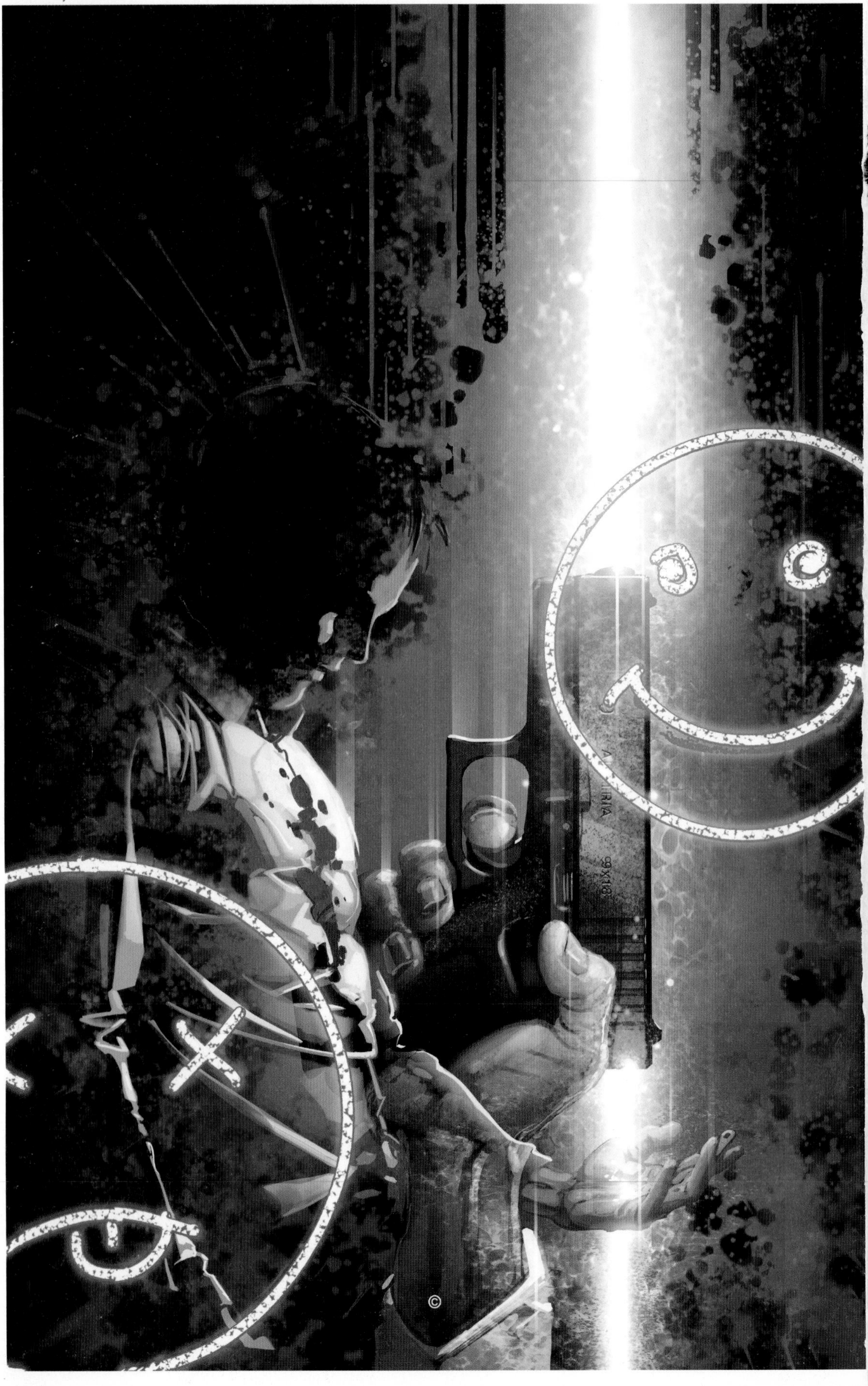